A DICTIONARY OF SELECTED ADVERBS FOR ALL AGES

ASHWANNIE HARRIPERSAUD

JESSICA SEERAJ	MAYLYN AMANDA BOOTOON	GAITRIE TULSI-MUTHAN

BlueRose ONE

Stories Matter

NewDelhi • London

For permissions requests or inquiries regarding this publication,
please contact:

BLUEROSE PUBLISHERS
www.BlueRoseONE.com
info@bluerosepublishers.com
+91 8882 898 898
+4407342408967

ISBN: 978-93-6452-672-2

Cover design: Daksh
Typesetting: Tanya Raj Upadhyay

First Edition: October 2024

Acknowledgment

We are indebted to all lexicographers that preceded us: from Samuel Johnson to Richard Allsopp and Walter Edwards. They led; we merely followed.

We would like to extend our heartfelt thanks to Professor Daizal R. Samad for his invaluable assistance and guidance in the completion of this work. His expertise and support were instrumental in bringing this project to fruition.

We would like to recognize ©2018 IPA Typefaces: Boulos SIL (metatext); Doulos SIL, IPA Kiel, IPA LS Uni (symbols) for the online publication of the IPA Alphabet from which reference was made to translate adjectives in our dictionary.

We would also like to recognize Cathy Votano ©NSW TAFE Commission 1993 for the online publication of the Phonetic Chart which was also referenced for the completion of our dictionary

About Our Dictionary

Background:

A Dictionary of Selected Adverbs for All Ages is designed to offer a resource that simplifies and clarifies the use of adverbs in language. Adverbs are crucial for adding detail and precision to both written and spoken communication. This dictionary provides accessible definitions and examples that cater to learners at various stages of language development. By covering a range of adverbs, from commonly used to those with detailed meanings, it supports vocabulary building and refines the ability to convey distinctions in expression. This resource is intended to assist readers in understanding and applying adverbs effectively, developing improved communication skills across different age groups.

Aim:

The aim of **A Dictionary of Selected Adverbs for All Ages** is to provide clear, accessible definitions and examples that amplify understanding and usage of adverbs across all age groups. By offering straightforward explanations and practical insights, the dictionary seeks to enrich vocabulary, improve communication skills, and support effective expression in both written and spoken language.

Scope:

This dictionary of selected adverbs contains a curated range of adverbs designed for readers of all ages. It includes definitions, usage examples, and contextual insights designed to support diverse learning needs. The scope covers adverbs that are frequently used and those essential for understanding complex language, aiming to enrich comprehension and application in everyday communication.

Rationale:

In an ever-evolving world of communication, adverbs play a crucial role in enriching our language by modifying verbs, adjectives, and other adverbs to convey distinction and clarity. This dictionary of selected adverbs is crafted to serve as a valuable resource for learners of all ages, providing clear and accessible definitions that strengthen understanding and application in various contexts.

Designed with the needs of diverse users in mind, this dictionary aims to bridge the gap between simple definitions and complex usage. For young learners, it offers straightforward explanations and examples that help build foundational vocabulary. For older students and adults, it provides deeper insight into adverbial details and their impact on meaning and tone.

Each entry is carefully selected to reflect a balance between commonly used and conceptually important adverbs, ensuring relevance and practicality. Definitions are accompanied by illustrative sentences that demonstrate how each adverb functions in different contexts.

Whether used as a learning tool, a reference guide, or a source of inspiration, this dictionary of selected adverbs aims to cultivate a greater appreciation of the subtleties of language and to empower users to express themselves with precision and creativity.

Definition of an Adverb

An adverb is a part of speech that modifies verbs, adjectives, or other adverbs, providing more information about how, when, where, or to what extent something happens.

Functions of Adverbs

1. Modifying Verbs:

Adverbs can describe how, when, where, or to what extent an action occurs.

Example: Hanna sings beautifully.

(Describes how Hanna sings.)

I. Modifying Adjectives:

Adverbs can modify adjectives to describe the intensity or degree of a quality.

Example: The test was extremely difficult.

(Describes the intensity of the difficulty.)

II. Modifying Other Adverbs:

Adverbs can modify other adverbs to adjust the degree of the modification.

Example: Arabelle ran very quickly.

(Describes how quickly Arabelle ran.)

Types of Adverbs

1. Adverbs of Manner:

Describe how an action is performed (quickly, softly, well, carefully, etc.).

*Example: Vince completed the project **efficiently**, and his team admired him for working so **diligently**.*

2. Adverbs of Time:

Indicate when an action occurs or its frequency (now, yesterday, often, soon, always, etc.).

*Example: We will start the meeting **promptly** at 10 a.m., and everyone should arrive on time.*

3. Adverbs of Place:

Describe the location or direction of an action (here, there, everywhere, nowhere).

*Example: The children played **outside** in the yard, and their parents watched from the porch.*

4. Adverbs of Degree:

Describe the intensity or degree of an action, adjective, or adverb (very, too, quite, almost).

*Example: The cake is **very** delicious.*

5. Adverbs of Frequency:

Indicate how often an action occurs (always, rarely, frequently, occasionally).

*Example: Shaun exercises **regularly**, and he also maintains a balanced diet to stay healthy.*

Formation of Adverbs

1. By Adding "-ly":

Many adverbs are formed by adding "-ly" to adjectives.

Examples: quickly (from quick), happily (from happy)

2. By Using Irregular Forms:

Some adverbs do not follow a standard pattern and may be irregular.

Examples: well (from good), fast (from fast)

Position in a Sentence

1. At the Beginning:

Adverbs can be placed at the start of a sentence for emphasis or to set the scene.

Example: **Suddenly**, *the lights went out.*

2. In the Middle:

Adverbs can appear between the subject and the main verb or after the verb.

Example: *She can* **always** *rely on her friends.*

3. At the End:

Adverbs can be placed at the end of a sentence to modify the whole sentence or the verb.

Example: *Grace finished her homework early, and then she went to bed* **quietly**.

Foreword

A Dictionary of Selected Adverbs is the most recent in a series of dictionaries written by Ashwannie Harripersaud and her team of undergraduate students who are also active teachers of English. This dictionary follows **A Dictionary of Selected Nouns** and **A Dictionary of Selected Adjectives**. The dictionaries are especially designed for teachers and students of secondary and primary schools, but it is also an invaluable teaching and learning tool for teachers and learners of English as a Second Language and English as a Foreign Language. As someone who teaches undergraduate university courses, I can say with certainty that these dictionaries will also serve undergraduates well.

The idea of focusing singularly on individual parts of speech in dictionaries is unique. Unlike traditional dictionaries, this series allows teachers and students to absorb each part of speech on its own before they move on to another. Eventually, student writing is informed and precise without confusion or muddle. Obviously, this idea of dictionaries of individual parts of speech saves time when the need arises to check on any word for meaning or accuracy in writing. Like Harripersaud's dictionaries that preceded it, this Harripersaud dictionary gives a thorough explanation of the respective parts of speech. This facilitates both teaching and learning by teachers and students, respectively.

Also, like Harripersaud's previous dictionaries, this Dictionary of Selected Adverbs offers pronunciation guidance by using the International Phonetic Alphabet. Moreover, it offers examples of the way each word may be used in sentences. This will be of immense use to both teachers and learners.

One of the things that I find most admirable about the way Ashwannie Harripersaud went about the compilation of these dictionaries is that she was willing to bring in undergraduates to participate in this series of projects. The idea is to have undergrads who rarely think about research and publication to do so, thereby establishing a habit of publishing, a hunger for academic inquiry. This is the kind of inclusivity that is not to be found at the university level where lecturers either talk incessantly about "research" that never sees the light of day and where publication is merely a means to promotion to a higher salary scale. Thus far, some seven undergraduates have been included in Harripersaud's lexicographical initiatives; their names and pictures on the covers. Kudos on this, Miss Harripersaud.

This Dictionary of Selected Adverbs, like the two dictionaries before it, will serve students and teachers well, but tools are useful only if and when they are used. If only policy-makers would take heed. If only.

Professor Daizal R. Samad
University of Guyana Berbice Campus
Tain, Corentyne,
Guyana

Aa

aback /abˈak/
to be taken by surprise or to be shocked or astonished by something unexpected
Example: She was taken aback by his sudden announcement.

abashedly /abˈaʃɪdli/
in a manner that shows embarrassment, shame, or unease
Example: She apologised abashedly after realising her mistake.

abeam /abˈiːm/
the direction perpendicular to the length of a ship or aircraft, often used in nautical or aviation contexts
Example: The ship sailed with the wind directly abeam.

abhorrently /ɑbˈhɔːrəntli/
doing something in a manner that is strongly detested, loathed, or regarded with intense dislike or disgust
*Example: He behaved abhorrently towards his co-workers, making
            offensive remarks, and displaying a lack of respect.*

abidingly /aˈbaɪdɪŋli/
in a manner that is enduring, lasting, or persistent
*Example: She remained abidingly faithful to her principles
            throughout her life.*

abjectly /ˈɑbdʒɛktli/
doing something in a manner that is extremely miserable, wretched, or lacking self-respect
*Example: He begged abjectly for forgiveness, kneeling before her
            with tears in his eyes.*

abloom /əˈbluːm/
in a state of blooming, blossoming, or flowering
Example: *The garden was abloom with colourful flowers in the springtime.*

ably /ˈaɪbli/
to do something skilfully, proficiently, or competently
Example: *She ably managed the project, ensuring that it was completed on time and within budget.*

abnormally /abnˈɔːməli/
to do something in a manner that deviates from what is considered normal or typical
Example: *Usain Bolt ran abnormally fast in the race, setting a new record for the event.*

aboard /abˈɔːd/
on or onto a ship, aircraft, train, or other vehicle
Example: *We went aboard the ship to start our cruise vacation.*

abominably /abˈɒmɪnəbli/
in a highly unpleasant, detestable, or morally offensive manner
Example: *He treated his employees abominably, showing no respect for their rights or well-being.*

aboriginally /ˌabəˈrɪdʒənlli/
relating to or in the manner of the original or indigenous inhabitants of a place
Example: *The tribe aboriginally inhabited the valley, living off the land and following ancient traditions.*

about /abˈaʊt/
approximately or nearly
Example: *There were about twenty people at the party.*

moving in a circular motion or in the vicinity
Example: The children were running about in the playground.
engaged in or occupied with
Example: She is about her work, preparing for the presentation.
used to introduce a topic or subject
Example: Let us talk about your plans for the weekend.

above /abˈʌv/
at a higher place or position
Example: The sun is shining from above.
higher in rank, authority, or position
Example: The CEO is seated above all the other executives.
more than or exceeding in quantity
Example: The temperature was above 90 degrees Fahrenheit.
in a previous part of a document or text
Example: As mentioned above, the project deadline is next Friday.

abreast /abrˈɛst/
side by side and keeping up with someone or something
*Example: They walked abreast down the street, chatting about their
             weekend plans.*

abroad /abrˈɔːd/
in or to a foreign country or countries
Example: She travelled abroad to study French literature.
in wide circulation or spread throughout
Example: Rumours about the incident were spread abroad.

absentmindedly /ˌabsentmˈaɪndɪdli/
to do something without paying attention or being mentally
preoccupied
*Example: She absentmindedly played with her hair while lost in
             thought during the meeting.*

absolutely /ˌæbsəlˈuːtli/
to emphasise certainty, completeness, or agreement
Example: I absolutely love chocolate ice cream.

absorbedly /absˈɔːbdli/
doing something with complete attention or deep concentration
*Example: He listened absorbedly to the lecturer, taking notes on
            every point.*

abstractedly /abˈstraktɪdlɪ/
in a manner that is not focused on one's surroundings or current
situation
*Example: Jack stared out the window abstractedly, his mind
            drifting far away from the meeting.*

abstractly /abstrˈaktli/
dealing with ideas, concepts, or theories rather than concrete, specific
things
*Example: He approached the problem abstractly, considering its
            theoretical implications rather than practical
            applications.*

absurdly /absˈɜːdli/
in a ridiculous, unreasonable, or nonsensical manner
Example: Sarah laughed absurdly at the idea that pigs could fly.

abundantly /abˈʌndəntli/
in large quantities or to a great degree
Example: The garden was abundantly filled with colourful flowers.

academically /ˌakədˈɛmɪkli/
pertains to matters related to education or scholarly pursuits
*Example: Gail excelled academically, earning top grades in all her
            classes.*

accentually /ɑkˈsentjʊəlli/
related to accents or emphasis in speech
Example: *The teacher spoke accentually, stressing certain syllables
to mimic a specific dialect.*

accessibly /aksˈɛsəbli/
in a way that is easy to approach, understand, or use
Example: *The museum designed its exhibits to be accessibly
arranged for visitors of all ages and backgrounds.*

accessorily /aksˈɛsərˌili/
something done in addition to the main action or purpose, like an
accessory
Example: *He added accessorily, mentioning a few extra details that
were not strictly relevant to the conversation.*

accidentally /ˌaksɪdˈɛntəli/
unintentionally or by chance
Example: *Jessica accidentally spilled her coffee on the table while
reaching for her phone.*

accordingly /akˈɔːdɪŋli/
in a manner that is appropriate to the circumstances or in a way that
corresponds to something else
Example: *The weather forecast predicted rain, so she packed
accordingly by bringing an umbrella.*

accountability /akˌaʊntəbˈɪlɪti/
in a manner that is responsible or answerable for one's actions
Example: *As a public official, she knew she had to act
accountability and transparently to maintain the trust of
the community.*

accurately /ˈakjʊrətli/
correctly or precisely
Example: *The scientist measured the temperature accurately to
ensure the validity of the experiment.*

accusatively /aˈkjuːzətɪvli/
doing or saying something in a manner that accuses or blames
someone
Example: *She looked at him accusatively when she found out he
had forgotten their anniversary.*

accusatorially /aˌkjuːzəˈtɔːrɪəlli/
speaking or acting in a manner that suggests accusation or blame
Example: *She stared at Jacob accusatorially, convinced that he was
the one who broke the vase.*

accusingly /akjˈuːzɪŋli/
in a way that suggests blame or accusation towards someone
Example: *"Where were you last night?" she asked accusingly, her
tone implying suspicion.*

acoustically /akˈuːstɪkli/
pertains to sounds or the properties of sound, particularly in a given
environment
Example: *The concert hall was designed acoustically to enhance
the clarity and richness of the music.*

acquisitively /aˈkwɪzɪtɪvli/
to do something in a way that shows a desire to acquire or possess
things
Example: *She looked at the display of jewellery in the window
acquisitively, her eyes lingering on the sparkling
diamonds.*

acrimoniously /ˌakrɪmˈəʊnɪəsli/
in a bitter, sharp, or harsh manner
*Example: After their argument, they parted ways acrimoniously,
            exchanging heated words and refusing to speak to each
            other.*

across /akrˈɒs/
from one side to the other, often implying movement or extension
over an area
*Example: Josh walked across the bridge to reach the other side of
            the river.*

acrostically /aˈkrɒstɪk kˈɔːli/
in a manner related to or involving an acrostic, in which certain letters
in each line form a word or words
*Example: The poet cleverly arranged the verse acrostically,
            spelling out a hidden message with the first letter of each
            line.*

actively /ˈaktɪvli/
in a proactive or engaged manner
*Example: The teenagers actively participate in community events,
            volunteering their time to help others.*

actually /ˈaktʃuːəli/
to emphasise the truth or reality of something, often to contrast it with
a mistaken belief or assumption
*Example: I thought I was lost, but I was actually just around the
            corner from my destination.*

acutely /akjˈuːtli/
in a way that is extremely sharp, intense, or keenly felt
*Example: Mary felt the pain acutely as she stubbed her toe on the
            corner of the table.*

additionally /adˈɪʃənəli/
in addition, or as an extra element or factor
Example: *Paula bought the groceries for dinner, and additionally, she picked up some flowers for the table.*

adequately /ˈadɪkwətli/
to a satisfactory or sufficient extent
Example: *George studied for the exam adequately and felt confident about his preparation.*

adhesively /adˈhiːsɪvli/
to do something in a manner that sticks or adheres
Example: *The tape was applied adhesively to ensure the poster stayed securely on the wall.*

adjacently /aˈdʒeɪsəntli/
in a position next to or near something else
Example: *The two houses were built adjacently, sharing a common wall.*

adjunctly /ˈadʒʌŋktli/
in a supplementary or additional manner
Example: *The engineer worked on the project adjunctly with his colleagues, contributing ideas and expertise to enhance the outcome.*

admirably /ˈadmərəblˌi/
in a praiseworthy or commendable way
Example: *She handled the difficult situation admirably, remaining calm and finding a solution that satisfied everyone involved.*

admittedly /adm'ɪtɪdli/
to acknowledge a fact or truth
*Example: Admittedly, I made a mistake by not double-checking the
details before submitting the report.*

adorably /ad'ɔ:rəbli/
doing something in an endearing, charming, or cute way
*Example: The toddler smiled adorably as she played with her
stuffed animals.*

adoringly /ad'ɔ:rɪŋli/
in a fashion expressing deep love, affection, or admiration
*Example: Ash looked at her pet adoringly, stroking its fur with
gentle care.*

adventurously /adv'ɛntʃərəsli/
in a bold, daring, or adventurous style
*Example: They decided to explore the unknown trails in the forest
adventurously, eager to discover new sights and
experiences.*

adverbially /ad'vɜ:bjəlli/
something being done in a way related to or resembling an adverb
*Example: She modified her speech adverbially, adding emphasis
and clarity with carefully chosen adverbs.*

adversely /adv'ɜ:sli/
in a way that has a negative or harmful effect
*Example: The company's profits were affected adversely by the
economic downturn.*

advisably /adv'aɪzəbli/
in a way that is wise or prudent, based on good advice or judgement

Example: *Betty decided to consult with a financial advisor before making any major investments, acting advisably to ensure her financial security.*

affectedly /aˈfektɪdli/
in a manner that is artificial, insincere, or exaggeratedly
Example: *She smiled affectedly when she saw him, trying too hard to appear happy.*

afresh /afrˈɛʃ/
to start again or anew, mostly after a pause or interruption
Example: *After their argument, they decided to begin their project afresh, with a renewed sense of cooperation.*

after /ˈaːfta/
to indicate a subsequent action in time or position
Example: *Sarah left the room, and John followed after.*

afterward /ˈaːftəwəd/
denotes an action or event occurring later in time or following another event
Example: *They went for a walk in the park, and afterward, they grabbed some ice cream.*

again /agˈɛn/
a repetition or returning to a previous state or action
Example: *Marvin forgot his keys at home, so he had to go back again to retrieve them.*

aggravatingly /ˈagrəveɪtɪŋli/
to describe something that causes irritation or annoyance
Example: *He tapped his fingers on the table aggravatingly, making it difficult for others to concentrate.*

aggressively /agrˈɛsɪvli/
describes actions or behaviour that are forceful, assertive, or hostile
*Example: The competitor entered the market aggressively,
                    undercutting prices and launching a massive advertising
                    campaign.*

ago /agˈəʊ/
indicates a period of time before the present moment
Example: She finished her homework an hour ago.

agonisingly /ˈagənaɪzɪŋli/
in a way that causes extreme physical or mental pain, distress, or
discomfort
*Example: She waited agonisingly for the test results, fearing the
                    worst.*

agreeably /agrˈiːəbli/
in a way that is pleasant or enjoyable manner, or in a way that is
satisfactory or in accordance with one's wishes or expectations
*Example: The weather was agreeably warm, perfect for a day at the
                    beach.*

ahead /ahˈɛd/
in a position in front of someone or something, or in advance of a
particular point in time or progress
Example: The car sped ahead of the truck on the highway.

all /ˈɔːl/
to indicate the entirety or completeness of something
Example: She ate all her dinner.
to refer to each individual member of a group
Example: All the students passed the exam.
to emphasise a quality or characteristic
Example: She is all too aware of the risks involved.

to indicate complete involvement or commitment
Example: Mark is giving his all to this project.
to indicate exclusively
Example: All I want is some peace and quiet.

allegedly /alˈɛdʒɪdli/
to indicate that something is claimed to be true or to have happened, but there is no concrete evidence to confirm it
Example: The suspect allegedly stole the jewellery from the store.

almost /ˈɔːlməʊst/
to indicate that something is very close to being the case or to reach a particular state or condition
Example: The project is almost complete; we just need to add a few final touches.

alone /alˈəʊn/
to indicate that someone or something is unaccompanied or isolated
Example: He was left alone in the dark forest.

along /alˈɒŋ/
to indicate movement or progress in a particular direction, often in parallel with someone or something else
Example: Gertrude walked along the beach, enjoying the sound of the waves.

aloud /alˈaʊd/
to describe something spoken audibly, so that it can be heard by others
Example: Jacob practised his speech aloud to ensure clarity and fluency.

already /ɑlrˈɛdi/

to show that something has happened, existed, or been done before a specific time or moment in the past, or that it has occurred earlier than expected

Example: Tricia has already eaten lunch, so she is not hungry.

alright /ɑlrˈaɪt/

satisfactory, acceptable, or in a satisfactory manner

Example: It is alright if you cannot make it to the party.

also /ˈɑlsəʊ/

to add more information or to indicate that something is in addition to what has already been stated

Example: The restaurant serves pasta dishes, and it also offers a selection of salads.

alternatively /ɑltˈɜːnətˌɪvli/

to suggest another option or possibility in place of the one already mentioned

Example: The team could pursue the current strategy, or alternatively, they could try a different approach.

altogether /ɑltəgˈɛðɐ/

to show the entirety or completeness of something

Example: The situation was altogether unexpected.

to describe a sum or combination of elements

Example: Jacque earned $50,000 altogether from his previous jobs.

always /ɑlweɪz/

to point out that something happens continuously or without exception, at all times, or on every occasion

Example: My grandmother always tells the best stories.

amazingly /amˈeɪzɪŋli/

to emphasise something that is surprising, extraordinary, or remarkable

Example: *Harry performed amazingly well in the competition, considering it was his first time.*

amblingly /ˈamblɪŋli/

something done in a relaxed, leisurely manner, often referring to walking at a slow and easy pace

Example: *The elderly couple strolled amblingly along the beach, enjoying the sunset.*

amorously /ˈamərəsli/

describes actions or behaviour that are related to or characterised by love, affection, or romantic feelings

Example: *The characters in the romance novel spoke amorously of their undying love.*

amply /ˈampli/

to a plentiful or sufficient degree, often indicating that something is provided in more than enough quantity or quality

Example: *Sue was amply awarded for her hard work with a generous award.*

analogically /ˌanəˈlɒdʒɪkəlli/

doing something by means of analogy, which involves drawing a comparison between two things to show a similarity

Example: *Hilary solved the maths problem analogically, drawing parallel to a similar problem she had encountered before.*

analytically /ˌanɐlˈɪtɪkli/

the process of examining or understanding something by breaking it down into its constituent parts, studying those parts in detail, and making logical connections or deductions

Example: *The mathematician approached the problem analytically,*
             breaking it down into smaller components to find a
             solution.

anatomically /ˌanatˈɒmɪkli/
the structure or organisation of the body, typically referring to the
arrangement of its parts or the study of its components
Example: *The doctor explained the injury anatomically, describing*
             the specific bones and muscles affected.

ancestrally /anˈsestrəlli/
something related to or inherited from one's ancestors, referring to
traits, customs, or characteristics passed down through generations
Example: *He felt a deep connection to the land, as his family had*
             lived there ancestrally for centuries.

anciently /ˈeɪnʃəntli/
something that occurred or existed in the distant past
Example: *The anciently written text provides insights into the*
             beliefs and practices of early society.

angelically /anˈdʒɛlɪkli/
an action or behaviour that is reminiscent of or characteristic of an
angel, connoting purity, goodness, or innocence
Example: *Grace smiled angelically, radiating warmth and kindness*
             to everyone around her.

angrily /ˈaŋgrɪli/
an action or behaviour done with anger or in a hostile manner
Example: *The customer complained angrily about the poor service.*

angularly /ˈaŋgjʊləli/
movement or positioning in a way that suggests angles or sharp
corners

Example: *The car turned angularly around the sharp bend in the*
            road.

animatedly /ˈanɪmeɪtɪdli/
actions or behaviours done with liveliness, enthusiasm, or excitement
Example: *The children laughed and played animatedly in the park,*
            full of energy.

annually /ˈanjuːəli/
happening once a year or on a yearly basis
Example: *The company conducts performance reviews annually to*
            assess employee progress.

anxiously /ˈaŋʃəsli/
actions or behaviour characterised by feelings of worry, unease, or
nervousness about an uncertain outcome
Example: *He paced anxiously back and forth, awaiting news from*
            the hospital.

any /ˈɛni/
to indicate one or some, without restriction or preference
Example: *Have you seen any good movies lately?*

anyhow /ˈɛnɪhˌaʊ/
to indicate that something will happen or be done despite any
obstacles or circumstances
Example: *I do not know how we'll get there, but we'll find a way*
            anyhow.
in a careless or haphazard manner; without concern for method or
order
Example: *Samantha completed the task, but it was done anyhow,*
            without following the instructions.

anymore /ˌɛnɪmˈɔː/
used in negative sentences to indicate that something that was once
true no longer applies
Example:　*We do not go out to eat as often anymore.*

anyway /ˈɛnɪwˌeɪ/
 a transition to a different topic
Example:　*I do not really like seafood. Anyway, have you decided*
　　　　　　where you want to go for dinner?
 to emphasise a point
Example:　*I told you to be careful, but you went ahead anyway.*
to express indifference or disregard for what has been previously
stated
Example:　*He did not listen to my advice; he did it his way anyway.*

anywhere /ˈɛnɪwˌeə/
any place or location, without specifying a particular one
Example:　*I could not find my keys anywhere in the house.*

apart /apˈɑːt/
to be separated or divided from something else
Example:　*The vase fell off the shelf and broke apart into several*
　　　　　　pieces.

apparently /apˈɑrəntli/
to indicate that something seems to be true based on the available
evidence or information, but it might not be confirmed
Example:　*Apparently, he is not coming to the party tonight.*

appropriately /aprˈəʊprɪətli/
doing something in a suitable or fitting manner, according to the
context or situation
Example:　*Martin dressed appropriately for the job interview,*
　　　　　　wearing a professional suit and tie.

approximately /aprˈɒksɪmətlˌi/
close to an exact value or amount, but not precisely
Example: *The journey will take approximately two hours by car.*

aptly /ˈaptli/
in a way that is particularly suitable, appropriate, or fitting for the situation or context
Example: *The comedian aptly captured the audience's attention with her witty jokes.*

arguably /ˈaːgjuːəbli/
to introduce a statement that is subject to debate or contention, implying that the statement may be true or valid, but not universally accepted
Example: *He is arguably the best player in the league, although opinions on this may vary.*

arrogantly /ˈarəgəntli/
describes behaviour characterised by an exaggerated sense of self-importance or superiority, often accompanied by disdain or disrespect towards others
Example: *He walked arrogantly into the meeting, acting as if he were above everyone else.*

ashore /aʃˈɔː/
the direction towards or onto the land from the water
Example: *We saw the dolphins swimming close to the boat before they leaped ashore.*

aside /asˈaɪd/
indicates movement or placement to one side
Example: *He stepped aside to let the other passengers board the bus first.*

to introduce a point that is separate from the main topic

Example: *Aside from his academic achievements, he is also a*
              talented musician.

astonishedly /ast'ɒnɪʃtli/

being in a state of astonishment or amazement

Example: *He stared astonishedly at the magician's disappearing*
              act.

astonishingly /ast'ɒnɪʃɪŋli/

in a manner that causes great surprise, wonder, or amazement

Example: *The results of the experiment were astonishingly*
              accurate, exceeding all expectations.

astray /astr'eɪ/

being off course or away from the correct path or direction

Example: *The hiker realised he had wandered astray from the*
              marked trail.

astringently /as'trɪndʒəntli/

doing something in a severe, strict, or stern way

Example: *The teacher spoke astringently to the students about the*
              importance of meeting deadlines.

something that is sharp, bitter, or harsh, especially in tone

Example: *The Professor criticised Mark's proposal astringently,*
              highlighting its impracticality and lack of feasibility.

asunder /as'ʌndɐ/

into separate parts or pieces

Example: *The storm tore the ship asunder, scattering its wreckage*
              across the ocean.

apart from each other

Example: *Their once strong friendship was torn asunder by*
              betrayal and mistrust.

into pieces violently or forcefully

Example: *The explosion ripped the building asunder, leaving*
            nothing but rubble.

atmospherically /ˌatməsfˈɛrɪkli/

something that pertains to or enhances the mood, feeling, or ambiance
of a particular place or environment

Example: *The dimly lit café was atmospherically perfect for a*
            romantic date.

atomically /atˈɒmɪkli/

pertains to something related to atoms, the smallest constituent units
of ordinary matter

Example: *The scientists studied the material's structure atomically,*
            examining the arrangement of individual atoms.

actions or processes that occur at the atomic level

Example: *Nanotechnology involves manipulating matter atomically*
            to create new materials and devices.

attributively /aˈtrɪbjʊtɪvli/

using an adjective to modify a noun, typically coming before the
noun it modifies

Example: *The adjective 'blue' in the phrase 'blue sky' is used*
            attributively, modifying the noun 'sky'.

audaciously /ɔːdˈeɪʃəsli/

doing something with boldness, daring, or fearless courage, often in a
way that is considered unconventional or risky

Example: *The artist audaciously combined different styles in her*
            painting, creating a unique masterpiece.

audibly /ˈɔːdəbli/

something that is done in a way that can be heard or perceived by the
ear

Example: Paul sighed audibly, expressing his frustration with the situation.

authentically /ɔ:θˈɛntɪkli/
doing something in a genuine, true, or original way, without imitation or falsehood
Example: The restaurant serves dishes authentically prepared according to traditional recipes from the region.

automatically /ˌɔ:təmˈatɪkli/
actions performed without conscious thought or effort, often because of a predetermined process, mechanism, or condition
Example: The lights in the hallway turn on automatically when someone enters.

aversely /aˈvɜ:sli/
doing something in a manner that shows strong dislike, opposition, or reluctance towards it
Example: She shook her head aversely when asked if she wanted to try the new food.

away /awˈeɪ/
indicates movement or direction from a particular place or position
Example: Austin walked away from the crowd.

awfully /ˈɔ:fəli/
to a great extent
Example: She is awfully talented at playing the piano.
in a manner inspiring awe, fear, or dread
Example: Luke looked awfully pale after hearing the bad news
an intensifier to express strong emphasis or exaggeration
Example: That was awfully rude of him to ignore your invitation.
in an unpleasant or objectionable manner

Example: *Shane behaved awfully towards his colleagues, causing*
             tension in the office.

awhile /aw'aɪl/
for a short period of time or temporarily
Example: *Justina sat on the bench for awhile, enjoying the*
             sunshine.

awkwardly /'ɔːkwədli/
in a clumsy or ungainly manner
Example: *He walked awkwardly in his new shoes.*
in a manner causing discomfort or embarrassment
Example: *Julia laughed awkwardly after telling a joke that no one*
             found funny.
in a way that is difficult to handle or manage
Example: *Grace answered the interview questions awkwardly,*
             stumbling over her words.
lacking grace or elegance
Example: *The dress hung awkwardly on her, not flattering her*
             figure.

axially /'aksɪəlli/
along or in relation to an axis
Example: *The wheel rotates axially around its central axis.*
in a manner that is central or fundamental
Example: *The research focuses axially on understanding genetic*
             mutations.
in a way that pertains to or follows a straight line
Example: *The technician inserted the probe axially into the soil to*
             measure moisture levels.

Bb

babyishly /ˈbeɪbɪɪʃli/
characteristic of a baby, often implying immaturity or childishness
Example: *She spoke babyishly, using simple words and high-pitched voice to communicate with the toddler.*

back /bˈak/
return to a previous position or state
Example: *The woman looked back at the old house nostalgically.*
in a backward direction
Example: *He stumbled back as the door swung open unexpectedly.*
in return or in response
Example: *She smiled back at him when he waved.*
to a previous time or situation
Example: *Let us go back to the beginning of the story.*
as support or assistance
Example: *She has had her friend back during the argument.*
as a reference to something past or behind
Example: *The store is located a few blocks back from the main street.*

backstage /bˈaksteɪdʒ/
in a theatrical context
Example: *The actors waited nervously backstage before making their entrance.*

backward /bˈakwəd/
in a direction toward the back or rear
Example: *The athlete stumbled backward after colliding with another player*
in a direction opposite to the usual or expected

Example: *The company's profits have been moving backwards in recent months.*

in a manner indicating a lack of progress or development

Example: *The country's education system is still backward compared to other developed nations.*

showing reluctance, hesitation, or lack of confidence

Example: *He was too backward to speak up during the meeting.*

to suggest a reversal or regression

Example: *The political reforms seem to be moving the country backward rather than forward.*

bacterially /bɑktˈiərɪəli/

related to the presence or actions of bacteria

Example: *The infection spread bacterially throughout the body, causing severe illness.*

resembling the behaviour or characteristics of bacteria

Example: *The population growth in the city was described as bacterially rapid, with exponential increases over a short period.*

influenced by bacterial presence or activity

Example: *The food spoiled bacterially due to improper storage and handling.*

involving bacterial processes or interactions

Example: *The scientists studied how bacterially mediated reactions contribute to foil fertility.*

badly /bˈadli/

poorly or inadequately

Example: *She performed badly in the exam because she did not study enough.*

in a severe or serious manner

Example: *He needed help badly after failing the exam for the third time.*

in a morally wrong or reprehensible way

Example: *Cheating on the exam reflects badly on Mary's integrity.*

in a way that causes harm or damage

Example: *Procrastinating badly affected her exam score.*

in a way that is difficult to endure or accept

Example: *She wanted to do well so badly that she could not sleep the night before the exam.*

very much or to a great extent

Example: *She badly wanted to pass the exam to make her parents proud.*

baldly /bˈɔːldli/

directly, without hesitation or subtlety

Example: *He baldly stated that he had no intention of attending the meeting.*

clearly, plainly, without embellishment

Example: *The facts were laid out baldly, leaving no room for interpretation.*

unadorned, lacking detail or decoration

Example: *The room was furnished baldly, with only a few chairs and a table.*

balmily /bˈɑːmili/

pleasantly warm and mild, like a gentle breeze or a soothing balm

Example: *The spring afternoon was balmily perfect for a picnic in the park.*

in a calming or soothing manner

Example: *Hermila spoke to the child balmily, trying to ease his pains.*

barbarously /bˈɑːbɐrəsli/

in a savage or brutal manner

Example: *The dictator's regime treated dissenters barbarously, often resorting to torture and executions.*

in a manner that is uncivilised or lacking refinement

Example: *The tribe's customs were viewed by outsiders as barbarously primitive.*

in an outrageous or shockingly inappropriate way

Example: *The comedian's jokes about the tragedy were considered barbarously insensitive.*

bareback /bˈeəbɑk/

riding a horse without a saddle

Example: *She loved to ride bareback through the fields, feeling the horse's muscles move beneath her.*

in a raw or unfiltered way

Example: *He spoke to her bareback, without sugar-coating his words or hiding his true feelings.*

barely /bˈeəli/

only just, almost not

Example: *The elderly woman barely made it to the bus stop in time, panting as she boarded.*

scarcely, hardly

Example: *The room was so dark that she could barely see her hand in front of her face.*

in a way that shows modesty or restraint

Example: *Nancy barely acknowledged his compliment, preferring to remain humble.*

barometrically /bˌarəʊmˈɛtrɪkɑːli/

related to changes in barometric pressure

Example: *The weather can be predicted barometrically by observing changes in pressure and its effects on the atmosphere.*

in a way that measures or indicates atmospheric pressure

Example: *The old barometer barometrically indicated a change in weather, with its needle dropping rapidly.*

basely /bˈeɪsli/

a morally low or dishonourable way

Example: *Gary betrayed his friend basely by spreading rumours about him.*

in a cowardly or despicable manner

Example: *The bully behaved basely by picking on those weaker than him.*

in a mean-spirited or malicious manner

Example: *She acted basely by sabotaging her colleague's chances for promotion.*

bashfully /bˈaʃfəli/

shyly or timidly, especially in social situations

Example: *Amy smiled bashfully when Tommy complimented her on her performance.*

modestly or self-consciously

Example: *Henry accepted the award bashfully, thanking everyone for their support.*

in a cute or charmingly embarrassed manner

Example: *The puppy wagged its tail bashfully after being praised for learning a new trick.*

basically /bˈeɪsɪkli/

in a fundamental or essential manner

Example: *The instructions for assembling the furniture were basically clear, but some steps were still confusing.*

in a simple or straightforward way

Example: *The problem can be solved basically by following these three steps.*

essentially or for the most part

Example: *The car is basically brand new; it only has a few miles on it.*

beamingly /bˈiːmɪŋli/

with a radiant or delighted expression

Example: *She looked at her new-born baby beamingly, filled with love and joy.*

with great enthusiasm or excitement

Example: *The children ran to their parents beamingly, excited to show them their artwork.*

to suggest satisfaction or contentment

Example: *The couple danced together beamingly, lost in the moment of happiness.*

beautifully /bjˈuːtɪfəli/

in a visually pleasing or attractive manner

Example: *The flowers bloomed beautifully in the garden, adding vibrant colours to the surroundings.*

in a skilful, graceful, or elegant manner

Example: *The dancer moved beautifully across the stage, executing each step with precision and grace.*

excellently or admirably

Example: *The symphony orchestra performed the piece beautifully, eliciting applause from the audience.*

becomingly /bɪˈkʌmɪŋli/

is appropriate, suitable, or pleasing

Example: *She dressed becomingly for the job interview, wearing a tailored suit and polished shoes.*

befittingly /bɪfˈɪtɪŋli/

is appropriate or suitable for a particular situation

Example: *The president's speech was befittingly solemn, given the gravity of the occasion.*

before /bɪfˈɔː/

in front of or ahead in position

Example: The manager stood before the audience to deliver his speech.

earlier in time

Example: I had never seen such beauty before.

in the presence of or in the sight of

Example: The burglar confessed his crime before the judge.

rather or sooner than

Example: I would die before I betray my principles.

prior to a specified time

Example: We need to finish this project before the deadline.

beforehand /bɪfˈɔːhɑnd/

in advance or prior to a specified time or event

Example: She always plans her trips beforehand to ensure everything goes smoothly.

beggarly /ˈbegəlɪ/

something being in a manner that is characteristic of a beggar, often implying poverty or meagreness

Example: The beggarly wages they received were not enough to support their families.

begrudgingly /bɪgrˈʌdʒɪŋli/

to do something reluctantly or with resentment

Example: Tommy begrudgingly admitted that his opponent had won the debate.

behaviourally /bɪhˈeɪvjərəli/

pertains to behaviour or actions, especially in the context of psychology or behavioural sciences

Example: The study aimed to investigate how certain factors influence behaviourally conditioned responses.

behind /bɪhˈaɪnd/
in a location to the rear
Example: *The dog ran behind the house.*
in a position that is slower or later in progress
Example: *She fell behind in her studies after getting sick.*
remaining after others have gone
Example: *He stayed behind to clean up the mess.*
late or overdue
Example: *She is behind on her rent payments.*
in a less advanced or developed state
Example: *The country is behind in technology compared to others.*

belatedly /bɪlˈeɪtɪdli/
something is done or occurring later than it should have been
Example: *She sent her birthday wishes belatedly, two weeks after
the actual date.*

believably /bɪlˈiːvəbli/
in a way that is convincing or credible
Example: *The actor portrayed the character believably, capturing
the emotions and nuances of the role.*

belligerently /bɪˈlɪdʒərəntli/
to describe an aggressive, hostile, or confrontational behaviour
Example: *The customer spoke belligerently to the cashier,
demanding a refund for the faulty product.*

below /bɪlˈəʊ/
indicates a position or level that is lower or less than something else
Example: *His performance in the exam was below average,
indicating a need for improvement.*

beneath /bɪnˈiːθ/
denotes a position that is lower or under something else

Example: *Beneath his tough exterior, he had a kind heart.*

beneficially /bˌɛnɪfˈɪʃəlˌi/
to describe actions or situations that are advantageous or helpful
Example: *Exercising regularly can beneficially impact both*
physical and mental health.

benignly /bɪnˈaɪnli/
to describe actions or situations that are gentle, kind, or harmless in
nature
Example: *The elderly librarian smiled benignly at the children as*
they entered the library.

besides /bɪsˈaɪdz/
in addition to; apart from
Example: *Besides studying for exams, Eric also works part-time at*
a café.

best /bˈɛst/
to indicate the highest degree or most favourable condition of
something
Example: *The team did their best to finish the project before the*
deadline.

better /bˈɛtɑ/
to indicate a higher degree or improved condition of something
compared to a previous state
Example: *She sings better than she did last year.*

beyond /bɪjˈɒnd/
to indicate something that is farther along in space, time, or degree
than a specified point or extent
Example: *His knowledge of physics goes beyond what is taught in*
textbooks.

biblically /ˈbɪblɪkəlli/
refers to actions, events, or concepts that are in accordance with or
related to the Bible or its teachings
*Example: The charity organisation operates biblically, following
                 principles of compassion and generosity outlined in the
                 scriptures.*

biennially /baɪˈenɪəlli/
occurring every two years
*Example: The conference is held biennially, attracting scholars and
                 researchers from around the world.*

bi-hourly /bˈaɪ aʊəli/
happening every two hours
*Example: The medication should be taken bi-hourly to manage pain
                 effectively.*
happening twice an hour
*Example: The bus service runs bihourly during peak times, with
                 buses departing every 30 minutes.*

bilaterally /baɪlˈatərəli/
involving or affecting two sides or parties equally or reciprocally
*Example: The trade agreement was negotiated bilaterally between
                 the two countries.*

billowingly /bˈɪləʊɪŋli/
to describe something moving or expanding in a large, rolling
manner, typically referring to clouds, smoke, or fabric
*Example: The smoke rose billowingly from the chimney, obscuring
                 the sky.*

bimonthly /ˈbaɪˈmʌnθli/
happening every two months

Example: *The magazine is published bimonthly, with new issues released in January, March, May, July, September, and December.*

happening twice a month

Example: *The employees receive their pay-checks bimonthly, on the 15ᵗʰ and the last day of each month.*

bindingly /ˈbaɪndɪŋli/

something done in a way that is legally or morally obligatory, requiring compliance or adherence

Example: *The decision of the arbitration panel was bindingly accepted by all involved parties.*

binocularly /bɪˈnɒkjʊləli/

using both eyes simultaneously

Example: *Gerald scanned the horizon binocularly, searching for any signs of movement.*

biologically /bˌaɪəlˈɒdʒɪkli/

relating to biology; the study of living organisms and their interactions with each other and their environments

Example: *The new species was classified biologically based on its genetic makeup and physical characteristics.*

bitingly /bˈaɪtɪŋli/

describes something done or said in a sharply critical, sarcastic, or harshly critical way

Example: *Ferdinand responded bitingly to the criticism, leaving some people feeling offended.*

bitterly /bˈɪtəli/

something done or experienced with strong resentment, anger, or disappointment

Example: *Justina cried bitterly when she heard the news of her friend's betrayal.*

biweekly /ˈbaɪˈwiːklɪ/
occurring every two weeks
Example: *She gets paid biweekly, receiving her pay-check every other Friday.*
occurring twice a week
Example: *The yoga class meets biweekly on Mondays and Wednesdays.*

bizarrely /bɪzˈɑːli/
describes something done or occurring in a strange, eccentric, or unconventional manner
Example: *The movie ended bizarrely, leaving the audience puzzled and confused.*

blamelessly /blˈeɪmləsli/
describes doing something without deserving blame or fault
Example: *Despite the accusations, she acted blamelessly throughout the entire ordeal.*

blandly /blˈɑndli/
doing something in a dull, uninteresting, or lacking in flavour or excitement way
Example: *He spoke blandly, lacking enthusiasm in his tone.*

blankly /blˈɑŋkli/
doing something in a way that lacks expression, emotion, or comprehension
Example: *She stared blankly at the computer screen, unable to recall what she had been working on.*

blasphemously /ˈblɑsfɪməsli/

in a manner that shows disrespect or irreverence towards something sacred or holy

Example: *He spoke blasphemously about the religious icon.*

to violate religious beliefs or principles

Example: *The artist depicted the prophet blasphemously in his artwork.*

blatantly /blˈeɪtəntli/

in a completely obvious and unashamed way, without attempt to conceal or disguise

Example: *She blatantly ignored the rules and continued to cheat during the game.*

in a flagrant or glaringly obvious manner, often used to describe something negative or offensive

Example: *The politician blatantly lied about his involvement in the scandal.*

blazingly /blˈeɪzɪŋli/

in an extremely fast or rapid manner, often with intense heat or speed

Example: *The car sped down the highway blazingly fast.*

in a way characterised by intense brightness or brilliance, as if on fire

Example: *The sun rose blazingly over the horizon, illuminating the landscape.*

bleakly /blˈiːkli/

in a desolate or grim fashion, without hope or optimism

Example: *Rose looked out at the stormy sea, feeling bleakly alone.*

in a cold or harshly uninviting mode

Example: *The landscape stretched out bleakly before them, devoid of any signs of life.*

blessedly /blˈɛsɪdli/

in a fortunate or blissful way, bringing happiness or relied

Example: *After a long day of work, I was blessedly greeted by my*
                  dog's wagging tail.

in a style that is favoured or protected by a divine power or higher force

Example: *The rain ceased, and the blessedly clear sky allowed us to*
                  enjoy the outdoor event.

blindingly /blˈaɪndɪŋli/

to an extreme or intense degree

Example: *The headlights were blindingly bright, making it difficult*
                  to see the road ahead.

blindly /blˈaɪndli/

without using sight or judgement

Example: *Gregory stumbled blindly through the dark forest, unable*
                  to see where he was going.

in an unreasoning, uncritical manner

Example: *They blindly accepted everything they were told without*
                  questioning it.

blissfully /blˈɪsfəli/

in a way that is full of joy or happiness

Example: *Martha danced blissfully in the warm sunlight, enjoying*
                  every moment of her vacation.

in a manner that is completely unaware of or unconcerned about potential problems or difficulties

Example: *Ignorant of the impending storm, they continued their*
                  picnic blissfully, laughing and chatting without a care in
                  the world.

blisteringly /blˈɪstərɪŋli/

extremely hot or intense

Example: *The sun beat down blisteringly, causing everyone to seek*
                  shade.

at a very fast pace or speed

*Example: The car sped down the highway blisteringly, leaving
             other vehicles far behind.*

blithely /blˈaɪðli/

in a carefree or cheerful fashion, showing a lack of concern or worry

*Example: Amy skipped blithely down the street, enjoying the
             sunshine, and ignoring her looming deadlines.*

in a casual or indifferent way, often implying a lack of awareness or consideration of consequences

*Example: Roy blithely ignored the warning signs and proceeded
             with his plan, unaware of the potential dangers ahead.*

bloody /blˈʌdi/

used as an intensifier, often to express strong emotion or emphasis

Example: The team fought bloody hard to win the championship.

used as an expletive, expressing anger, frustration, or annoyance

Example: Bloody hell, I cannot believe I missed the last train!

bluntly /blˈʌntli/

in a direct and straightforward manner, often without tact or consideration for feelings

*Example: Anna bluntly told Jonathan that his idea was impractical
             and would never work.*

in a manner characterised by a lack of sharpness or keenness

*Example: The knife cut bluntly through the soft fruit, making it
             difficult to slice cleanly.*

blushingly /ˈblʌʃɪŋli/

in a way that shows embarrassment or shyness, often accompanied by blushing

*Example: Wendy replied blushingly when Mark complimented her
             on her performance.*

in a manner that is rosy or flushed, resembling the appearance of someone who is blushing

Example: *The sky turned blushingly pink as the sun began to set.*

boastfully /bˈəʊstfəli/

involves bragging or boasting about one's achievements, abilities, or possessions

Example: *Bill spoke boastfully about his recent promotion, exaggerating his accomplishments.*

characterised by excessive pride or arrogance

Example: *Sarah strutted boastfully around the room, flaunting her expensive jewellery.*

bodily /bˈɒdɪli/

in a physical or corporeal way, relating to the body

Example: *Deon lifted the heavy box bodily, using his strength to carry it.*

entirety, as a whole, or as a single unit

Example: *The entire team was bodily transported to the competition venue by bus.*

boisterously /ˈbɔɪstərəsli/

in a loud and enthusiastic manner, often with a lot of noise and activity

Example: *The children played boisterously in the yard, laughing, and shouting as they chased each other.*

in a cheerful and lively manner, with high spirits and exuberance

Example: *The party guests danced boisterously to the upbeat music, thoroughly enjoying themselves.*

boldly /bˈəʊldli/

in a brave and confident way, without fear or hesitation

Example: *Arty boldly stepped onto the stage and delivered her speech with conviction.*

in a striking or conspicuous way, often involving strong or vivid features

Example: *The artist used bold colours and shapes to create a visually stunning masterpiece.*

boringly /bˈɔːrɪŋli/

in a dull or uninteresting way

Example: *The lecture was delivered boringly, causing many students to struggle to stay awake.*

in a tedious or monotonous fashion

Example: *Tom spoke boringly about his daily routine, with no variation or enthusiasm in his tone.*

botanically /bətˈanɪkli/

anything related to botany, the scientific study of plants

Example: *The researcher discussed the plant's structure botanically, focusing on its reproductive organs and cellular composition.*

boyishly /bˈɔɪʃli/

describes behaviour or characteristics that are reminiscent of a young boy

Example: *Mike grinned boyishly as he recounted his adventures from the weekend camping trip.*

braggingly /brˈagɪŋli/

describes someone boasting or showing off

Example: *Walter spoke braggingly about his new job, emphasising his high salary and impressive title.*

bravely /brˈeɪvli/

to perform an action with courage or boldness

Example: *Despite her fear of heights, Kim climbed bravely to the top of the mountain.*

brazenly /brˈeɪzənli/

conveys a sense of boldness, shamelessness, or audacity

Example: *The thief brazenly walked into the store and stole a laptop in broad daylight.*

breathlessly /brˈɛθləsli/

describes an action or state done or experienced with anticipation, excitement, or exhaustion

Example: *Kerry waited breathlessly for the results of the competition, her heart pounding with nervousness.*

breathtakingly /brˈɛθteɪkɪŋli/

something that is stunningly beautiful, awe-inspiring, or impressive

Example: *The view from the mountaintop was breathtakingly beautiful, with snow-capped peaks stretching as far as the eye could see.*

briefly /brˈiːfli/

denotes a short duration or a concise manner

Example: *The athlete paused briefly to catch his breath before continuing the race.*

brightly /brˈaɪtli/

with a strong, vivid, or intense light

Example: *The stars twinkled brightly in the night sky, creating a beautiful spectacle.*

in a cheerful or optimistic way

Example: *Drew laughed brightly, enjoying the company of her friends on a sunny day.*

with intelligence or skill

Example: *The student answered the question brightly, demonstrating a deep understanding of the topic.*

brilliantly /brɪˈlɪəntli/

in a manner that is exceptionally bright or shining

Example:　*The diamonds sparkled brilliantly under the spotlight.*

in an approach that is exceptionally clever, talented, or skilful

Example:　*Pam solved the puzzle brilliantly, impressing everyone with her intelligence.*

in a way that is exceptionally successful or outstanding

Example:　*The musician performed brilliantly at the concert, receiving a standing ovation from the audience.*

briskly /brɪˈɪskli/

in a quick and energetic manner, with speed and efficiency

Example:　*Winifred walked briskly to catch the bus, her footsteps echoing on the pavement.*

broadly /brɔˈɔːdli/

widely or extensively

Example:　*The news of their engagement spread broadly throughout the community.*

in a general or overall mode

Example:　*Quincy smiled broadly, happy to see her old friend again.*

in a liberal or tolerant manner

Example:　*Kelvin approached the topic broadly, considering multiple perspectives before forming his opinion.*

brokenly /brɔˈəʊkənli/

in a fragmented or disjointed manner, indicating interruption or discontinuity

Example:　*Heather spoke brokenly, pausing frequently to collect her thoughts.*

in a faltering or uneven manner, suggesting emotional distress or physical impairment

Example:　*Trayon sang brokenly, his voice cracking with sorrow.*

brotherly /brˈʌðəli/

in a way characteristic of brothers, showing familial affection or camaraderie

Example: *They hugged each other brotherly after not seeing each other for years.*

in a supportive or protective way

Example: *Sam offered his friend brotherly advice when he was going through a tough time.*

in a harmonious or cooperative manner

Example: *The teammates worked together brotherly to achieve victory in the championship game.*

brutally /brˈuːtəli/

in a way that is extremely harsh, cruel, or violent

Example: *The dictator brutally suppressed any form of dissent among the population.*

in a blunt or straightforward manner, without consideration for feelings or sensitivities

Example: *The critic brutally criticised the actor's performance in the play, leaving him feeling demoralised.*

in a manner that is unrelenting or relentless, often causing severe physical or emotional harm

Example: *The storm brutally battered the coastal town, leaving behind a trail of destruction.*

bulkily /bˈʌlkɪli/

in a fashion that is large, cumbersome, or unwieldy in appearance or movement

Example: *The old wardrobe, with its bulkily built frame, was difficult to manoeuvre up the narrow staircase.*

burdensomely /ˈbɜːdnsəmli/

in a mode that imposes a heavy load or obligation, causing difficulty or hardship

Example: *The taxes were burdensomely high, making it challenging*
                    for small businesses to thrive.

in a way that feels oppressive or overwhelming due to excessive
weight or responsibility

Example: *Carrying the heavy backpack burdensomely, Harvey*
                    struggled to keep up with the rest of the hiking group.

in a manner that causes mental or emotional strain due to excessive
worry or concern

Example: *The constant demands of his job weighed burdensomely*
                    on his mind, affecting his sleep and overall well-being.

burningly /bˈɜːnɪŋli/

in a manner that suggests intense heat or burning sensation

Example: *The sun shone burningly on the desert, making the heat*
                    almost unbearable.

with strong intensity or passion

Example: *Sarah spoke burningly about her passion for the cause,*
                    conveying deep commitment.

busily /bˈɪzɪlˌi/

in a way that indicates active, energetic, or industrious engagement in
tasks or activities

Example: *The students were busily working on their assignments,*
                    hardly noticing the time passing by.

crowded or filled with activity

Example: *The market was busily bustling with shoppers, vendors,*
                    and merchants.

being preoccupied or occupied with numerous tasks or
responsibilities

Example: *Wyatt typed busily on his laptop, trying to finish his work*
                    before the deadline.

buzzingly /bˈʌzɪŋli/

filled with a low, continuous humming sound, resembling the noise of bees or machinery

Example: *The city streets were buzzingly alive with the sounds of traffic and people going about their day.*

lively, vibrant, or filled with excitement

Example: *The party was buzzingly energetic, with music, laughter, and conversation filling the air.*

Cc

calmingly /kˈɑːmɪŋli/
an action performed in a soothing or tranquil way
Example: *She spoke calmingly, her gentle voice easing the tension in the room.*

calmly /kˈɑːmli/
an action or manner performed in a relaxed, composed, and tranquil way, often in a situation where one might expect stress or excitement
Example: *Despite the chaos around her, she faced the situation calmly.*

candidly /kˈandɪdli/
speaking or behaving in a frank, open, and sincere way, without reservation or pretence
Example: *He candidly admitted his faults, eager to make amends and move forward with honesty.*

cannily /kˈanɪli/
in a shrewd or clever way, showing good judgement or resourcefulness
Example: *He cannily invested in the stock market, earning significant profits by carefully analysing trends and making strategic decisions.*
in a cautious or careful way, with awareness of potential risks or consequences
Example: *She cannily navigated through the busy streets, always aware of potential hazards and obstacles.*
in a knowing or sly way, often with a sense of craftiness or cunning
Example: *He cannily manipulated the situation to his advantage, subtly influencing others without them realising it.*

cantankerously /kənˈtaŋkərəsli/
an action that is ill-tempered, quarrelsome, or contentious
Example: *He cantankerously refused to compromise, insisting on having his way in every matter.*

capably /kˈeɪpəbli/
performing an action competently, proficiently, or skilfully
Example: *She capably managed the project, ensuring everything was completed on time and within budget.*

capaciously /kəˈpeɪʃəsli/
having a large capacity or ample space
Example: *The closet was built capaciously, with enough room to store all her clothes and shoes.*

to be open-minded or accommodating, able to hold or accept a wide range of ideas
Example: *She listened capaciously to her friend's differing opinions, considering them with an open mind and respect.*

in a manner that is extensive or expansively, covering a wide range or scope
Example: *The library was built capaciously, housing an extensive collection of books on various subjects.*

generously or lavishly; providing abundantly or plentifully
Example: *The picnic basket was packed capaciously with sandwiches, fruits, and snacks for the day at the beach.*

capitally /ˈkapɪtlɪ/
in a way that is excellent, superb, or outstanding
Example: *Pat performed capitally in the final round of the competition, impressing the judges with her skill and precision.*

relates to or involves the death penalty

Example: The debate focused on the issue of whether certain crimes
should be punished capitally with the death penalty.

pertains to the capital city or the principal city of a country

Example: London is capitally important as it serves as the capital
city of the United Kingdom.

in a manner that is financially profitable or advantageous

Example: Investing in renewable energy sources can be capitally
beneficial in the long run, both economically and
environmentally

to be politically or strategically important

Example: The bridge was situated capitally, connecting two major
cities, and facilitating trade and communication between
them

captivatingly /ˈkaptɪveɪtɪŋli/

performing an action in a captivating or enchanting way; can hold
one's attention or interest in a charming or irresistible way

Example: The magician performed captivatingly, holding the
audience spellbound with his mesmerising tricks.

carefully /kˈeəfəli/

shows caution or prudence, avoiding mistakes or accidents

Example: She walked carefully along the icy path, making sure not
to slip on the frozen ground.

demonstrates attention to detail or thoroughness

Example: Tom read the instructions carefully before assembling the
furniture, ensuring each piece was put together correctly.

shows consideration for others or sensitivity to their feelings

Example: She listened carefully to her friend's concerns, offering
support, and understanding during their difficult time.

suggests thoughtfulness or deliberation

Example: The supervisor spoke carefully, choosing his words with
precision to convey his message clearly and effectively.

protecting or preserving something valuable or fragile

Example: The store attendant wrapped the delicate vase carefully
in bubble wrap before packing it away for storage.

carelessly /kˈeələsli/
shows lack of attention or thoughtfulness
Example: She carelessly left her phone on the table, only to realise
later that it was missing.
shows lack of caution or recklessness
Example: He carelessly drove through the red light, risking an
accident.
shows lack of regard or consideration for others
Example: Sam carelessly disrupted the quiet atmosphere of the
library by speaking loudly on his phone.

demonstrates lack of neatness or precision
Example: The painter painted the walls carelessly, leaving streaks
and drips of paint all over the floor.
shows lack of responsibility or accountability
Example: She carelessly forgot to lock the door, leading to the theft
of valuable items from her home.

caringly /kˈeərɪŋli/
performing an action with concern, kindness, or affection towards
others
Example: The nurse caringly tended to the sick child, soothing their
discomfort with gentle words and gestures.

carnally /kˈɑːnəli/
actions or behaviours that are related to or involve physical desires or
pleasures, particularly those of a sexual nature
Example: He desired her carnally, consumed by lustful thoughts.

carousingly /kˈɑraʊsɪŋli/
involves boisterous and festive behaviour, often accompanied by loud laughter and revelry
Example: *The friends laughed carousingly as they shared stories around the campfire.*

cartographically /ˌkɑːtəʊˈgrafɪkəlli/
actions or processes that pertains to the creation, study, or analysis of maps or charts
Example: *The geographer cartographically mapped the region's terrain to better understand its topography.*

casually /kˈɑʒuːəli/
in a relaxed or informal way, without formality or seriousness
Example: *They chatted casually over coffee, enjoying each other's company without any pressure or expectations.*
without much thought, attention, or concern; in a nonchalant or indifferent way
Example: *He casually tossed his keys on the table, not noticing they landed dangerously close to the edge.*
without careful planning or preparation; in an improvised or spontaneous way
Example: *She decided to cook dinner casually, throwing together whatever ingredients she had in the fridge.*
without strict adherence to rules or conventions
Example: *He dressed casually for the party, opting for jeans and a t-shirt instead of formal attire.*

categorically /kˌatɪgˈɒrɪkli/
to emphasise the certainty or definitiveness of a statement or action
Example: *She denied the allegations categorically, asserting her innocence without hesitation.*

catholically /ˈkæθəlɪkɑli/

without narrowness or restriction

Example: *He approached his studies catholically, exploring a wide range of topics and perspectives to gain a comprehensive understanding.*

consistent with the principles or practices of the Catholic Church

Example: *The couple decided to raise their children catholically, attending church services regularly and instilling Catholic values in their upbringing.*

in a comprehensive or inclusive manner, considering a wide range of perspectives or beliefs

Example: *The committee approached the issue catholically, considering various viewpoints and opinions before deciding.*

causally /kˈɔːsəli/

indicating a relationship between two or more events where one event brings about another

Example: *She explained the concept causally, illustrating how changes in weather patterns directly affect crop yields.*

the principle that every event is caused by preceding events and causes subsequent events

Example: *The scientist analysed the data causally, tracing the chain of causation to understand the origins of the phenomenon*

caustically /kˈɔːstɪkli/

a sharp, sarcastic, or biting tone

Example: *Jane responded caustically to his criticism, her words dripping with sarcasm and disdain.*

harsh criticism or commentary

Example: *The reviewer's caustically negative remarks about the film left many disappointed fans questioning their own opinions.*

cautiously /kˈɔːʃəsli/

in a careful or prudent manner, exercising caution

Example: *I cautiously approached the wild animal to avoid startling it*

cavalierly /ˌkavəˈlɪəli/

displaying arrogance or disregard for others' feelings

Example: *He cavalierly dismissed her concerns, showing no regard for her feelings*

celestially /sɪˈlestjəlli/

relating to the celestial body, such as stars, planets, or heavenly bodies

Example: *The astronomer gazed celestially at the night sky, studying the movements of the stars.*

centennially /senˈtenjəlli/

events or occurrences that happen once every hundred years

Example: *The town celebrates its founding centennially with a grand parade and fireworks display.*

centrally /sˈɛntrəli/

something occurring at, in, or from the centre

Example: *The town square is centrally located, making it easily accessible from all directions.*

cerebrally /sərˈiːbrəli/

things related to or involving the brain, intellect, or mental processes

Example: *He approached the problem cerebrally, analysing it with logic and reason.*

ceremonially /ˌsɛrɪmˈəʊnɪəli/
actions or events performed according to a formal or ritualistic
procedure, often with symbolic significance
Example: *The flag was ceremonially raised at dawn, marking the*
beginning of the national holiday.

ceremoniously /ˌsɛrɪmˈəʊnɪəsli/
actions or events performed with formal observance of ceremonial
practices or customs
Example: *The king ceremoniously knighted the brave soldier,*
honouring his valour in battle.

certain /sˈɜːtən/
definitely; without doubt
Example: *I am certain that I locked the door before leaving the*
house this morning.
in a particular or specific manner
Example: *The CEO handled the situation with a certain grace,*
calming everyone down with her composed demeanour.

certainly /sˈɜːtənli/
without doubt; definitely
Example: *She will certainly attend the meeting tomorrow; she*
confirmed it multiple times.
used to indicate agreement or affirmation
Example: *"Can I count on your help?" "Certainly, I'll be there to*
assist you."

chance /tʃˈɑːns/
randomly or by luck
Example: *They bumped into each other at the airport by chance*
after years of not seeing each other.
possibly or potentially

Example: *There's a chance of rain later today, so you might want to*
             bring an umbrella just in case.

riskily or hazardously

Example: *Jim took a chance by investing all his savings into the*
             new start-up, hoping for a big return on his investment.

changeably /tʃˈeɪndʒəbəli/

in a way that varies or fluctuates

Example: *The weather in this region tends to be changeably*
             unpredictable, with frequent shifts between sunshine and
             rain

chaotically /keɪˈɒtɪkli/

actions or processes that are characterised by chaos, disorder, or lack
or organisation

Example: *The children played chaotically in the yard, their toys*
             scattered everywhere and laughter filling the air.

characteristically /kˌarɪktərˈɪstɪkli/

actions or behaviours that are typical or characteristic of a particular
person, thing, or situation

Example: *She characteristically arrived early to the meeting,*
             prepared and ready to contribute to the discussion.

charitably /tʃˈarɪtəbli/

a sense of compassion, empathy, and consideration for the well-being
of others

Example: *She donated charitably to the local homeless shelter,*
             providing warm meals and clothing for those in need.

charmingly /tʃˈɑːmɪŋli/

actions or behaviours that are pleasing, delightful, or attractive in a
way that captivates or wins over others

Example: *The young couple smiled charmingly at each other as*
they danced under the stars.

chastely /ˈʧeɪstli/
doing something in a morally pure or virtuous manner
Example: *He admired her chastely from afar, respecting her*
boundaries and values.

cheap /ʧˈiːp/
something that is obtained or done at a low cost or with little expense
Example: *He found a cheap apartment in the city, allowing him to*
save money for other expenses.

cheaply /ʧˈiːpli/
something that is obtained or done at a low cost or with little expense
Example: *Jenny decorated her apartment cheaply by shopping at*
thrift stores and repurposing old furniture.

cheerfully /ʧˈiəfəli/
doing something in a fashion that is full of cheer or happiness
Example: *She greeted her friends cheerfully, her smile lighting up*
the room.

cheerily /ʧˈiərɪli/
doing something in a bright, lively, or cheerful way
Example: *The children skipped cheerily through the park, enjoying*
the sunshine and fresh air.

cheeringly /ʧˈiərɪŋli/
doing something in a manner that uplifts or encourages others, by
providing support, comfort, or inspiration
Example: *She spoke cheeringly to her friend, offering words of*
encouragement during a difficult time.

chemically /kˈɛmɪkli/

actions or processes that relate to chemistry or involve chemical substances

Example: *The scientist analysed the compound chemically, identifying its molecular structure and properties.*

chiefly /tʃˈiːfli/

primarily or mainly; the most important or significant aspect that occurs at a greater extent than anything else

Example: *She was chiefly responsible for organising the event, overseeing all the major details and decisions.*

childishly /tʃˈaɪldɪʃli/

characteristics of a child, often implying immaturity, naivety, or simplicity

Example: *He responded childishly to criticism, pouting, and refusing to listen to reason.*

chirpily /tʃˈɜːpɪli/

characterised by chirping or making bird-like sounds

Example: *The birds chirpily greeted the dawn, filling the air with their cheerful melodies.*

conveying a sense of cheerfulness or liveliness

Example: *She chirpily invited her friends over for a weekend barbecue, eager to spend time together and enjoy good food.*

chivalrously /ʃˈɪvəlrəsli/

behaving in a noble, respectful, and honourable way, often with a sense of protecting or defending others

Example: *Tommy chivalrously held the door open for the elderly lady, showing kindness and respect towards her.*

choicely /ˈtʃɔɪslɪ/

to describe doing something in a carefully selected or chosen manner

Example: She decorated her room choicely, selecting each piece of
furniture and decor with great care and consideration

chorally /kɒˈrɑːlli/

describes actions or events that are performed or executed
collectively by a group of people, similar to how a choir or chorus
sings or performs together in unison

Example: The students sang chorally during the school assembly,
their voices blending harmoniously in song.

chromatically /krəʊmˈatɪkli/

actions, changes, or variations that occur in a manner akin to the
progression of colours in a chromatic scale

Example: The artist painted the landscape chromatically, using a
wide range of colours to capture the vibrant beauty of the
scene.

churlishly /ˈtʃɜːlɪʃli/

describes behaviour that is rude, surly, or ill-mannered

Example: He responded churlishly to the waiter's polite inquiry,
snapping at him without cause.

circularly /sˈɜːkjʊləli/

something done or happening in a circular manner, often involving a
sequence of events or actions that repeat or return to the starting point

Example: The debate continued circularly, with each side restating
their arguments without making progress toward a
resolution.

to describe a process or argument that lacks a clear direction or
conclusion, instead going around in circles without making progress

Example: Their discussion about the project's budget went
circularly, with everyone repeating the same points and
no decision being reached.

something that is arranged or organised in a circular shape or pattern

Example: The tables in the conference room were arranged
circularly to facilitate better communication among the
attendees.

clairvoyantly /kleə'vɔɪəntli/

gaining knowledge or insight about events, situations, or information through psychic or intuitive means rather than through conventional sensory channels

Example: She predicted the outcome of the game clairvoyantly,
astonishing everyone with her accurate foresight.

clammily /kl'amɪli/

describes something done or happening in a damp, sticky, or unpleasantly moist manner

Example: His hands felt clammily cold as he stepped out of the
chilly water.

clashingly /kl'aʃɪŋli/

describes something done in a manner that involves clashes or conflicts, either in terms of sound, style, appearance, or ideas

Example: The two artists' styles clashed in the collaborative
project, resulting in a disjointed final product.

classically /kl'asɪkli/

adherence to principles, forms, or aesthetics within a particular field, such as classical music, art, literature, or architecture

Example: She dressed classically in a black dress and pearls for the
formal event, exuding timeless elegance.

cleanly /ˈklenlɪ/

describes something done or happening in a way that is neat, tidy, or without causing mess or disorder

Example: *She wiped the kitchen counters cleanly, leaving them sparkling and free of crumbs or spills.*

actions or outcomes that are achieved smoothly, efficiently, and without complications

Example: *He executed the project plan cleanly, meeting all deadlines and delivering excellent results ahead of schedule.*

clearly /klˈiəli/

doing something in a manner that is transparent, easy to understand, or free from ambiguity

Example: *She explained the concept clearly, breaking down complex ideas into simple terms that everyone could grasp*

doing something in a way that is distinct, sharp, or easily perceivable

Example: *The singer enunciated each word clearly, allowing the audience to hear every lyric with perfect clarity.*

doing something in a fashion that is complete, thorough, or without obstruction

Example: *The road signs were placed clearly along the highway, ensuring drivers could navigate the route without confusion.*

clemently /ˈkleməntli/

leniency, gentleness, or benevolence in one's behaviour or attitude towards others

Example: *The judge clemently granted the first-time offender a reduced sentence, considering their remorse and efforts towards rehabilitation.*

cleverly /klˈɛvəli/

using one's intelligence, wit, or resourcefulness to achieve a desired outcome effectively or to solve a problem creatively

Example: *She cleverly solved the puzzle by thinking outside the box and finding an unexpected solution.*

clinically /klˈɪnɪkli/

a focus on facts, data, and evidence, without emotion or bias.

Example: *The scientist examined the results clinically, analysing the data without allowing personal biases to influence the interpretation.*

clockwise /klˈɒkwaɪz/

a direction of movement that follows the same direction as the hands of a clock, which is typically from left to right

Example: *He turned the knob clockwise to tighten it and secure the door shut.*

closely /klˈəʊsli/

doing something in a manner that is near

Example: *She followed closely behind her friend as they navigated through the crowded streets of the city.*

a close examination, scrutiny, or observation of something

Example: *The detective studied the crime scene closely, searching for any clues that could lead to solving the case.*

cloudily /klˈaʊdli/

obscured by clouds

Example: *The view of the mountains was cloudily obscured by the thick fog that had rolled in.*

to be unclear, vague, or uncertain

Example: *His explanation of the new policy was cloudily worded, leaving many employees confused about its implications.*

clumsily /klˈʌmzɪli/

is done in a graceless, awkward, or inept way

Example: *He clumsily bumped into the table, spilling his drink in the process.*

coarsely /kˈɔːsli/

a lack of finesse, delicacy, or precision in behaviour or execution

Example: *John coarsely interrupted the conversation with his loud and inappropriate remarks.*

coaxingly /ˈkəʊksɪŋli/

done in a gentle, persuasive, or seductive way, often with the intention of persuading someone to do something

Example: *She smiled coaxingly, hoping to convince her friend to join her on the adventure.*

coequally /kəʊˈiːkwəlli/

is equal or equivalent to something else in value, status, importance, or some other aspect

Example: *Both candidates are coequally qualified for the position, making the decision difficult for the hiring committee*

cogently /kˈəʊdʒəntli/

the ability to express ideas or points of view in a way that is persuasive and compelling

Example: *The speaker cogently argued his case, persuading the audience to reconsider their stance on the issue.*

cognizably /ˈkɒgnɪzəbli/

a change, action, or situation is evident or observable, often to the extent that it can be readily identified and understood by others

Example: *The impact of the new policy was cognizably evident in the improved efficiency of the department.*

coherently /kəʊhˈiərəntli/
ideas, arguments, or statements are presented in a clear,
understandable, and connected manner, with logical connections
between them
Example: *The manager explained her plan coherently, outlining
                each step in a logical sequence that everyone could
                follow.*

coincidentally /kəʊˌɪnsɪdˈɛntəli/
happens by chance or accident, often unexpectedly or without prior
planning
Example: *Coincidentally, we ran into each other at the grocery
                store just as I was thinking about calling you.*

coincidently /kəʊˈɪnsɪdəntli/
happens by chance or accident, often unexpectedly or without prior
planning
Example: *He happened to arrive at the same restaurant
                coincidently when his friend was having lunch.*

coldly /kˈəʊldli/
a detached, distant, or indifferent attitude toward others or a situation
Example: *She greeted him coldly, making it clear that their
                previous argument was still unresolved.*

collectedly /kəˈlektɪdli/
maintaining a sense of poise, composure, and clarity of mind, despite
external pressures or distractions
Example: *Even amid chaos, Jane spoke collectedly, calming those
                around her with her composed demeanour.*

collectively /kəlˈɛktɪvli/
the combined efforts, resources, or contributions of multiple
individuals or entities towards a common goal or outcome

Example: *The team worked collectively to achieve their sales*
             targets for the quarter, pooling their skills and efforts to
             reach success.

colourfully /kˈʌləfəli/
expressed in a vivid, vibrant, or lively manner, often involving a rich
array of colours
Example: *The artist painted the landscape colourfully, capturing*
             the vibrant hues of the sunset in every brushstroke.

comelily /kˈʌmlˈɪli/
pleasant, or attractive to look at
Example: *The flowers were arranged comelily in a vase, creating a*
             beautiful centrepiece for the table.

comfortably /kˈʌmftəbli/
relaxed, at ease, or without discomfort
Example: *Robert sank into the soft armchair comfortably, enjoying*
             the feeling of relaxation after a long day.

comically /kˈɒmɪkli/
an action, situation, or expression which elicits laughter or
amusement from others
Example: *The comedian delivered his jokes comically, leaving the*
             audience roaring with laughter throughout the entire
             show.

commandingly /kəˈmɑːndɪŋli/
something done in an authoritative, assertive, or dominating way
Example: *The general spoke commandingly, instilling confidence*
             and respect among his troops.

commercially /kəmˈɜːʃəlˌi/

activities relating to commerce, business, or trade with the intention of generating profit or financial gain

Example: *The company launched its new product commercially, aiming to capture a larger market share and increase revenue.*

commonly /kˈɒmənli/

something that occurs or is done frequently, regularly, or widely

Example: *It is commonly known that breakfast is the most important meal of the day.*

compactly /kəmpˈaktli/

tightly packed or densely arranged

Example: *She folded the clothes compactly to fit them all into the suitcase for her trip.*

in a way that uses or fills only a small amount of space

Example: *Sue packed her belongings compactly into the small storage bin, making sure to utilise every inch of available space.*

comparably /kˈɒmpərəbli/

similarity or equivalence in relation to another thing or situation

Example: *The new smartphone is comparably priced to its competitors, offering similar features at a competitive cost.*

comparatively /kəmpˈarətˌɪvli/

something done or happening in a manner that involves making comparisons with something else, often to highlight differences, and similarities

Example: *She performed comparatively better on the second exam after studying more diligently.*

compassionately /kəmpˈaʃənətli/
a genuine caring attitude and a willingness to alleviate suffering or offer support to those in need
Example: *The doctor spoke compassionately to the patient, explaining their diagnosis and treatment options with kindness and empathy.*

competently /kˈɒmpɪtəntli/
an action or manner of behaviour that is done with skill, proficiency, or capability
Example: *Tommy completed the project competently, demonstrating his expertise and attention to detail.*

competitively /kəmpˈɛtɪtɪvli/
done in a competitive or rivalry-driven way
Example: *The company priced its products competitively to attract more customers in the market.*

complacently /kəmplˈeɪsəntli/
a sense of contentment or satisfaction with one's current situation, accompanied by a lack of concern for improvement or change
Example: *He sat complacently on the couch, ignoring the mounting pile of work that needed to be done.*

completely /kəmplˈiːtli/
is total, absolute, or without exception
Example: *She was completely unaware of the surprise party planned for her birthday.*

compliantly /kəmplˈaɪəntli/
in a way that conforms to rules, regulations, or requests, often without resistance or objection
Example: *The employees filled out the paperwork compliantly, following the company's procedures without hesitation.*

comprehensively /kˌɒmprɪhˈɛnsɪvli/

with thoroughness and attention to detail

Example: The report comprehensively analyses the data.

a wide range or scope

Example: Aria studied comprehensively for the exam, covering all
the topics.

includes all relevant factors, elements, or aspects

Example: The policy addresses the issue comprehensively,
considering various perspectives.

conceivably /kənsˈiːvəbli/

to indicate that something is possible within the realm of imagination
or belief

Example: Conceivably, we could finish the project ahead of
schedule if we work efficiently.

conclusively /kənklˈuːsɪvli/

something that is done or settled in a clear and final matter

Example: The DNA evidence conclusively proved his innocence,
leading to his exoneration.

concurrently /kənkˈʌrəntli/

describing events, actions, or situations occurring at the same moment
in time

Example: The two teams were playing their respective matches
concurrently on adjacent fields.

confidently /kˈɒnfɪdəntli/

doing something with self-assurance, certainty, or conviction

Example: Amy answered the question confidently, knowing she had
prepared well.

a manner of behaviour or action that is assertive and fearless, often in
the face of challenges or uncertainties

Example: *Fred approached the task confidently, undeterred by*
potential obstacles.

describing something done or decided upon firmness and decisiveness, without doubt or second-guessing

Example: *She confidently accepted the job offer, knowing it was the*
right decision.

suggesting a sense of reliance or trust in one's own abilities, judgements, or beliefs

Example: *He confidently led the team, inspiring trust, and respect*
among its members.

conscientiously /kˌɒnsɪˈɛnʃəsli/

referring to doing something with careful attention to detail, thoroughness, and dedication

Example: *He conscientiously reviewed each document, ensuring*
accuracy and completeness before submitting them to the
client.

someone who carries out their responsibilities or obligations with a sense of moral duty or ethical principles

Example: *She conscientiously volunteered at the local animal*
shelter every weekend, driven by her deep compassion for
animals in need.

a commitment to acting in accordance with one's conscience or moral principles

Example: *The nurse conscientiously refused to administer the*
experimental treatment, as it conflicted with her ethical
beliefs.

consciously /kˈɒnʃəsli/

referring to doing something with awareness, purpose, or deliberate intent

Example: *She consciously made the decision to start eating*
healthier, opting for fruits and vegetables instead of junk
food.

describing a state of being fully aware or mindful of one's thoughts, actions, or surroundings

Example: *He walked through the forest consciously, taking in the sights and sounds of nature with a clear mind.*

consecutively /kəns'ɛkjuːt ˌɪvli/
describing events or actions that occur one after another in uninterrupted order

Example: *The team won the championship title consecutively for three years, showcasing their dominance in the sport.*

suggesting that something occurs repeatedly or continuously for a specified number of times

Example: *She completed her daily workout routine consecutively for a month, leading to significant improvements in her strength and stamina.*

consequently /k'ɒnsɪkwəntli/
referring to something that happens as a direct outcome or consequence of a preceding action, event, or condition

Example: *He missed the bus, and consequently, he arrived late to work.*

conservatively /kəns'ɜːvət ˌɪvli/
describing an action or approach that is characterised by carefulness, restraint, or prudence

Example: *Graham invested conservatively, preferring low-risk options.*

referring to something done or viewed in a manner that aligns with traditional or conventional norms or values

Example: *He dressed conservatively for the job interview.*

indicating a degree or extent that is not excessive or radical

Example: *The budget was planned conservatively to avoid overspending.*

suggesting a demeanour or attitude that is reserved, understated, or not overly expressive

Example: *The teacher spoke conservatively, revealing only what was necessary.*

considerably /kəns'ɪdərəbli/
to a notably large extent or degree

Example: *The temperature dropped considerably overnight, causing frost to form on the windows.*

considerately /kəns'ɪdərətli/
in a thoughtful and respectful manner, showing concern for the feelings and needs of others

Example: *He considerately held the door open for the elderly woman, allowing her to enter the building with ease.*

consistently /kəns'ɪstəntli/
in a steady and regular way, without variation or fluctuation

Example: *Joe consistently wakes up early to exercise before starting his day.*

conspicuously /kənsp'ɪkjuːəsli/
in a way that is easily noticeable or clearly visible, often suggesting something is intentionally done to attract attention or stand out

Example: *She wore a conspicuously bright red hat, making it easy for her friends to spot her in the crowd.*

constantly /k'ɒnstəntli/
continuously or without interruption

Example: *She checked her phone constantly throughout the day*
Regularly or frequently occurring

Example: *He constantly visits his favourite coffee shop for his morning caffeine fix.*

continually /kənt'ɪnjuːəli/

repeatedly or frequently over a period

Example: *The dog barked continually throughout the night, keeping the neighbours awake.*

in an ongoing or persistent manner

Example: *She strives continually for self-improvement, always seeking new challenges and opportunities to grow.*

continuously /kənt'ɪnjuːəsli/

in an uninterrupted or unbroken manner

Example: *The river flowed continuously, never ceasing in its journey downstream.*

in a constant or unchanging way

Example: *The air conditioner hummed continuously, maintaining a steady temperature throughout the room.*

conveniently /kənv'iːnɪəntli/

in a way that is easy or suitable for a particular purpose

Example: *She conveniently scheduled her dentist appointment for the afternoon, allowing her to finish her work before heading to the clinic.*

in a way that is opportune or advantageous

Example: *He conveniently found a parking spot right in front of the store, making his shopping trip quick and easy.*

conversely /kənv'ɜːsli/

in a way that shows contrast or opposite relation

Example: *She prefers hot weather; conversely, her sister enjoys the cold.*

in a way that presents an opposing viewpoint or perspective

Example: *She argued for stricter regulations on environmental protection; conversely, her colleague advocated for more lenient policies to support economic growth.*

convincingly /kənvˈɪnsɪŋli/

in a manner that persuades or impresses others with its truth or validity

Example: *The lawyer presented the evidence convincingly, leaving the jury with no doubt about the defendant's innocence.*

in a way that is compelling or plausible

Example: *She explained her theory convincingly, providing logical reasoning and evidence to support her claims.*

coolly /kˈuːli/

in a calm, composed, or unemotional manner

Example: *Despite the unexpected news, she reacted coolly, maintaining her composure, and assessing the situation calmly.*

in a fashionable or stylish manner

Example: *He strolled into the party coolly, dressed in a sharp suit and exuding confidence with every step.*

correctly /kərˈɛktli/

in an accurate or precise manner

Example: *She followed the instructions correctly, resulting in a perfectly baked batch of cookies.*

in accordance with what is right, proper, or expected

Example: *He answered all the questions on the exam correctly, demonstrating a strong understanding of the material.*

correspondingly /kˌɒrɪspˈɒndɪŋli/

in a manner that corresponds or matches something else

Example: *With more rainfall, the level of humidity in the air increases correspondingly.*

in a manner that is proportionate or in relation to something else

Example: *As the demand for a product rises, the price often increases correspondingly.*

courageously /kʌrˈeɪdʒəsli/

in a brave or fearless manner

Example: *She courageously stood up to the bully, refusing to back down.*

in a manner showing strength of character and determination

Example: *The soldiers fought courageously on the battlefield, never losing hope.*

craftily /krˈɑːftɪli/

in a sly, cunning, or deceitful manner

Example: *The thief craftily stole the jewels without anyone noticing.*

in a skilful or clever manner, often with a hint of trickery or deception

Example: *The magician craftily performed the illusion, leaving the audience in awe.*

crazily /krˈeɪzɪli/

in a wild or frenzied manner

Example: *The children ran crazily around the playground, full of energy and excitement.*

in an irrational or eccentric manner

Example: *She laughed crazily at the joke, unable to control her amusement.*

creatively /kriːˈeɪtɪvli/

inventively or imaginatively

Example: *Sarah approached the project creatively, generating innovative ideas to solve the problem.*

with originality or artistic flair

Example: *The chef cooked creatively, experimenting with flavours and presentation to delight diners.*

credibly /krˈɛdɪbli/

in a believable or convincing way

Example: *The scientist presented her research findings credibly,*
             backed by solid evidence.
in a trustworthy or reliable manner
Example: *The news anchor reported the story credibly, ensuring*
             accuracy and impartiality.

credulously /ˈkredjʊləsli/
in a gullible or easily believing way
Example: *The scammer took advantage of the credulously trusting*
             nature of the elderly couple.
in a naively or uncritically accepting manner
Example: *The conspiracy theory was embraced credulously by*
             some, despite lacking evidence.

creepingly /ˈkriːpɪŋli/
slowly and surreptitiously advancing
Example: *The vines crept creepingly up the walls of the old castle,*
             reclaiming it inch by inch.

criminally /krˈɪmɪnəli/
involves or relates to criminal behaviour or activity
Example: *Sam was driving criminally, weaving in and out of traffic*
             at high speeds.
is morally reprehensible or deserving of severe condemnation
Example: *It is criminally irresponsible to leave a child unattended*
             in a dangerous situation.

crisply /krˈɪspli/
is sharp or distinct, often with clear articulation or definition
Example: *Rosy spoke crisply, enunciating each word with*
             precision.
is fresh or invigorating, often with a sense of liveliness or efficiency
Example: *The morning air felt crisply cold as Desma stepped*
             outside.

critically /krˈɪtɪkli/
involves careful analysis, evaluation, or judgement
Example: *It is important to think critically about the information*
                presented to us before forming opinions.
indicating the severity or seriousness of a situation or condition
Example: *The patient's condition deteriorated critically overnight,*
                requiring immediate medical attention.

crookedly /krˈʊkɪdli/
is not straight or aligned properly
Example: *The picture hung crookedly on the wall, tilting to the left.*
is dishonest or deceitful
Example: *The politician smiled crookedly as he made promises he*
                had no intention of keeping.

crossly /krˈɒsli/
showing annoyance or irritation
Example: *The teacher croosly scolded the students for talking*
                during the lesson.
indicating displeasure or frustration
Example: *Rudolph muttered crossly to himself as he struggled to*
                untangle the knots in the rope.

crucially /krˈuːʃəlˌi/
is vitally important or essential
Example: *The meeting tomorrow will be crucially significant for*
                finalising the budget.
plays a crucial or decisive role in a situation
Example: *The timing of the announcement was crucially strategic,*
                maximising its impact on public opinion.

crudely /krˈuːdli/
in a rough or unrefined manner

Example: *Luke painted the fence crudely, with uneven strokes and*
             splatters of paint.
in a simple or unsophisticated way
Example: *The diagram was crudely drawn, making it difficult to*
             understand the concept.

cruelly /krˈuːəlˌi/
involves causing pain, suffering, or harm deliberately
Example: *The bully laughed cruelly as he taunted the younger*
             children.
showing a lack of empathy or compassion
Example: *The dictator ruled his country cruelly, suppressing*
             dissent and violating human rights.

cryptically /krˈɪptɪkli/
is mysterious, enigmatic, or difficult to understand
Example: *Ben spoke cryptically, dropping hints without revealing*
             the full truth.
suggestive of hidden or secret knowledge
Example: *The symbols carved into the ancient stone were*
             cryptically encoded, requiring decryption to reveal their
             significance.

culinarily /kjˈʊlɪnərili/
related to cooking or cuisine
Example: *Kim is culinarily skilled, able to prepare a variety of*
             dishes from different cuisines.
concerning culinary arts or practices
Example: *Henry travelled to France to study culinarily under*
             renowned chefs in Paris.

culturally /kˈʌltʃərəli/
related to culture or cultural practices

Example: *The festival is culturally significant, showcasing various*
                  aspects of local culture and heritage.
reflecting the customs, beliefs, and values of a particular society or
group
Example: *The museum exhibit explores culturally significant*
                  artefacts from different civilizations around the world.

cunningly /kˈʌnɪŋli/
in a clever or skilful way, often with a hidden motive or intent
Example: *The fox cunningly outsmarted the hunter by leading him*
                  into a trap.
in a sly or deceitful manner, with a desire to deceive or manipulate
Example: *Jacob spoke cunningly, carefully choosing his words to*
                  manipulate the situation in his favour.

curiously /kjˈʊrɪəsli/
in a way that shows an eager desire to know or learn something
Example: *The child looked curiously at the strange object, wanting*
                  to know what it was.
is unusual or strange, often arousing interest or suspicion
Example: *The cat tilted its head curiously, watching the bird*
                  perched on the fence.

currently /kˈʌrəntli/
at the present time; now
Example: *I am currently studying for my exams.*

curtly /kˈɜːtli/
in a brief or abrupt manner, often with rudeness
Example: *The boss spoke curtly to the employees, dismissing their*
                  questions without consideration.

customarily /kˌʌstəmˈɛrəli/
is unusual or habitual according to custom or tradition

Example: In our family, we customarily gather for dinner every Sunday evening.

cynically /sˈɪnɪkli/
expresses distrust or scepticism about motives or sincerity
Example: The politician cynically manipulates public opinion to further his own agenda.
shows contempt for accepted standards or beliefs, often with a belief that people are motivated purely by self-interest
Example: Laura looked at the charity event cynically, suspecting ulterior motives behind the organisers' actions.

Dd

daftly /ˈdɑːftli/
in a silly or foolish manner
*Example: She daftly wore her winter coat in the middle of summer,
much to the amusement of her friends.*

daily /dˈeɪli/
occurring every day or pertaining to each day
Example: She takes a walk daily to enjoy the fresh air.

daintily /dˈeɪntɪli/
in a delicate, graceful, or refined way
*Example: She sipped her tea daintily, holding the cup with her
pinky finger extended.*

damnably /dˈamǝbli/
in a manner that is extremely bad or deserving of condemnation
*Example: His actions were damnably reckless, putting everyone at
risk.*

damply /ˈdampli/
in a slightly wet or moist manner
Example: The clothes hung damply on the line, not quite dry yet.

dancingly /ˈdɑːnsɪŋli/
in a manner resembling dancing, often implying grace, liveliness, or
rhythmic movement
Example: The leaves fluttered dancingly in the autumn breeze.

dangerously /dˈeɪndʒǝrǝsli/
in a manner that is likely to cause harm or poses a risk

Example: He drove dangerously fast on the icy roads.

daringly /dˈeərɪŋli/
in a bold or adventurous fashion
Example: She daringly climbed the steep cliff without any safety gear.

darkly /dˈɑːkli/
in a way that is obscure, mysterious, or grim
Example: The clouds gathered darkly, casting an ominous shadow over the landscape.

dartingly /ˈdɑːtɪŋli/
describes doing something in a quick or sudden manner
Example: The lizard moved dartingly across the sunlit rocks, avoiding the predator.

dashingly /dˈaʃɪŋli/
describes doing something in a lively, stylish, or bold way
Example: The actor appeared dashingly on the red carpet, charming everyone with his impeccable suit and confident demeanour.

dazzlingly /dˈazəlɪŋli/
describe something done in a way that is very bright, striking, or impressive
Example: The fireworks display at the celebration was dazzlingly colourful, lighting up the night sky with bursts of vibrant hues and sparkling patterns.

deadly /dˈɛdli/
extremely or very
Example: She was deadly serious about her intentions to pursue a career in medicine.

causing or capable of causing death

Example: *The cobra's venom is deadly, capable of killing a person within hours if left untreated.*

deafly /ˈdefli/
unresponsively or inattentively to sound

Example: *The child stared at the screen, deafly ignoring his mother's calls.*

in a manner that shows a lack of awareness or consideration for sound

Example: *He walked through the bustling market, deafly oblivious to the noise around him.*

dearly /dˈiəli/
with deep affection

Example: *She cherished her grandmother dearly and visited her every chance she got.*

at a great cost or expense

Example: *She paid dearly for her mistake, facing severe consequences.*

deathly /ˈdeθlɪ/
extremely or very

Example: *She was deathly afraid of the dark.*

in a manner resembling death or causing death

Example: *The deathly silence of the abandoned house sent shivers down my spine.*

with lethal effect

Example: *The poison had a deathly effect, causing symptoms of severe paralysis within minutes.*

debonairly /ˌdebəˈneəli/
in a charming, suave, or sophisticated manner

Example: *He greeted his date at the restaurant debonairly, with a warm smile and a confident handshake.*

deceitfully /dɪˈsiːtfʊlli/

actions done in a deceptive, dishonest, or misleading manner

Example: *The salesman deceitfully promised a lifetime warranty on the faulty product.*

deceivingly /dɪsˈiːvɪŋli/

in a way that gives a false impression or appearance

Example: *The magician's tricks were deceivingly simple, making it seem like anyone could do them.*

decidedly /dɪsˈaɪdɪdli/

unequivocally or unquestionably

Example: *The evidence presented in court was decidedly against the defendant, leaving no room for doubt.*

in a distinctive or noticeable manner

Example: *The artist's style was decidedly modern, with bold colours and abstract shapes.*

emphatically or with emphasis

Example: *She nodded decidedly, indicating her strong agreement with the proposal.*

certainly, or definitely

Example: *The evidence presented in court was decidedly against the defendant, leading to a guilty verdict.*

deceivably /dɪsˈiːv ˈeɪbəli/

in a manner that can be misleading or deceptive

Example: *Her innocent smile was deceivably sweet.*

in a way that invites deception or misinterpretation

Example: *The appearance of the old house was deceivably quaint.*

in a manner that can lead to being deceived.

Example: *The website layout was deceivably professional.*

decimally /ˈdesɪməlɪ/
relates to or involves decimals, which are numbers expressed in a decimal system
Example: The teacher explained the multiplication of fractions decimally, emphasising the importance of understanding decimal notation.

declaratively /dɪˈklɑrətɪvli/
in a manner that states or asserts something clearly
Example: He explained the procedure declaratively.
assertively or with confidence
Example: She spoke declaratively about her beliefs.
in a way that functions as a statement
Example: The sentence was structured declaratively.

decoratively /dˈɛkrətˌɪvli/
in a decorative or ornamental manner
Example: She arranged the flowers decoratively on the table.
with a focus on enhancing appearance or beauty
Example: The curtains were hung decoratively to complement the room's colour scheme.
in a manner that adds embellishment or embellishes
Example: He carved the wood decoratively with intricate patterns.

decorously /dˈɛkərəsli/
in a manner that shows proper behaviour or etiquette
Example: The guests behave decorously during the formal dinner.
in a way that is socially appropriate
Example: She spoke decorously at the ceremony.
with propriety or respectability
Example: He dressed decorously for the job interview.

decreasingly /dˈiːkriːsɪŋli/
decrease or reduction in temperature

Example: *The temperature outside is decreasingly pleasant as*
        winter approaches.

decrease or reduction in interest rates

Example: *Interest rates are decreasingly favourable for new home*
        buyers.

decrease or reduction in popularity

Example: *The trend shows that this product is decreasingly popular*
        among consumers.

decrease or reduction in efficiency

Example: *The old machinery is decreasingly efficient compared to*
        newer models.

decrease or reduction in support

Example: *Funding for the arts has been decreasingly available*
        over the past decade.

decretorily /dɪˈkriːtərɪli/

something done in a manner that is authoritative, final, or based on an official decree or order

Example: *The judge ruled decretorily, leaving no room for appeal*
        or further discussion.

decussately /ˈdekəseɪtli/

something arranged in a pattern resembling an X or crossing, typically referring to botanical or anatomical structures

Example: *The veins in the leaf were arranged decussately, forming*
        a distinct X-shaped pattern.

dedicatedly /ˈdedɪkeɪtɪdli/

to do something with strong commitment, focus, and wholehearted devotion

Example: *She dedicatedly studied for her medical boards every day*
        for six months, resulting in her highest score yet.

deducibly /dɪˈduːsəbli/
in a manner that can be inferred or reasoned logically
Example: *The solution to this maths problem is deducibly derived*
from the given information.

deductively /dɪˈdʌktɪvli/
a method of reasoning or argumentation that proceeds logically from
general principles to specific conclusions
Example: *The detective approached the case deductively, starting*
with the broader evidence and then narrowing down to
specific suspects.

deeply /dˈiːpli/
to a great depth
Example: *He breathed deeply before diving into the pool.*
profoundly or intensely
Example: *She was deeply moved by the farewell speech.*
to a great extent or seriousness
Example: *Sam is deeply involved in the community project.*
with great insight or understanding
Example: *He deeply understands the complexities of the issue.*

defensively /dɪfˈɛnsɪvli/
an action done in a manner intended to defend or protect
Example: *The team played defensively, focusing on protecting their*
goal against the opponent's attacks.

deferentially /dˌɛfərˈɛnʃəlˌi/
an action done with respect or submission to someone else's authority
or opinion
Example: *She spoke deferentially to her mentor, acknowledging his*
wisdom and experience in the field.

definitely /dˈɛfɪnətli/
to express certainty or emphasis
Example: *I will definitely attend the party tonight*

definitively /dɪfˈɪnɪˌɪvli/
to express finality or decisiveness
Example: *The detective definitively concluded that the suspect was at the scene of the crime.*

deftly /dˈɛftli/
doing something skilfully and with ease
Example: *She deftly handled the delicate surgery, showcasing her years of experience and steady hands*

degenerately /dɪˈdʒenərɪtli/
in a morally corrupt or depraved way
Example: *He lived degenerately, indulging in all manner of vice and excess.*
in a manner that shows a decline from a former good state
Example: *The once beautiful garden was now degenerately overgrown and neglected.*
in a way that demonstrates a loss of normal qualities or standards
Example: *The debate deteriorated degenerately into personal attacks and insults.*

degradingly /dɪˈɡreɪdɪŋli/
doing something in a way that diminishes someone's dignity, respect, or value
Example: *The manager spoke to the employee degradingly, making them feel worthless and insignificant.*

dejectedly /dɪdʒˈɛktɪdli/
in a sad or depressed way
Example: *He sighed dejectedly after hearing the bad news.*

with a sense of defeat or discouragement
Example: *She walked dejectedly out of the office after being passed over for the promotion.*
showing lack of hope or enthusiasm
Example: *The team left the field dejectedly after their crushing defeat.*

delectably /dɪlˈɛktəbli/
in a deliciously enjoyable way
Example: *The chef prepared the meal delectably, using fresh herbs and spices.*
in a manner that is highly pleasing or delightful
Example: *The dessert was presented delectably, with a beautiful garnish.*
in a way that is enticing or appetising
Example: *He described the dish delectably, making everyone eager to try it.*

deliberately /dɪlˈɪbərətli/
to do something intentionally, on purpose, or with careful consideration.
Example: *The child deliberately knocked over the tower of blocks, watching them fall with a mischievous grin.*

delicately /dˈɛlɪkətli/
to do something in a gentle, careful, or sensitive manner.
Example: *She opened the antique music box delicately, so as not to damage its delicate interior.*

deliciously /dɪlˈɪʃəsli/
to do something in a way that is very enjoyable or pleasant, often in reference to taste, smell, or a pleasurable experience

Example: *The chef sautéed the vegetables deliciously, adding just the right amount of seasoning to enhance their natural flavours.*

delightedly /dɪlˈaɪtɪdli/
to do something with great pleasure or joy
Example: *The children delightedly ran to the ice cream truck when they heard the familiar jingle.*

delightfully /dɪlˈaɪtfəli/
to do something in a way that causes delight or is very pleasant and enjoyable
Example: *She sang delightfully at the concert, captivating the audience with her beautiful voice and expressive performance.*

deliriously /dɪlˈɪrɪəsli/
to do something in a way that is wildly excited, ecstatic, or frenzied, often to the point of losing control or being irrational
Example: *The fans cheered deliriously as their team scored the winning goal in the championship match.*

demandingly /dɪˈmɑːndɪŋli/
to do something in a way that requires much effort, attention, or time, often with a sense of insistence or high standards
Example: *The professor demandingly scrutinised each student's research paper for thoroughness and accuracy.*

demissly /dɪˈmɪsli/
to do something in a humble or lowly manner, often showing submission or dejection
Example: *Sarah demissly accepted the criticism, her head bowed in humility.*

demonstratively /dɪˈmɒnstrətɪvli/

to do something in a way that clearly shows one's feelings or intentions, often through expressive or emphatic actions

Example: *She hugged her friend demonstratively to express her joy at seeing him after a long time apart.*

dependably /dɪpˈɛndəbli/

in a reliable, trustworthy, or consistent manner

Example: *The old car may not be flashy, but it starts dependably every morning, getting me to work without fail.*

deprecatingly /ˈdɛprəˌkeɪtɪŋli/

to do something in a manner that expresses disapproval or modesty about oneself or something else

Example: *He smiled deprecatingly when complimented on his achievements, attributing them to luck rather than skill.*

depressingly /dɪprˈɛsɪŋli/

to do something in a manner that causes feelings of sadness, despair, or hopelessness

Example: *The news of the job cuts spread depressingly through the office, leaving everyone anxious about their future.*

deservedly /dɪzˈɜːvɪdli/

in a manner that is rightfully or justly earned, usually because of one's actions or qualities

Example: *Jane studied diligently for the exam and deservedly received an A grade.*

despairingly /dɪspˈeərɪŋli/

to do something in a manner that shows despair, hopelessness, or deep sadness

Example: *After searching for hours, she looked around despairingly, realising she had lost her most treasured possession.*

desperately /dˈɛspərətli/
to do something in a way that shows a great sense of urgency, intense desire, or extreme need
Example: *Pam searched desperately for her lost keys, fearing she would be late for her appointment.*

despondently /dɪsˈpɒndəntli/
to do something in a manner that shows feelings of hopelessness, dejection, or discouragement
Example: *Tom sat despondently on the bench, feeling defeated after receiving the rejection letter.*

destructively /dɪstrˈʌktɪvli/
to do something in a manner that causes harm, damage, or destruction
Example: *The earthquake destructively ravaged the coastal town, leaving behind widespread devastation.*

determinedly /dɪtˈɜːmɪnˌɪdli/
to do something in a resolute, unwavering, or firm manner, typically showing strong motivation or resolve
Example: *She tackled the difficult project determinedly, working late into the night to meet the deadline.*

detestably /dɪˈtɛstˈeɪbəli/
to do something in a manner that is deserving of strong dislike or hatred. It describes actions that are reprehensible or morally offensive
Example: *The politician's actions were detestably self-serving, betraying the trust of the people who had elected him.*

diagonally /daɪˈagənəli/
indicates movement, direction, or position along a diagonal line,
which runs at an angle between two non-adjacent corners or sides
Example: *The chess piece moves diagonally across the board,*
            capturing the opponent's pawn.

dialectically /ˌdaɪəˈlektɪkəlli/
something done in a manner that involves reasoning or
argumentation, especially in the context of philosophy or discussion
involving opposing viewpoints
Example: *The students were encouraged to analyse the novel*
            dialectically, considering the conflicting perspectives of
            the characters in their discussions.

diametrically /dˌaɪəmˈɛtrɪkli/
in complete opposition or directly opposite in nature
Example: *Her political views are diametrically opposed to those of*
            her colleague.

diatonically /daɪəˈtɒnɪkli/
something related to the natural scale of eight tones, whether music or
speech
Example: *The melody was composed entirely diatonically, adhering*
            strictly to the natural
scale without any chromatic alterations.

differentially /ˌdɪfəˈrenʃəlli/
in a manner that varies or differs depending on circumstances,
conditions, or individuals
Example: *The medicine is prescribed differentially based on the*
            patient's age and medical history.

differently /dˈɪfrəntli/
in a way that is not the same as another way, or in a manner that
varies or contrast with something else
Example: *She approached the problem differently than her*
colleagues, offering a unique perspective.

differingly /ˈdɪfəɪŋli/
in a manner that is different or varied from one another
Example: *The twins may look alike, but they behave differingly.*

digressively /daɪˈgresɪvli/
to do something in a manner that departs from the main topic or
subject, often by going off on a tangent or discussing unrelated
matters
Example: *During the lecture, the professor spoke digressively*
about his recent vacation, veering off the main topic of
the course for a few minutes.

diligently /dˈɪlɪdʒəntli/
to do something in a careful, conscientious, and thorough manner,
with persistent effort and attention to the detail
Example: *Sarah diligently studied for hours every day to prepare*
for the upcoming exam.

dingily /dˈɪnʒli/
something done in a dull, dirty or shabby manner, often associated
with a lack of brightness or cleanliness
Example: *The artist dingily painted the landscape, using dull and*
muted colours to convey a sense of desolation.

diplomatically /dˌɪpləmˈatɪkli/
doing something in a tactful, skilful, or sensitive manner, especially
in situations where there may be different opinions or potential for
conflict

Example: The ambassador diplomatically addressed the sensitive issue, skilfully navigating through the differing opinions to reach a peaceful resolution.

directly /daɪrˈɛktli/
in a straight line or street park
Example: She walked directly to the store without stopping.
immediately or without delay
Example: Please call me directly if you have any questions.
explicitly or clearly
Example: She stated her opinion directly without hesitation.
precisely or exactly
Example: The bus arrives directly at 9:00 AM.
straightforwardly or honestly
Example: She answered the question directly without evasion.

dirtily /ˈdɜːtɪlɪ/
actions done in a manner that is unclean, sullied, or more morally questionable
Example: He dirtily neglected to wash his hands after using the restroom, which made everyone around him uncomfortable.

dirty /dˈɜːti/
in a soiled or unclean manner
Example: He came home from playing outside and was all dirty.
in a morally or ethically questionable manner
Example: The politician played dirty to win the election.
in a sexually suggestive or lewd manner
Example: The comedian told jokes that were too dirty for the children.
in a dishonest or unfair manner
Example: They made money dirty with illegal activities.
in a mean spirited or malicious manner

Example: They spoke to each other dirty, hurting feelings.

disagreeably /dˌɪsɐgrˈiːəbəli/
in a way that is unpleasant, causing discomfort, annoyance, or disagreement
Example: The medicine tasted disagreeably bitter, causing the child to grimace at the unpleasant flavour.

disapprovingly /dˌɪsɐprˈuːvɪŋli/
doing something in a manner that shows disapproval or disfavour towards someone or something
Example: The teacher looked at the student disapprovingly when he found out that the assignment was not done

disarmingly /dɪsˈɑːmɪŋli/
something done in a way that removes suspicion or hostility, often by being charming, friendly, or sincere
Example: She spoke disarmingly about her mistakes, diffusing the tension in the room with her sincere and open-hearted approach.

disbelievingly /dˌɪsbɪlˈiːvɪŋli/
doing something in a manner that shows disbelief or scepticism towards something
Example: He raised an eyebrow disbelievingly when told the improbable story.

discontentedly /ˈdɪskənˈtentɪdlɪ/
doing something in a manner that shows dissatisfaction or unhappiness with the situation
Example: She sighed discontentedly as she looked at the messy room.

discouragingly /dɪsˈkʌrɪdʒɪŋli/

something done in a manner that causes discouragement or a lack of hope

Example: *The coach shook his head discouragingly after seeing the team performance in practice.*

discourteously /dɪsˈkɜːtjəsli/

doing something in a manner that is rude, impolite, or lacking in manners

Example: *He spoke discourteously to the waiter when his order was delayed.*

discreetly /dɪskrˈiːtli/

to do something in a careful, cautious, or subtle manner, especially to avoid causing embarrassment or offence

Example: *She discreetly slipped a note into his hand during the meeting.*

dishonestly /dɪsˈɒnɪstli/

doing something in a deceitful, fraudulent, or untruthful manner

Example: **The employee dishonestly recorded lower sales figures to embezzle funds**

disrespectfully /dˌɪsrɪspˈɛktfəli/

doing something in a manner that shows a lack of respect or regard for someone or something

Example: *The student spoke disrespectfully to the teacher, ignoring their instructions.*

doctorally /ˈdɒktərəlli/

to describe actions or behaviours associated with a doctorate or a scholarly approach

Example: *She approached the research problem doctorally,*
conducting thorough literature reviews and rigorous
analysis.

doctrinally /dɒkˈtraɪnlli/
something done in accordance with a particular doctrine, belief
system, or set of principles, especially those of a religious or
ideological nature
Example: *The group followed the guidelines doctrinally, adhering*
strictly to the teachings of their faith.

dogmatically /dɒgmˈatɪkli/
doing something in a manner that asserts beliefs or principles as if
they are true and not open to discussion or debate
Example: *He dogmatically insisted that his political ideology was*
the only correct perspective.

domestically /dəmˈɛstɪkli/
related to the house or household
Example: *He enjoys spending his weekends domestically, working*
on home improvement projects.
related to internal affairs of a country
Example: *The president's primary focus was on addressing*
domestic issues like health care and education.

dorsally /ˈdɔːsəlli/
in a position or direction towards the back or upper side of an orgasm
Example: *The shark has a prominent fin located dorsally.*

double /dˈʌbəl/
twice in quantity or degree
Example: *She received double the amount of her usual pay-check*
this month.

doubly /dˈʌbli/
in a double manner or to twice the extent
Example: *She was doubly sure to check the locks before going to bed.*

doubtfully /dˈaʊtfəli/
in a manner that expresses uncertainty, hesitation, or lack of conviction
Example: *Despite the optimistic forecasts, he doubtfully questioned the project's success.*

doubtless /dˈaʊtləs/
without doubt; to indicate a high level of confidence or certainty about something
Example: *He looked at the dark clouds doubtfully, unsure if the picnic would still happen.*

down /dˈaʊn/
to a lower position or level
Example: *She carefully climbed down the ladder.*
along a path or direction
Example: *They walked down the winding road towards the village.*
the ground or a sitting position
Example: *The dog laid down on the ground to cool off.*
reduced in amount or intensity
Example: *The noise in the room gradually went down after the meeting started.*
in writing or recording
Example: *She jotted down the important notes during the lecture.*

downhill /ˈdaʊnˈhɪl/
in the direction down a slope or towards a lower place
Example: *The cyclists sped downhill, enjoying the rush of the descent.*

downright /dˈaʊnraɪt/
completely, absolutely, or to an extreme degree, often emphasising
something negative
Example: His behaviour was downright rude during the meeting.

downstairs /ˈdaʊnˈsteəz/
to or on a lower floor of a building, typically the ground floor in a
multi-story building
Example: She went downstairs to answer the doorbell.

downstream /dˈaʊnstriːm/
in the direction of the current of a stream or river
*Example: The small boat drifted downstream, carried effortlessly
            by the flowing water.*
in a sequence or process later in the series
*Example: The factory inspected the product downstream to ensure
            quality before packaging.*

downward /dˈaʊnwəd/
movement towards a lower position or level
*Example: The plane began its downward descent towards the
            airport runway.*
decline or decrease in amount, quality, or value
*Example: The company's profits have been on a downward trend
            for the past quarter.*
physically in a downward direction
*Example: The hikers carefully climbed downward from the steep
            cliff.*

dramatically /drəmˈatɪkli/
in a striking or significant manner, often involving noticeable change
or impact

Example: The temperature dropped dramatically as the storm
approached.

dreadfully /drˈɛdfəli/
in a manner that causes great fear, apprehension, discomfort, or
distress
Example: She waited dreadfully for the exam results, fearing the
worst.

dreadingly /drˈɛdɪŋli/
in a manner that expresses fear, apprehension, or dread about
something that is anticipated or expected to happen
Example: He looked at the approaching deadline dreadingly,
unsure if he could finish the project on time.

dreamily /drˈiːmɪli/
doing something in a manner characterised by dreaminess or a state
of being lost in pleasant thoughts or fantasies
Example: She gazed out of the window dreamily, lost in the beauty
of the sunset.

dreamingly /drˈiːmɪŋli/
to describe actions or states that are reminiscent of dreaming or being
lost in a dream-like state
Example: He walked through the garden dreamingly, imagining
himself in a mystical forest filled with enchanted
creatures.

drearily /drˈiərɪli/
something done in a dull, gloomy, or depressing manner, often
suggesting a lack of enthusiasm or cheerfulness
Example: The rain fell drearily outside, matching his mood as he
stared out the window.

droppingly /drˈɒpɪŋli/

in the manner of something that drops

Example: *The old tree branches swayed droppingly in the breeze, shedding their leaves with each gust of wind.*

droopingly /drˈuːpɪŋli/

something done in a drooping or sagging manner, indicating a lack of energy or vitality

Example: *The flowers in the garden hung droopingly after a long day of scorching heat.*

drowsily /drˈaʊsɪli/

actions or states done in a sleepy or half-asleep manner, often indicating a feeling of tiredness or drowsiness

Example: *Pam blinked drowsily while trying to stay awake during the late-night movie.*

drudgingly /ˈdrʌdʒɪŋlɪ/

relates to performing something in a laborious, dull, or tedious manner, often implying that the task is burdensome or unpleasant

Example: *John cleaned the garage drudgingly, knowing it would take hours to organise everything.*

drunkenly /drˈʌŋkənli/

actions or behaviours that are done under the influence of alcohol, often characterised by unsteady movements, impaired judgement, or slurred speech

Example: *He stumbled drunkenly down the street, unable to walk straight after a night of heavy drinking.*

dryly /ˈdraɪli/

in a humorously sarcastic or ironic manner

Example: *"Is that your idea of a joke?" she asked dryly, raising an eyebrow as she spoke.*

in a matter-of-fact or unemotionally straightforward manner
Example: *He stated the facts dryly, without any hint of emotion or exaggeration.*

dubiously /djˈuːbɪəsli/
in a manner that expresses doubt, scepticism, or uncertainty about something
Example: *He accepted the offer dubiously, wondering if it was too good to be true.*

dully /dˈʌli/
lacking brightness or shine; in a dull manner
Example: *The old coin glinted dully in the dim light of the antique shop.*
lacking interest, excitement, or enthusiasm; in a boring or uninteresting manner
Example: *She listened dully to the lecture, finding the topic completely unengaging.*
in a manner that lacks sharpness or clarity; in a subdued or muted way
Example: *The distant thunder rumbled dully in the grey sky, foretelling the coming storm.*

duly /djˈuːli/
in accordance with what is required or expected, often implying that something has been done promptly, correctly, or formally
Example: *Sam completed the paperwork duly and submitted it to the office before the deadline.*

dumbly /dˈʌmli/
without speaking; silently
Example: *She stared dumbly at the unexpected gift, unable to find words to express her gratitude.*
in a manner lacking intelligence or understanding

Example: *Joe stood there dumbly, unable to comprehend the instructions given to him.*

in a manner lacking the ability to communicate effectively

Example: *She looked at him dumbly, unable to respond to his question due to her inability to speak.*

durably /djˈɔːrəbəli/

in a manner that is strong, lasting, or able to withstand wear, pressure, or damage over time

Example: *The house was constructed durably with sturdy materials to withstand harsh weather conditions for decades.*

duskily /dˈʌskili/

in a way resembling dusk, or dimly lit

Example: *The room was duskily lit by a single candle, casting shadows across the walls.*

in a manner that suggests darkness or shadowiness

Example: *The room was illuminated duskily, casting long shadows across the floor as the sun set outside.*

dutifully /djˈuːtɪfəli/

In a way that shows obedience, respect, or fulfilment of one's duty or responsibility

Example: *Sarah dutifully completed her chores every evening without complaint.*

dyingly /ˈdaɪɪŋli/

in a manner that pertains to dying or approaching death

Example: *The patient looked at his family dyingly, knowing his time was drawing near.*

in an intense or fervent manner, as if one is passionately longing or yearning for something

Example: *She pleaded with him dyingly to reconsider his decision, desperate for him to stay.*

dynamically /daɪˈæmɪkli/

in a way that is characterised by energy, vigour, change, or action

Example: *The dancers moved dynamically across the stage, showcasing their agility and synchronised movements.*

Ee

each /ˈiːtʃ/
every one of two or more people or things, considered separately
*Example: Each student received a certificate for their outstanding
            performance in the competition.*

eagerly /ˈiːɡəli/
with keen or enthusiastic desire or interest
*Example: The children eagerly awaited the arrival of Santa Claus
            on Christmas Eve.*

early /ˈɜːli/
before the expected or usual time
Example: Pat woke up early to catch the sunrise at the beach.
at the beginning of a period
*Example: He arrived at the meeting early to ensure he had time to
            prepare his presentation.*

earnestly /ˈɜːnəstli/
with sincere and intense conviction
*Example: She earnestly apologised for the misunderstanding,
            hoping to mend their friendship.*
seriously and with deep feeling
*Example: The Mayor earnestly pledged to support the community
            in rebuilding after the disaster.*

earthly /ˈɜːθli/
in relation to the physical world or human life on Earth
*Example: His ambitions were not tied to earthly desires; instead, he
            sought spiritual enlightenment.*
used for emphasis in expressions meaning no possible way or reason

Example: There's no earthly reason why she would turn down such a generous offer.

earthward /ˈɜːθwəd/
toward the Earth or ground
Example: The bird swooped earthward, gliding gracefully as it descended to land on a branch.

earthwards /ˈɜːθwədz/
toward the Earth or ground
Example: The apple fell from the tree, tumbling earthwards.

easily /ˈiːzɪli/
without difficulty or effort
Example: She finished the puzzle easily, smiling at her quick success.
readily or likely
Example: The old bridge could easily collapse under the weight of a heavy truck.
comfortably or without strain
Example: The spacious lounge allowed them to sit easily for hours, enjoying their conversation.

east /ˈiːst/
the direction toward the east, one of the four cardinal points of the compass
Example: They walked east, following the rising sun.

easterly /ˈiːstəli/
in or toward the east
Example: The ship sailed in an easterly direction, heading for the distant shores.

eastward /ˈiːstwəd/
toward the east
Example: *The birds flew eastward, chasing the morning light.*

eastwardly /ˈiːstwədli/
toward the east or in an eastward direction
Example: *The river flows eastwardly, winding through the valley.*

eastwards /ˈiːstwədz/
toward the east
Example: *The caravan continued its journey eastwards, seeking*
             new opportunities.

easy /ˈiːzi/
without difficulty or effort
Example: *She found the maths problem surprisingly easy to solve.*
in a relaxed manner
Example: *He leaned back in his chair, taking it easy after a long*
             day at work.
gently or carefully
Example: *She handled the fragile vase with an easy touch, afraid it*
             might break.

eccentrically /ɛksˈɛntrɪkli/
in a manner that is unconventional, unusual, or deviates from the
norm
Example: *He dressed eccentrically, wearing mismatched socks and*
             a hat shaped like a pineapple.

ecclesiastically /ɪˌkliziˈɑstɪkli/
in a manner that relates the church or clergy
Example: *The cathedral was decorated ecclesiastically, with*
             intricate stained glass and ornate altar furnishings.

eclectically /ɪˈklɛktɪkli/
in a manner that draws from a diverse range of sources or styles
Example: *She decorated her apartment eclectically, blending vintage furniture with modern art pieces.*

economically /ˌiːkənˈɒmɪkli/
in a way that relates to economics or finance
Example: *The country's policies were designed to grow economically, focusing on improving*
employment and reducing inflation.
using resources efficiently or sparingly
Example: *She managed her household economically, finding ways to save on groceries and utilities each month.*
in a concise or brief manner
Example: *Jessica explained the complex concept very economically, using just a few well-chosen words.*

ecstatically /ɛkstˈatɪkli/
in the state of extreme happiness or joy
Example: *She hugged her best friend ecstatically upon hearing the good news.*
with intense enthusiasm or exhilaration
Example: *Sarah danced ecstatically when she received her acceptance letter to her dream college.*

edgeways /ˈɛdʒweɪz/
with the edge or side foremost; sideways
Example: *He turned the book edgeways to fit it on the shelf.*
in terms of time or space; with consideration of depth or breadth
Example: *They discussed the project's details edgeways, exploring every aspect before deciding.*

edgewise /ˈɛdʒwaɪz/
in a narrow direction, usually referring to fitting into a small space

Example: He managed to slide the large box edgewise through the narrow doorway.

with difficulty, often in terms of being able to speak or be heard

Example: She could not get a word in edgewise during the heated debate.

edgingly /ˈedʒɪŋli/

cautiously or gradually moving

Example: He approached the wild animal edgingly, careful not to startle it.

narrowly or marginally

Example: They won the game edgingly, with just one point difference.

editorially /ˌɛdɪtˈɔːrɪəli/

in the matter of an editor

Example: The article was revised editorially to ensure accuracy and clarity.

relating to the content or opinions of an editorial

Example: The newspaper expressed its stance on the policy change editorially.

educationally /ˌɛdʒuːkˈeɪʃənəli/

anything associated with education or the process of educating

Example: The school organised an educationally enriching field trip to the science museum.

eerily /ˈɪərɪli/

in a strange and frightening manner

Example: The abandoned house stood eerily silent on the hill, surrounded by overgrown weeds.

in a way that causes unease or discomfort

Example: Her smile faded, leaving the room feeling eerily quiet.

effectively /ɪfˈɛktɪvli/
in a manner that achieves the desired result
Example: *The new marketing strategy effectively increased sales by 20%.*
in a way that is efficient and successful
Example: *She managed the team effectively, ensuring all deadlines were met ahead of schedule.*

effectually /ɪfˈɛktʃuːəli/
in a manner that achieves the desired effect or result
Example: *The new sales strategy effectually increased the company's revenue.*
thoroughly or efficiently
Example: *The maid cleaned the entire house effectually, leaving no corner untouched.*

effeminately /ɪˈfemɪnɪtli/
in a manner traditionally associated with femininity
Example: *She walked effeminately, with delicate gestures and a graceful stride.*
in a way that is considered unmanly or overly delicate
Example: *He spoke effeminately, using a high-pitched voice and expressive hand gestures.*

effervescently /ˌefəˈvesntli/
in a lively and enthusiastic manner
Example: *She greeted everyone effervescently, spreading cheer wherever she went.*
in a way that is literally bubbly or fizzy
Example: *The effervescently sparkling water danced in the sunlight.*

efficaciously /ˌefɪˈkeɪʃəsli/

in an effective manner

Example: *The new medicine worked efficaciously to relieve her*
            pain within minutes.

successfully producing the intended result

Example: *The new training program proved to be efficacious in*
            improving employee performance.

efficiently /ɪfˈɪʃəntli/

in a manner that achieves maximum productivity with minimal waste

Example: *The factory reorganised its production line to operate*
            more efficiently, reducing waste and increasing output.

in a way that is effective and well-organised

Example: *She managed the project efficiently, ensuring tasks were*
            completed on time and within budget.

effortlessly /ˈɛfətləsli/

in a manner that requires little or no effort

Example: *She played the piano effortlessly.*

with ease and skill

Example: *He effortlessly solved the complex maths problem,*
            demonstrating his proficiency in the subject.

egotistically /ˌɛgətˈɪstɪkəli/

in a self-centred or self-important manner

Example: *John spoke egotistically about his achievements, ignoring*
            everyone else's contributions.

with an excessive focus on oneself

Example: *She pursued her goals egotistically, often disregarding*
            the needs and opinions of others.

egregiously /ɪgrˈiːdʒəsli/
in an outstandingly bad or shocking manner
Example: *The company's failure to address safety concerns was
egregiously irresponsible.*
to an extraordinary or glaring degree
Example: *The politician's misuse of public funds was egregiously
unethical.*

eighthly /ˈeɪtθli/
to indicate something in the eighth place or order in a sequence
Example: *Eighthly, we need to review the financial projections for
next quarter.*

either /ˈaɪðɐ/
indicating a choice between two options
Example: *You can either have tea or coffee with your breakfast.*
used to emphasise alternatives
Example: *You can either go to the movies or stay home and relax.*
used in negative constructions to mean 'also' or 'too'
Example: *She does not like coffee, and I don't either.*

elastically /ɪˈlɑstɪkːəli/
in a flexible or resilient manner
Example: *The rubber band stretched elastically to accommodate
the expanding load without breaking.*
adapting or responding smoothly to changes
Example: *Her team responded elastically to the sudden changes in
project requirements, adjusting their strategies
seamlessly.*

elatedly /ɪˈleɪtɪdli/
in a joyful or ecstatic manner
Example: *She hugged her friend elatedly upon hearing the good
news.*

with a sense of great satisfaction or happiness

Example: *He elatedly accepted the award for his outstanding achievements in research.*

electively /ɪˈlektɪvli/

by choice or preference

Example: *She chose to take the advanced course electively, to further her skills in*

programming.

in a manner that allows for choice or selection

Example: *He decided to pursue the elective course in photography to expand his skills in visual arts.*

electrically /ɪlˈɛktrɪkli/

involving electricity or electrical power

Example: *The city was powered electrically, ensuring continuous supply during the storm.*

in a manner that is energetic, exciting, or thrilling

Example: *The atmosphere at the concert was electrically charged as the band began to play.*

relating to electrical equipment or devices

Example: *The electrically powered car silently glided down the road.*

electronically /ˌɛlɪktrˈɒnɪkli/

involving electronic technology

Example: *She submitted her job application electronically through the company's website.*

using electronic devices or equipment

Example: *The documents were signed electronically using a digital signature.*

in a manner that relates to electronic systems or processes

Example: *He transferred the funds electronically to his friend's bank account.*

elegantly /ˈɛlɪgəntli/

in a graceful and stylish manner, showing refinement or sophistication

Example: *She walked into the room elegantly, wearing a flowing gown that caught everyone's attention.*

elementally /ˌɛlɪˈmɛntlli/

something fundamental, basic, or essential to the nature of something else

Example: *The principle of fairness is elementally important in any democratic society.*

elfishly /ˈɛlfɪʃli/

to describe actions or behaviours reminiscent of elves, often implying playfulness, mischief, or a whimsical nature

Example: *She elfishly rearranged the ornaments on the Christmas tree.*

elliptically /ɪlˈɪptɪkli/

doing something in an elliptical manner, which can mean using elliptical shapes or forms

Example: *The artist painted the landscape elliptically, capturing the rolling hills and curved riverbanks with gentle brushstrokes.*

expressing something in a concise or indirect way

Example: *He spoke elliptically about his future plans, leaving his intentions unclear to the audience.*

eloquently /ˈɛləkwəntli/

to express oneself fluently, persuasively, and with grace or skill in speech or writing

Example: *She eloquently defended her position during the debate, persuading the audience with well-reasoned arguments.*

else /ˈɛls/
something different or additional
Example: *I have finished all my homework; now, what else can I do to help?*
an alternate or different situation
Example: *If this plan fails, we will have to consider what else we can do to solve the problem.*

elsewhere /ˈɛlsweə/
in or to another place
Example: *She could not find her keys at home, so she looked for them elsewhere.*

elsewise /ɛlsˌwaɪz/
in a different manner, or otherwise
Example: *He was advised to approach the problem elsewise, considering alternative solutions.*

elusively /ɪˈluːsɪvli/
to describe actions or behaviours that are difficult to grasp, understand, or pin down
Example: *The answer to the puzzle remained elusively hidden, despite several attempts to solve it.*

elvishly /ˈelvɪʃli/
to describe actions or characteristics that resemble or are characteristic of elves, often suggesting playfulness, mischief, or a magical quality
Example: *She danced elvishly through the forest, leaving a trail of laughter and wonder behind her.*

embarrassedly /ɪmˈbarəstli/
to describe actions or behaviours that show embarrassment or shame

Example: Pam apologised embarrassedly after realising her
            mistake in front of everyone.

eminently /ˈɛmɪnəntli/
to a high degree, notably, or conspicuously
Example: The eminently talented musician impressed the audience
            with her remarkable performance.

emotionally /ɪmˈəʊʃənəli/
actions or states related to emotions, feelings, or sentiment
Example: She reacted emotionally to the news of her friend's
            illness, feeling deeply saddened.

emotionlessly /ɪˈməʊʃən,lesli/
describes actions or behaviours lacking emotion or feeling, often
            characterised by a lack of expression or affect
Example: He delivered the news emotionlessly, his face betraying
            no hint of the turmoil inside him.

empathetically /ˌɛmpɐθˈɛtɪkli/
doing something in a manner that shows understanding and sharing of
another person's feelings or emotion
Example: She empathetically listened to her friend's problems,
            offering support and reassurance.

emphatically /ɛmfˈatɪkli/
doing something in a forceful, clear, or definite way, often to show
importance or urgency
Example: She shook her head emphatically to convey her strong
            disagreement with the proposal.

emptily /ˈɛmptɪli/
doing something in a way that lacks substance, meaning, or emotion;
it often conveys a sense of hollowness or lack of genuine feel

Example: *Paul apologised emptily without truly acknowledging his mistake.*

enchantingly /ɪnˈʧɑːntɪŋli/
doing something in a way that is charming, captivating, or delightful
Example: *The garden was enchantingly lit with fairy lights, creating a magical atmosphere.*

encouragingly /ɛnkˈʌrɪdʒɪŋli/
doing something in a way that gives support, confidence, or hope to someone
Example: *She smiled encouragingly at her student before the exam, boosting his confidence.*

encroachingly /ɪnˈkrəʊʧɪŋli/
doing something in a way that gradually intrudes or trespasses on something or someone else's space, rights, or territory
Example: *The vines from the neighbouring garden were encroachingly creeping over the fence into our yard.*

endearingly /ɛndˈɪərɪŋli/
doing something in a way that inspires affection or love, often through charming, sweet, or lovable behaviour
Example: *She greeted everyone at the party endearingly, with warm hugs and genuine compliments.*

endlessly /ˈɛndləsli/
doing something in a way that seems to have no end, limit or conclusion
Example: *The children ran around the playground endlessly, full of energy and excitement.*
perpetually or continuously
Example: *The waves crashed endlessly against the shore, creating a soothing sound.*

endurably /ɪnˈdjʊərəbli/

doing something in a way that can be tolerated or endured

Example: *The pain was endurably mild after taking painkillers.*

bearably

Example: *Despite the heat, the air conditioning made the room endurably cool.*

enduringly /ɪnˈdjʊərɪŋli/

doing something in a way that lasts for a long time or can withstand the test of time

Example: *Their enduringly strong friendship has lasted through many ups and downs over the years.*

persistently

Example: *She enduringly pursued her dream of becoming a doctor, despite facing many challenges.*

endways /ˈendweɪz/

Something positioned or oriented with one end foremost or vertically

Example: *The vase fell endways off the shelf, shattering on the floor.*

endwise /ˈendwaɪz/

in the direction of or with one and foremost

Example: *He pushed the heavy box endwise through the narrow doorway.*

energetically

doing something with a lot of energy, vigour, or enthusiasm

Example: *She danced energetically all night at the party, enjoying every moment on the dance floor.*

engagedly /ɪnˈgeɪdʒdli/

doing something with interest, attentiveness, or involvement

Example: The students listened engagedly as the teacher explained
           the complex scientific concept.

engagingly /ɪnˈgeɪdʒɪŋli/
doing something in a charming, attractive, or appealing manner that
captures attention or interest
Example: The author engagingly narrated the story, drawing in the
           audience with vivid descriptions and relatable
           characters.

enjoyably /ɛndʒˈɔɪəbli/
in a way that provides pleasure or satisfaction
Example: They spent the afternoon enjoyably, exploring the scenic
           hiking trails in the park.

enormously /ɪˈnɔːməslɪ/
to a very great extent or degree
Example: **The elephant was enormously large compared to the
           other animals in the zoo.**

enough /ɪˈnʌf/
sufficiently
Example: She had enough food to last the entire weekend camping
           trip.
to a satisfactory extent
Example: I have studied enough for the exam and feel confident
           about it.
to a degree that is suitable or desirable
Example: She earns enough money to comfortably support her
           family.
in an excessive manner
Example: He ate enough at the buffet to make himself
           uncomfortably full.

enterprisingly /ˈentəpraɪzɪŋli/

in a bold, energetic, or resourceful manner, especially in pursuing opportunities or overcoming challenges

Example: The team enterprisingly tackled the project,
*   demonstrating their creativity and determination to*
*   succeed.*

entertainingly /ˌentəˈteɪnɪŋli/

in a manner that is enjoyable, amusing, or engaging

Example: The comedian entertainingly performed a stand-up
*   routine that had the audience laughing.*

enthrallingly /ɪnˈθrɔːlɪŋli/

in a captivating or spellbinding manner, holding someone's attention completely

Example: The novel's plot unfolded enthrallingly, keeping readers
*   glued to its pages until the very end.*

enthusiastically /ɛnθjˌuːzɪˈastɪkli/

with great energy, excitement, and eagerness

Example: She enthusiastically cheered for her favourite team
*   during the championship game.*

enticingly /ɪnˈtaɪsɪŋli/

in a way that is tempting, attractive, or inviting, usually to encourage someone to do something or to get their attention

Example: The aroma of freshly baked cookies wafted enticingly
*   from the kitchen, drawing everyone in.*

entirely /ɪnˈtaɪəlɪ/

completely, wholly, or to the fullest extent

Example: Roy was entirely focused on finishing his project before
*   the deadline.*

enviously /ˈenvɪəsli/
in a way that shows envy or jealousy, typically desiring something possessed by another
Example: She looked enviously at her friend's new car, wishing she could afford one too.

environmentally /ɪnˌvaɪərənˈmentlli/
actions or behaviours that are mindful of or beneficial to the environment
Example: The company is committed to using environmentally friendly packaging to reduce its carbon footprint.

epicurean /ˌepɪkjʊəˈriːən/
relates to enjoyment of fine food and drink, often with an emphasis on refined tastes and pleasures
Example: The restaurant's menu catered to epicurean tastes, offering a selection of gourmet dishes and rare wines.

epidemically /ˌepɪˈdemɪkəlli/
in a manner related to epidemics, often involving the rapid spread of a disease affecting many people
Example: The healthcare system responded epidemically to the outbreak.

episcopally /ɪˈpɪskəpəlli/
pertains to bishops or the office of a Bishop in a religious context, typically within the structure or hierarchy of the Christian Church
Example: The episcopally ordained minister led the congregation in a solemn ceremony at the cathedral.

equally /ˈiːkwəlɪ/
in a manner that is fair, impartial, or without bias, often indicating something shared or distributed evenly

Example: *They divided the cake equally among all the guests at the party.*

equitably /ˈɛkwɪtəbli/
in a fair and impartial manner, ensuring justice and fairness in distribution or treatment
Example: *The company's policy ensures that all employees are paid equitably for their work, regardless of gender or background.*

equivalently /ɪˈkwɪvələntli/
in a manner that is equal in value, significance, or effect
Example: *The two candidates' qualifications were evaluated equivalently during the hiring process.*

equivocally /ɪˈkwɪvəkəlli/
in a way that is ambiguous, uncertain, or unclear, often with the intention to deceive or mislead
Example: *Joey answered the question equivocally, leaving everyone unsure of his true intentions.*

erectly /ɪˈrektli/
in an upright or vertical position, typically referring to posture or the state of being upright
Example: *He stood erectly during the ceremony, showing his respect and attentiveness.*

ergonomically /ˌɜːgənˈɒmɪkli/
relates to the design or arrangement of items (such as furniture or equipment) to maximise efficiency and comfort, especially in relation to human use
Example: *The new office chairs were designed ergonomically to support proper posture and reduce back strain.*

erotically /ɪrˈɒtɪkli/

pertains to actions or behaviours that are related to sexual desire or arousal

Example: *The movie depicted an erotically charged scene between the two main characters.*

erratically /ɛrˈatɪkli/

in a manner that is irregular, unpredictable, or inconsistent

Example: *The stock prices moved erratically throughout the day.*

erroneously /ɪˈrəʊnjəsli/

in a mistaken or incorrect manner, typically due to a misunderstanding or misinformation

Example: *She erroneously believed the event was on Friday, but it was actually scheduled for Saturday.*

esoterically /esəˈterɪkli/

in a way that is understood or intended by only a small group of people with specialised knowledge or interests

Example: *He spoke esoterically about quantum mechanics, leaving the audience bewildered by the complex concepts.*

especially /ɪsˈpeʃəlɪ/

particularly, primarily, or notably

Example: *She loves animals, especially cats.*

essentially /ɪˈsenʃəlɪ/

fundamentally, in essence, or primarily

Example: *Water is essentially composed of hydrogen and oxygen molecules.*

estimably /ˈɛstɪməbli/

in a worthy or commendable manner, indicating something deserving of respect or admiration

Example: *She has contributed estimably to the community through*
her volunteer work and charitable donations.

eternally /iːˈtɜːnlli/
without end, forever, or for an infinite duration
Example: *Their love for each other will remain eternally strong.*

ethically /ˈeθɪkəlli/
pertains to actions or behaviours that are in accordance with
principles of right and wrong, especially as they relate to moral
values and standards
Example: *The company prides itself on operating ethically,*
ensuring fair treatment of employees.

ethnically /ˈeθnɪkəlli/
something related to ethnicity or characteristic of a particular ethnic
group
Example: *The traditional dance was ethnically inspired,*
showcasing the rich cultural heritage of the community.

euphorically /juːˈfɒrɪkli/
in the state of intense happiness, excitement, or joy
Example: *Jessica hugged her teammates euphorically after their*
team won the championship.

evasively /ɪˈveɪsɪvli/
in a way that avoids giving a direct answer or response, often due to
reluctance, deceit, or a desire to conceal information
Example: *She evasively skirted around the issue of her involvement*
in the project, refusing to provide clear details.

even /ˈiːvən/
equal or level

Example: *Make sure the table legs are adjusted so that it stands*
even.

surprisingly or unexpectedly (used to emphasise the contrast)
Example: *She did not even say goodbye before leaving.*

in a consistent or uniform manner
Example: *He brushed his hair until it was smooth and even.*

to emphasise something extending to a particular point or extend
Example: *The trail continued to the summit, even reaching above*
the tree line.

used for emphasis or confirmation
Example: *He did not believe it at first, but now he even saw it with*
his own eyes.

inclusive or including everyone or everything
Example: *The invitation was extended to friends and family, even*
colleagues.

without pause or interruption continuously
Example: *She continued working, sewing the fabric even as the sun*
sets.

evenly /ˈiːvənlɪ/
in an equal, uniform, or balanced manner
Example: *He distributed the candies evenly among his friends.*

eventually /ɪˈventʃəlɪ/
at some later time, especially after a series of events or delays
Example: *Eventually, the rain stopped, and the sun came out.*

ever /ˈevə/
at any time; at all time
Example: *Have you ever been to Paris?*
continuously; always
Example: *She is ever hopeful, no matter the circumstances.*
increasingly; more and more
Example: *The mountain peak seemed ever distant as they climbed.*

evermore /ˈevəˈmɔː/
to denote forever or for all future time
Example: Their love would last evermore.

everywhere /ˈevrɪweə/
being present or found in all places or locations
Example: Flowers were blooming everywhere in the garden.

evidently /ˈevɪdəntlɪ/
something that is clearly or obviously true, apparent or evident based
on the available evidence or circumstances
Example: Ruby was evidently pleased with the surprise party.

exactly /ɪgˈzɑktlɪ/
precisely; accurately
Example: He knew exactly what to say.
in a manner that is true or correct without any deviation
Example: The puzzle pieces fit together exactly.
to emphasise agreement or alignment with someone else's statement
Example: "Exactly! That's what I was trying to explain."
used to intensify a statement or to indicate emphasis
Example: She knew exactly how to handle the situation.

exaggeratedly /ɪgˈzadʒəreɪtɪdlɪ/
to do something in an exaggerated or overly dramatic manner
Example: Jessica sighed exaggeratedly when she heard the news.

exasperatingly /ɪgˈzɑːspəreɪtɪŋli/
describes something that causes irritation or annoyance
Example: The constant delays were exasperatingly frustrating.

exceedingly /ɪkˈsiːdɪŋlɪ/
to a very great degree or extent

Example: *Susan was exceedingly happy with her exam results.*

excellently /ˈeksələntli/
in a very good or outstanding manner
Example: *She performed excellently in the piano recital.*

exceptionally /ɪkˈsepʃənlɪ/
in a way that is unusually good or outstandingly well
Example: *The team played exceptionally well and won the championship.*

excessively /ɪkˈsesɪvli/
in a way that is more than necessary, appropriate, or usual
Example: *She spent excessively on clothes last month.*

excitedly /ɛksˈaɪtɪdli/
an action done with enthusiasm, eagerness, or anticipation
Example: *She jumped up and down excitedly when she heard the news.*

exclusively /ɪksˈkluːsɪvlɪ/
solely, only, or restrictedly to a particular thing or group, excluding others
Example: *The VIP lounge is exclusively for first-class passengers.*

expansively /ɪksˈpansɪvli/
in a way that is open, wide-ranging, or with the willingness to share extensively
Example: *Charles spoke expansively about his travels across Europe.*

expectantly /ɪksˈpektəntli/
in a way that shows eager anticipation or expectation

Example: *Jessica waited expectantly for the arrival of her long-lost friend.*

expertly /ˈekspɜːtli/
in a highly skilled or knowledgeable manner
Example: *The chef expertly prepared a gourmet meal.*

explicitly /ɪksˈplɪsɪtli/
clearly, directly, or in a way that leaves no room for confusion or doubt
Example: *The rules were explicitly stated before the game began.*

expressively /ɪksˈpresɪvli/
in a manner that conveys emotions, feelings, or meanings effectively
Example: *Pat sang expressively, conveying the sadness of the song's lyrics.*

expressly /ɪksˈpresli/
for a particular purpose, explicitly, or specifically
Example: *The package was sent expressly for next-day delivery.*

exquisitely /ˈekskwɪzɪtli/
in a very beautiful, delicate, or finely detailed manner
Example: *The dress was exquisitely crafted with intricate lace details.*

extensively /ɪksˈtensɪvlɪ/
in a thorough or comprehensive manner, covering a large area, range, or scope
Example: *They searched extensively for the missing keys throughout the house.*

extraordinarily /ɪksˈtrɔːdnrɪlɪ/
done exceptionally or remarkably

Example: The team's performance was extraordinarily impressive.

extremely /ɪksˈtriːmlɪ/
to a very great degree or extent
Example: The weather was extremely hot during the heatwave.

Ff

fabulously /ˈfɑbjʊləsli/
to describe something done to an exceptional degree, often implying something that is very good or impressive
Example: She danced fabulously at the recital, captivating everyone in the audience.
to describe something done in a manner that is fantastical or reminiscent of myths
Example: The magician performed fabulously, conjuring creatures that seemed straight out of a legend.

facially /ˈfeɪʃəlli/
something done in a manner that pertains to the face
Example: She smiled facially, her expression revealing genuine happiness.
to describe something conveyed or interpreted through facial expressions
Example: He reacted facially, his raised eyebrows conveying surprise.

factually /ˈfæktʃʊəlli/
to imply that something is accurate, true, and supported by factual evidence
Example: The report was factually correct, with all statements backed by solid evidence.
to describe something related to or consistent of facts
Example: The article was factually informative, providing clear and accurate data.

fadedly /fˈeɪdɪd/
to describe something that appears dim, pale, or less vibrant, often due to the passage of time or wear

Example: *The old photograph was fadedly beautiful, its colours dimmed by time.*

to describe an action or state that is weak, lacking in strength or intensity

Example: *She smiled fadedly, barely masking her exhaustion.*

faint-heartedly /ˈfeɪntˈhɑːtɪdlɪ/

to describe actions carried out with the lack of courage or confidence

Example: *He faint-heartedly asked for help, unsure if anyone would listen.*

to describe actions performed with the lack of determination or conviction

Example: *She faint-heartedly attempted the challenge, unsure if she could succeed.*

faintly /ˈfeɪntlɪ/

to describe something that is not strong or intense, often barely perceptible

Example: *The scent of flowers drifted faintly through the open window.*

to describe something that is not clear or is only just visible or audible

Example: *He could faintly hear distant music playing.*

something that is vague or not pronounced

Example: *She remembered faintly the events of that long-ago summer.*

fairly /ˈfeəlɪ/

doing something impartially, without favouritism or bias

Example: *Sarah assessed the candidates fairly, focusing solely on their qualifications.*

to describe something to a moderate degree, not extremely but sufficiently

Example: *She did fairly well on the exam, scoring just above average.*

something being clearly or noticeably so
Example: *The stars were fairly visible in the dark night sky.*

faithfully /ˈfeɪθfʊlɪ/
performing actions with steadfast allegiance or reliability
Example: *He served the company faithfully for over twenty years.*
doing something in a manner that is true to the original, without deviation
Example: *John faithfully recreated the author's intricate style in his translation of the novel.*
Performing actions consistently over time
Example: *Pat faithfully attended yoga classes every Tuesday for the past five years.*

fallibly /fˈɑləbəli/
something done with the potential for error or imperfection
Example: *She acknowledged that her conclusions were fallibly based on limited information.*

falsely /ˈfɔːlslɪ/
to imply that something is not true or is based on false information.
Example: *He was accused falsely of stealing the missing money from the office.*
to describe actions or statements intended to deceive or mislead others
Example: *She falsely claimed to have a degree from a prestigious university on her resume.*

familiarly /fəˈmɪljəlɪ/
to imply a casual or relaxed approach, often between people who know each other well
Example: *He greeted his old friend familiarly, with a warm hug and a big smile.*
in a way that shows knowledge or recognition

Example: She spoke familiarly about the characters in the book.

famously /ˈfeɪməslɪ/
to imply that something is known by many people, often for a specific reason
Example: He famously declared that he would never give up, inspiring others with his
unwavering determination.
to describe actions or achievements that are highly praised or celebrated
Example: The artist famously painted the iconic portrait that now hangs in museums around the world.

fantastically /fɑnˈtɑstɪkəlli/
to imply something done with creativity or imagination, often in a way that is unreal or whimsical
Example: The children's book was fantastically illustrated, bringing magical creatures to life on every page.
to describe something done to an exceptional degree, often implying admiration or praise
Example: She performed fantastically well in her piano recital, impressing everyone with her skill.
in a bizarre or extraordinarily strange manner
Example: The magician pulled a rabbit out of his hat fantastically, leaving the audience in awe and disbelief.

far /fɑː/
at or to considerable distance in space or time
Example: Their house is located far from the city centre, requiring a long commute every day.
to a great extent or degree
Example: She was willing to go far to achieve her dreams, even if it meant facing significant challenges along the way.
very much or by a great deal

Example: *Jessica cares far too deeply about what others think of her.*

to describe actions or situations that are removed in some way

Example: *The political scandal seemed far from affecting residents' daily lives.*

farther /ˈfɑːðə/

at or to a greater distance in space or time

Example: *She decided to walk farther into the forest to explore its hidden trails.*

to emphasise a greater amount or level of something

Example: *Sam wanted to push himself farther in his training to improve his endurance.*

something that is more removed or distant

Example: *The campground was farther from the city than they had anticipated.*

farthest /ˈfɑːðɪst/

at or to the greatest distance in space or time

Example: *The farthest star visible to the naked eye is over 4 light-years away from Earth.*

to the greatest extent or degree

Example: *He reached the farthest point in his career, achieving success beyond his wildest dreams.*

to the most remote or extreme point

Example: *The hikers trekked to the farthest corners of the national park.*

fashionably /fˈaʃənəbli/

to indicate that something is done in a way that is currently trendy or in vogue

Example: *She dressed fashionably for the event, wearing the latest styles and accessories.*

to describe actions or behaviours that align with what is currently popular or accepted as stylish

Example: *She arrived fashionably late to the party, making a grand entrance that caught everyone's attention.*

fast /fɑːst/

doing something in a short amount of time

Example: *Roy completed his homework fast so he could go out and play with his friends.*

to imply that something is done in a way that is fixed or stable

Example: *The boat was anchored fast to the dock, ensuring it would not drift away.*

to describe processes or changes that occur swiftly

Example: *The company adapted fast to the new market demands, implementing changes within weeks.*

fatally /ˈfeɪtlli/

in a manner leading to death

Example: *He was fatally injured in the car accident and did not survive.*

in a way that leads to failure or disaster

Example: *His decision to ignore safety protocols proved fatally wrong when the machine malfunctioned.*

irrevocably or irreversibly

Example: *The error in the software code fatally compromised the security of the entire network.*

fatly /ˈfɑtli/

in a rich or abundant manner

Example: *The land was fatly endowed with natural resources.*

to describe something done in a way that emphasises physical bulk or fatness

Example: *The cat lay fatly on the cushion, barely moving.*

favourably /ˈfeɪvərəbli/

in a way that shows approval or support

Example: *The committee reviewed the proposal favourably,*
             impressed by its thoroughness and potential impact.

to the advantage or benefit of someone or something

Example: *The recent economic policies have impacted the company*
             favourably, leading to increased profits.

in a manner that indicates a positive outcome or result

Example: *Her presentation was received favourably by the*
             audience, resulting in a standing ovation.

favouredly /ˈfeɪvədli/

in a manner that shows preference or favour

Example: *The candidate was viewed favouredly by the interview*
             panel.

with advantages or benefits

Example: *John was born into a favouredly wealthy family.*

fawningly /ˈfɔːnɪŋli/

in an excessively flattering or servile manner

Example: *He spoke fawningly to his boss, hoping to curry favour*
             for a promotion.

to describe behaviours aimed at winning someone's approval through
insincere praise or attention

Example: *She smiled fawningly at the celebrity, hoping to impress*
             them with compliments.

fearfully /ˈfɪəfʊlli/

an action done in a manner marked by fear, anxiety, or concern

Example: *He approached the haunted house fearfully, unsure of*
             what he might find inside.

extremely or very much

Example: *She feared for her safety fearfully as the storm intensified*
             outside.

federally /ˈfedərəlli/

actions, regulations, or context that pertain to the national government of a country, especially in a federal system where power is divided between a central authority and constituent regions

Example: *The law was passed federally, applying to all states equally under national jurisdiction.*

to imply that something is being done or regulated by the federal government or opposed to state or local governments

Example: *The project was funded federally, ensuring consistency and oversight across all participating states.*

feebly /ˈfiːbli/

to indicate that something is done with little strength, energy, or effectiveness

Example: *He tried to lift the heavy box, but only managed to lift it feebly off the ground.*

in an unconvincing or inadequate way

Example: *She argued feebly against the proposal, unable to present strong evidence to support her case.*

feelingly /ˈfiːlɪŋlɪ/

to indicate something is expressed or done in a manner that shows strong feelings or emotional intensity

Example: *She spoke feelingly about her childhood memories, her voice trembling with emotion.*

to imply that an action is performed with a profound appreciation or empathy for the subject

Example: *He spoke feelingly about the hardships faced by refugees, demonstrating a deep understanding of their struggles.*

femininely /ˈfemɪnɪnli/

to indicate that something is done in a way that aligns with qualities or behaviours typically attributed to women

Example: She dressed femininely in a flowing dress and delicate
              jewellery for the party.

actions or expressions that exhibit gentleness, grace, or other
attributes, often culturally linked to femininity

Example: Jane moved femininely, with a softness and grace that
              captivated everyone in the room.

ferociously /fəˈrəʊʃəsli/

to indicate that something is done with great intensity, aggression, or
savagery

Example: The lioness defends her cubs ferociously against the
              approaching predator.

actions performed with a high degree of energy, enthusiasm, or
tenacity

Example: Daniel tackled his studies ferociously, determined to
              excel in his exams.

fervently /ˈfɜːvəntli/

to indicate that something is done with great enthusiasm, zeal, or
emotion

Example: She prayed fervently for her friend's recovery from
              illness.

to imply that an action is performed sincerely and with strong
conviction

Example: He fervently believed in the cause and dedicated his life
              to advocating for social justice.

festally /ˈfestlli/

to indicate that something is done in a way that is joyous, festive, or
appropriate for a celebration

Example: The town was decorated festally for the annual summer
              carnival.

to imply that actions are performed with a celebratory and joyful
attitude

Example: *They danced festally around the bonfire, celebrating the*
　　　　　　successful completion of their project.

fetishistically /ˌfet.ɪˈʃɪs.tɪ.kəl.i/
to indicate that something is done with a focus on an object, body
part, or practise that is the subject of fetishist interest
Example: *He collected shoes fetishistically, amassing hundreds of*
　　　　　　pairs from different eras and cultures.
to imply that an action is performed with an intense, often irrational,
attachment or obsession
Example: *She cleaned her car fetishistically every weekend,*
　　　　　　ensuring it was spotless inside and out.

feudally /ˈfjuːdlli/
to indicate that something is done in a way that pertains to or is
characteristic of the feudal system, a mediaeval social structure with a
hierarchy of lords, vassals, and serfs
Example: *The land was divided feudally among the lords and*
　　　　　　peasants.
actions or situations that resemble the social, economic, or political
structure of the feudal era
Example: *The distribution of resources was managed feudally.*

feverously /ˈfiːvərəsli/
to indicate that something is done with the characteristics or
symptoms associated with fever, such as high body temperature,
restlessness, or delirium
Example: *She tossed and turned feverously in bed, unable to find*
　　　　　　relief from her illness.
actions performed with great urgency, excitement, or enthusiasm
Example: *The team worked feverously to meet the project deadline,*
　　　　　　putting in extra hours to ensure success.

fiducially /fɪˈdjuːʃjəlli/
something done in accordance with the legal or ethical obligations of trust and loyalty, especially in financial or legal contexts
Example: He managed the company's finances fiducially, always putting the interests of the shareholders first.
an action performed with integrity and faithfulness to the trust placed in someone or something
Example: The lawyer handled the client's estate fiducially, ensuring every decision was made with their best interests in mind.

fiercely /ˈfɪəsli/
something done with great strength, aggression, or determination
Example: Ruby defended her thesis fiercely, arguing every point with passion and conviction.
actions performed with intense feelings or emotions, such as anger, love, or dedication
Example: The mother fiercely protected her children from any harm, showing unwavering dedication and love.
an action carried out with a strong desire to win or overcome challenges
Example: He competed fiercely in the race, pushing himself to the limit to cross the finish line first.

fifthly /ˈfɪfθlɪ/
to enumerate items in a sequence, like "fifth"
Example: Fifthly, we need to discuss the budget allocation for the upcoming project phase.

fightingly /ˈfaɪtɪŋli/
something done with an aggressive or confrontational attitude, often in a physical or metaphorical sense
Example: He approached the negotiation fightingly, determined to defend his position and secure a better deal.

actions performed with a strong will or readiness to confront challenges or opposition

Example: *Kim faced the difficult task fightingly, refusing to give up despite the obstacles in her way.*

figuratively /ˈfɪɡjʊrətɪvli/

to indicate that something is expressed in a non-literal or symbolic sense, often to create a vivid or imaginative comparison

Example: *Her smile lit up the room figuratively, spreading warmth and happiness among everyone present.*

finally /ˈfaɪnəlɪ/

indicating that something happens or is achieved after a long-awaited or anticipated period

Example: *Finally, after years of hard work, she graduated from college with honours.*

the outcome or resolution of a situation

Example: *The court's decision was reached, finally ending the long legal dispute.*

as a concluding point; to sum up

Example: *After months of preparation, the team finally launched their product.*

financially /faɪˈnɑnʃəlli/

to indicate that something is done or understood from a financial perspective

Example: *She was financially secure after years of diligent saving and investing.*

actions taken to manage or handle money or investments

Example: *They decided to invest in solar panels to benefit financially in the long run.*

to indicate that something has financial consequences or impacts

Example: *Their decision to buy a new car will affect them financially for years to come.*

fine /faɪn/

to indicate that something meets a standard or expectation

Example: *The essay was fine, meeting all the requirements for the assignment.*

in a subtle or delicate manner

Example: *She adjusted the details of the painting with fine brushstrokes, adding depth and texture.*

to indicate that something is done with accuracy or attention to detail

Example: *Jessica did a fine job of organising the event, paying attention to every detail.*

in good health or spirits

Example: *Despite the accident, she was fine and did not sustain any injuries.*

finely /ˈfaɪnli/

to indicate that something is done with precision, detail or subtlety

Example: *She carved the intricate design finely into the wood, revealing every delicate detail.*

something being divided into small parts or particles

Example: *The flour was finely ground, creating a smooth and even texture for baking.*

to suggest that something is of high quality or skilfully executed

Example: *James dressed finely for the occasion, showcasing his impeccable taste in fashion.*

finitely /ˈfaɪnaɪtli/

concepts or actions that have limits or boundaries, specifically in terms of quantity, extent, or duration

Example: *The resources available for the project are finitely allocated.*

firmly /ˈfɜːmli/

in a strong, steady, or resolute manner

Example: *She firmly believed in standing up for what was right, no matter the consequences.*

physical actions or conditions where something is held or fixed securely in place

Example: *He held onto the railing firmly as he climbed the stairs.*

without hesitation or uncertainty

Example: *She firmly declined the offer, knowing it was not right for her.*

first /ˈfɝst/

to indicate something happens before others in a sequence or as a priority

Example: *She was the first to arrive at the party, eager to greet the host.*

actions or occurrences that happened or are done for the initial time

Example: *Her first attempt at baking cookies turned out surprisingly well.*

to suggest that something is of utmost importance or significance

Example: *Safety is always our first priority when conducting experiments in the lab.*

before all others in time, order, or rank.

Example: *She was the first student to arrive at the school every morning.*

to indicate priority or precedence over other factors

Example: *Roy's first concern was to ensure the safety of everyone involved.*

first-hand /ˈfɜːstˈhænd/

directly from the original source or personal experience

Example: *She learned about the incident first-hand from witnesses who were present at the scene.*

firstly /ˈfɝstli/

as the first point or item in a series

Example: Firstly, let us review the main objectives of our project.
to imply a chronological or logical order of events or actions
Example: Firstly, he prepared the ingredients before starting to cook dinner for his family.

fitly /ˈfɪtli/
to indicate that something is done in a way that is fitting or suitable for the circumstances
Example: The decorations were arranged fitly for the elegant wedding reception.
actions or behaviours that are executed in a manner that is correct or proper
Example: She responded fitly to the criticism, addressing each point with clarity and professionalism.

fittingly /ˈfɪtɪŋli/
in a manner that is appropriate or suitable
Example: The retiring teacher was fittingly honoured with a heartfelt speech.
in a manner that is proper or correct
Example: The award was fittingly presented to the top performer of the year.

fivefold /ˈfaɪvfəʊld/
to five times the previous amount or size
Example: She increased her savings fivefold by investing wisely over the past decade.
in five parts or pieces
Example: The package was divided fivefold, with each section carefully labelled for distribution.

fixedly /ˈfɪksɪdlɪ/
something done in a way that is not subject to change or movement

Example: *He stared fixedly at the painting, captivated by its*
intricate details and vibrant colours.

to suggest that someone is directing their attention or gaze steadily
and intently

Example: *She watched fixedly as the magician performed his tricks.*

flagrantly /ˈfleɪɡrəntli/

an action that is done openly and without any attempt to hide or cover
it up

Example: *He flagrantly ignored the no-smoking sign and lit a*
cigarette in the non-smoking area.

to emphasise that a behaviour is shockingly noticeable and often
without regard for norms or expectations

Example: *The politician flagrantly misuses public funds for*
personal gain.

flakily /ˈflɑːkəli/

a behaviour that is erratic, unpredictable, or unreliable

Example: *Her plans were often flakily organised, causing confusion*
among her friends.

the physical property of being flaky, often used to describe food
textures

Example: *The pastry was flakily baked, with layers that crumbled*
delicately with each bite.

flamingly /ˈfleɪmɪŋli/

something done with great fervour, energy, or emotion

Example: *He defended his position flamingly, passionately arguing*
for his beliefs in the heated debate.

something that is visually very bold or vivid, often with a sense of
being on fire or very bright

Example: *The sunset painted the sky flamingly, casting vibrant hues*
of red and orange across the horizon.

a behaviour that is outrageously bold or offensive

Example: She responded flamingly to the criticism, causing a stir
with her bold and confrontational attitude.

flaringly /ˈfleərɪŋli/

to describe how something widens or spreads out suddenly

Example: The fire spread flaringly through the dry grass.

to describe something that is visually striking, like a bright light or
colour

Example: The fireworks lit up the night sky flaringly, dazzling
everyone with bursts of colour and light.

flashily /flaʃiːli/

suggesting something is done in a way intended to attract attention or
impress others, often through excessive display

Example: He arrived at the party flashily dressed in a bright red
suit and glittering gold shoes.

to imply a lack of subtlety, with a focus on bright, extravagant, or
tacky display

Example: She decorated her apartment flashily with neon lights
and bold patterns.

flashingly /ˈflaʃɪŋli/

to indicate that something is done with a noticeable, intense
brightness

Example: The diamond ring sparkle flashingly in the sunlight,
catching everyone's attention.

an action done in a way that seeks to attract attention through a gaudy
or extravagant display

Example: She entered the room flashingly, wearing a sequined
gown and a large-feathered hat.

flat /ˈflɑt/

totality or completeness

Example: Her tire went completely flat, forcing her to pull over to the side of the road.

doing something in a clear and unambiguous manner

Example: She stated her opinion flat, leaving no room for misunderstanding.

something done evenly or uniformly

Example: The chef spread the frosting on the cake flat, ensuring it covered every inch smoothly.

an action done in a dull or monotonous manner

Example: His voice was flat as he read the script, lacking emotion or enthusiasm.

referring to time or measurements

Example: The lease was signed for a flat rate of $1000 per month.

flatly /ˈflatli/

to imply a firm, unequivocal stance

Example: She flatly refused to attend the meeting without a valid reason.

a manner of speaking or acting that is straightforward and unambiguous, often without concern or diplomacy

Example: He responded flatly to the criticism, stating that he disagreed with their assessment.

an action done in a dull, uninterested, or monotonous manner

Example: She answered the phone flatly, lacking any enthusiasm in her voice.

flatteringly /ˈflatərɪŋli/

something that is done or said to make someone feel good about themselves or to enhance their image

Example: He complimented her flatteringly on her new haircut, making her smile with delight.

how something is presented to make it look more appealing or attractive

Example: *The dress was tailored flatteringly to accentuate her figure.*

flauntingly /ˈflɔːntɪŋli/
to imply that someone is deliberately displaying their possessions, achievements, or qualities to attract attention or impress others
Example: *She flauntingly displayed her new car by parking it right in front of the office building.*
to emphasise that an action is done without shame or modesty, often to provoke envy or admiration
Example: *She flauntingly displayed her vacation photos on social media.*

flawlessly /ˈflɔːləsli/
to suggest that something is done with extreme accuracy, precision, or skill, without any errors or flaws
Example: *She performed the dance routine flawlessly, impressing the judges with her precision and grace.*
something that proceeds without interruptions or disruptions, in a manner that is exceptionally well-executed
Example: *The concert proceeded flawlessly, with each musician playing their part perfectly.*

fleetingly /ˈfliːtɪŋli/
to indicate that something happens or is perceived for only a short duration
Example: *She caught a fleetingly glimpse of the shooting star before it disappeared into the night sky.*
to describe how something or someone appears or passes by quickly without lingering
Example: *The deer appeared fleetingly at the edge of the forest before darting away into the trees.*

fleetly /ˈfliːtli/

to describe movement that is fast and efficient

Example: *John ran fleetly across the field, easily outpacing his
                competitors.*

actions or processes that are carried out with speed and efficiency

Example: *She completed the task fleetly, finishing well ahead of
                schedule.*

flimsily /ˈflɪmzɪli/

to suggest that something is not sturdy or well-made, often implying
                it might break or fail easily

Example: *The makeshift tent was flimsily constructed, barely
                holding up against the strong wind.*

to refer to arguments, explanations, or justifications that are not well-
                founded or are easily refuted

Example: *His excuse for being late was flimsily constructed and fell
                apart under questioning.*

to imply a lack of substance or weight

Example: *The evidence supporting his claim was flimsily presented
                and did not convince anyone.*

flirtatiously /flɜːtˈeɪʃəsli/

behaviour that is light-hearted, coy, or subtly suggestive to engage
someone romantically or playfully

Example: *She winked flirtatiously at him across the room, teasingly
                twirling her hair.*

flittingly /flˈɪtɪŋli/

to describe movements or actions that happen quickly and without
lingering

Example: *The butterfly moved flittingly from flower to flower in the
                garden.*

to refer to something that is experienced or noticed momentarily,
without lasting impact or presence

floatingly /ˈfləʊtɪŋli/
moving or drifting lightly, like something that floats on water or air
Example: *The feather drifted floatingly down from the tree branch, carried by a gentle breeze.*
being in a state of suspension or lack of a definite place
Example: **She moved through the room floatingly, as if untethered from the ground.**
Moving in a smooth, effortless, or elegant way
Example: *The dancer moved across the stage, floatingly, as if gliding on air.*

florally /ˈflɔrəli/
done in a way that relates to or resembles flowers
Example: *She decorated the room florally, with fresh blooms in every corner.*
featuring designs or motifs of flowers
Example: *The curtains were patterned florally, with vibrant roses and daisies.*

fluently /ˈfluəntli/
done in a way that is smooth and effortless
Example: *She spoke fluently in French, effortlessly switching between languages.*
speaking or writing a language easily and accurately
Example: *He could communicate fluently in Mandarin, impressing everyone with his command of the language.*
in a manner that flows without interruption
Example: *She spoke English fluently, without any pauses or hesitations.*

fluffily /flˈʌfili/

done in a way that is soft to the touch and light and texture

Example: The kitten's tail swayed fluffily as it played with the yarn.

having the visual characteristics of being fluffy

Example: The clouds drifted fluffily across the bright blue sky.

done in a way that is light and gentle

Example: The feathers floated fluffily to the ground.

fluidly /ˈfluːɪdli/

moving or functioning without friction or interruption

Example: The dancer moved fluidly across the stage.

performing an action in a continuous, graceful manner

Example: The pianist's fingers moved fluidly over the keys.

foamingly /fˈəʊmɪŋli/

in a way that produces or is covered with foam

Example: The waves crashed foamingly against the shore.

displaying bubbles or froth

Example: The soda spilled, fizzing foamingly over the rim of the glass.

showing intense emotion or activity, often in a turbulent way

Example: He ranted foamingly about the injustice he faced.

focally /ˈfəʊkəlli/

done with concentration on a particular point or area

Example: The investigation was focally centred on the suspect's alibi.

pertaining to the central point of interest or activity

Example: The discussion was focally about the budget cuts.

in a way that relates to the main point or region of interest

Example: The artist emphasized the details focally, highlighting the portrait's expression.

fondly /ˈfɑndli/
demonstrating a warm and loving attitude
Example: *She looked fondly at the old photograph of her grandparents.*
showing care and tenderness
Example: *He patted his dog fondly on the head before leaving for work.*
recalling something with fond memories and affection
Example: *She fondly remembered her childhood summers spent at the lake.*

foolishly /ˈfulɪʃli/
acting in a way that shows a lack of wisdom or common sense
Example: *He foolishly spent all his savings on unnecessary gadgets.*
behaving in a way that is silly or unwise
Example: *She foolishly ignored the warning signs and ventured into the forest alone after dark.*
taking unnecessary risks or acting carelessly
Example: *Daniel foolishly drove without a seatbelt, ignoring the safety regulations.*

forbiddingly /fəbˈɪdɪŋli/
acting in a way that goes against rules or regulations
Example: *The couple met forbiddingly in the shadows of the old oak tree.*
doing something that is considered taboo or socially unacceptable
Example: *They kissed forbiddingly in the dimly lit corner.*
engaging in activities that are explicitly disallowed
Example: *He accessed the forbiddingly restricted section of the website, ignoring the warning not to proceed.*

forcefully /ˈfɔrsfəli/
doing something with a strong physical or emotional impact

Example: *She closed the door forcefully behind her, unable to contain her frustration any longer.*

doing something in a way that leaves no doubt or hesitation

Example: *The teacher explained the concept forcefully to ensure everyone understood.*

acting decisively and assertively

Example: *The CEO intervened forcefully to resolve the conflict among the team members.*

forcibly /ˈfɔrsəbli/

acting with strength to achieve something

Example: *The police had to forcibly remove the protestors from the building to restore order.*

achieving something despite opposition or unwillingness

Example: *The new policy was implemented forcibly despite strong objections from the staff.*

in a manner that involves coercion or necessity

Example: *Jenny was forcibly removed from the premises by security after causing a disturbance.*

forebodingly /fˈɔːbəʊdɪŋli/

acting or speaking in a way that indicates a sense of impending danger or trouble

Example: *The dark clouds gathered forebodingly, signalling an approaching storm.*

done in a way that creates a sense of unease or apprehension

Example: *He looked at her forebodingly, his expression hinting at troubling news to come.*

acting or speaking as if aware of a future negative event

Example: *She spoke forebodingly about the ominous signs of an economic downturn.*

forever /fɚˈɛvɚ/

continuing indefinitely into the future

Example: *Their love for each other was meant to last forever.*

without ever ending or changing

Example: *The mountains stood tall, seemingly forever unchanged by time.*

without interruption or cessation

Example: *She promised to love him forever, unwavering in her commitment.*

at all times; throughout all times

Example: *Her smile will remain in my heart forever.*

forgetfully /fəˈgetfʊlli/

acting without paying attention to the task at hand, often due to preoccupation with other thoughts

Example: *She forgetfully left her keys on the kitchen counter as she rushed out the door.*

failing to give proper care or attention, leading to omission or oversight

Example: *He forgetfully neglected to water the plants, and they wilted in the sun.*

acting without considering the potential consequences or necessary details

Example: *She forgetfully signed the document without reading the fine print.*

performing actions in a haphazard or sloppy manner due to lack of attention or concern

Example: *He forgetfully packed his bag, leaving out important items he needed for the trip.*

forlornly /fəˈlɔːnli/

in a way that shows sorrow or unhappiness

Example: *She looked out the window forlornly as the rain poured down.*

with a sense of hopelessness or despondency

Example: *He sat forlornly on the bench, feeling utterly defeated.*

exhibiting feelings of isolation or abandonment

Example: *The abandoned puppy whimpered forlornly in the empty alley.*

showing a lack of optimism or expectation for a positive outcome

Example: *She stared forlornly at the empty mailbox, knowing the letter would never come.*

formally /ˈfɔɹməli/

used to describe actions or behaviours that follow official or traditional standards

Example: *He formally addressed the committee with a prepared speech.*

refers to behaving with propriety and respect, often in social or professional settings

Example: *She shook hands formally with each guest as they arrived.*

indicates a meticulous or methodical approach, often in academic, technical, or scientific contexts

Example: *The report was formally structured with clear sections and citations.*

pertains to actions performed with a sense of ritual or ceremony

Example: *The president formally inaugurated the new building with a ribbon-cutting ceremony.*

formerly /ˈfɔrmɚli/

used to indicate that something was the case in the past but is no longer true

Example: *James formerly worked as a teacher before switching careers to become a chef.*

refers to a time that has already elapsed

Example: *The city was formerly known as New Amsterdam before it was renamed New York.*

formidably /ˈfɔrmədəbli/

indicates doing something in a manner that causes others to feel apprehension or awe

Example: The boxer faced his opponent formidably, with a fierce and unyielding stance.

describes actions performed with a level of difficulty or challenge that is significant

Example: Sarah tackled the advanced maths problem formidably, using complex formulas and techniques.

refers to doing something in a powerful, impressive, or commandingly

Example: The champion boxer fought formidably in the ring, displaying his powerful and commanding presence.

forth /ˈfɔɹθ/

moving ahead or progressing

Example: The project is moving forth smoothly despite initial setbacks.

emerging or being made visible

Example: The sun came forth from behind the clouds, brightening the sky.

continuing to move forward or advance

Example: He stepped forth confidently, ready to face whatever challenges lay ahead.

departing from a specific location

Example: The ship set forth from the harbour at dawn, beginning its journey across the sea.

forthwith /ˈfɔɹθ ˈwɪθ/

indicates something should be done at once, without any hesitation or pause

Example: The judge demanded the verdict be delivered forthwith, to ensure justice was swiftly served.

emphasising promptness and urgency in carrying out an action

Example: The emergency services were instructed to respond to the call forthwith, as lives were at stake.

fortnightly /ˈfɔrtˌnaɪtli/
refers to an event or action that occurs once every two weeks
Example: The magazine is published fortnightly, so it comes out every two weeks.

fortunately /ˈfɔːʧnɪtli/
indicates that something happened in a favourable or fortunate manner
Example: Fortunately, the rain stopped just in time for the outdoor wedding ceremony.
expresses relief or gratitude for a positive outcome
Example: Fortunately, he found his lost wallet at the lost and found counter.

forward /ˈfɔrwɜd/
moving in the direction that faces ahead
Example: She took a step forward to get a closer look at the painting.
ahead in time or order
Example: Please send me the report two days forward from today.
continuing or progressing
Example: The project is moving forward smoothly, with each milestone achieved on schedule.
showing confidence or readiness
Example: He approached the challenge with a forward attitude, ready to tackle any obstacles in his way.
to send or pass along
Example: Please forward the email to the entire team for review.

fourfold /ˌfɔɹˈfoʊld/
used to indicate a multiplication or increase by four

Example: *The company's profits increased fourfold after implementing the new marketing strategy.*

divided into four equal parts

Example: *He folded the paper neatly, creating a fourfold brochure for the event.*

fourthly /ˈfɔɹθli/

indicates the placement of something as the fourth in a sequence

Example: *Fourthly, we need to discuss the budget allocation for the upcoming project phase.*

foxily /fˈɒksili/

actions or behaviours done in a cunning or sly manner

Example: *She foxily convinced him to buy the more expensive car by highlighting its "exclusive" features.*

fractionally /ˈfrakʃənlli/

used to describe something that occurs or changes in a very small amount or increment

Example: *The temperature increased fractionally, just enough to notice a slight difference in the room.*

indicates something that is extremely small or subtle in nature

Example: *He adjusted the microscope fractionally to get a clearer view of the cell structure.*

fractiously /ˈfrakʃəsli/

indicates behaviour characterised by being easily annoyed, argumentative, or contentious

Example: *The tired toddler began to behave fractiously after missing his afternoon nap.*

describes actions or behaviours that are unruly, rebellious, or difficult to manage

Example: *The children argued fractiously over who would get the last piece of cake at the party.*

fragilely /ˈfradʒaɪlli/

describes actions or conditions that are delicate, easily damaged, or prone to breaking

Example: *She held the antique vase fragilely; afraid it might slip from her grasp.*

indicates something that is susceptible to harm or damage

Example: *The butterfly landed fragilely on the delicate flower petals.*

fragility /fradʒˈɪlɪti/

refers to the quality of being delicate, easily broken, or fragile

Example: *The artist's sculpture captured the fragility of a delicate flower petal.*

indicate the state of being weak, frail, or easily affected

Example: *The delicate glass figurine was handled with extreme care due to its fragility.*

describe a situation or condition that is unstable or precarious

Example: *The economy's fragility was evident in the wake of the stock market crash.*

fragrantly /ˈfreɪgrəntli/

describes something done with a pleasing aroma

Example: *The flowers bloomed fragrantly, filling the garden with their sweet scent.*

indicates something that emits a noticeable and enjoyable smell

Example: *The flowers bloomed fragrantly, filling the air with their sweet scent.*

frankly /ˈfraŋkli/

indicates speaking or expressing oneself truthfully and directly, without reservation or evasion

Example: *Frankly, I do not think the proposal is a good idea for our company's future growth.*

emphasises being sincere and straightforward in speech

Example: *She spoke frankly about her feelings, not holding*
                  anything back.

used to introduce a statement or opinion that may be blunt or direct

Example: *Frankly, I do not think that is a good idea.*

frantically /ˈfrɑnəkəli/

describes actions that are characterised by extreme urgency, anxiety, or panic

Example: *She searched frantically for her misplaced keys before*
                  realising they were in her pocket.

indicates doing something with great intensity or fervour

Example: *The firefighters worked frantically to contain the*
                  spreading wildfire before it reached the nearby town.

fraudulently /ˈfrɔduləntli/

describes actions or behaviours that involve deceit, trickery, or dishonesty

Example: *He was accused of fraudulently altering the financial*
                  records to hide the company's losses.

indicates actions done with the purpose of misleading others for personal gain

Example: *She was caught fraudulently using someone else's credit*
                  card information to make online purchases.

freakishly /ˈfriːkɪʃli/

describes actions or events that deviate from normal expectations

Example: *The freakishly warm weather in December confused*
                  everyone.

indicates behaviour or occurrences that are strangely or unnaturally different

Example: *He possessed freakishly strong muscles that allowed him*
                  to lift heavy weights effortlessly.

free /ˈfrɪ/

describes something that is given or available without charge

Example: The museum offers free admission on Sundays to encourage more visitors.

indicates a state of being unrestricted or not constrained

Example: After finishing his exams, he finally felt free to relax and enjoy the summer break.

describes movement or action that is uninhibited

Example: The horse galloped free across the open field, enjoying the freedom to run without reins.

refers to something that is done openly or without secrecy

Example: They freely shared their opinions during the open forum, fostering a constructive discussion.

freely /ˈfrili/

doing something without any restrictions or limitations

Example: The children played freely in the open field, enjoying the freedom to run and explore.

to indicate a willingness to do something or give something without expecting anything in return

Example: She freely offered her help to anyone in need, expecting nothing in return.

something that is available without cost or restriction

Example: The information is freely accessible to all users, without any fees or barriers.

acting without feeling obligated to follow specific rules or norms

Example: She spoke freely, unencumbered by the formalities of the event.

freezingly /ˈfriːzɪŋli/

to refer to something that is very cold in temperature, often to the point of causing freezing or intense coldness

Example: The wind blew freezingly across the snow-covered landscape.

to describe something that is emotionally cold, distant, or hostile
Example: *Her freezingly indifferent response to his heartfelt*
apology hurt him deeply.

frequently /ˈfriːkwəntli/
happening many times; on many occasions
Example: *She frequently visits her grandmother on weekends to*
spend time together.
at regular intervals; consistently
Example: *He checks his email frequently throughout the day to stay*
updated on work matters.

fresh /ˈfrɛʃ/
referring to something that has happened, been done, or acquired very recently
Example: *The bakery just delivered a fresh batch of bread this*
morning.
used to describe actions done in a lively, brisk, or vigorous manner
Example: *He approached the project with a fresh enthusiasm,*
eager to tackle the challenges ahead.
used to indicate something happening or occurring without delay or hesitation
Example: *He provided a fresh response to the question, showing his*
quick thinking and readiness.

freshly /ˈfrɛʃli/
refers to something that has been done, made, or acquired not long before
Example: *She served freshly baked cookies to her guests, straight*
out of the oven.
indicates that something is in a state of freshness or is fresh in quality
Example: *The salad was made with freshly picked lettuce and*
tomatoes from the garden.
used to describe actions that are done with energy or vigour

Example: She sprinted across the finish line, her legs moving
freshly despite the long race.

fretfully /ˈfrɛtfəli/
used when someone is irritated or annoyed, often showing signs of
discontent
Example: She paced fretfully around the room, unable to find her
misplaced keys.
reflecting concern or on ease, often accompanied by restlessness
Example: The parents waited fretfully at the hospital, hoping for
news about their child's condition.
showing signs of agitation or restlessness, often due to discomfort or
dissatisfaction
Example: She kept checking the clock fretfully, worried about
missing her flight.

friendly /frˈɛndli/
acting in a way that is affable, welcoming, or amicable towards others
Example: The neighbours are very friendly and always greet each
other with a smile.
creating an atmosphere of openness and approachability
Example: The hotel staff provided friendly assistance to all guests,
making everyone feel welcome.
showing readiness to help or work together harmoniously
Example: She offered friendly advice to her colleague on how to
solve the problem effectively.

frightenedly /ˈfraɪtndli/
acting or reacting with fear or apprehension
Example: She glanced frightenedly over her shoulder, afraid of
what might be lurking in the shadows.
showing signs of being alarmed or distressed due to fear
Example: The child clung to his mother frightenedly during the
thunderstorm.

frightfully /frˈaɪtfəli/

to describe something that is causing great fear or apprehension

*Example: The haunted house looked frightfully eerie in the
                moonlight.*

to emphasise the intensity of something, often negative or unpleasant

*Example: She felt frightfully nervous before her first public
                speaking engagement.*

used as an intensifier; like "very" or "extremely" in emphasising the
degree of something

Example: Mark was frightfully good at playing the piano.

frigidly /ˈfrɪdʒɪdli/

referring to temperatures that are icy, freezing, or extremely cold

*Example: The air was frigidly cold, causing frost to form on the
                windowpanes.*

describing someone's behaviour that is aloof, unfriendly, or lacking
warmth or emotion

*Example: She greeted him frigidly, barely making eye contact or
                offering a smile.*

used to describe actions or responses that are cold, indifferent, or
unenthusiastic

Example: He responded frigidly to her suggestion.

friskily /frˈɪskili/

engaging in a manner that is lively and spirited

Example: The puppy bounded friskily around the yard.

acting with vigour or enthusiasm

*Example: She danced friskily to the upbeat music, enjoying the
                lively rhythm.*

moving or behaving in lively and animated way

Example: The foal pranced friskily around the field.

approaching something with a cheerful or carefree attitude

Example: *She greeted the day friskily, ready to tackle whatever challenges came her way.*

frivolously /ˈfrɪvələsli/
doing something in a way that is not serious or significant
Example: *She spent money frivolously on unnecessary gadgets.*
behaving in a way that shows a lack of seriousness or responsibility
Example: *He frivolously ignored his deadlines.*
approaching something with little regard for its gravity or consequences
Example: *She frivolously accepted the dare without considering the potential risks involved.*

frolicsomely /ˈfrɒlɪksəmli/
engaging in activities with a sense of fun, light-heartedness, and energy
Example: *The kittens frolicsomely pounced on each other's tails.*
acting with enthusiasm and zest, often in a carefree or unrestrained manner
Example: *The children ran frolicsomely through the sprinklers on a hot summer day.*

frontally /frˈʌntəli/
engaging with something or someone by facing them directly
Example: *The teacher addressed the class frontally to ensure everyone could hear and see her clearly.*
dealing with a problem or issue openly and directly
Example: *The manager decided to address the team's concerns frontally during the meeting.*
referring to something that pertains to the front or forward-facing aspect
Example: *The painting depicts the subject frontally, emphasizing their facial features.*

frontwards /frˈʌntwədz/
referring to the act of moving forward or towards the front
Example: He took a step frontwards, eager to see what was ahead.
describing something that faces or points towards the front
Example: The chair was placed frontwards, facing the stage.
indicating progress or advancement in a forward direction
Example: She focused on moving frontwards in her career.

frostily /ˈfrɒstɪlɪ/
referring to someone's demeanour or behaviour that lacks warmth or
friendliness
Example: She greeted him frostily, barely making eye contact.
describing interactions that are formal, reserved, or unapproachable
*Example: He responded frostily to her suggestion, keeping the
               conversation brief.*
indicating a coolness or iciness in attitude that may convey
disapproval or displeasure
*Example: She frostily declined his invitation, making her
               disapproval clear.*

frothily /frˈɒθili/
describing something that is covered with froth or foam
*Example: The cappuccino was served frothily, with a thick layer of
               foam on top.*

frowningly /frˈaʊnɪŋli/
doing something in a way that expresses disapproval, displeasure, or
concern, typically by furrowing one's brows and displaying a frown
*Example: He looked at the mess frowningly, clearly unhappy with
               the situation.*

frozenly /ˈfrəʊznli/
doing something in a manner that suggests being stiff, immobile, or
without emotion, as if frozen

Example: *She stood frozenly, unable to react to the shocking news.*

frugally /ˈfruːɡəlli/
doing something in a way that saves money or resources
Example: *They lived frugally, saving most of their income for future*
investments.
using only a small amount of something
Example: *She applied the paint frugally, ensuring it covered the*
entire surface with minimal waste.

fruitfully /frˈuːtfəli/
something done in a way that produces good results or yields a
positive outcome
Example: *The team worked together fruitfully to complete the*
project ahead of schedule.
yielding benefits or profits, often in a financial sense
Example: *The new marketing strategy proved fruitfully effective.*
achieving desired outcomes or success in an endeavour
Example: *Her efforts were finally rewarded fruitfully when she*
received the promotion.

fruitlessly /frˈuːtləsli/
performing an action that does not achieve the desired outcome
Example: *She searched fruitlessly for her lost keys throughout the*
house.
doing something in a way that does not produce any significant or
useful results
Example: *Despite their efforts, they searched fruitlessly for a*
solution to the problem.
engaging in activities that do not lead to any productive or beneficial
outcome
Example: *He spent hours scrolling through social media fruitlessly*
instead of studying for his exam.

frumpily /frˈʌmpili/
in a way that lacks style or fashion sense
Example: She showed up to the party frumpily dressed.
in a manner that appears worn out, untidy, or neglected
*Example: After a long day of work, she arrived home frumpily
            dressed and ready to relax.*
in a way that is plain, dull, or unfashionably drab
Example: He dressed frumpily for the casual Friday at the office.

frumpishly /ˈfrʌmpɪʃli/
in a way that lacks style or fashion sense
*Example: She walked into the party frumpishly, wearing old jeans
            and a faded T-shirt.*
in a manner that is plain, dull, or lacking in elegance
*Example: She attended the gala frumpishly, wearing a simple dress
            and minimal makeup.*
in a way that appears untidy or poorly maintained
*Example: She arrived at the meeting frumpishly, with wrinkled
            clothes and unkempt hair.*

frustratedly /frʌstrˈeɪtɪdli/
acting in a manner that expresses annoyance or anger due to being
unable to accomplish something
*Example: She sighed frustratedly when the internet connection
            dropped.*
acting with a sense of disappointment or discouragement due to
obstacles or setbacks
*Example: He frustratedly threw his hands up in the air, unable to
            figure out the solution.*
showing signs of agitation or vexation due to feeling hindered or
blocked in achieving a goal
Example: She paced frustratedly in the waiting room.

full /fʊl/

to indicate completeness or entirety

Example: The grocery bag was full.

to indicate that something is filled to its maximum capacity

Example: The concert hall was full, with not a single empty seat left.

to describe actions or feelings that are intense or strong

Example: After the thrilling victory, their hearts were full of joy and excitement.

to indicate directness or straightforwardness in communication

Example: She gave a full explanation of the project.

to describe something that is already in use or taken

Example: All the parking spots were full, so I had to park on the street.

fully /fʊli/

to indicate that something is done to the maximum extent or degree

Example: She was fully prepared for the exam after studying all night.

to describe actions that are done in a thorough or exhaustive manner

Example: He fully understood the requirements after reading the entire document carefully.

to indicate that something is done without any reservations or exceptions

Example: Sarah fully accepted the responsibility for the mistake and apologized sincerely.

to describe actions or qualities that are carried out with maximum effort or effectiveness

Example: He tackled the project fully, ensuring every detail was meticulously addressed.

fulsomely /ˈfʊlsəmli/

to describe something done in an exaggerated or insincere manner, often implying excessive flattery or praise

Example:　　She thanked him fulsomely for the smallest favour.
to describe something given or expressed in a lavish or generous manner
Example:　　The host welcomed the guests fulsomely.
to indicate something done in an overly elaborate or profuse way
Example:　　She apologized fulsomely, showering him with
　　　　　　　compliments and gifts to make amends.

fumblingly /fˈʌmblɪŋli/
doing something in a manner that lacks dexterity or skill often, resulting in mistakes or mishandling
Example:　　He fumblingly tried to assemble the furniture.
performing an action with hesitation or uncertainty, as if unsure of how to proceed
Example:　　He fumblingly searched for her keys in her purse.
doing something in a way that demonstrates a lack of proficiency or competence
Example:　　He fumblingly attempted to tie the knot.

fumingly /fjˈuːmɪŋli/
acting or speaking with visible or intense anger
Example:　　Jessica left the room fumingly after an argument with her
　　　　　　　colleague.
performing an action with irritation or annoyance
Example:　　She typed out the email fumingly, frustrated by the
　　　　　　　repeated delays in the project.

functionally /fˈʌŋkʃənəli/
to describe something in a way that relates to its practical use or purpose, rather than its form or aesthetics
Example:　　The new smartphone was designed functionally.
to describe something in terms of its operational or mechanical aspects

Example: The engineer analysed the machine functionally, focusing on its efficiency and performance.

to describe something in a manner that achieves its intended purpose effectively and efficiently

Example: The redesigned website was structured functionally, making navigation intuitive and enhancing user experience.

fundamentally /fˌʌndəmˈɛntəli/

to describe something in its most basic or essential form

Example: Freedom of speech is fundamentally important in a democratic society.

to describe something as being a fundamental or inherent characteristic

Example: Education is fundamentally important for personal growth and development.

to describe something in terms of its foundational principles or core concepts

Example: The debate focused fundamentally on the ethical implications of the new policy.

to describe a change or transformation that affects the essence or core of something

Example: The discovery of electricity fundamentally changed the way people lived and worked.

furiously /fjˈɔːrɪəsli/

acting or moving with extreme anger or rage

Example: John slammed the door furiously after the argument.

performing an action with great energy or force

Example: She typed furiously to finish her assignment before the deadline.

moving or progressing very quickly or rapidly

Example: The car sped furiously down the highway.

further /fˈɜːðɐ/

to indicate an increase in amount, degree, or extent

Example: *She walked further into the forest to explore its depths.*

to indicate something happening to a greater extent or degree

Example: *He emphasized the need for further improvements in their strategy to achieve better results.*

to introduce additional information or points

Example: *He added further details to support his argument during the debate.*

to indicate movement or progress in a forward direction

Example: *She decided to walk further along the trail to explore more of the scenic route.*

to indicate something happening at a more distant time or place

Example: *They planned to discuss the matter further during their next meeting.*

furthermore /fˌɜːðəmˈɔː/

introducing a supplementary or additional point

Example: *She enjoyed painting as a hobby; furthermore, it helped her relax after a long day at work.*

to indicate something that adds to or supports the previous statement

Example: *She loves reading; furthermore, she finds it helps her to unwind after a busy day.*

to emphasise that there is more to consider or to explain

Example: *His qualifications were impressive, and furthermore, his experience in the field made him an ideal candidate for the job.*

furthest /fˈɜːðəst/

to indicate physical distance

Example: *The furthest point of their hike was the summit of the mountain.*

to indicate degree or amount

Example: *She went the furthest in the math competition, solving the most difficult problems.*

to indicate the most distant point in time or space

Example: *The campsite is located at the furthest end of the hiking trail.*

furtively /fˈɜːtɪvli/

performing an action in a way that is intended to avoid attention or observation

Example: *He glanced around furtively before slipping the note into her bag unnoticed.*

acting in a manner that is characterised by deceit or secrecy

Example: *She checked her phone furtively during the meeting, hoping no one would notice.*

doing something with caution or weariness

Example: *He peeked furtively around the corner before entering the dark alley.*

fussily /fˈʌsili/

doing something with excessive attention to trivial details

Example: *She arranged the flowers fussily, ensuring each stem was precisely positioned in the vase.*

acting with nervousness or agitation, often over minor issues

Example: *She rearranged the table settings fussily, making sure every fork and spoon was perfectly aligned.*

doing something with a strong desire for precision or perfection

Example: *He adjusted the alignment of the painting fussily, making sure it was perfectly centred on the wall.*

Gg

gaddingly /gˈɑdɪŋli/
in a way that involves moving restlessly or aimlessly from place to place, often in pursuit of pleasure or entertainment
Example: She wandered gaddingly through the city.

gaily /ˈgeɪlɪ/
in a cheerful or light-hearted manner
Example: The children laughed gaily as they played in the park.
in a bright or colourful way
Example: The flowers bloomed gaily in the vibrant garden.

gainfully /gˈeɪnfəli/
in a way that is profitable, beneficial, or providing a gain, especially in terms of employment or occupation
Example: She was gainfully employed as a software engineer at a leading tech company.

gainlessly /gˈeɪnlˈɛsli/
in a way that does not provide any gain, profit, or advantage
Example: He spent his savings gainlessly on frivolous purchases.

gallantly /gˈɑləntli/
acting with boldness or valour often in the face of danger
Example: The firefighter gallantly rushed into the burning building to save the trapped family.
behaving in a manner that is considerate, courteous, and respectful, often towards women
Example: He gallantly opened the door for her, offering a warm smile.
exhibiting a sense of nobility or grandeur in action or appearance
Example: The knight rode gallantly across the battlefield.

gamely /ˈɡeɪmli/
showing courage and determination, often in challenging or adverse situations
Example: Despite the heavy rain, she gamely continued the marathon.
approaching tasks or challenges with energy and a positive attitude
Example: He gamely tackled the difficult project with enthusiasm.

garishly /ˈɡeərɪʃli/
in a way that is overly vivid and glaring, often considered unattractive or in bad taste
Example: The house was decorated garishly with neon colours and flashing lights.
in a manner that is showy or flashy, lacking subtlety or elegance
Example: The garishly decorated room was filled with bright, mismatched colours and patterns.

garrulously /ˈɡarʊləsli/
in a way that involves talking a lot, often about trivial matters
Example: He garrulously recounted every detail of his vacation.
speaking in a lengthy, roundabout, or repetitive manner
Example: The professor garrulously explained the theory.

gaspingly /ˈɡɑːspɪŋlɪ/
breathing in a rapid, laboured, or desperate manner, often due to surprise, exertion, or excitement
Example: She reached the finish line gaspingly, having run the marathon without stopping.
reacting with a sharp intake of breath, often accompanied by a sense of shock or disbelief
Example: He gaspingly watched as the magician pulled a rabbit out of the hat.

gate-wise /gˈeɪt:wˈaɪzli/

referring to the direction or method of entering or exiting through gates

Example: *The hikers proceeded gate-wise through the narrow entrance to the trail.*

acting in a way that mimics the movement or function of gates

Example: *The automatic doors opened gate-wise as shoppers approached the store entrance.*

gaudily /gˈɔːdɪli/

characterised by excessive or tastelessly bright colours, patterns, or decorations

Example: *She wore a gaudily patterned shirt that clashed with her skirt.*

displaying a lack of restraint or subtlety in appearance or style

Example: *The room was decorated gaudily with oversized, brightly coloured furniture and ornate fixtures.*

gawkishly /gˈɔːkʃli/

acting in a manner that lacks grace or finesse

Example: *He danced gawkishly at the party, tripping over his own feet.*

behaving in a manner that attracts attention due to being socially inexperienced or unaware

Example: *She gawkishly asked the CEO a question that revealed her lack of knowledge about the industry.*

gayly /ˈgeɪli/

describing actions or behaviours that are cheerful, carefree, or filled with happiness

Example: *The children skipped gayly through the meadow, laughing and chasing butterflies.*

referring to something that is adorned with bright colours or decorations

Example: *The float in the parade was decorated gayly with*
                 balloons and ribbons.

gelidly /ˈʤelɪdli/

describing something done with an icy or freezing quality

Example: *The wind blew gelidly across the tundra, chilling us to*
                 the bone.

acting with a cold, detached, or indifferent attitude

Example: *She responded to his questions gelidly, showing little*
                 emotion or interest in the conversation.

generally /dʒˈɛnərəli/

referring to something that happens in most cases or is true for the majority of situations

Example: *He generally wakes up early in the morning to exercise*
                 before work.

describing something in a general or nonspecific way, without focusing on details

Example: *He generally prefers to take the lead in group projects*
                 without getting into the specifics.

accepted or understood by the majority

Example: *The guidelines were generally agreed upon by all team*
                 members before implementation.

generically /dʒənˈɛrɪkli/

referring to something in a broad or undefined way, without specific details or distinctions

Example: *He store sold a range of generically labelled canned*
                 vegetables without brand names.

relating to characteristics or qualities that are typical of a category rather than specific to an individual member

Example: *The advertisement described the product generically.*

describing something, such as a product, that is not identified by a trademarked brand name but is instead referred to by its general type or category

Example: *He bought a generically labelled pain reliever at the pharmacy.*

generously /dʒ'ɛnərəsli/

in a way that shows readiness to give more of something, especially money, than is strictly necessary or expected

Example: *She donated generously to the charity.*

providing something in ample or plentiful amounts

Example: *The chef sprinkled the dish generously with fresh herbs before serving it.*

demonstrating a broad-minded, forgiving, or gracious attitude

Example: *He always speaks generously of others.*

genetically /dʒɛn'ɛtɪkli/

pertaining to the characteristics or traits inherited from one's parents through genes

Example: *Genetically, she inherited her father's blue eyes and her mother's curly hair.*

involving the alteration or manipulation of an organism's genetic material

Example: *The new strain of rice is genetically modified to resist pests and grow in harsh conditions.*

genially /dʒ'iːnɪəli/

exhibiting warmth, kindness, and a pleasant disposition

Example: *He greeted his guests genially, offering them a warm smile and a handshake.*

demonstrating affability and a welcoming attitude towards others

Example: *He genially invited everyone to join in the festivities, making sure everyone felt included.*

genteelly /ʤenˈtiːlli/
exhibiting characteristics associated with high social standing, elegance, and good manners.
Example: She carried herself genteelly at the gala, displaying impeccable manners and grace.
demonstrating sophisticated taste and decorum
Example: She hosted the dinner party with genteel sophistication.
behaving with an exaggerated sense of propriety and gentility
Example: She spoke genteelly, always using polite and refined language.

gently /ʤˈɛntli/
performing actions with a light touch or minimal force
Example: She brushed her hair gently to avoid tangling it further.
showing care, compassion, and consideration in behaviour or speech
Example: She spoke gently to comfort her friend who was feeling upset.
proceeding slowly and smoothly, without sudden changes or harshness
Example: The boat rocked gently on the calm lake.

genuinely /ʤˈɛnjuːɪnli/
expressing real feelings or thoughts without pretence or deceit
Example: She smiled genuinely upon receiving the unexpected compliment from her colleague.
indicating something is real, true, or exactly as it appears or is claimed to be
Example: He genuinely apologized for the misunderstanding.
acting in a way that is natural and uncontrived
Example: She genuinely expressed her gratitude, and her smile reflected her sincere appreciation.

geocentrically /ˌdʒəʊ sˈɛntrɪk ˈɔːli/

viewing or considering something from a perspective where Earth is the central point, especially in astronomy

Example: It was believed geocentrically that the sun and other planets revolved around the Earth.

describing an approach or viewpoint that aligns with the idea that the Earth is at the centre of the universe

Example: The geocentrically oriented model placed Earth at the centre of celestial movements.

geographically /dʒˌɪəgrˈafɪkli/

something related to geography or the physical features of a specific place or region

Example: The country is geographically diverse, with mountains, plains, and coastal areas.

geologically /dʒˌɪəlˈɒdʒɪkli/

pertains to the processes, events, or phenomena related to geology, which is a study of the Earth's physical structure, history, and processes

Example: The canyon was formed geologically over millions of years by the erosion of rock layers.

geometrically /dʒˌiːəʊmˈɛtrɪkli/

describing how something is structured or shaped according to geometric principles

Example: The garden was designed geometrically, with perfectly symmetrical beds and pathways.

describing the arrangement or positioning of objects in space

Example: The chairs were arranged geometrically around the conference table for the meeting.

describing how quantities or figures change according to geometric progression or principles

Example: *The pattern of the tiles on the floor was arranged*
             geometrically.

germanely /dʒɜːˈmeɪnli/
something is germane if it is directly related to or appropriate for the topic at hand
Example: *She brought up a point that was germanely to the*
             discussion.
used to describe information, comments, or actions that are pertinent and contribute meaningfully to the current context
Example: *His feedback was germanely focused on the project's key*
             objectives.
indicates that something is fitting or suitable for the situation or discussion
Example: *Her suggestion was germanely timed, addressing a*
             critical aspect of the ongoing debate.

ghastly /ɡˈɑːstli/
used to describe something that is shockingly bad, dreadful, or terrifying
Example: *The horror movie featured ghastly scenes that left the*
             audience on edge throughout the night.
indicates extreme unpleasantness or horror
Example: *The ghastly sight of the abandoned, dilapidated house*
             sent chills down my spine.
describes something that is deeply disturbing or frightening
Example: *The ghastly scream echoed through the empty hallway,*
             sending shivers down my spine.

ghostly /ɡˈəʊstli/
to relate to something that is eerie, spectral, or reminiscent of ghosts or the supernatural
Example: *The ghostly figure appeared at the window, sending*
             shivers down my spine.

to describe something that is very faint, pale, or lacking in substance, as if it were ghost-like

Example: *The ghostly outline of the mountains appeared in the misty morning haze.*

to describe actions or occurrences that evoke a sense of haunting or unease

Example: *The ghostly whispers in the old mansion made my hair stand on end.*

giddily /ˈgɪdɪlɪ/

referring to a physical sensation of feeling light-headed or unsteady, often due to excitement or rapid movement

Example: *She spun around giddily after receiving the unexpected news of her promotion.*

to describe behaviour that is marked by joy, excitement, frivolity, often enough in a playful or superficial way

Example: *The children laughed giddily as they played in the park on a sunny afternoon.*

to describe actions or emotions that are excessively exuberant or enthusiastic

Example: *He giddily accepted the award, his excitement evident to everyone in the room.*

gigantically /dʒaɪgˈɑntɪkli/

to describe something that is exceptionally large or huge in size

Example: *The cruise ship was gigantically anchored at the port, towering over nearby boats.*

to indicate something of gigantic proportions or immense magnitude

Example: *The skyscraper rose gigantically above the city skyline.*

to describe something that is extremely big or extensive

Example: *The gigantically sprawling shopping mall boasted over 300 stores.*

gigglingly /gˈɪɡlɪŋli/

to refer to the action of laughing in a high-pitched, nervous, or restrained manner

Example: The children ran through the park, gigglingly chasing each other in a game of tag.

to describe laughter or amusement that is light-hearted and without seriousness

Example: She responded gigglingly to his playful joke.

to imply laughter that is accompanied by a sense of mischief or playful teasing

Example: The students exchanged answers gigglingly during the exam.

gingerly /dʒˈɪndʒəli/

indicating that someone is handling something delicately to avoid causing damage or injury

Example: She picked up the fragile vase gingerly, afraid it might break if handled too roughly.

to describe an action done tentatively or with slight reluctance, often due to uncertainty or fear

Example: He approached the edge of the cliff gingerly.

provide a short simple sentence example of the word gingerly which means

Example: She gingerly tested the hot water with her fingers before stepping into the bath.

girlishly /gˈɜːlɪʃli/

to refer to behaviour or actions that are characteristic of a young girl

Example: She giggled girlishly at the sight of the fluffy puppy playing in the park.

to describe behaviour that is flirtatious or coy, typically in a way that is perceived as characteristic of girls or young women

Example: She smiled girlishly, twirling her hair as she flirted with him at the party.

to imply actions or expressions that are innocent, naive, or charmingly childlike

Example: *She skipped girlishly down the path, picking wildflowers along the way.*

glacially /ˈgleɪsjəlli/
describing movement or change that happens at an extremely slow pace, like the movement of a glacier

Example: *Progress on the construction project moved glacially.*

to refer to actions or processes that resemble or are characteristic of glaciers, such as their slow, grinding movements

Example: *The negotiations between the two countries proceeded glacially, with each side reluctant to compromise.*

to describe behaviour or interactions that are emotionally distant or unresponsive, akin to the coldness associated with glaciers

Example: *After the argument, their communication was glacially polite but lacked warmth or sincerity.*

gladly /glˈɑdli/
to indicate a readiness or eagerness to do something without hesitation or reluctance

Example: *She gladly accepted the job offer, excited to start her new role at the company.*

to denote doing something with joy or pleasure

Example: *He gladly helped his friend move into her new apartment.*

to imply performing an action or fulfilling a request with a sense of satisfaction or content

Example: *She gladly volunteered to organise the charity event.*

glamorously /glˈa.mərəsli/
to describe something that is stylish, fashionable, and visually appealing in a luxurious or sophisticated way

Example: *She arrived at the gala glamorously dressed in a shimmering gown and sparkling jewellery.*

to imply an air of charm, allure, or charisma, often associated with the world of fashion, entertainment, or luxury

Example: *The movie star arrived at the red-carpet event glamorously dressed in a stunning designer gown.*

to denote an appealing or captivating appearance or demeanour

Example: *She smiled glamorously, her confident demeanour catching everyone's attention at the party.*

glancingly /ɡlˈɑːnsɪŋli/

to describe something that is done quickly or in passing, without delving deeply into details

Example: *He only mentioned the issue glancingly during the meeting, not wanting to dwell on it.*

to refer to a literal glance or glance-like movement, but more often figuratively to mean indirectly or tangentially

Example: *She addressed the controversial topic only glancingly in her speech.*

glaringly /ɡlˈeərɪŋli/

to emphasise that something stands out and is easily noticed, often due to its striking nature

Example: *The typo in the headline was glaringly obvious to everyone who read the newspaper.*

to denote something that is done in a way that is perceived as shocking or offensive because it is so evident

Example: *Her absence from the meeting was glaringly disrespectful, given her role in the project.*

glassily /ɡlˈɑːsili/

describing something that is smooth, shiny, or reflective like glass

Example: *The lake's surface shimmered glassily under the morning sun.*

to imply a lack of expression or emotion, akin to the cold, smooth surface of glass.

Example: *He stared at her glassily, his face devoid of any hint of emotion or reaction.*

gleefully /glˈiːfəli/

to denote a state of excitement or pleasure, often accompanied by a sense of satisfaction or anticipation

Example: *The children ran gleefully through the park.*

to imply a playful or mischievous enjoyment of something

Example: *She opened the gift gleefully, eager to see what surprise awaited inside.*

glidingly /ˈglaɪdɪŋli/

to describe something that moves or progresses in a smooth and fluid manner

Example: *The skater moves glidingly across the ice, executing graceful spins and jumps.*

to imply a movement or action that is characterised by grace and poise

Example: *She danced glidingly across the stage, captivating the audience with her elegant movements.*

to suggest a movement that is quiet and almost imperceptible

Example: *The cat crept glidingly through the tall grass, stalking its prey with silent determination.*

glintingly /glˈɪntɪŋli/

describing something that shines briefly, usually reflecting light

Example: *The diamond ring glintingly caught her eye as it sparkled in the sunlight.*

to imply something that is noticeable or strikingly evident, often in a fleeting or momentary way

Example: *Her eyes glintingly betrayed her excitement as she talked about her upcoming vacation.*

glisteringly /ˈɡlɪstərɪŋli/

to describe something that is sparkling or shining with a bright and intense light

Example: *The glisteringly polished silverware gleamed under the chandelier's light.*

to imply something that has a dazzling or spectacular quality

Example: *The glisteringly beautiful fireworks lit up the night sky.*

to describe something that is visually impressive or captivating

Example: *The glisteringly decorated Christmas tree was the highlight of the holiday party.*

glitteringly /ɡlˈɪtərɪŋli/

to describe something that reflects light in a way that is bright and noticeable

Example: *The chandelier in the ballroom glitteringly illuminated the grand hall, adding an air of elegance to the event.*

to imply something that is adorned or presented in a flashy, extravagant, or showy manner

Example: *The car showroom displayed glitteringly polished vehicles under bright showroom lights.*

to describe something that is visually striking or captivating, often due to its beauty or attractiveness

Example: *The sunset over the ocean was glitteringly beautiful.*

gloatingly /ˈɡləʊtɪŋlɪ/

to describe someone expressing or showing satisfaction or pleasure, especially when feeling triumphant over someone else's failure or discomfort

Example: *He grinned gloatingly as he watched his rival's project fail miserably.*

to imply a kind of pleasure derived from someone else's misfortune or suffering

Example: *She gloatingly recounted her opponent's mistakes, revelling in their misfortune.*

used to describe someone who is visibly revelling in their own success or victory

Example: *After winning the championship, he walked gloatingly around the arena.*

globally /glˈəʊbəli/
referring to something that applies to or affects the entire world or a large portion of it

Example: *The pandemic had a globally significant impact on economies.*

to describe an approach or perspective that considers all aspects or elements of a situation

Example: *The environmental treaty was negotiated globally to address climate change on a comprehensive scale.*

something that is spread across the entire globe or present everywhere on Earth

Example: *The impact of deforestation is felt globally, affecting ecosystems and climate patterns worldwide.*

gloomily /glˈuːmɪli/
to describe something done with a sense of sadness or despair

Example: *He sighed gloomily as he looked out at the rainy weather.*

to imply a situation or atmosphere that is bleak, depressing, or lacking in hope

Example: *She stared out the window gloomily, feeling trapped by the grey skies and persistent rain.*

to denote a perspective or viewpoint that focuses on the darker aspects of the situation

Example: *He spoke gloomily about the future, emphasizing the challenges and uncertainties ahead.*

gloriously /glˈɔːrɪəsli/
to denote something that is impressive, beautiful, or awe-inspiring

Example: *The sunrise over the mountains was gloriously colourful.*

to describe something done with exceptional skill, success, or achievement

Example: *She performed gloriously in the final match, scoring three goals, and leading her team to victory.*

to imply a sense of triumph, happiness, or pride

Example: *The team celebrated gloriously after winning the championship, lifting the trophy high in the air.*

glossily /glˈɒsɪli/

describing something that has been polished or treated to appear smooth and shiny

Example: *The furniture in the showroom gleamed glossily under the bright lights.*

to imply a surface that is sleek and attractive, often in a stylish or fashionable manner

Example: *The car's glossily polished exterior reflected the sunlight, giving it a sleek and luxurious appearance.*

to describe something that is done with a polished or refined finish

Example: *The artist applied paint glossily to create a smooth and shiny surface on the canvas.*

gloweringly /glˈaʊərɪŋli/

to denote someone looking at someone or something with a fierce or threatening stare

Example: *He stood in the doorway gloweringly, his arms crossed, clearly displeased with the situation unfolding before him.*

to imply an attitude or demeanour that is characterised by hostility or resentment

Example: *He answered the questions gloweringly, clearly irritated by the interrogation.*

glowingly /ˈgləʊɪŋli/

to describe praise or approval that is expressed with great admiration or satisfaction

Example: *The manager spoke glowingly about the team's performance.*

to imply a literal or figurative glow that suggests something is shining or standing out positively

Example: *The city skyline glowed glowingly as the sun set behind the skyscrapers.*

to denote a manner or tone that is optimistic, hopeful, or full of positivity

Example: *She spoke glowingly about her future, excitedly outlining her ambitions and dreams.*

glumly /glˈʌmli/

to describe someone's demeanour or expression that reflects unhappiness or disappointment

Example: *The child sat glumly in the corner after losing the game.*

to imply a mood of silent discontent or dissatisfaction

Example: *After losing the game, they walked back to the locker room glumly, each player reflecting on what went wrong.*

to describe actions or statements that lack energy or optimism

Example: *She nodded glumly when asked about her plans for the weekend.*

gluttonously /ˈglʌtnəsli/

to describe eating or consuming something in large quantities or with excessive eagerness

Example: *He ate the cake gluttonously.*

indulging in something to the point of excess, not necessarily limited to food

Example: *He spent the afternoon shopping gluttonously, buying far more clothes than she actually needed.*

gnashingly /nˈaʃɪŋli/
to describe actions where teeth are ground together forcefully, often out of frustration, anger, or pain
Example: *He clenched his teeth gnashingly as he struggled to finish the difficult puzzle.*

goadingly /gˈəʊdɪŋli/
to refer to actions that intentionally provoke or stimulate someone, often to elicit a response or reaction
Example: *She smirked goadingly, knowing her words would provoke him into an argument.*
urging someone on or pushing them forward, especially in a competitive context
Example: *The coach shouted goadingly at the team, encouraging them to push harder in the final minutes of the game.*

good /gˈʊd/
to indicate proficiency or effectiveness in performing an action
Example: *She is very good at playing the piano.*
describing the extent or completeness of an action
Example: *He did a good job cleaning the kitchen thoroughly.*
denoting that something meets acceptable standards
Example: *The soup tasted good, seasoned just right with a comforting warmth.*
used to describe the positive outcome or effect of something
Example: *The rain was good for the garden, helping the plants grow strong and healthy.*
indicating a large extent or degree
Example: *She has a good amount of experience in her field, having worked for over a decade in various roles.*

goofily /gˈuːfili/
performing actions in a way that is humorous or lacks seriousness

Example: He grinned goofily as he attempted to juggle oranges,
              entertaining his friends with his playful antics.

acting in a way that is not graceful or is somewhat awkward

Example: She walked goofily across the stage, tripping over her
              own feet but laughing it off with the audience.

doing something that is absurd or ludicrous, often in a way that draws
attention

Example: The clown goofily danced around the stage.

gorgeously /gˈɔːdʒəsli/

describing something done with striking beauty or appeal

Example: She looked gorgeously elegant in her evening gown.

conveying a sense of luxury, richness, or opulence

Example: The hotel lobby was gorgeously decorated with marble
              floors, crystal chandeliers, and plush velvet couches.

highlighting something done with grandeur or impressiveness

Example: The fireworks display was gorgeously orchestrated.

goutily /gˈaʊtili/

performing actions that indicate discomfort or difficulty due to gout

Example: He winced goutily as he tried to put on his shoe.

describing actions done with the symptoms or effects of gout, such as
stiffness or pain, often in the joints

Example: He moved goutily, his knee visibly swollen and causing
              him discomfort with each step.

gracefully /grˈeɪsfəli/

performing actions with beauty and smoothness, often implying a
pleasing appearance or movement

Example: She danced across the stage gracefully.

acting with composure and self-assuredness

Example: Despite the unexpected question, she answered
              gracefully, showing no sign of hesitation or uncertainty.

moving or behaving in a way that is gentle and smooth, without abruptness or harshness

Example: *The ballerina leapt gracefully across the stage, her movements flowing with effortless elegance.*

interacting with others in a polite, respectful, and kind way

Example: *She gracefully thanked each guest for attending her party, making them feel appreciated and welcome.*

gracelessly /gɹˈeɪsləsli/

performing actions in a way that is uncoordinated or lacks smoothness

Example: *He stumbled gracelessly as he tried to navigate the narrow pathway in the dark.*

acting in a way that is not aesthetically pleasing or elegant

Example: *She fell gracelessly into the chair, her movements awkward and unrefined.*

behaving or moving in a way that lacks sophistication or refinement

Example: *He exited the stage gracelessly, tripping over the microphone cord in front of the entire audience.*

interacting with others in a way that lacks politeness or respect

Example: *She spoke gracelessly to the customer, displaying impatience and rudeness.*

handling situations without consideration for others' feelings or the social context

Example: *He handled the delicate issue of layoffs gracelessly, causing unnecessary distress among the team.*

graciously /grˈeɪʃəsli/

acting with warmth, compassion, and a willingness to help others

Example: *She graciously accepted the award and thanked everyone who supported her throughout her career.*

behaving in a respectful and considerate way

Example: *He graciously offered his seat to the elderly woman on the bus.*

performing actions with poise, elegance, and refinement

Example: *She graciously accepted the compliment and thanked everyone for their kind words.*

responding to situations in a pleasant, amiable, or favourable way

Example: *He graciously offered to help with the project, demonstrating his willingness to contribute positively.*

showing leniency, compassion, or forgiveness

Example: *She graciously forgave him for the mistake, showing her compassionate nature.*

gradually /ɡrˈadʒuːəli/

indicating that something happens little by little rather than all at once

Example: *The temperature gradually dropped throughout the evening as the sun set.*

describing a process that proceeds in small, incremental steps

Example: *She gradually improved her piano skills by practising every day for a year.*

showing a steady, continuous movement or change in a certain direction

Example: *The sun gradually descended below the horizon, painting the sky in hues of orange and pink.*

suggesting a smooth, consistent, and unhurried progression

Example: *Over time, she gradually became more confident in her new role at work.*

Emphasising that changes occur so slowly that they are almost unnoticed until they accumulate

Example: *The patient's health gradually improved with each passing day, showing steady signs of recovery.*

grammatically /ɡramˈatɪkli/

performing actions in a way that follows the accepted rules and conventions of grammar

Example: *He wrote his essay grammatically, checking for errors in spelling and punctuation before submitting it.*

concerning aspects or elements of grammar

Example: *She struggled with speaking grammatically correct*
             sentences in the new language class.

considering or evaluating something based on its grammatical
properties or correctness

Example: *The teacher evaluated the essay not only for content but*
             also grammatically to ensure clarity and precision.

grandiosely /ˈɡrɑndɪəʊsli/

in an impressive or magnificent in appearance or style, especially
pretentiously

Example: *He spoke grandiosely about his modest achievements.*

with exaggerated grandeur or pompousness

Example: *She grandiosely declared herself the best artist in the*
             entire city.

grandly /ɡrˈɑndli/

in a grand or impressive way

Example: *The ballroom was grandly decorated for the gala.*

in an ambitious or extravagant way

Example: *He grandly announced his plan to travel the world in a*
             private jet.

with an air of importance or superiority

Example: *She grandly waved off their concerns, confident in her*
             decision.

in a way that shows grandeur or splendour, often with a sense of
showiness

Example: *The fireworks lit up the sky grandly, dazzling everyone*
             below.

granularly /ˈɡrɑnjʊləli/

in a detailed or specific way

Example: *The data was analysed granularly to identify subtle*
             patterns.

with attention to small components or elements

Example: *She granularly reviewed each section of the report for accuracy.*

in a manner that breaks something down into smaller parts

Example: *The data was analysed granularly, breaking it down into smaller, more specific components.*

graphically /grˈafɪkli/

in a very clear and detailed manner, often in a way that is vivid or explicit

Example: *The novel graphically described the intense battle scenes.*

using visual representations such as graphs, diagrams, or illustrations

Example: *The data was presented graphically to illustrate the trends over time.*

in the way that pertains to graphics or visual art

Example: *She explained the concept graphically using sketches and diagrams.*

in a manner that is striking or dramatic, often to the point of being shocking or gruesome

Example: *The movie depicted the crime scene graphically, showing every detail of the gruesome murder.*

gratefully /grˈeɪtfəli/

with gratitude or thankfulness

Example: *She accepted the award gratefully, thanking everyone who supported her.*

in a way that shows appreciation or thanks

Example: *He gratefully accepted their help during a difficult time.*

expressing a sense of relief or pleasure

Example: *She gratefully sighed after finishing her final exams.*

gratifyingly /grˈatɪfˌaɪŋli/

in a manner that provides pleasure or satisfaction

Example: *He was gratifyingly surprised by the positive feedback on his presentation.*

in a way that gives a sense of accomplishment or fulfilment

Example: *She completed the project gratifyingly, feeling a deep sense of accomplishment and fulfilment.*

gratingly /grˈeɪtɪŋli/

in a manner that is irritating or annoying

Example: *His constant complaining was gratingly annoying during the entire trip.*

in a harsh or unpleasant way, often referring to sound

Example: *The screeching of the chalk on the blackboard was gratingly unpleasant.*

gravely /grˈeɪvli/

in a serious or solemn manner

Example: *The doctor delivered the news about the patient's condition gravely, emphasizing the seriousness of the situation.*

to a degree that is serious or concerning

Example: *The doctor's expression turned gravely when discussing the test results.*

in a way that is sombre or dignified

Example: *She spoke gravely at the memorial service, honouring her late grandfather with heartfelt words.*

great /grˈeɪt/

to a very large or considerable extent

Example: *She has a great deal of experience in managing large-scale projects.*

extremely well, very satisfactorily

Example: *He performed great in his exams, scoring top marks in all subjects.*

greatly /ɡrˈeɪtli/

to a great extent; very much; significantly

Example: *She greatly appreciated the support she received during her difficult times.*

in a notable or important manner; profoundly

Example: *His discovery greatly impacted the field of medicine.*

in a way that shows enthusiasm or intensity

Example: *She was greatly excited about the opportunity to perform on stage, her enthusiasm evident in every movement.*

greedily /ɡrˈiːdɪli/

in a way that shows excessive or insatiable desire, especially for food or possessions

Example: *The child greedily grabbed all the cookies from the plate before anyone else could have one.*

in a manner that eagerly seeks or consumes something in large quantities

Example: *The investor greedily bought up stocks during the market dip, hoping for a quick profit.*

grimly /ɡrˈɪmli/

in a stern or serious manner; without showing any humour or amusement

Example: *He nodded grimly as he delivered the bad news to the team.*

in a way that indicates grimness or harshness; in a manner that suggests hardship or difficulty

Example: *She tightened her grip on the umbrella and walked grimly through the pouring rain.*

in a way that is forbidding or daunting, with a sense of menace or threat

Example: *The soldiers stared grimly at the approaching storm.*

grossly /ɡrˈəʊsli/

in a coarse, vulgar, or offensive manner

Example: *His jokes were grossly inappropriate for the formal gathering.*

to an excessive or exaggerated degree; greatly or significantly

Example: *The company's profits were grossly underestimated in the initial projections.*

flagrantly or conspicuously; in a way that is obviously wrong or offensive

Example: *The company's actions were grossly unethical, clearly violating industry standards.*

in a manner that relates to total amounts or quantities, typically without deductions

Example: *He was grossly overcharged for the repair work on his car.*

grotesquely /ɡrəʊtˈɛskli/

refers to something that is oddly shaped, exaggerated, or outlandish in appearance

Example: *The cartoon character was drawn grotesquely, with wildly exaggerated features and proportions.*

describes actions or behaviours that are excessively distorted or exaggerated, often to the point of being absurd

Example: *His attempt at imitating a celebrity ended up being grotesquely exaggerated.*

indicates something that is offensive, shocking, or morally repugnant

Example: *The movie depicted scenes of violence in a grotesquely graphic manner.*

in a hideously distorted manner

Example: *The mask was crafted grotesquely, with exaggerated features that were*

unsettling to look at.

in a manner evoking a sense of the grotesque

Example: *The actor portrayed the villain grotesquely, with*
                   exaggerated gestures and a sinister laugh.

growlingly /grˈaʊlɪŋli/
describe a sound or voice that is deep, harsh, and aggressive, often
indicating anger or hostility
Example: *The dog greeted strangers growlingly, protecting its*
                   territory.
refers to a voice or manner of speaking that expresses dissatisfaction
or discontent, often in a low, murmuring tone
Example: *He responded growlingly to the criticism, clearly*
                   displeased with the feedback.
describes a deep, resonant sound resembling a growl, often associated
with animals or machinery
Example: *The engine of the old car rumbled growlingly as it*
                   struggled up the hill.
indicates a low-pitched or throaty sound that is audible and
pronounced
Example: *He spoke growlingly under his breath, clearly frustrated*
                   with the situation.

grudgingly /grˈʌdʒɪŋli/
describes actions or behaviours that are done with a sense of
hesitation or resistance
Example: *She grudgingly agreed to help with the project, despite*
                   her busy schedule.
indicates doing something while feeling annoyed or displeased about
it
Example: *He grudgingly admitted his mistake, knowing he had to*
                   apologize.
refers to admitting something reluctantly or unwillingly, often due to
being unable to deny the truth
Example: *She grudgingly accepted that she needed to ask for help*
                   with her studies.

used to describe actions or behaviours done with envy or begrudging admiration

Example: *She grudgingly acknowledged her rival's impressive achievement.*

grumpily /grˈʌmpɪli/

describes someone's demeanour or behaviour characterised by a mood of discontent, often accompanied by grumbling or complaints

Example: *John answered the phone grumpily, annoyed at being disturbed during his nap.*

refers to someone's mood that is marked by irritability or a tendency to be easily annoyed

Example: *He grumpily muttered complaints about the weather as he trudged through the rain.*

indicates a mood that is gloomy or sulky, typically showing a lack of enthusiasm or willingness to engage

Example: *She grumpily declined the invitation to the party, preferring to stay home alone.*

describes someone's expression or actions that convey dissatisfaction or displeasure

Example: *He grumpily slammed the door shut behind him, clearly upset about something.*

gruntingly /grˈʌntɪŋli/

describes a noise that is deep, rough, and often made in a manner like a grunt

Example: *The exhausted athlete gruntingly lifted the heavy weights during his training session.*

refers to a sound or mannerism that mimics the vocalisation of an animal, typically a pig or similar creature

Example: *The toddler gruntingly imitated the sound of a pig while playing with his toy farm animals.*

indicates a sound made during physical exertion or effort, often accompanied by a low, involuntary vocalisation

Example: *The weightlifter gruntingly lifted the barbell, pushing*
himself to reach his personal best.

describes speech or communication that is unclear, difficult to
understand, or poorly articulated

Example: *He gruntingly muttered his response, making it hard to*
decipher what he was trying to say.

guiltily /ˈgɪltɪlɪ/

describes actions, expressions or behaviour that indicates someone is
experiencing guilt or remorse

Example: *She glanced guiltily at the broken vase.*

indicates behaviour that betrays awareness of having done something
wrong or forbidden

Example: *He ate the last cookie guiltily, hoping no one would*
notice.

refers to actions or expressions that reveal a sense of shame about
one's actions or choices

Example: *She smiled guiltily when asked about her secret late-night*
snack.

guiltlessly /ˈgɪltlɪsli/

describes actions or behaviours that are performed without any sense
of wrongdoing or moral culpability

Example: *Jane enjoyed the dessert guiltlessly, knowing she had*
stuck to her diet all week.

indicates behaviour or actions that are free from any guilt or
responsibility

Example: *He indulged in a day of relaxation guiltlessly, having*
completed all his tasks ahead of schedule.

describes actions or behaviours that do not induce feelings of guilt in
others

Example: *She accepted the compliment guiltlessly, knowing it was*
genuinely meant.

gullibly /gˈʌləbəli/

describes someone who believes things too easily or is quick to accept information without sufficient evidence or scepticism

Example: *He gullibly fell for the online scam promising instant wealth without questioning its legitimacy.*

indicates actions or behaviours that demonstrate a lack of critical thinking or judgement when faced with information or claims

Example: *She gullibly believed the sales pitch without checking the product reviews first.*

refers to someone who is overly trusting and susceptible to manipulation or deceit

Example: *He gullibly handed over his credit card information to the caller claiming to be from tech support.*

gurglingly /gˈɜːglɪŋli/

describes actions or sounds that resemble the noise of a liquid moving or bubbling

Example: *The stream flowed gurglingly over the smooth rocks.*

indicates actions, speech, or sounds that mimic or evoke the sound of gurgling

Example: *The baby laughed gurglingly as she played with her toys in the bathtub.*

gushingly /gˈʌʃɪŋli/

describes behaviour or speech that is overly enthusiastic, often to the point of being effusive or exaggerated

Example: *She greeted her favourite actor gushingly, showering him with compliments and praise.*

indicates expressing emotions such as love, admiration, or gratitude in a very demonstrative or a sentimental way

Example: *She thanked her friend gushingly for the surprise birthday party.*

refers to expressing praise or compliments in a manner that is effusive and unrestrained

Example: *Jessica complimented her friend gushingly on her*
             beautiful artwork.

describes actions or speech that are characterised by strong emotional
expression or sentimentality

Example: *She spoke gushingly about her favourite movie,*
             expressing her deep emotional connection to the story
             and characters.

gymnastically /dʒɪmnˈɑːstɪkˈɔːli/

describes movements, exercises, or activities characteristic of
gymnastics

Example: *The dancer moved gymnastically across the stage,*
             displaying the grace and flexibility of a gymnast.

indicates actions or movements that involve agility, flexibility, and
coordination, like those required in gymnastics

Example: *She performed gymnastically, effortlessly leaping over*
             the hurdles.

refers to actions or movements that demonstrate physical skill or
acrobatic prowess

Example: *He navigated the obstacle course gymnastically,*
             showcasing his remarkable agility and balance.

Hh

habitually /həbˈɪtʃuːəli/
something that is done often or frequently
Example: *She habitually drinks coffee every morning.*
in a way that follows established customs or practises
Example: *He habitually removes his shoes before entering the house.*
following a set routine or pattern
Example: *She habitually goes for a run after work.*
done in the same way over time
Example: *He habitually checks his emails first thing in the morning.*
referring to an action performed due to habit rather than conscious decision
Example: *She habitually twirls her hair when she is thinking.*

haggardly /ˈhɑɡədli/
looking exhausted or fatigue
Example: *He looked haggardly after working late nights all week.*
appearing thin and drawn, often from hunger, worry or suffering
Example: *She stared haggardly into the mirror, her face gaunt and eyes sunken.*
showing signs of stress or anxiety
Example: *He spoke haggardly, his voice trembling with worry.*

haggishly /ˈhɑɡɪʃli/
acting or looking like a witch or an old, ugly woman
Example: *She cackled haggishly, her eyes gleaming with mischief.*
appearing menacing or unattractive in a way that might remain one of a hag
Example: *The old woman grinned haggishly; her face twisted in an eerie smile.*

behaving in a malevolent or spiteful way
Example: He haggishly plotted his revenge.
acting in a way that is harsh or disagreeable
Example: She scolded him haggishly, her tone sharp and unkind.

half /hˈɑːf/
to some extent but not completely
Example: The project is half finished and still needs a lot of work.
dividing something into two equal parts
Example: She cut the apple in half and gave one piece to her friend.
roughly or about
*Example: The movie is half over, so we should be ready for the big
            twist soon.*
to a moderate extent
*Example: He was only half interested in the topic, not fully
            engaged.*

halfway /hˈɑːfweɪ/
in or at the middle of a distance
*Example: They stopped for a break when they were halfway
            through their hike.*
in or at the middle of a period or process
Example: She checked her progress halfway through the project.
being an equal distance from two points
Example: The new coffee shop is halfway between our two offices.
not fully or completely
*Example: The novel was only halfway completed when the deadline
            arrived.*

haltingly /hˈɒltɪŋli/
doing something with pauses, uncertainty, or a lack of smoothness
*Example: She spoke haltingly, searching for the right words to
            explain her idea.*
showing signs of stopping or losing strength

Example: *The engine ran haltingly before finally sputtering to a*
             stop.

handily /hˈɑndɪli/
achieving something without much difficulty
Example: *She solved the puzzle handily, finishing it in just a few*
             minutes.
being easily accessible or available
Example: *The tools were handily stored in the garage, ready for*
             use.
doing something with skill and competence
Example: *He handled the tricky negotiations handily, impressing*
             everyone with his expertise.

handsomely /hˈɑndsʌmli/
in a way that shows largesse or abundance
Example: *She was handsomely rewarded for her hard work on the*
             project.
performing an action with skill and proficiency
Example: *He played the piano handsomely, captivating the entire*
             audience with his skill.
done in a way that is aesthetically pleasing or well-proportioned
Example: *The house was handsomely decorated with elegant*
             furniture and tasteful art.
in a manner that is polite and considerate
Example: *He handsomely complimented her work, showing genuine*
             appreciation.

haphazardly /hɑphˈɑzədli/
without a specific pattern or plan
Example: *The papers were scattered haphazardly across the desk.*
done without careful consideration or precision
Example: *He haphazardly assembled the shelf, resulting in a*
             wobbly and uneven structure.

in the chaotic or untidy manner

*Example: The books were stacked haphazardly on the floor,
            creating a mess in the room.*

without uniformity or consistency

*Example: The colours were painted haphazardly on the wall,
            creating a mismatched pattern.*

haplessly /ˈhɑplɪsli/

in a way that shows bad luck or misfortune

*Example: He haplessly dropped his phone, and it shattered on the
            pavement.*

in a manner that shows a lack of control or ability to improve the
situation

*Example: She haplessly tried to fix the broken vase, only making
            the situation worse.*

without achieving success or desired outcomes

*Example: Despite his efforts, he haplessly attempted to fix the car
            but could not get it to start.*

happily /hˈɑpɪli/

experiencing or expressing happiness

Example: She smiled happily as she opened her birthday gift.

with a sense of satisfaction or contentment

*Example: He sat back happily after finishing the final chapter of his
            book.*

with a positive or upbeat attitude

*Example: She greeted everyone happily at the party, full of energy
            and cheer.*

happening in a way that turns out well or is beneficial

*Example: The project, which seemed difficult at first, happily
            concluded ahead of schedule.*

hard /hˈɑːd/

doing something with a lot of energy or determination

Example: *She worked hard to complete the assignment before the*
              deadline.

doing something that is difficult or challenging

Example: *The exam was so hard that many students struggled to*
              finish it on time.

in a way that is firm or solid

Example: *The rock was too hard to break with just a hammer.*

in a manner that is severe or critical

Example: *He spoke hard about the mistakes in the report,*
              emphasizing their seriousness.

doing something with considerable force

Example: *She hit the ball hard, sending it flying over the fence.*

harder /hˈɑːdɐ/

doing something with increased exertion or determination compared
to before

Example: *He practiced harder each day to improve his skills.*

experiencing or facing more challenges or obstacles

Example: *The second half of the race was harder, with steeper hills*
              and stronger winds.

applying more force or energy

Example: *She pushed harder on the pedal to make the bike go*
              faster.

acting or responding with greater severity

Example: *The coach became harder on the team after their poor*
              performance.

hardly /hˈɑːdli/

only just or to a very small extent

Example: *She could hardly believe the news when she heard it.*

in a manner that is almost not the case

Example: *The team hardly had time to celebrate before starting the*
              next game.

something done with great effort or challenge

Example: *He hardly managed to lift the heavy box by himself.*
referring to something that is almost non-existent
Example: *There was hardly any milk left in the jug.*

harmlessly /hˈɑːmləsli/
acting or being in a way that is safe and does not result in physical or emotional damage
Example: *The cat playfully pounced on the toy, harmlessly batting it around.*
doing something in a way that poses no danger or threat
Example: *The children laughed and harmlessly threw water balloons at each other.*
doing something in a way that does not offend or upset others
Example: *He joked harmlessly about the weather, making everyone smile without causing any offence.*

harmonically /hɑːmˈɒnɪkli/
in a manner that pertains to musical harmony, which involves the combination of different musical notes played or sung simultaneously to produce a pleasing sound
Example: *The choir sang harmonically, blending their voices to create a rich, pleasing sound.*
referring to elements that are in harmony or agreement with each other in a broader context
Example: *The colours in the room were chosen harmonically, creating a soothing and balanced atmosphere.*
in the context of harmonic series or harmonic functions, referring to relationships or sequences that follow harmonic principles
Example: *The architect designed the building harmonically, ensuring the proportions followed principles of harmonic sequences.*

harmoniously /hɑːˈməʊnjəsli/
to imply that something is done in a way that is pleasingly consistent and orderly, often referring to music or sounds that are pleasant when hear together
Example: *The choir sang harmoniously, creating a beautiful and soothing melody.*
to suggest that actions, thoughts, or relationships are in a state of peaceful coexistence or agreement
Example: *The team worked harmoniously to complete the project on time.*
refers to situations where there is no disagreement or tension, and everything proceeds smoothly
Example: *The siblings played harmoniously in the garden all afternoon.*

harshly /hˈɑːʃli/
acting or speaking with great severity, often causing discomfort or distress
Example: *The teacher spoke harshly to the students for not completing their assignments.*
something unpleasant to the senses, particularly sound
Example: *The wind howled harshly through the trees.*
treating someone with a lack of kindness or with sharp, critical language
Example: *The critic judged the performance harshly, pointing out every flaw.*
referring to something that is unrelievedly severe in appearance or conditions
Example: *The desert sun beat down harshly, with no shade in sight.*

hastily /hˈeɪstɪli/
doing something quickly, often without taking the necessary time or care

Example: *She hastily packed her bags and rushed to catch the train.*

to suggest that actions or decisions are made impulsively or rashly

Example: *He hastily agreed to the plan without considering the consequences.*

referring to an action done in a rush or brisk way, often under pressure

Example: *She hastily signed the contract without reading the details.*

hatefully /hˈeɪtfəli/

showing strong animosity or aversion towards someone or something

Example: *He spoke hatefully about his rival, showing no respect or kindness.*

acting in a way meant to hurt or offend others

Example: *She looked at him hatefully after he made the hurtful comment.*

with malice or ill will

Example: *He stared hatefully at the person who had wronged him.*

something done in a way that is extremely disagreeable or offensive

Example: *The graffiti on the wall was written hatefully, filled with offensive slurs.*

haughtily /hˈɔːtɪli/

in an arrogantly superior manner

Example: *She haughtily dismissed their concerns, believing herself above their worries.*

With condescension or disdain

Example: *He haughtily ignored their requests, confident in his own superiority.*

in a proud or lofty manner

Example: *She walked haughtily into the room, confident and unbothered by others.*

hauntedly /hˈɔːntɪdli/

in a manner suggestive of being troubled or tormented

Example: *She looked at him hauntedly, her eyes reflecting her inner turmoil.*

actions or expressions that seem influenced by supernatural presences

Example: *He spoke hauntedly of the shadowy figures he claimed to have seen in the old house.*

with an appearance of suffering from persistent fear or anxiety

Example: *Her face looked hauntedly as she recounted the terrifying ordeal.*

hauntingly /hˈɔːntɪŋli/

to imply that something leaves a deep, memorable impression, often tinged with sadness or beauty

Example: *The melody played hauntingly, lingering in their minds long after it ended.*

something that is reminiscent of ghosts or the supernatural, often creating a spooky or unsettling atmosphere.

Example: *The old mansion stood hauntingly in the moonlight, casting eerie shadows.*

something that keeps coming back to one's mind, often in a disturbing or poignant way

Example: *The ghost story haunted him hauntingly, replaying in his mind long after he heard it.*

hazily /hˈeɪzɪli/

something that is not clearly defined or easily understood

Example: *He remembered the details hazily, struggling to piece together the events of the night.*

something that is not distinct or sharply visible, often due to physical haze or fog

Example: *The mountains appeared hazily through the thick morning fog.*

in a confused or disoriented manner

Example: *She hazily wandered through the streets, unsure of her*
            surroundings.

headily /hˈɛdɪli/
in an intoxicating or exhilarating manner
Example: *The scent of the blooming flowers filled the air headily,*
            making everyone feel elated.
impulsively or recklessly
Example: *He headily spent his savings on a flashy car.*
in a manner that affects the senses strongly
Example: *The perfume was applied headily, overwhelming*
            everyone in the room.
with a strong or potent influence
Example: *The novel's dramatic ending headily influenced her*
            thoughts for days.

headlong /hˈɛdlɒŋ/
moving with the head leading the body, often in a literal physical
sense
Example: *Jim dove headlong into the pool, his body cutting through*
            the water with great speed.
acting quickly, often without careful thought or consideration
Example: *He plunged headlong into the project, eager to get*
            started despite the risks.
moving with great momentum or force, often in a way that is difficult
to control
Example: *The car skidded headlong into the intersection, unable to*
            stop before crashing into the side barrier.

healthily /hˈɛlθɪli/
in a manner that promotes physical health
Example: *She ate healthily by including lots of fruits and vegetables*
            in her diet.
in a way that supports mental or emotional well-being

Example: *They communicated healthily, always listening and supporting each other.*

in a way that is robust or vigorous

Example: *The children played healthily in the park, full of energy and enthusiasm.*

actions taken with moderation and thoughtfulness, contributing to overall well-being

Example: *She managed her work-life balance healthily, ensuring she had time for both relaxation and productivity.*

heartedly /hˈɑːtɪdli/

with full commitment or enthusiasm

Example: *He supported the project wholeheartedly, giving it his best effort.*

with sincerity and earnestness

Example: *She apologized heartedly, genuinely regretful for her mistake.*

with emotional depth or intensity

Example: *He sang the song heartedly, pouring all his emotions into the performance.*

heartily /hˈɑːtɪli/

with great enthusiasm or energy

Example: *They laughed heartily at the comedian's jokes.*

with sincerity and genuine feeling

Example: *She heartily congratulated her friend on the promotion.*

in a thorough or complete manner

Example: *He heartily enjoyed the meal, savouring every bite.*

with strong agreement or support

Example: *The audience heartily applauded the speaker's inspiring message.*

heartlessly /hˈɑːtləsli/

acting in a way that shows no sympathy or concern for others

Example: She heartlessly ignored their pleas for help, focusing only
on her own needs.

in a manner that is harsh or unkind

Example: He heartlessly criticized her performance in front of the
entire team.

heatedly /ˈhiːtɪdlɪ/

showing strong feelings, often of anger or passion

Example: They argue heatedly about the best way to solve the
problem.

engaging in something with great enthusiasm or intensity

Example: She discussed her favourite book heatedly, unable to hide
her excitement.

heavenly /hˈɛvənli/

describing something that is extremely enjoyable or wonderful

Example: The dessert was heavenly, with its rich chocolate and
creamy texture.

pertaining to celestial divine aspects

Example: The choir sang a heavenly melody that seemed to reach
the stars.

heavily /hˈɛvili/

describing something that is done with great physical weight or
impact

Example: She breathed heavily after running the marathon.

indicating a significant extent or quantity

Example: The project was heavily dependent on the new software
for success.

suggesting a burdened or cumbersome movement

Example: He walked heavily across the room, exhausted from the
long day.

describing something that is done with great intensity or severity

Example: *The storm rained heavily throughout the night, causing*
             widespread flooding.

heavy /hˈɛvi/
intensely or strongly
Example: *The decision had a heavy impact on the entire team.*
with great weight or impact
Example: *The heavy box fell off the shelf with a loud thud.*

hectically /hˈɛktɪkli/
describing actions that are done with great speed and disorganisation,
often due to being overwhelmed or rushed
Example: *She packed her bags hectically, trying to catch her flight*
             on time.
indicating a high level of activity, often with a sense of urgency or
lack of control
Example: *The office was working hectically to meet the last-minute*
             deadline.

hedonistically /hˌɛdənˈɪstɪkli/
acting with the primary aim of seeking enjoyment and sensory
gratification
Example: *They spent the weekend hedonistically, indulging in*
             luxury and fine dining.
engaging in activities or behaviours that emphasise personal pleasure
and comfort
Example: *He lived hedonistically, prioritizing his comfort and*
             pleasure above all else.

heedfully /ˈhiːdfʊlli/
paying close attention to details or instructions
Example: *She listened heedfully to the professor's lecture, taking*
             careful notes.

acting with awareness and consideration, often to avoid mistakes or danger

Example: *He drove heedfully through the foggy streets to avoid any accidents.*

heedlessly /ˈhiːdlɪsli/

acting without regard for potential consequences or the importance of the situation

Example: *She heedlessly skipped the safety briefing, not realizing the risks involved.*

behaving in a way that shows a lack of consideration for the risks or impacts of one's actions

Example: *He heedlessly threw the papers into the air, causing them to scatter everywhere.*

heftily /hˈɛftɪli/

describing actions performed with considerable physical power

Example: *He heftily lifted the heavy suitcase onto the truck.*

indicating a large amount or degree

Example: *The project budget was heftily increased to cover additional costs.*

heinously /hˈeɪnəsli/

describing actions that are extremely immoral or atrocious

Example: *The crime was heinously brutal, shocking the entire community.*

indicating an act that is highly objectionable or severe in its negative impact

Example: *The company's actions were heinously damaging to the environment.*

hellishly /hˈɛlɪʃli/

describing something that is unbearably bad or challenging

Example: *The hike was hellishly difficult, with steep climbs and harsh weather.*

indicating a high degree of discomfort or trouble

Example: *The traffic jam was hellishly long, causing them to be hours late.*

hellward /hˈɛlwˈɔːd/

moving or directing oneself in the direction of hell, often used metaphorically or in a literary context

Example: *The character's actions seemed to lead him hellward, as he made increasingly destructive choices.*

describing behaviour that is seen as leading to severe consequences or moral degradation

Example: *His reckless decisions sent him hellward, leading to a life of regret and hardship.*

helpfully /hˈɛlpfəli/

acting in a way that aids or benefits others

Example: *She answered the questions helpfully, ensuring everyone understood the instructions.*

doing something that adds value or makes a task easier

Example: *He helpfully organized the files, making it easier for the team to find what they needed.*

helplessly /hˈɛlpləsli/

demonstrating an inability to change or control circumstances

Example: *She watched helplessly as the storm damaged her house.*

acting in a way that reveals a lack of control or capacity to affect outcomes

Example: *He shook his head helplessly, unable to find a solution to the problem.*

hence /hˈɛns/

indicating a conclusion or result based on what has been previously stated

Example: *The roads were icy; hence, the school was closed for the day.*

referring to a point in time that will occur because of the current situation

Example: *The project will be completed by next week; hence the deadline is Friday.*

henceforth /hˈɛnsfɔːθ/

referring to a point in time that will occur because of the current situation

Example: *The rules will be enforced strictly henceforth to ensure fairness.*

here /hˈiə/

indicating the current or specific location where the speaker is

Example: *Please come here and join us at the table.*

referring to the present moment or situation

Example: *Here, we are discussing the new project guidelines.*

referring to the specific context being addressed

Example: *Here, the term "efficiency" refers to reducing waste in production.*

hereabout /hˈiəɐbˈaʊt/

referring to the vicinity or general area near the current location

Example: *I live hereabout, just a few blocks away from the park.*

referring to the general time close to the present or a specific event

Example: *The new policy was implemented hereabout last year.*

hereby /hˈiəbaɪ/

used to indicate that something is being done or declared through the action or document currently being referred to

Example: *I hereby resign from my position, effective immediately.*
emphasising that the action or declaration is being made through the document or statement itself

Example: *We hereby confirm the terms of our agreement as outlined in this letter.*

herein /hɪərˈɪn/
referring to something contained within the current text or document
Example: *The details of the contract are specified herein.*
indicating that something is included or addressed within the scope of the current context
Example: *The responsibilities of each team member are outlined herein.*

hereinafter /ˈhɪərɪnˈɑːftə/
referring to something that will be mentioned or addressed later in the same document or text
Example: *The term "contractor" shall hereinafter refer to the individual or company hired for the job.*
indicating that further details or references will be provided later in the document
Example: *The procedures will be described hereinafter in section three of this manual.*

hereinto /hˈiəˈɪntʊ/
referring to entering or being inside a specific location or area mentioned previously in the text
Example: *The information should be entered hereinto as indicated in the guidelines.*

hereon /hˈiərɒn/
referring to something related to or situated on the current document or piece of text

Example: *Please sign hereon to confirm your acceptance of the*
           terms.

indicating something pertaining to this subject or context being
discussed or referred to in the current document

Example: *The responsibilities of the parties involved are detailed*
           hereon.

hermetically /hɜːmˈɛtɪkli/

referring to something that is tightly sealed to prevent the passage of
air or other substances

Example: *The jar was hermetically sealed to keep the food fresh.*

suggesting a state of being cut off or insulated from external factors

Example: *The company operated hermetically, with no outside*
           influences affecting its decisions.

hesitatingly /ˈhezɪteɪtɪŋlɪ/

acting with uncertainty or reluctance, often due to doubt or fear

Example: *She spoke hesitatingly, unsure of how her words would*
           be received.

indicating a lack of confidence that results in slow or deliberate action

Example: *He hesitatingly approached the podium, nervous about*
           his speech.

hiddenly /ˈhɪdnli/

performing an action in a way that avoids detection

Example: *She hiddenly placed the note under his desk.*

something done in a way that is not immediately apparent or obvious

Example: *The treasure was hiddenly concealed behind the old*
           painting.

hideously /hˈɪdiəsli/

describing something that is visually repulsive

Example: *The monster's face was hideously deformed.*

describing something that causes shock, horror, or disgust

Example: *The crime scene was hideously gruesome.*
used to emphasise the degree of something negative
Example: *The exam was hideously difficult.*

high /hˈaɪ/
refers to a position for above ground or a lower level
Example: *The kite flew high in the sky.*
indicates a significant degree or amount
Example: *The cost of living is very high.*
refers to a situation of authority or status
Example: *He holds a high position in the company.*
refers to a state of great joy or excitement, sometimes due to drugs
Example: *The music made him feel incredibly high.*
used to describe something done with great intensity or volume.
Example: *The speakers were blasting music at a high volume.*

higher /hˈaɪɐ/
indicates a position or place that is more elevated than another
Example: *The hill is higher than the surrounding land.*
refers to a superior position or status
Example: *She was promoted to a higher rank in the organization.*
indicates a large amount, degree, or intensity
Example: *The temperature today is higher than yesterday.*

highly /hˈaɪli/
indicates a significant level or amount
Example: *She is highly skilled in graphic design.*
refers to strong approval or commendation
Example: *The movie was highly praised by critics.*
indicates superior quality or standard
Example: *The hotel is highly rated for its luxurious amenities.*
refers to a status of significant power or influence
Example: *He is a highly influential leader in the community.*

hilariously /hɪlˈeərɪəsli/
to describe something that provokes a lot of laughter
Example: *The comedian's jokes were hilariously funny.*

hintingly /hˈɪntɪŋli/
to give subtle clues or hints rather than stating something outright
Example: *She hintingly suggested that he should reconsider his decision.*
referring to something indirectly or implying it without explicit mention
Example: *He hintingly referred to his plans for a surprise party.*

hissingly /hˈɪsɪŋli/
to describe an action done in a way that involves or resembles a hiss
Example: *She spoke hissingly through clenched teeth.*

historically /hɪstˈɒrɪkli/
something is considered or analysed from a historical perspective
Example: *Historically, the city was a major trade centre.*
something that is based on documented historical evidence
Example: *The building is historically significant due to its age and architecture.*
the way something has evolved or been shaped by historical events over time
Example: *The region's culture has been historically shaped by various invasions.*

hitherto /hˈɪðətˌuː/
referring to a point in time extending up to the present
Example: *The project had hitherto remained a secret.*

hoarsely /hˈɔːsli/
describes speaking or sounding in a way that is harsh and lacks smoothness, often due to vocal strain or illness

Example: *He spoke hoarsely after cheering at the concert.*

refers to producing sound or speech that is not clear or smooth due to a hoarse voice

Example: *She answered the phone hoarsely, struggling to speak clearly.*

hoggishly /ˈhɒgɪʃli/

Example: *He ate the entire pizza hoggishly, leaving nothing for anyone else.*

relates to the way a hog behaves, often in a messy or unclean manner.

Example: *The kids played hoggishly in the mud, leaving their clothes covered in dirt.*

holily /hˈəʊlɪlɪ/

to describe actions or behaviours performed in a way that reflects religious piety or sanctity

Example: *She prayed holily every morning before breakfast.*

to imply living or acting according to a strict moral or spiritual code

Example: *He lived holily, following a strict set of spiritual principles.*

home /hˈəʊm/

describes returning to or being at one's own house or dwelling

Example: *After a long trip, it felt wonderful to be home.*

implies doing something in a way that feels natural or instinctive, like the comfort of home

Example: *He completed the task with a home touch, making it look effortless and familiar.*

refers to moving towards a specific goal or target

Example: *She kept her eyes on the target, aiming home with every shot.*

homelily /hˈəʊmlˈɪli/

this describes something done in a way that is modest or lacking in sophistication, reflecting the simplicity often associated with home life

Example: *The dinner was prepared homelily, with simple*
ingredients and a warm, comforting touch.

homely /hˈəʊmli/

implies actions or styles that evoke a sense of cosiness or domesticity

Example: *The cottage had a homely charm, with cosy blankets and*
warm, inviting colours.

homeopathically /hˌəʊmiːəpˈɑθɪkli/

describes methods or actions that align with the principles of homoeopathy, which involves treating diseases with very diluted substances

Example: *He treated his allergies homeopathically with tiny doses*
of natural extracts.

implies doing something in a way that follows the homoeopathic approach or philosophy

Example: *She approached her health issues homeopathically,*
favouring natural remedies over conventional medicine.

homeward /hˈəʊmwəd/

describes movement or direction leading back to one's place of residence

Example: *They started their homeward journey after the party*
ended.

honest /ˈɒnɪst/

expressing oneself or behaving in a way that is straightforward and free from deceit

Example: *She gave an honest answer to the question.*

refers to actions done with integrity and without manipulation

Example: *He made an honest effort to solve the problem.*

honestly /ˈɒnɪstli/

describe speaking or behaving with honesty, without deception or exaggeration

Example: *She spoke honestly about her feelings on the matter.*

expressing oneself with genuine intent and without pretence

Example: *He honestly shared his true thoughts on the project.*

honourably /ˈɒnərəbli/

behaving or acting in a way that reflects high moral standards and integrity

Example: *She acted honourably by returning the lost wallet she found.*

emphasises actions that reflect respect and uphold one's dignity

Example: *He conducted himself honourably during the negotiation, respecting everyone's views.*

performing actions with a commitment to ethical and principled behaviour

Example: *The soldier served honourably throughout his career.*

hopefully /hˈəʊpfəli/

describes doing something with a sense of optimism or desire for a positive outcome

Example: *She submitted her application hopefully, believing she would get the job.*

hopelessly /hˈəʊpləsli/

describes actions or attitudes that reflect despair or a sense of futility

Example: *He looked hopelessly at the wrecked car, knowing it could not be repaired.*

refers to situations that are so bad they seem impossible to fix or improve

Example: *The project seemed hopelessly out of control with so many errors.*

acting in a way that indicates an awareness of inevitable failure or lack of success

Example: *She smiled hopelessly as she saw the exam results.*

horizontally /hˌɒrɪzˈɒntəli/

describes movement or orientation that is parallel to the horizon or the ground

Example: *The picture was hung horizontally on the wall.*

horribly /hˈɒrɪbli/

describes something done in a way that is very disturbing or upsetting

Example: *The movie ended with a horribly shocking twist.*

actions or situations that provoke intense fear or dread

Example: *The haunted house was horribly frightening.*

something done poorly or badly

Example: *The cake turned out horribly, with a burnt crust and raw centre.*

horridly /hˈɒrɪdli/

describes actions or situations that are extremely unpleasant or offensive

Example: *The room smelled horridly of mould and decay.*

implies something done in a manner that is exceptionally poor or dreadful

Example: *The movie was horridly edited, making it hard to follow.*

horrifically /hɒrˈɪfɪkli/

describes actions or events that evoke a strong sense of fear, shock, or disgust

Example: *The crime scene was horrifically gruesome, leaving everyone in shock.*

implies something done in an exceptionally poor or dreadful manner

Example: *The play was horrifically staged, with poorly executed scenes and dialogue.*

refers to actions or situations that are startlingly bad or shocking

Example: *The customer service was horrifically unhelpful.*

horrifyingly /hˈɒrɪfˌaɪŋli/

describing something that instils a deep sense of fear, shock, or disgust

Example: *The documentary revealed horrifyingly graphic images of the disaster.*

emphasising the intensity of the shock or distress caused by something

Example: *The news report was horrifyingly detailed, leaving viewers deeply unsettled.*

highlighting the severe unpleasantness or awfulness of something

Example: *The conditions in the overcrowded shelter were horrifyingly bad.*

hospitably /hɒspˈɪtəbəli/

describing actions that show warmth, kindness, and generosity to guests and strangers

Example: *They welcomed their guests hospitably, offering refreshments and a comfortable seat.*

emphasising the provision of comfort, care, and friendliness to visitors

Example: *The host greeted everyone hospitably, ensuring they felt at ease and well-cared-for.*

indicating an openness to accepting others and making them feel at home

Example: *She spoke hospitably, making the new neighbours feel immediately welcome and included.*

hostilely /ˈhɒstaɪlli/

describing actions that are openly unfriendly or aggressive

Example: He responded hostilely to the criticism, raising his voice, and crossing his arms.

indicating a stance or reaction that is against something or someone

Example: She reacted hostilely to the new policy, voicing a strong objection at the meeting.

connoting a sense of danger or threat through one's actions or demeanour

Example: The dog growled hostilely, warning us to stay away.

hotly /hˈɒtli/

describing actions or expressions carried out with strong feelings, such as anger, excitement, or enthusiasm

Example: They debated the issue hotly, each side passionately defending their viewpoint.

indicating a situation characterised by heat or intense activity

Example: The two teams hotly pursued the championship title throughout the season.

highlighting situations that are highly contested or eagerly pursued

Example: The issue was hotly debated at the town meeting.

describing something done quickly or with great urgency.

Example: She hotly finished her homework before the deadline.

hourly /ˈaʊəli/

describing something that happens once per hour

Example: The bus arrives at the station hourly.

however /haʊˈɛvɐ/

used to indicate a shift or contrast from what was previously stated

Example: The weather was sunny in the morning; however, it started raining in the afternoon.

used to indicate the extent or manner of something

Example: He did not enjoy the movie; however, he appreciated the special effects.

used to add a nuance or qualification to a previous statement

Example: *She is a great cook; however, she rarely has time to prepare elaborate meals.*

hugely /hjˈuːdʒli/
describing something that is very large in scale or impact
Example: *The project was hugely successful, surpassing all expectations.*
used to emphasise the intensity or magnitude of an action or quality
Example: *She was hugely excited about her upcoming vacation.*
indicating a high level of enthusiasm, importance, or influence
Example: *The new policy was hugely influential in shaping the company's future.*

humanely /hjuːmˈeɪnli/
describing actions done in a way that is caring and considerate of the well-being of others
Example: *The shelter humanely euthanized the animals to prevent their suffering.*
referring to actions that uphold ethical treatment and respect for individuals' rights
Example: *The workers were treated humanely, with fair wages and safe conditions.*

humanly /hjˈuːmənli/
describing actions or qualities that are typical of human behaviour or experience
Example: *It is humanly impossible to predict every outcome with certainty.*
referring to what can be achieved or managed by humans, acknowledging natural limitations
Example: *The rescue team did everything humanly possible to find the missing hikers.*

humbly /hˈʌmbli/

describing actions or expressions that reflect a humble attitude, without boasting or claiming undue importance

Example: *She humbly accepted the award, thanking everyone who helped her.*

indicating behaviour that is polite and shows regard for others, often acknowledging one's own limitations or lower status

Example: *He humbly apologized for his mistake and asked for forgiveness.*

reflecting a lack of extravagance or showiness, often implying simplicity

Example: *The artist lived humbly, focusing more on his craft than on luxury.*

humiliatingly /hjˈuːmɪlˌɪeɪtˌɪŋli/

describing actions or situations that lead to a sense of shame or degradation

Example: *She was humiliatingly defeated in the final round of the competition.*

referring to actions that strip someone of their self-respect or dignity

Example: *He was humiliatingly exposed in front of his colleagues for his mistake.*

humorously /hjˈuːmərəsli/

describing actions, comments, or situations that elicit laughter or amusement

Example: *She humorously described her mishap at the party, making everyone laugh.*

indicating that something is done with a humorous attitude or intention

Example: *He humorously imitated the boss's voice to lighten the mood.*

referring to actions or speech that use wit to entertain or provoke thought

Example: She humorously pointed out the irony in the situation, making everyone think and smile.

hungrily /hˈʌŋgrɪli/

describing the way someone eats or looks at food when they are very hungry

Example: He ate the pizza hungrily, devouring every slice.

referring to a passionate or fervent longing for something, not necessarily food

Example: She looked hungrily at the travel brochures, dreaming of her next adventure.

indicating an eager or enthusiastic approach to an activity or opportunity

Example: He hungrily seized every opportunity to advance his career.

hurriedly /hˈʌrɪdli/

describing actions done rapidly, often due to a lack of time or urgency

Example: She packed her bags hurriedly, trying to catch her flight.

indicating that something is done without taking sufficient time or care

Example: He wrote the report hurriedly, missing several important details.

reflecting a state of urgency or stress that accelerates the piece of actions

Example: They left the building hurriedly as the fire alarm went off.

hurtfully /hˈɜːtfəli/

describing actions or words that lead to psychological hurt or distress

Example: His comments were hurtfully direct, leaving her in tears.

referring to actions that result in physical or emotional injury

Example: The argument escalated hurtfully, causing both a lot of emotional pain.

indicating behaviour that is intentionally or unintentionally offensive or hurtful

Example: *She spoke hurtfully, not realizing how her words would affect him.*

hushedly /hˈʌʃtli/

describing actions or speech carried out in a soft or low tone to avoid making noise

Example: *They talked hushedly in the library to avoid disturbing the other readers.*

referring to communication or behaviour that is discrete or confidential

Example: *The two friends whispered hushedly about the surprise party.*

indicating a quiet or respectful attitude in response to something significant or solemn

Example: *The audience listened hushedly as the speaker shared the emotional story.*

huskily /hˈʌskili/

describing speech that is deep, rough, or slightly raspy, often due to vocal strain or a cold

Example: *He spoke huskily after cheering loudly at the concert all night.*

referring to a voice or sound that is low and resonant, often conveying emotion or intensity

Example: *She sang the final notes huskily, filled with deep emotion.*

indicating that speech or behaviour is affected by physical effort or strong feelings, such as excitement or sadness

Example: *He answered the phone huskily, his voice still rough from the night before.*

hyperactively /hˌaɪpərˈaktɪvli/
referring to behaviour characterised by unusually high levels of
activity or movement
Example: The children played hyperactively in the park.
indicating actions driven by a heightened state of excitement or
nervousness
*Example: She paced hyperactively around the room, unable to calm
her nerves before the big presentation.*
describing behaviour that reflects symptoms or traits commonly
associated with hyperactivity, such as difficulty staying still or focus
*Example: He fidgeted hyperactively during the long meeting,
struggling to stay still.*

hyperbolically /ˌhaɪpɜːˈbɒlɪkəlli/
describing actions, speech, or descriptions that involve hyperbole or
extreme exaggeration
*Example: He hyperbolically claimed that the book was so
captivating it could change the world.*
referring to expressions or descriptions that go beyond the normal
level of intensity for effect
*Example: She hyperbolically said she had waited an eternity for her
coffee to arrive.*
indicating that the statements or claims are meant to be understood
figuratively, not as factual truth
*Example: He hyperbolically claimed he could run faster than a
speeding train.*

hypnotically /hɪpnˈɒtɪkli/
describing actions or effects that can put someone into a trance or a
state of heightened suggestibility
*Example: The rhythmic music played hypnotically, lulling the
audience into a trance-like state.*
referring to something that captures attention in a way that is almost
spellbinding or entrancing

Example: The dancer moved *hypnotically, captivating everyone*
             with her graceful performance.
indicating behaviour or presentation that resembles the influence or
characteristics of hypnosis
Example: His voice was delivered *hypnotically, making it hard for*
             the audience to look away.

hypocritically /hˌɪpəkrˈɪtɪkli/
describing actions or statements that involve pretending to hold moral
standards or beliefs that one does not actually follow
Example: He criticized others for being late, but *hypocritically, he*
             was always tardy himself.
referring to behaviour that outwardly appears virtuous or righteous,
but is self-serving or deceptive
Example: She spoke *hypocritically about the importance of honesty,*
             while secretly hiding her own deceit.
indicating actions that contradict the values or principles one publicly
and espouses
Example: He preached about environmental conservation but
             hypocritically drove a gas-guzzling SUV.

hypothetically /hˌaɪpəθˈɛtɪkli/
referring to discussions or considerations that involve imagined or
theoretical situations rather than actual events
Example: *Hypothetically, if she won the lottery, she would buy a*
             house on the beach.
indicating that something is being discussed as an assumption or
theoretical possibility rather than a fact
Example: *Hypothetically, if everyone worked from home, traffic*
             congestion would decrease
significantly.
describing statements or arguments that are made based on assumed
or proposed conditions

Example: Hypothetically, if the company doubled its budget, it could expand into new markets.

hysterically /hɪstˈɛrɪkli/
describing behaviour marked by intense, uncontrollable emotions such as fear, anxiety, or joy
Example: She laughed hysterically at the joke, unable to control her laughter.
referring to actions that are overly dramatic or unreasonable, often due to emotional overload
Example: He reacted hysterically to the minor setback, as if it were a major disaster.
indicating actions or responses that are chaotic or frenzied due to emotional upheaval
Example: She called her friends hysterically after losing her phone.

Ii

iambically /ɪˈambɪkli/

describing something done according to the iambic metre, which is a pattern of unstressed and stressed syllables

Example: *He spoke the incantation iambically, giving a rhythmic and almost musical quality to his words*

pertains to actions or expressions that follow the iambic rhythm, such as the structure of lines in poetry written in iambic metre

Example: *She recited the poem iambically, creating a gentle, rhythmic flow.*

icily /ˈaɪsɪli/

describes something done in a way that is physically cold or chilly

Example: *She stared at him icily, her gaze as cold as the winter wind.*

refers to behaviour or speech that is emotionally distant, unfriendly, or unkind, conveying a lack of warmth

Example: *He responded icily, making it clear he was upset.*

indicates a lack of concern or emotional involvement, often appearing detached or indifferent

Example: *She greeted him icily, barely acknowledging his presence.*

idealistically /aɪdˈiəlˈɪstɪkli/

describes actions, thoughts, or attitudes that are guided by idealism, which involves pursuing high ideals or principles, often not grounded in practical realities

Example: *He spoke idealistically about creating a world without poverty.*

refers to behaviour or viewpoints that prioritise or focus on ideal standards or perfect outcomes, often at the expense of practicality or realism

Example: *She approached the project idealistically, aiming for perfect results despite the challenges.*

ideally /aɪˈiəli/
refers to something done in a manner that represents an ideal or perfect situation, as close to the best possible outcome as can be
Example: *Ideally, we would finish the work by tomorrow.*
describes actions or conditions that align with an ideal or theoretical standard, often in a way that may not be practical or realistic
Example: *Ideally, everyone would have a perfect work-life balance, though it is often difficult to achieve.*
indicates behaviour or approaches that reflect one's highest values, beliefs, or principles, even if they are not always achievable in practice
Example: *He handled the situation ideally, staying true to his principles even when it was tough.*

identically /aɪˈɛntɪkli/
describes actions or situations that are performed or occur in the same manner or form without any differences
Example: *The twins dressed identically for the party, wearing matching outfits.*
refers to something done in a way that matches exactly or replicates another thing perfectly
Example: *The two designs were printed identically, with every detail matching perfectly.*
indicates that two or more items or actions are so similar that they cannot be differentiated from one another
Example: *The two documents were identical, with each page appearing identically the same.*

idiotically /ˌɪdɪˈɒtɪkli/
describes actions or behaviour that are carried out in a way that is considered very silly or lacking in common sense

Example: *He acted idiotically, forgetting the important details of*
              the plan.

refers to doing something without proper thought or logic, often
resulting in impractical or nonsensical outcomes

Example: *She spent all her savings on a gadget that idiotically did*
              not work as promised.

indicates that something is done in a way that is characteristic of or
comparable to idiotic behaviour

Example: *He responded idiotically, ignoring the clear instructions,*
              and making the situation worse.

idly /ˈaɪdli/

refers to doing something without purpose or effort, often
characterised by a lack of activity or engagement

Example: *He sat idly by the window, watching the rain without any*
              aim.

describes actions or behaviour that are performed without any
specific aim or useful outcome, often seen as wasted time

Example: *She wandered idly through the park, not sure what she*
              wanted to do.

ignobly /ɪgnˈəʊbəli/

refers to actions performed in a way that is morally low or
contemptible, lacking in honour or dignity

Example: *He acted ignobly by betraying his friends for personal*
              gain.

describes behaviour or actions that are considered unprincipled or
selfish, lacking nobility or ethical standards

Example: *She behaved ignobly, spreading rumours to harm her*
              rival's reputation.

indicates doing something in a manner that is characteristic of or
consistent with low or dishonourable qualities

Example: *He treated his colleagues ignobly, undermining their*
              efforts to advance his own position.

ignorantly /ˈɪgnərəntli/
refers to actions or statements made without proper knowledge, understanding, or awareness of the facts or details
Example: *He spoke ignorantly about the topic, not knowing the full background or details.*
describes behaviour or opinions that are based on a lack of information or education, often leading to incorrect or misguided conclusions
Example: *She ignorantly dismissed the new policy without understanding its benefits.*

illegally /ɪlˈiːgəli/
refers to actions or behaviours that are done in a way that breaches legal regulations or statutes
Example: *"He was fined for driving illegally in a restricted area.*
describes activities that are prohibited or unauthorised according to legal standards
Example: *They were caught selling goods illegally at the market.*
indicates behaviour or actions that go against established legal requirements or prohibitions
Example: *He was arrested for operating a business illegally without a license.*

illegibly /ɪlˈɛdʒəbəli/
refers to writing or text that is unclear or messy to the point where it cannot be easily deciphered
Example: *The note was so illegible that no one could read it.*
describes text or handwriting that is so poorly written or formatted that it is hard to interpret or understand.
Example: *Her handwriting was so illegible that I could not make out a single word.*

illicitly /ɪlˈɪsɪtli/

refers to actions or behaviours that are conducted in violation of laws or regulations

Example: *He was caught illicitly downloading copyrighted material.*

describes activities that are not only illegal but also considered improper or unethical by societal standards

Example: *They were illicitly trading in restricted goods.*

indicates that something is done without permission or in a concealed manner, often to evade detection or compliance with rules

Example: *She was caught using the software illicitly, without a proper license.*

illogically /ɪˈlɒdʒɪkəlli/

refers to actions or statements that do not follow a rational or reasoned structure, making them inconsistent or contradictory

Example: *His argument was illogically constructed and did not make sense.*

describes behaviour or arguments that do not adhere to principles of clear and consistent reasoning, often resulting in flawed or irrational conclusions

Example: *She responded illogically, jumping to conclusions without any evidence.*

illusively /ɪˈluːsɪvli/

refers to actions or presentations that generate a misleading or deceptive appearance, making things seem different from reality

Example: *The magician's tricks made the impossible appear illusively possible.*

describes something that provides an illusion or false impression, often causing confusion or misunderstanding

Example: *The painting's depth was illusively created.*

pertains the actions or expressions that are based in imaginative or fanciful ideas rather than practical or realistic considerations

Example: *Her illusively grand plans for the project were more*
                   fantasy than feasible.

illustratively /ˈɪləstreɪtɪvli/
refers to presenting something in a way that helps explain or clarify a concept, often using examples or visual aids to make it clearer
Example: *She explained the process illustratively, using charts and*
                   diagrams to clarify her points.
describes actions or explanations that involve the use of illustrative materials or methods to support or enhance understanding
Example: *His lecture was illustratively detailed, including graphs*
                   and images to aid comprehension.
indicates that something is done in a way that visually represents or depicts a point or idea
Example: *The book illustratively shows the historical events*
                   through detailed maps and drawings.

imaginatively /ɪmˈadʒɪnətˌɪvli/
refers to actions or expressions that demonstrate originality and creativity, often involving novel ideas or approaches
Example: *She designed the costumes imaginatively, using vibrant*
                   colours and unique patterns.
describes behaviour or work that uses imagination to create or interpret things in unique or unusual ways
Example: *The artist illustratively painted the scene in a way that*
                   was both imaginative and original.
indicates that something is done with a sense of inspiration or visionary thinking, often leading to innovative or artistic outcomes
Example: *He solved the problem imaginatively, coming up with a*
                   creative and unconventional solution.

imitatively /ˈɪmɪtətɪvli/
refers to actions or behaviours that involve imitation, often replicating the style, manner, or characteristics of something or someone else

Example: She sang imitatively, mimicking the vocal style of her
favourite artist.

describes behaviour or practises that are characterised by copying or
emulating another's actions or methods

Example: His work was imitatively like the famous painter's style.

indicates that something is done in a way that reflects an effort to
reproduce or mirror and existing example or model

Example: The design was imitatively based on the classic
architectural style.

immaculately /ɪmˈakjʊlətli/

refers to something that is done or maintained in an exceptionally
clean or pristine condition, free from any dirt or imperfections

Example: Her house was immaculately clean, with everything in its
place.

describes actions or results that are carried out to perfect accuracy or
attention to detail, without any errors or mistakes

Example: He completed the project immaculately, with no errors or
oversights.

indicates that something is done with such high standards of
perfection that is beyond reproach or criticism

Example: Her performance was immaculately executed, leaving no
room for criticism.

immaturely /ˌɪməˈtjʊəli/

refers to behaviour or actions that are characteristic of someone who
is not fully grown or has not reached emotional or psychological
maturity

Example: He reacted immaturely to the criticism.

describes actions or decisions that are made with a level of thought or
understanding that is not yet fully developed or refined

Example: He handled the situation immaturely, lacking the
judgment needed to resolve it effectively.

indicates behaviour that is naive or lacking in the complexity typically associated with more mature individuals

Example: *His response was immaturely simplistic, missing the deeper implications of the problem.*

immeasurably /ɪmˈɛʒərəbli/

refers to something so extensive or significant that it cannot be quantified or assessed accurately

Example: *Her gratitude was immeasurably great, beyond any measure or words.*

describes something that surpasses the ability to be measured or assessed, often implying great magnitude or intensity

Example: *The beauty of the landscape was immeasurably stunning.*

indicates that the degree or amount is so vast or profound that it exceeds any standard method of measurement

Example: *His impact on the community was immeasurably positive.*

immediately /ɪmˈiːdɪətli/

refers to actions or events occurring instantly or without any lapse of time

Example: *He responded immediately to the emergency call.*

indicates that something is situated right next to or near something else

Example: *The store is immediately adjacent to the café.*

describes actions or responses that occur directly, without involving any additional stages or intermediaries

Example: *She made the decision immediately, without consulting anyone else.*

refers to doing something right at the moment it is required or needed

Example: *He addressed the issue immediately when it arose.*

immensely /ɪmˈɛnsli/

refers to something that is done or felt to an extraordinarily large degree or intensity

Example: *The movie was immensely popular, drawing huge crowds.*

describes a situation or condition that is extremely significant or intense

Example: *She was immensely grateful for all the support she received.*

imminently /ˈɪmɪnəntli/

refers to something that is expected to occur very soon or in the near future

Example: *The storm is expected to hit imminently.*

describes a situation or event that is on the verge of happening, implying urgency or immediate anticipation

Example: *The project deadline is imminently approaching, so we need to finish up quickly.*

immorally /ɪmˈɒrəli/

refers to actions or behaviours that are considered unethical or wrong according to moral standards

Example: *He acted immorally by deceiving his friends for personal gain.*

describes behaviour that is perceived as lacking in moral integrity or righteousness

Example: *She behaved immorally by exploiting her colleagues for her own benefit.*

immovably /ɪmˈuːvəbli/

refers to something that is fixed or stationary, incapable of being shifted or relocated

Example: *The statue stood immovably in the centre of the square.*

describes an attitude or position that is firm and resistant to change, often indicating strong conviction or determination

Example: *He remained immovably committed to his principles, despite the opposition.*

impartially /ɪmpˈɑːʃəlˌi/

refers to actions or judgments made without favouritism or prejudice, treating all parties equally

Example: The judge listened impartially to both sides of the case before deciding.

describes behaviour or decisions made based on objective criteria rather than personal feelings or interests

Example: The referee judged the match impartially, ensuring fair play for both teams.

impatiently /ɪmpˈeɪʃəntli/

refers to a state of being annoyed or restless because of waiting or not getting what one wants in a timely manner

Example: He tapped his foot impatiently while waiting for the train to arrive.

describes an attitude of being eager or anxious for something to happen, often resulting in a sense of urgency

Example: She waited impatiently for the announcement.

impeccably /ɪmpˈɛkəbli/

refers to actions or conditions carried out with no errors or imperfections, demonstrating exceptional quality

Example: She dressed impeccably for the formal event, looking flawless from head to toe.

describes behaviour or performance that adheres to the highest standards, showing no faults or deficiencies

Example: He performed the routine impeccably, with flawless precision and grace.

imperatively /ɪmˈpɛrətɪvli/

Refers to actions or statements that are made with a sense of urgency or authority, often conveying that something must be done

Example: The doctor advised imperatively that he start the
medication immediately.

describes actions taken with a pressing need or importance, often
suggesting that the situation requires immediate attention

Example: The manager spoke imperatively, stressing that the
project must be completed by the end of the day.

imperceptibly /ɪmpəsˈɛptəbli/

refers to changes or actions that occur so slowly or subtly that they
are barely perceptible

Example: The light in the room dimmed imperceptibly as the sun
set.

describes something happening in a way that is not discernible
through ordinary observation or measurement

Example: The paint dried imperceptibly, making the transition
between colours barely noticeable.

imperfectly /ɪmpˈɜːfɛktl̩i/

refers to actions or conditions that are done with errors or
imperfections, lacking in complete accuracy or excellence

Example: He completed the project imperfectly, with several
mistakes and missing details.

describes something that does not fully meet the required or ideal
standard, showing some level of inadequacy

Example: The instructions were followed imperfectly, leading to
some errors in the final result.

indicates that the result or process is marred by some level of
imperfection or defect

Example: The sculpture was crafted imperfectly, with a few visible
flaws.

impersonally /ɪmˈpɜːsnlli/

refers to actions or communications that are done without expressing
personal feelings or connections

Example: The email was written impersonally, lacking any personal touch or warmth.

describes interactions or evaluations that are carried out without regard for individual preferences or relationships

Example: The performance was assessed impersonally, focusing only on objective criteria without considering personal effort.

impetuously /ɪmˈpetjʊəsli/

refers to actions taken quickly and without careful considerations, often driven by impulse rather than thought

Example: He acted impetuously, deciding on the spot without thinking it through.

describes behaviour characterised by a strong, spontaneous force or enthusiasm, often resulting in rapid or unplanned actions

Example: She bought the car impetuously, driven by a sudden burst of excitement.

indicates actions performed with a lack of self-control or deliberation, showing impulsive or emotional reactions

Example: He shouted impetuously, reacting to the news before he had a chance to think about it.

impishly /ɪmpˈɪʃli/

refers to behaviour characterised by playful troublemaking or minor pranks, often with a sense of harmless fun

Example: He smiled impishly as he hid his friend's keys.

describes actions or expressions that involve a certain degree of audacity or impudence, often done with a sense of light-heartedness

Example: She spoke impishly, making a cheeky comment that made everyone laugh.

implausibly /ɪmplˈɔːzəbli/

refers to actions, statements, or scenarios that are difficult to accept as true or reasonable due to their improbability

Example: *His excuse for being late was implausibly far-fetched and*
hard to believe.

describe something that is presented or argued in a manner that does
not align with common sense or logical reasoning

Example: *The story was implausibly dramatic, with events that*
stretched the bounds of reality.

implicitly /ɪmplˈɪsɪtli/

refers to something understood or assumed without being explicitly
mentioned or detailed

Example: *Her agreement was implicitly understood when she*
nodded in response to the proposal.

describes actions or beliefs based on underlying assumptions or
accepted norms, without explicitly examining them

Example: *He trusted the plan implicitly, without questioning its*
details or feasibility.

indicates a degree of trust or acceptance without needing further
proof or explanation

Example: *She implicitly trusted her friend's advice.*

impliedly /ɪmplˈaɪdli/

refers to something that is suggested or inferred without being
explicitly expressed

Example: *His silence impliedly agreed with the proposal.*

describes an action or understanding that occurs because of indirect
hints or suggestions

Example: *Her smile impliedly suggested that she was pleased with*
the outcome.

imploringly /ɪmplˈɔːrɪŋli/

refers to actions or expressions made with a sense of earnestness and
emotional intensity, often begging, or pleading for something

Example: *He looked at her imploringly, begging for a second*
chance.

describes behaviour characterised by a strong, heartfelt appeal or request

Example: *She spoke imploringly, asking for help with a desperate tone in her voice.*

impolitely /ɪmpəlˈaɪtli/

refers to behaviour or speech that lacks courtesy or politeness, often coming across as offensive or inappropriate

Example: *He interrupted the meeting impolitely, cutting off others before they could finish speaking.*

describes actions that disregard the usual rules of social interaction, leading to a lack of tact or propriety

Example: *She addressed the guest impolitely, ignoring the common etiquette for introductions.*

importantly /ɪmpˈɔːtəntli/

refers to actions or statements that convey or acknowledge the significance of a matter or issue

Example: *Importantly, we need to address the budget concerns before finalizing the project.*

describes how something is done with a focus on its crucial nature or impact

Example: *She emphasized the changes importantly, highlighting their crucial impact on the team's success.*

importunely /ɪmˈpɔːtjuːnli/

refers to actions or behaviour characterised by relentless or excessive insistence, often to the point of being annoying or intrusive

Example: *He called her importunely, repeatedly asking for updates despite her clear instructions to wait.*

describes requests or demands made in a manner that is irritating or inappropriate due to their excessive nature

Example: *He asked for a raise importunely, repeatedly pressing the issue even after being told no.*

imposingly /ɪmˈpəʊzɪŋli/

refers to actions or appearances that are grand, impressive, or authoritative, often elicited admiration or awe

Example: The statue stood imposingly in the centre of the plaza.

describes behaviour or presentation that projects strength, dignity, or significance, making a notable impact on others

Example: She spoke imposingly at the conference, commanding
respect with her confident demeanour.

impossibly /ɪmpˈɒsəbli/

refers to situations or conditions that appear to be beyond the realm of possibility due to their extreme nature

Example: The task seemed impossibly difficult, with challenges that
appeared insurmountable.

describes something that is so extreme or improbable that it challenges belief or comprehension

Example: The mountain was impossibly steep, making the climb
seem almost beyond belief.

indicates an action or scenario that seems unreasonable or beyond the bounds of rational thought

Example: The solution was impossibly complex, defying any
reasonable attempt at resolution.

imprecisely /ˌɪmprɪsˈaɪsli/

referring to actions or statements that are not specific or detailed, leading to a general or vague understanding

Example: The instructions were imprecisely given, leaving
everyone confused about the next steps.

describes information or descriptions that are vague or ambiguous, lacking precision

Example: The report was imprecisely written, with details that were
unclear and vague.

indicates a lack of thoroughness or carefulness in execution or communication

Example: *He calculated the figures imprecisely, leading to errors in the final report.*

impressionably /ɪmprˈɛʃənəbli/

refers to being open to persuasion or easily swayed by external factors or opinions

Example: *She listened impressionably to the speaker, quickly adopting his views on the topic.*

describes behaviour or relations that are notably affected by external stimuli or influences

Example: *Children are often impressionably affected by the characters they see on television.*

impressively /ɪmprˈɛsɪvli/

refers to actions, performances, or presentations that are done in a way that leaves a strong, positive impression on others

Example: *She performed the song impressively, captivating the entire audience with her talent.*

describes something done in a manner that is striking or outstanding, often standing out due to its quality or impact

Example: *The building was designed impressively, with a sleek and modern architecture that stood out.*

indicates that something is done with a high level of proficiency or talent that commands attention

Example: *He solved the complex problem impressively, demonstrating remarkable skill and insight.*

improbably /ɪmprˈɒbəbli/

refers to events, situations, or outcomes that seem highly improbable or not easily accepted as true

Example: *The team won the game improbably, against all odds and predictions.*

describes occurrences or scenarios that do not conform to what is expected or considered probable

Example: *The two old friends met improbably at a remote village while traveling.*

improperly /ɪmprˈɒpəli/

refers to actions or behaviour that do not conform to accepted standards, norms, or expectations

Example: *He disposed of the chemicals improperly, ignoring safety regulations.*

describes conduct that violates established rules, regulations, or ethical guidelines

Example: *She was reprimanded for using company resources improperly.*

indicates something done in a manner that is mistaken or flawed

Example: *The form was filled out improperly, leading to delays in processing.*

improvisationally /ˌɪmprəvaɪzˈeɪʃənəli/

refers to actions or performances that are done spontaneously or without pre-planning, relying on creativity and adaptability

Example: *He played the jazz solo improvisationally, creating a unique and spontaneous melody.*

describes actions or approaches that are marked by making things up as one goes along, rather than following a predefined script or plan

Example: *The actors performed improvisationally, creating their lines and scenes on the spot.*

imprudently /ɪmˈpruːdəntli/

refers to actions or decisions made without careful consideration of potential risks or consequences

Example: *He invested all his savings imprudently, without researching the risks involved.*

describes behaviour that shows a lack of wisdom or planning, often leading to undesirable outcomes

Example: She spoke imprudently at the meeting, revealing sensitive information that should have been kept confidential.

impulsively /ɪmpˈʌlsɪvli/

refers to actions taken spontaneously and without forethought, often based on immediate feelings or desires

Example: He bought the expensive gadget impulsively, without checking his budget first.

describes actions or decisions made quickly, without deliberation or thorough analysis

Example: She signed up for the class impulsively, deciding on a whim without researching the course.

indicates behaviour that is marked by a lack of restraint and an inclination to act on instinct rather than reason

Example: He impulsively quit his job after a heated argument with his boss.

impurely /ɪmˈpjʊəli/

refers to actions or conditions characterised by a lack of cleanliness or purity, often including contaminants or impurities

Example: The ingredients were mixed impurely, resulting in a product with unwanted contaminants.

describes behaviour or practises that are tainted by unethical or immoral influences, lacking moral purity

Example: His decisions were made impurely, driven by personal gain rather than ethical considerations.

in /ˈɪn/

indicates being inside or within something

Example: The cat is in the box.

refers to a period or moment within which something occurs

Example: She finished her homework in an hour.

describes a state or situation
Example: He is in trouble.
refers to something currently popular or fashionable
Example: Bright colours are in this season.
indicates involvement or engagement in an activity
Example: She is in a meeting.

inaccurately /ɪnˈakjʊrətli/
refers to statements or descriptions that are incorrect or misleading
Example: The report was filled with inaccurately presented data.
indicates data or measurements that are not exact or precise
Example: The measurements were recorded inaccurately.
describes actions or representations that do not accurately reflect the truth
Example: The movie portrays the historical event inaccurately.

inactively /ɪnˈaktɪvli/
describes performing an action or role with minimal effort or activity
Example: He sat inactively during the meeting.
indicates a state of being passive or not actively involved
Example: The account has been inactively managed for months.
implies doing something with little or no energy or enthusiasm
*Example: She worked on the project inactively, showing little
enthusiasm.*

inadequately /ɪnˈadɪkwətli/
describes something done in a way that is not enough to meet the standard or requirement
Example: The report was completed inadequately.
indicates that something is done in a manner that is not up to expected standards
Example: The meal was prepared inadequately.
refers to actions that do not achieve the desired effect or result
Example: The solution was inadequately addressing the problem.

inadvertently /ɪnædvˈɜːtəntli/

describes something done without intention or deliberate effort

Example: She inadvertently left her keys at home.

refers to results or consequences that happen by mistake rather by design

Example: The email was sent to the wrong person inadvertently.

indicates occurrences that happen without prior planning or awareness

Example: He inadvertently walked into the wrong meeting room.

inappropriately /ˌɪnæprˈəʊpriətli/

actions or conduct that are not appropriate for the context or setting

Example: She dressed inappropriately for the formal event.

behaviour that is socially unacceptable or offensive

Example: His comments were inappropriately rude.

responses or reactions that are not fitting for the situation or circumstances

Example: Her laughter was inappropriately loud during the serious
*   discussion.*

inaptly /ɪnˈæptli/

describes something done in a manner that is not appropriate for the context

Example: He inaptly chose a casual outfit for the job interview.

indicates that something is done in a way that is not suitable or correct

Example: The instructions were inaptly written, causing confusion.

inarguably /ɪnˈɑrguəbli/

indicates that something is so certain or obvious that it cannot be refuted

Example: The sun is inarguably the centre of our solar system.

refers to a fact or truth that is accepted without controversy

Example: She is inarguably the best player on the team.

inasmuch /ɪnəsmˈʌtʃ/
indicates the degree or scope to which something is true or applicable
Example: The plan is effective inasmuch as it addresses all major concerns.
used to acknowledge or consider certain conditions or facts
Example: The proposal is acceptable, inasmuch as it meets our budget constraints.
used to express that something is valid only to the extent of a particular condition or fact
Example: The policy is useful inasmuch as it applies to our current needs.

inattentively /ˌɪnəˈtentɪvli/
refers to doing something without paying full attention
Example: He answered the questions inattentively and missed several details.
indicates a failure to notice or address details due to being careless or distracted
Example: She filled out the form inattentively, leading to several errors.
describes actions performed without proper care or consideration
Example: He drove inattentively, almost missing the turn.

inaudibly /ɪnˈɔːdəbli/
describes speech or sounds that are so quiet or muffled that they cannot be heard
Example: She spoke inaudibly, and no one could hear her response.
refers to actions or communications done in such a subtle or faint manner that they are not perceptible
Example: He nodded inaudibly to show his agreement.

incandescently /ˈɪnkɑnˈdesntli/
to describe an action performed in a radiant or glowing manner
Example: The candle burned incandescently, casting a warm glow throughout the room.

incapably /ɪnkˈeɪpəbəli/
performing a task in a way that demonstrates an inability to do it well
Example: He handled the equipment incapably, causing several mistakes during the operation.
acting or speaking in a way that shows a general lack of competence
Example: She spoke incapably about the project, revealing her lack of understanding of the details.
doing something in an ineffective or insufficient manner
Example: He attempted to fix the car incapably, resulting in more damage than before.

incautiously /ɪnkˈɔːʃəsli/
acting in a way that shows a lack of carefulness or prudence.
Example: She spoke incautiously about the sensitive topic.
engaging in behaviour that is careless or heedless of potential dangers
Example: He drove incautiously in the rain.
doing something impulsively without proper forethought
Example: She invested incautiously in the stock market.

incessantly /ɪnsˈɛsəntli/
something happening continuously or without breaks
Example: The rain fell incessantly, drenching everything in sight throughout the day.
an action that is done continuously or without stopping
Example: He talked incessantly about his new project.
something that goes on endlessly or with cessation
Example: The dog barked incessantly through the night, keeping everyone awake.

incidentally /ˌɪnsɪdˈɛntəli/

monitoring something that is not the main topic but is related or relevant

Example: *Incidentally, while discussing the new software, she mentioned the upcoming company event.*

introducing additional information that is not central to the main discussion

Example: *Incidentally, I found your lost keys while cleaning the garage.*

referring to something that happens by accident or as a secondary consequence

Example: *Incidentally, while looking for the book, she discovered an old letter hidden in its pages.*

incitingly /ɪnsˈaɪtɪŋli/

in a manner that encourages or stimulates a particular action or feeling

Example: *The speech was delivered incitingly, motivating the audience to act on the*

issue.

in a way that prompts or motivates others to act or respond

Example: *The coach spoke incitingly, rallying the team to give their best performance.*

inclusively /ɪnklˈuːsɪvli/

describing something that encompasses all parts or members of a group

Example: *The policy was designed inclusively, addressing the needs of every department in the company.*

referring to a manner that includes all relevant aspects or items

Example: *The report was written inclusively, covering all aspects of the project from start to finish.*

involving all types or categories, often used in contexts related to diversity and inclusivity

Example: *The curriculum was designed inclusively, incorporating*
             diverse perspectives and materials from various cultures.

incoherently /ɪnkəʊhˈɪərəntli/
expressing thoughts or ideas in a manner that is difficult to
understand due to a lack of logical flow
Example: *He spoke incoherently after the long day, his sentences*
             jumbling together without clear meaning.
communicating or behaving in a fragmented or disconnected manner,
where ideas or statements do not follow a clear order
Example: *She replied incoherently during the interview, jumping*
             from one topic to another without clear connections.

incompetently /ɪnkˈɒmpɪtəntli/
performing tasks in a way that shows a deficiency in the required
skills or expertise
Example: *He handled the technical issues incompetently, causing*
             further delays in the project.
carrying out actions without achieving the desired results due to a
lack of competence
Example: *The chef cooked the meal incompetently, resulting in*
             undercooked and poorly seasoned dishes.
acting in a manner that reflects poor performance or professionalism
Example: *The customer service representative handled the*
             complaint incompetently, failing to resolve the issue
             effectively.

incompletely /ɪnkəmplˈiːtli/
something that is done or presented only in part, not in its entirety
Example: *The report was submitted incompletely, missing several*
             key sections and data.
referring to actions or efforts that do not cover all aspects or details
Example: *The instructions were followed incompletely, leaving out*
             important steps needed for the project.

describing something that is not fully completed or resolved

*Example: The puzzle remained incompletely assembled, with
            several pieces still missing.*

inconsequentially /ɪnˈkɒnsɪkwəntli/

acting or occurring in a way that does not have a major impact or importance

*Example: The comment was inconsequentially made, having little
            effect on the outcome of the meeting.*

pertaining to actions or points that do not have significant relevance to the main issue

*Example: The discussion about office decorations was
            inconsequentially included in the meeting.*

describing something that is considered trivial or unimportant

*Example: The minor error in the report was addressed
            inconsequentially.*

inconsiderately /ˌɪnkənˈsɪdərɪtli/

acting in a way that shows a lack of consideration for others, such as speaking or behaving in a manner that disregards others' feelings or situations

Example: He spoke inconsiderately about her personal issues.

acting in a way that ignores accepted social norms or practices, leading to discomfort or inconvenience for others

*Example: She parked inconsiderately in the disabled spot, causing
            inconvenience for those who needed it.*

engaging in behaviour that does not consider the possible negative effects or repercussions on others

*Example: He talked loudly on the phone inconsiderately, disturbing
            everyone in the quiet library.*

inconsolably /ɪnkˈɒnsəʊləbəli/

being unable to find relief or comfort from deep sorrow or sadness

Example: She cried inconsolably after hearing the news.

exhibiting an inability to be comforted despite attempts to soothe or reassure

Example: *The child sobbed inconsolably, despite his parents' best efforts to calm him down.*

inconveniently /ɪnkənvˈiːnɪəntli/

occurring at the time that is problematic or unsuitable, causing disruption or trouble

Example: *The power outage happened inconveniently during the important presentation.*

situated in a place that makes access or use difficult, leading to inconvenience

Example: *The mailbox was placed inconveniently far from the entrance, making it a hassle to use.*

creating any form of difficulty or hassle that disrupts normal activities or plans

Example: *The road was closed inconveniently for maintenance.*

incorrectly /ɪnkərˈɛktli/

doing something in a manner that is not accurate or true, such as making an error in a calculation or statement

Example: *He answered the question incorrectly, providing the wrong information on the test.*

acting in a way that does not adhere to expected standards or norms, leading to mistakes or inappropriate outcomes

Example: *She filled out the form incorrectly, leading to delays in processing her application.*

providing information or answers that are not precise or correct

Example: *The technician diagnosed the problem incorrectly, resulting in further issues with the equipment.*

incorrigibly /ɪnkˈɒrɪdʒəbəli/

acting in a way that is persistently bad or problematic, and unable to be changed or corrected

Example: *He behaved incorrigibly, repeatedly making the same mistakes despite numerous warnings.*

having a characteristic or tendency that is ingrained and resistant to change

Example: *He was incorrigibly stubborn, refusing to change his mind no matter the evidence presented.*

engaging in habits or patterns that are deeply entrenched and resistant to modification

Example: *She continued to smoke incorrigibly, despite numerous attempts to quit.*

increasingly /ɪnkrˈiːsɪŋli/

describing something that is becoming more intense, frequent, or significant overtime

Example: *The weather has been getting increasingly warmer as summer approaches.*

indicating a steady or progressive change in quality or state

Example: *Her confidence was increasingly noticeable with each successful presentation.*

suggesting that something is gaining importance or becoming more prevalent

Example: *Social media is increasingly influencing public opinion and trends.*

incredibly /ɪnkrˈɛdɪbli/

to emphasise a high degree of intensity of something

Example: *The view from the mountaintop was incredibly breath-taking.*

to suggest that something is so surprising or unusual that it is hard to believe

Example: *The magician's performance was incredibly impressive.*

to indicate that something is remarkably or extraordinarily different from the norm

Example: *The new smartphone features were incredibly advanced.*

incredulously /ɪnkrˈɛdjʊləsli/

acting or responding in a way that indicates doubt or surprise about something that seems hard to believe

Example: She looked at the news incredulously, unable to believe the unexpected announcement.

demonstrating an attitude of scepticism or mistrust towards a statement or situation

Example: He responded incredulously to the claim, doubting its truthfulness.

reacting to something that is highly improbable or surprising with a sense of astonishment

Example: She stared incredulously at the lottery ticket, amazed that she had won the grand prize.

incrementally /ˌɪnkrɪmˈɛntəli/

describing a process where changes or improvements happen in small, steady amounts over time

Example: The company increased its sales incrementally, seeing gradual growth each quarter.

indicating that progress or development happens in a series of minor, manageable steps rather than in large, sudden changes

Example: The software was improved incrementally, with new features added in small, regular updates.

referring to making minor adjustments or changes that accumulate over time

Example: The team made incremental improvements to the design.

incurably /ɪnkjˈɔːrəbəli/

referring to a medical condition or illness that cannot be treated or remedied

Example: The patient was diagnosed with an incurably rare disease.

describing a problem or defect that is so severe or ingrained that it cannot be fixed or improved

Example: The system's design flaws were incurably problematic.

indebtedly /ɪnˈdetɪdli/

acting in a way that expresses thankfulness or appreciation for something received

Example: He nodded indebtedly, deeply grateful for the generous assistance.

performing an action as a response to a sense of duty or obligation due to receiving help or a favour

Example: She worked extra hours indebtedly to repay her colleague for covering her shift.

indecently /ɪnˈdiːsntli/

acting in a manner that is socially unacceptable or offensive, such as true vulgarity or obscenity

Example: He spoke indecently in the meeting.

behaving in a way that is not suitable or respectful in each context, often violated norms of decency.

Example: She dressed indecently for the formal event.

indecisively /ˌɪndɪˈsaɪsɪvli/

acting in a way that shows hesitation or difficulty in choosing a course of action

Example: He responded indecisively when asked about his weekend plans.

exhibiting a lack of commitment or clarity, often changing one's mind frequently or failing to make a definitive decision

Example: She chose the restaurant indecisively, wavering between several options before finally making a choice.

indeed / ɪnˈdid/

used to confirm or agree with the previous statement, often adding emphasis

Example: *The movie was fantastic; indeed, it was one of the best films I have ever seen.*

used to add emphasis to a statement, sometimes highlighting the truth or significance of what has been said

Example: *The hike was challenging; indeed, it tested every bit of our endurance.*

indefinitely / ɪnˈdɛfənətli/

referring to a time with no definite end or specified limit

Example: *The meeting was postponed indefinitely due to scheduling conflicts.*

indicating an unspecified or vague extent or scope, without clear boundaries or limits

Example: *The project was put on hold indefinitely, with no clear timeline for its resumption.*

used to express ambiguity or lack of clarity about a situation or condition

Example: *The future of the old building remains undecided indefinitely, leaving its fate uncertain.*

independently / ɪndɪˈpɛndəntli/

acting or functioning without relying on others

Example: *She completed the project independently, without needing any help from her colleagues.*

operating or making decisions without external influence or control

Example: *The start-up operates independently, making all strategic decisions without interference from investors.*

performing an action in isolation from other concurrent actions or factors

Example: The team worked independently on their tasks, each
focusing on their own section of the project.

indicatively /ɪnˈdɪkətɪvli/
performing an action in a way that suggests or points to something
Example: Her raised eyebrow indicatively suggested that she was
sceptical of the proposal.
acting in a manner that represents or reflects a condition or
characteristic
Example: The increase in sales numbers indicatively reflected the
success of the new marketing strategy.
providing information or clues in a way that suggests something
indirectly
Example: His nervous laughter indicatively hinted at his discomfort
with the question.

indifferently /ɪnˈdɪfrəntlɪ/
acting in a way that shows no particular interests or enthusiasm
Example: She shrugged indifferently at the news, showing no
interest in the outcome.
displaying a neutral or unremarkable attitude without preference or
strong feelings
Example: He answered the question indifferently, with no strong
feelings either way.
showing an apathetic or detached response, often implying a lack of
care or concern about the outcome
Example: She glanced indifferently at the broken vase, not caring
about the damage.

indignantly /ˌɪnˈdɪgnəntˌli/
acting in a way that shows strong displeasure or offence
Example: She spoke indignantly when her ideas were dismissed
without consideration.
demonstrating feelings or moral outrage or indignation

Example: *He protested indignantly when he was accused of*
cheating.
reacting with a sense of injustice or insult, often driven by a brief that
something wrong or unfair has occurred
Example: *She reacted indignantly to the unfair criticism of her*
work.

indirectly / ˌɪndɚ-ˈɛktˌli/
describing something that is not achieved through a direct method or
approach
Example: *He suggested the idea indirectly, hinting at it rather than*
stating it outright.
referring to something that is implied rather than explicitly stated.
Example: *Her comment indirectly referred to his previous mistakes.*
indicating actions or effects that occur through a circuitous or less
obvious route
Example: *The new policy indirectly affected employee morale by*
changing work conditions.

individually / ˌɪndɪˈvɪdjʊəlli/
referring to actions or attributes that apply to each person or item one
at a time
Example: *Each student was evaluated individually for their unique*
strengths.
describing something that relates to the specific qualities or traits of
each individual entity
Example: *The dogs were trained individually to address their*
specific needs.
highlighting that something is done or considered in a manner that
distinguishes each part or person from others
Example: *The teacher met with each student individually to discuss*
their progress.

indoors /ˈɪnˌdɔrz/
describing activities or conditions that take place inside the building
Example: We decided to play board games indoors due to the rain.
indicating that something is situated or happening within the confines
of any enclosed space, such as a home, office, or other building
Example: The children spent the afternoon indoors, playing in the
living room.

industrially /ˌɪnˈdəstriəli/
describing something done in a way that proteins to or characteristic
of industrial processes
Example: The factory was industrially designed to maximize
efficiency and output.
referring to activities or practices related to the industrial sector
Example: The city industrially developed its waterfront to support
new factories.
indicating that something is done on a large scale, like the scale of
industrial production
Example: The company industrially manufactured thousands of
units each day.

ineffectively /ˌɪnɪˈfektɪvli/
indicating that an action is carried out in a way that does not produce
the intended effect
Example: The new strategy was implemented ineffectively, failing
to improve sales.

inevitably /ˌɪˈnɛvətəbli/
when something is bound to happen due to the nature of things or
circumstances
Example: The meeting was inevitably delayed due to the
unexpected traffic jam.
when something is expected to occur because of a particular set of
conditions

Example: *Given the team's poor performance, a loss was inevitably expected.*

in a way that does not fail to happen

Example: *The sun will inevitably rise each morning.*

inexplicably / ˌɪnɪksˈplɪkəbli/

when something happens without an obvious cause or explanation

Example: *The lights flickered inexplicably during the storm.*

when an event or behaviour occurs in a way that defies logical or rational explanation

Example: *He was inexplicably calm despite the chaotic situation.*

infinitely /ˈɪnfənətli/

describing something that has no limits or bounds

Example: *The universe seems infinitely vast and mysterious.*

referring to something that goes on indefinitely

Example: *The road stretched infinitely into the horizon.*

used to emphasise a very high degree of a quality

Example: *She was infinitely grateful for his help.*

informally / ˌɪnˈfɔrməli/

describing actions or behaviours that lack strict rules or official protocols

Example: *They decided to meet informally for coffee to discuss the project.*

referring to interactions or communications that are less structured or rigid

Example: *They chatted informally about their weekend plans.*

when something is done in a manner that deviates from formal standards or conventions

Example: *He addressed the group informally, without using any official titles.*

infrequently /ˌɪnˈfrikwəntli/
describing something that happens not often or with low frequency
Example: They meet infrequently, only a few times a year.
referring to events that occur intermittently or with irregularity
Example: She visits her hometown infrequently, about once every
few years.

inherently /ɪnˈhɪərəntli/
referring to traits or characteristics that are naturally a part of
something
Example: The job is inherently challenging due to its complex
nature.
indicating that something is true or exists because of the nature of the
thing itself
Example: The project is inherently risky because of its
unpredictable outcomes.

initially /ˌɪˈnɪʃəli/
describing an action or situation that occurs at the start of something
Example: Initially, the team faced many challenges in the new
project.
referring to something that takes place during the early part of a
process or period
Example: Initially, the weather was clear, but it later turned
stormy.

innocently /ˈɪnəsəntli/
acting without knowledge of wrongdoing or guilt
Example: She smiled innocently when asked about the missing
cookies.
doing something without any intention to harm or offend
Example: He had asked the question innocently, not meaning to
upset anyone.
showing a lack of awareness or sophistication

inquiringly /ɪnˈkwaɪərɪŋli/
in a manner that shows curiosity or desire for information
Example: She looked at him inquiringly, waiting for an explanation.

inquisitively /ɪnˈkwɪzɪtɪvli/
performing an action with a sense of curiosity or questioning
Example: She looked at the old map inquisitively, wondering where it might lead.
acting in a manner that seeks detailed information or understanding
Example: He asked inquisitively about the mechanics of the antique clock.

insanely /ɪnˈseɪnli/
to an extreme or excessive degree
Example: The roller coaster ride was insanely fast and thrilling.
in a manner that is irrational or chaotic
Example: He laughed insanely, his behaviour growing more erratic by the minute.
describing actions or states that are intense or frenzied
Example: She worked insanely to meet the tight deadline.

insatiably /ɪnsˈeɪʃɪəbəli/
acting with an unappeasable or endless craving
Example: He read books insatiably, never seeming to get enough.
engaging in an activity with a continuous and unfulfilled need or appetite
Example: She was insatiably curious, always asking questions and seeking new knowledge.

insecurely /ˌɪnsɪˈkjʊəli/

in a manner that is not securely fixed or stable

Example: *The ladder wobbled insecurely as he climbed it.*

acting with a lack of confidence or assurance

Example: *She spoke insecurely, doubting her own words.*

inside /ˌɪnˈsaɪd/

referring to something happening or existing within the boundaries of an enclosed space

Example: *The cat stayed inside the cosy house during the storm.*

indicating something is located within an object or container

Example: *The keys were hidden inside the drawer.*

referring to something happening within a figurative or abstract boundary

Example: *The team worked inside the project's tight deadlines.*

inspiringly /ɪnspˈaɪərɪŋli/

performing an action in a manner that motivates or encourages others

Example: *She spoke inspiringly, uplifting everyone with her words of hope.*

acting or presenting in a way that stimulates enthusiasm or positive feelings

Example: *His dedication to the cause was inspiringly evident in his passionate speeches.*

instantly /ˈɪnstəntli/

occurring or being done at once, with no time lapse

Example: *The lights turned off instantly when the switch was flipped.*

happening without any waiting period or pause

Example: *She received the email instantly after clicking send.*

instead / ɪnˈstɛd/
to indicate that something is being used or done in a place of
something else
Example: She chose tea instead of coffee for breakfast.
used to show that one action or choice is being made rather than
another
Example: He went for a walk instead of watching TV.
used to suggest that something different from what might be
anticipated is happening
*Example: Instead of feeling nervous, she was excited for the new
             challenge.*

instinctively / ɪnˈstɪŋktɪvˌli/
acting in a way that is automatic or done without deliberate thought,
often driven by innate impulses
Example: She instinctively reached out to catch the falling glass.
performing an action based on inherent tendencies or instinct
*Example: The dog instinctively guarded its owner's home from
             intruders.*
acting in a manner that reflects a deep, often subconscious
understanding or knowledge
Example: He instinctively knew how to calm the upset child.

intellectually / ˌɪntɪˈlektjʊəlli/
referring to actions or activities that engage or pertain to the mind or
cognitive processes
*Example: She challenged herself intellectually by tackling complex
             puzzles.*
describing something done in a way that demonstrates or requires
intellectual capacity
*Example: The debate was conducted intellectually, with careful
             analysis and reasoned arguments.*
involving a focus on ideas, theories, or academic aspects

Example: *He engaged intellectually with the latest research in his*
               field.

intelligently / ˌɪnˈtɛlɪdʒəntli/
acting or making decisions in a way that reflects good judgement and
understanding
Example: *She responded intelligently to the complex question*
               during the interview.
handling tasks or situations with skill and thoughtfulness
Example: *He managed the project intelligently, ensuring every*
               detail was carefully considered.
engaging in a process or activity with careful consideration and
mental acuity
Example: *The scientist approached the problem intelligently,*
               analysing all the data before drawing conclusions.

intelligibly / ˌɪnˈtɛlədʒəbli/
speaking or writing in a manner that is easy to comprehend
Example: *She explained the instructions intelligibly, making sure*
               everyone understood the task.
conveying thoughts or ideas in a way that is easily grasped by others
Example: *He spoke intelligibly about the complex topic, making it*
               accessible to the audience.

intendedly /ɪnˈtɛndɪdli/
performing an action with a specific purpose or goal in mind
Example: *She intendedly included extra details in the report to*
               ensure clarity.
acting in a way that reflects a conscious decision or plan
Example: *He intendedly arrived early to set up the meeting room*
               before anyone else.

intensely / ˌɪnˈtɛnsli/
performing an action with a high degree of emotion or force

Example: She focused intensely on her painting, lost in her creative process.

engaging in an activity with concentrated attention or effort

Example: He studied intensely for the final exams to ensure he passed with flying colours.

experiencing or presenting something with great clarity or prominence

Example: The colours in the sunset were intensely vivid, creating a breath-taking view.

intentionally /ˌɪnˈtɛnʃənəli/

doing something on purpose, with a specific intention or goal

Example: She intentionally left the door open to let in some fresh air.

acting with clear intent or premeditation

Example: He intentionally skipped the meeting to avoid a difficult discussion.

intently /ˌɪnˈtɛntli/

doing something with concentrated attention or deep interest

Example: She listened intently to the speaker's every word.

engaging in an activity with a strong, purposeful mindset

Example: He worked intently on the project to meet the deadline.

interchangeably /ˌɪntɚˈtʃeɪndʒəbli/

using different terms, items, or methods as replacements for each other

Example: You can use "email" and "electronic mail" interchangeably.

performing actions or using objects that serve the same purpose or function

Example: The terms "soda" and "pop" are often used interchangeably.

interestingly /ˈɪntɚˌɛstɪŋli/
describing something that is intriguing or holds interest
Example: *Interestingly, the book was written by the same author as the movie.*
highlighting a point or fact that is unusual or significant
Example: *Interestingly, the rare bird was spotted in the city park.*

intermittently /ˌɪntɚˈmɪtəntli/
happening or occurring sporadically, with breaks or gaps in between
Example: *The rain fell intermittently throughout the afternoon.*
appearing or functioning in a stop-and-start manner rather than continuously
Example: *The lights flickered intermittently during the storm.*

internally /ˌɪnˈtɚnəli/
pertaining to processes or conditions inside an organisation or system
Example: *The company is working on improving its internally communication system.*
referring to something happening or located within the interior of a physical object
Example: *The machine's problems were traced to issues internally with its wiring.*
describing feelings, thoughts, or processes occurring within an individual
Example: *She struggled internally with her decision to move away.*

internationally /ˌɪntəˈnɑʃənlli/
involving or extending across multiple countries
Example: *The company expanded its operations internationally to reach new markets.*
pertaining to or recognised on a global scale
Example: *The film received internationally acclaimed reviews for its exceptional storytelling.*
involving interactions or relations between different countries

Example: *The conference focused on issues of internationally trade and diplomacy.*

intimately /ˈɪntəmətli/
acting or interacting with a high degree of personal closeness or familiarity
Example: *They knew each other intimately from years of working together.*
having a deep and thorough understanding of a subject or situation
Example: *She understood the topic intimately after years of research.*
pertaining to private or personal matters, often with an emotional or confidential element
Example: *He shared his intimately personal feelings with his closest friend.*

intricately /ˈɪntrəkətli/
done in a manner that involves many interconnected parts or details
Example: *The artist intricately carved patterns into the wooden sculpture.*
involving intricate or elaborate relationships or structures
Example: *The plot of the novel was intricately woven with multiple subplots.*

intrinsically /ˌɪnˈtrɪnsɪkəli/
pertaining to qualities or characteristics that are fundamental and inherent to something
Example: *The beauty of the artwork is intrinsically linked to its unique design.*
describing attributes that are an essential part of something's nature
Example: *Honesty is intrinsically important to building trust.*

introvertedly /ˈɪntɹəvˌɜːtɪdli/

acting in a way that reflects introversion, such as being reserved or withdrawn

Example: *She introvertedly preferred quiet nights at home over large social gatherings.*

displaying behaviours or preferences that align with an introverted personality, such as focusing on internal thoughts rather than external interactions

Example: *He introvertedly spent most of his free time reading rather than socializing.*

intuitively /ɪnˈtuɪtɪvli/

acting or understanding something through instinctive knowledge rather than analytical thinking

Example: *She intuitively knew how to fix the problem without any instructions.*

performing an action in a way that feels natural or automatic

Example: *He intuitively reached for the light switch in the dark room.*

invariably /ɪnˈvɛɹiəli/

describing something that always happens in the same way

Example: *She invariably drinks coffee every morning before work.*

referring to a situation or outcome that remains constant across different circumstances

Example: *The sun invariably rises in the east.*

inward /ˈɪnwɜd/

moving or directed towards the inner part or centre

Example: *She looked inward to find peace and clarity.*

pertaining to internal thoughts, emotions, or reflections

Example: *His inward thoughts were focused on solving the problem.*

inwardly /ˈɪnwɚdli/

pertaining to thoughts, emotions, or processes occurring within a person rather than externally observable actions

Example: *She was inwardly anxious about the upcoming exam, despite her calm exterior.*

involving aspects that are not visible or external, but are part of a person's inner world

Example: *He was inwardly excited about the surprise, even though he did not show it outwardly.*

inwards /ˈɪnwədz/

moving or directed towards the interior or centre of a space

Example: *The path curved inwards towards the centre of the garden.*

focusing or directing attention toward one's inner self or internal aspects

Example: *She turned her attention inwards to reflect on her personal goals.*

irately /aɪˈreɪtli/

acting or responding with visible anger or frustration

Example: *He irately demanded an explanation for the mistake.*

displaying irritation or displeasure in one's actions or tone

Example: *She spoke irately when the issue was not resolved promptly.*

ironically /aɪˈrɑnɪkli/

describing a situation where the outcome is opposite to what one would expect, often highlighting a contrast between appearance and reality

Example: *Ironically, the fire station burned down while the firefighters were away.*

expressing something in a manner that is intended to be understood as the opposite of what is literally said, often for humorous or critical effect

Example: *Ironically, he praised the messy room for its "organizational creativity."*

irrationally /ˌɪˈrɑʃənəli/
acting or thinking in a manner that lacks rational thought or reason

Example: *She irrationally avoided the meeting out of fear, despite knowing it was important.*

making decisions or exhibiting behaviour based on emotions rather than reason

Example: *He irrationally spent all his savings on a spontaneous trip.*

irregularly /ˌɪˈrɛgjələ-li/
occurring at an even or inconsistent intervals

Example: *The bus arrived irregularly, making it difficult to plan the trip.*

exhibiting irregularity or lack of uniformity in shape, size, or arrangement

Example: *The tiles were laid out irregularly, giving the floor a unique pattern.*

irresolutely /ɪˈrezəluːtli/
acting in a way that reflects hesitation or indecision

Example: *She walked irresolutely towards the podium, unsure of what to say.*

exhibiting a lack of resolve or firmness in decision making

Example: *He approached the decision irresolutely, unable to commit to a single option.*

irresponsibly /ˌɪrəˈspɑnsəbli/

acting in a way that shows a disregard for responsibilities or consequences

Example: *He irresponsibly left the door unlocked, putting everyone at risk.*

displaying a lack of careful thought or consideration in decision making or actions

Example: *She irresponsibly spent all her savings without planning for the future.*

irreverently /ɪˈrevərəntli/

acting or speaking in a manner that shows a lack of respect for something that is typically held in high regard

Example: *He irreverently joked about the solemn ceremony, upsetting many guests.*

treating serious or solemn matters in a way that is more casual or unserious than might be expected

Example: *She irreverently made light of the serious issue during the meeting.*

irrevocably /ˌɪˈrɛvəkəbli/

referring to something that cannot be reversed or altered once it has occurred

Example: *The decision was irrevocably final, and there was no turning back.*

denoting a state or action that is fixed and unchangeable

Example: *The contract was irrevocably signed, binding both parties to its terms.*

irritably /ˈɪrɪtəbli/

acting in a way that shows irritation or frustration

Example: *She answered the question irritably after being interrupted several times.*

displaying a tendency to become easily irritated or agitated

Example: *He spoke irritably when his colleague kept asking the*
           same question.

irritatingly /ˈɪrɪteɪtɪŋli/
acting or being in a manner that provokes irritation
Example: *The constant noise from the construction site was*
           irritatingly disruptive.
exhibiting qualities or behaviours that are bothersome or annoying
Example: *She irritatingly tapped her pen throughout the entire*
           meeting.

isolatedly /ˈaɪsəleɪtɪdli/
performing an action or existing in a manner that is separate from
others or in a solitary context
Example: *He worked isolatedly in his home office to focus on the*
           project.
addressing or handling something in a manner that treats it as a
separate case or entity
Example: *The issue was isolatedly addressed to ensure it did not*
           affect the overall project.

Jj

jadedly /ˈʤeɪdɪdli/

done in a way that reflects tiredness or fatigue from repeated exposure or experience

Example: She listened jadedly to the same old complaints.

done with a sense of cynicism or a lack of idealism, often due to past experiences that have led to a more negative or sceptical outlook

Example: He jadedly dismissed the politician's promises as empty rhetoric.

done in a manner that lacks the freshness or excitement that might have been present earlier, showing that the individual has become less responsive or interested over time

Example: She jadedly flipped through the magazine, barely glancing at the pages.

jaggedly /ˈʤɑgdli/

describing something done in a manner that is uneven or rough, similar to the appearance of jagged edges

Example: The mountain peaks rose jaggedly against the sky.

referring to actions or movements that are not smooth, but instead marked by abrupt or irregular changes

Example: The dancer moved jaggedly across the stage, her motions sharp and unpredictable.

jinglingly /ʤ ˈɑŋgəlɪŋli/

referring to sound that is jarring or unpleasant, like metal objects clinging together

Example: The keys fell janglingly to the floor.

pertaining to behaviour or effects that are irritating or troublesome, often metaphorically

Example: The loud arguments from the neighbours rang janglingly through the thin walls.

jarringly /ˈʤɑːrɪŋli/

referring to something done in a way that is unpleasant or dissonant, often causing discomfort or irritation

Example:　*The alarm went off jarringly, disrupting the peaceful morning.*

describing something that stands out starkly or disruptively from its surroundings or context

Example:　*The bright neon sign jarringly clashed with the old-fashioned storefronts.*

jauntily /ˈʤɔntəli/

done in a way that is upbeat and spirited

Example:　*He walked down the street jauntily, whistling a cheerful tune.*

reflecting a stylish or fashionable demeanour, often suggesting an effortless charm

Example:　*She wore her hat jauntily tilted to one side, adding a touch of flair to her outfit.*

jazzily /ʤˈæzɪli/

done with a sense of flair or vibrancy, often associated with the lively and rhythmic qualities of jazz music

Example:　*The dancer moved jazzily across the floor, her steps full of rhythm and energy.*

jealously /ˈʤɛləsli/

done in a way that shows envy or possessiveness towards someone else's success, possessions, or relationships

Example:　*She looked jealously at her friend's new car, wishing it were hers.*

referring to a manner of being excessively protective or guarding something with great care and concern

Example: He guarded his grandmother's heirloom jealously, ensuring it was never out of sight.

jeeringly /ʤ'iərɪŋli/
done in a way that makes fun of someone or something with derision
Example: The crowd jeeringly mocked the player after his missed shot.
showing disrespect or disdain through remarks or behaviours
Example: She spoke jeeringly about the new policy, dismissing it as a waste of time.

jejunely /ʤɪ'ʤuːnli/
done in a way that is uninspiring or uninteresting
Example: His presentation was jejunely delivered, leaving the audience uninterested.
reflecting a superficial or simplistic approach, lacking depth or complexity
Example: The article was jejunely written, offering only a basic overview without any deeper insights.

jerkily /ʤ'ɜːkili/
referring to movements that are sudden and sharp, often lacking smoothness
Example: The robot moved jerkily, its gears grinding with each abrupt shift.
describing actions that are inconsistent or fragmented, with noticeable pauses or interruptions
Example: He spoke jerkily, struggling to find the right words between long pauses.

jestingly /'ʤestɪŋli/
done with the intention of being funny or amusing
Example: He jestingly teased his friend about the silly hat she was wearing.

made without serious intent, often to entertain or lighten the mood

Example: *She jestingly claimed she could beat everyone in the game.*

jocularly /ˈdʒɒkjʊləli/

done with the intention of being funny or light-hearted

Example: *He jocularly remarked that he would need a crane to lift all the birthday presents.*

made with a sense of fun or amusement, not meant to be taken seriously

Example: *She jocularly suggested they should all dress as pirates for the meeting.*

jointly /ˈdʒɔɪntli/

done in partnership or cooperation with others

Example: *They jointly managed the project to ensure its success.*

indicating that two or more people or groups are collectively responsible for something

Example: *The two companies are jointly responsible for the new product's development.*

describing an action that involves multiple contributors working together

Example: *The teams worked jointly to complete the research study.*

jokingly /ˈdʒoʊkɪŋli/

when something is said or done in a light-hearted, humorous manner, often to amuse or entertain

Example: *She jokingly claimed she could cook dinner in five minutes.*

when actions or statements are made with the intention of being funny or amusing, rather than factual or earnest

Example: *He jokingly said he would never finish the marathon, even though he was training hard.*

jollily /dʒ'ɒlili/
when an action is done with a sense of cheerfulness or happiness
Example: She jollily greeted everyone at the party with a big smile.
with a sense of merriment or joy, often in a way that suggests a
carefree or spirited attitude
Example: They jollily sang holiday songs around the fireplace.

jolly /'dʒɑli/
done in a happy, cheerful, or spirited manner.
Example: He greeted everyone with a jolly laugh at the party.
in a carefree, happy way often indicating a lack of seriousness
Example: They jolly joked about their upcoming vacation plans.

joltingly /dʒ'əʊltɪŋli/
done in a way that causes a sudden and unexpected movement or
impact
Example: The car came to a joltingly abrupt stop at the red light.
in a manner that physically jars or shakes, often due to sudden force
or impact
Example: The elevator joltingly jerked as it started moving.

joshingly /dʒ'ɒʃɪŋli/
relates to actions or remarks made in a playful, teasing, or joking
manner
*Example: He joshingly teased his friend about missing the game-
                winning shot.*

journalistically /ˌdʒɝnə'lɪstɪkəli/
done with standards, techniques, or practises typical of journalism,
such as thorough research, fact-checking, and objective reporting
*Example: She journalistically covered the story, ensuring all facts
                were accurate and sources verified.*

jovially /ˈdʒəʊvjəlli/

done in a way that is happy and full of good spirits

Example: *He jovially joined the party, spreading cheer with his infectious laughter.*

in a joyful, lively, and carefree manner

Example: *They jovially danced around the room, celebrating their friend's birthday.*

with a warm and sociable attitude, often making others feel comfortable and welcome

Example: *He greeted the guests jovially, making everyone feel instantly at home.*

joyfully /ˈdʒɔɪfəli/

done in a manner that expresses or reflects happiness and contentment

Example: *She joyfully accepted the award, her face beaming with delight.*

in a way that shows or conveys deep pleasure or satisfaction

Example: *They joyfully celebrated their anniversary with a grand party.*

with an upbeat, positive attitude that often includes excitement or exuberance

Example: *He joyfully announced the news of his promotion to his friends.*

joylessly /ˈdʒɔɪlɪsli/

done in a way that lacks pleasure, contentment, or joy

Example: *She completed the task joylessly, her enthusiasm clearly faded.*

in a manner that appears bleak, dull, or uninspired

Example: *He worked joylessly through the paperwork, his mind clearly elsewhere.*

exhibiting a lack of enthusiasm or positive emotion, often due to dissatisfaction or monotony

Example: *She answered the questions joylessly, her interest clearly waning.*

joyously /ˈʤɔɪəsli/
done with a sense of great happiness and pleasure
Example: *They joyously welcomed the new year with fireworks and celebration.*
with high spirits and energetic enthusiasm
Example: *She joyously danced around the room; her excitement evident in every step.*

jubilantly /ˈʤuːbɪləntli/
done with a sense of victory or success, often following an achievement or accomplishment
Example: *They jubilantly cheered when their team won the championship.*
in a way that expresses immense happiness and elation
Example: *He jubilantly shouted with joy after hearing the good news.*
with high spirits and energetic enthusiasm, often showing outward signs of joy
Example: *The crowd jubilantly celebrated the festival, dancing and singing all night.*
reflecting a festive or celebratory mood, often marked by loud and enthusiastic expressions
Example: *The children jubilantly sang birthday songs, their voices ringing through the house.*

Judaically /ʤuˈdɪʃəli/
pertains to actions or behaviour associated with Jewish practises, customs, or perspectives
Example: *The rabbi spoke Judaically about the significance of the holiday traditions.*

judgmentally /dʒʌdʒmˈɛntəli/
done in a way that involves making critical evaluations or
assessments, often with a tendency to judge others harshly
Example: *She judgmentally commented on her co-worker's outfit,*
finding it unprofessional.
exhibiting a tendency to form opinions or make decisions based on
personal standards or criteria
Example: *He judgmentally evaluated the new policy based on his*
own experiences and biases.
involving careful consideration or analysis, though this can
sometimes carry a negative connotation of being overly critical
Example: *She looked judgmentally at the report, finding faults in*
every section.

judicially /dʒuˈdɪʃəli/
done in a way that relates to the legal system or court proceedings,
often involving formal procedures and considerations
Example: *The case was judicially reviewed to ensure all legal*
procedures were followed.
performed with fairness and neutrality, similar to how judges are
expected to make decisions based on evidence and law
Example: *The committee judicially assessed the applications,*
considering each one impartially.

judiciously /dʒuˈdɪʃəli/
done in a thoughtful manner that considers various factors and
potential consequences
Example: *She judiciously chose her words to avoid any*
misunderstandings.
executed with the insight and foresight to make sensible and
appropriate choices
Example: *He judiciously invested his savings, carefully evaluating*
each opportunity.

juicily /dʒˈuːsili/

referring to something that is juicy or has a lot of juice, often used to describe food

Example: The watermelon was sliced and served juicily, dripping with sweet juice.

describing something presented with a lot of detail, excitement, or vividness, often in a figurative sense

Example: She described the vacation juicily, detailing every exciting adventure and vibrant sunset.

done in a manner that is particularly attractive or indulgent, often with the connotation of sensory pleasure

Example: The chef prepared the steak juicily, ensuring it was tender and full of rich flavours

jumblingly /dʒˈʌmblɪŋli/

done in a way that is chaotic or lacking in order, resulting in confusion, or mixing of elements

Example: The notes were jumblingly scattered across the desk.

performed in a manner that causes or reflects confusion, often leading to a tangled or mixed-up result

Example: He jumblingly arranged the papers, leaving them in a disorganized mess.

done in a random or careless manner, without systematic organisation or structure

Example: The books were jumblingly stacked on the shelf, with no apparent order.

jumpily /dʒˈʌmpili/

done in a manner that reflects anxiety or unease, often resulting in jittery or erratic movements

Example: She answered the phone jumpily, her hands trembling with nerves.

exhibiting signs of restlessness or fidgetiness, often involving quick, twitchy movements

Example: *He paced jumpily around the room, unable to sit still.*
in a way that involves abrupt or jerky motions, often reflecting a lack of smoothness or coordination

Example: *The car started jumpily down the bumpy road, jolting with each bump.*

juridically /dʒʊˈrɪdɪkli/
pertains to actions or behaviours related to the legal system or principles of law

Example: *The case was evaluated juridically to ensure it complied with all legal standards.*

just /ˈdʒəst/
refers to something happening at a specific moment or in a precise manner

Example: *The train arrived just in time for the meeting.*
indicates a small or minimal amount, often suggesting that something is only barely sufficient or achievable

Example: *She had just enough money to buy the book.*
describes something that happened a short time ago

Example: *He had just finished dinner when the phone rang.*
often used to emphasise fairness or equality

Example: *Everyone should just have the same opportunities.*
used to indicate something that is straightforward or not complex

Example: *Just follow these simple instructions.*

justifiably /dʒˈʌstɪfˌaɪəbəli/
done in a manner that is supported by valid reasons or evidence

Example: *Her concerns were justifiably addressed in the meeting.*
performed in a way that is deemed appropriate or necessary based on the situation

Example: *He was justifiably praised for his hard work.*
indicating that an action or belief is correct or acceptable given the context

Example: She was justifiably confident about her decision.

justly /ˈdʒəstli/
done in a manner that is impartial and equitable, ensuring fairness and adherence to principles of justice
Example: All students were justly rewarded for their efforts.
in a way that is deserved or warranted based on the situation or circumstances
Example: He was justly recognized for his contributions.
in accordance with the law or legal standards
Example: The defendant was justly acquitted by the court.
reflecting correctness and appropriateness in relation to moral or ethical standards
Example: Her actions were justly praised for their moral integrity.

Kk

kaleidoscopically /kəˌlaɪdəˈskɒpɪkəlli/
to describe something that changes in a complex, colourful, or shifting pattern
Example: The cityscape appeared kaleidoscopically as the lights danced across the buildings.

karmically /kˈɑːmɪkli/
describing actions or events that are thought to be influenced by or connected to past actions, implying a cause-and-effect relationship based on one's actions
Example: He believed the good fortune was karmically related to his past generosity
referring to something that is viewed through the lens of karma, suggesting that the situation or behaviour is considered in terms of moral or spiritual consequences
Example: She felt karmically rewarded for her kindness to others.
describing something that occurs because of one's previous deeds or choices, reflecting the idea that current experiences are shaped by past actions
Example: He saw his current success as karmically linked to his hard work in the past.

keenly /ˈkinli/
describing someone who is highly attentive, eager, or enthusiastic about something
Example: She listened keenly to every detail of the lecture.
referring to an acute or highly perceptive awareness
Example: He was keenly aware of the team's growing frustration.
indicating a strong emotional or intellectual response
Example: He keenly felt the weight of his responsibilities.

kiddingly /ˈkɪdɪŋli/

indicating that something is said or done with humour or not to be taken seriously

Example: *He was just kiddingly suggesting that they should go to Mars.*

suggesting that the intent behind the statement or action is light-hearted or meant to amuse

Example: *She kiddingly claimed she could win the race in a minute.*

kinda /ˈkɪndə/

to indicate that something is somewhat true or partially true, but not completely

Example: *I am kinda tired after the long day.*

expressing that something is not exactly or fully what is being described, often implying a lack of certainty or precision

Example: *The movie was kinda interesting, but not what I expected.*

to convey that something is slightly or moderately in a certain way

Example: *The dress is kinda stylish, but not quite my taste.*

kind-heartedly /ˈkaɪndˈhɑːtɪdli/

describing actions that are motivated by genuine kindness and concern for others

Example: *He kind-heartedly offered to help with her heavy bags.*

indicating that the way something is done reflects a key ring and empathetic attitude

Example: *She kind-heartedly listened to her friend's problems.*

kindly /ˈkaɪndli/

describing actions or behaviours done with kindness or generosity

Example: *He kindly offered to drive us home.*

to indicate that something is done with courtesy or thoughtfulness

Example: *She kindly answered all their questions.*

referring to an approach or attitude that is gentle and welcoming

Example: *He kindly greeted the new neighbours with a warm smile.*

kinesthetically /ˌkɪnəsˈθɛtɪkli/
describing something that involves or is associated with bodily motion or physical activity
Example: She learns kinesthetically by using hands-on activities.
referring to experiences or actions that engage the body's sense of movement and position
Example: He kinesthetically explored the dance steps through practice and repetition.

kinetically /kɪnˈɛtɪkli/
referring to something involving the energy of motion
Example: The ball moved kinetically across the field with great speed.
describing actions or phenomena involving motion or dynamic processes
Example: The machine operates kinetically, with its parts moving smoothly and efficiently.
to describe processes or actions that are characterised by motion or change
Example: The gears in the engine work kinetically to power the vehicle.

kingly /ˈkɪŋli/
referring to actions or behaviours that are majestic, dignified, or regal
Example: He made a kingly entrance at the gala, commanding everyone's attention.
indicating a way of doing things that displays a high level of respect, authority, or importance
Example: She was treated with a kingly honour during the ceremony.
describing actions that reflect noble qualities or greatness associated with royalty

Example: *His kingly generosity was evident in the grand charity*
event he hosted.

kinky /kˈɪŋkili/
describing actions or behaviours that are unusual or not mainstream
Example: *She has a taste for quirky, kinky fashion choices.*
referring to activities or preferences that involve unconventional or
non-mainstream sexual interests
Example: *They explored kinky activities as part of their*
relationship.

kittenishly /ˈkɪtnɪʃli/
describe actions that are light-hearted, playful, or spirited, similar to
how a kitten might behave
Example: *She kittenishly pounced on her friend's lap, pretending to*
be a playful cat.
referring to actions that are charming or slightly naive, evoking the
cute and gentle nature of a kitten
Example: *He smiled kittenishly, his innocent charm endearing*
everyone around him.

knavishly /ˈneɪvɪʃli/
describe actions that are done with cunning or trickery, reflecting
deceitful behaviour
Example: *He knavishly tricked his friends into thinking it was their*
turn to pay.

kneelingly /nˈiːlɪŋli/
describing actions or behaviours carried out with the person in a
kneeling position
Example: *She approached the altar kneelingly to offer her prayers.*
in a humble or submissive manner
Example: *He kneelingly asked for forgiveness, showing his*
sincerity and humility.

knightly /ˈnaɪtli/
referring to actions or behaviour that reflected honour, bravery, and
chivalry traditionally associated with knights
*Example: He acted in a knightly manner, always protecting those in
          need.*
describing conduct that is noble, courteous, and respectful similar to
the ideals of knighthood
*Example: His knightly conduct earned him respect from everyone
          he met.*

knit-wise /nˈɪtwˈaɪz/
referring to the orientation or way stitches are worked or observed in
a knitting project
*Example: Make sure to work the pattern knit-wise for a smooth
          texture.*
describe actions or instructions that align with standard knitting
practises
*Example: To create the ribbing, knit the stitches knit-wise as
          instructed.*

knobbly /nɒbli/
referring to a surface or texture that is characterised by small,
protruding bumps or knobs
Example: The knobbly surface of the rock made it difficult to hold.
describing something that has a textured surface with raised rounded
areas
Example: The knobbly sweater felt interesting against my skin.

knottily /ˈnɒtɪli/
referring to something that involves or is affected by literal nuts or
complex entanglements
Example: The rope was tied knottily, making it hard to unravel.

describing actions or situations that are complicated or difficult to resolve, like how "knotty" describes complex problems or issues
Example: The negotiations proceeded knottily, with many issues still unresolved.

knowably /nˈəʊəbəli/

referring to something that is accessible or understandable through knowledge or awareness
Example: The answer was knowably clear once we reviewed the data.
describing something that is identifiable or discernible based on available information
Example: The solution was knowably effective after the results were analysed.

knowingly /ˈnoʊɪŋli/

describe actions performed with full understanding of their nature or consequences
Example: He knowingly broke the rules to achieve his goal.
indicating that an action was done deliberately, with the intent to achieve a particular outcome
Example: She knowingly chooses the difficult path to test her limits.
referring to behaviour that reflects an understanding of a situation or information
Example: He knowingly addressed the issue, aware of its complexities.

knowledgeably /ˈnɑlɪdʒəbli/

describing actions or statements made with deep knowledge or expertise in a particular subject
Example: She answered the questions knowledgeably, drawing on her years of experience.
referring to actions or contributions that reflect an informed perspective

Example: He spoke knowledgeably about the latest advancements
in technology.

kookily /ˈkuːkɪli/
describing actions or behaviours that are only unusual or strange in a
whimsical or unconventional way
Example: He dressed kookily for the party, wearing a mix of bright,
mismatched patterns.

koranically /kəˈrɑnɪkli/
referring to actions, behaviours, or practises that align with the
principles, laws, or guidance provided in the Quran
Example: She lived koranically, following the teachings and
guidance of the Quran in her daily life.

Ll

labially /ˈleɪbjəlli/
sounds produced with the involvement of the lips, such as bilabial sounds like "p," "b," and "m"
Example: *The speech therapist explained that the sound "b" is produced labially.*
how certain phonetic or articulatory features are influenced by lip movement or lip configuration
Example: *The vowel was pronounced labially, with the lips rounded to shape the sound.*
describing the action or modification of sounds based on lip positioning and movement
Example: *The consonant was modified labially, requiring the lips to come together for articulation.*

laboriously /ləˈbɔriəsli/
performing a task in a way that requires considerable physical or mental effort
Example: *She laboriously hand-washed all the dishes after the party.*
doing something in a manner that is slow and requires careful attention to detail
Example: *He laboriously edited each page of the manuscript to ensure accuracy.*
engaging in an activity that is challenging or demanding
Example: *They laboriously built the model from thousands of tiny pieces.*

labouredly /ˈleɪbədli/
describing an action done with significant physical or mental exertion
Example: *He labouredly carried the heavy boxes up the stairs.*

referring to a process that is done with difficulty or in a way that is not smooth or easy

Example: She spoke labouredly, struggling to find the right words.

indicating that the task is challenging and requires a lot of effort to accomplish

Example: The artist labouredly painted each detail of the intricate mural.

lackadaisically /ˌlakəˈdeɪzɪkəlli/

doing something in a manner that is careless or indifferent, showing little motivation or engagement

Example: He approached his work lackadaisically, missing several important deadlines.

acting with a sense of sluggishness or unconcern, often due to a lack of urgency or care

Example: She completed the assignment lackadaisically, with little regard for the quality of her work.

performing tasks without the necessary attention to detail or effort

Example: He cleaned the room lackadaisically, leaving dust in every corner.

lacklusterly /ˈlakˌlʌstəli/

doing something in a manner that is monotonous or uninspiring

Example: The presentation was delivered lacklusterly, with no enthusiasm or energy.

performance or exhibiting qualities that are flat or unexciting

Example: She performed lacklusterly, failing to engage the audience.

describing something that appears drab or unremarkable, often in a figurative sense

Example: The movie ended lacklusterly, failing to leave a memorable impression.

laconically /ləˈkɒnɪkəlli/

conveying information using very few words

*Example: He replied laconically, "No comment," and walked
             away.*

providing responses or statements that are direct and to the point,
sometimes perceived as blunter or impolite

*Example: She answered laconically, "I don't know," showing little
             interest in the discussion.*

lacteally /ˈlɑktɪəlli/

describing something that has a milk-like appearance or quality

Example: The soft, white cheese had a lacteally smooth texture.

ladylike /ˈleɪdiˌlaɪk/

acting in a way that aligns with traditional expectations of female
grace, refinement, and decorum

*Example: She spoke in a ladylike manner, with polite words and
             graceful gestures.*

demonstrating manners, appearance or behaviour that reflect elegance
and sophistication

*Example: Her ladylike demeanour impressed everyone at the
             formal event.*

exhibiting reserved or modest behaviour that aligns with traditional
feminine norms

*Example: She always dressed in a ladylike fashion, favouring
             modest and elegant outfits.*

laggingly /ˈlɑgɪnli/

performing an action with noticeable delay or slowness

*Example: The team was laggingly completing their tasks, causing
             the project to fall behind schedule.*

moving or progressing at a slower rate than others or compared to a
standard

Example: *He was laggingly catching up with the rest of the group during the hike.*

demonstrating a lack of timeliness or efficiency relative to a target or expectation

Example: *The software update was laggingly implemented, missing its expected launch date.*

lamely /ˈleɪmli/

acting or speaking with a lack of effectiveness or strength

Example: *He lamely attempted to explain his absence.*

providing a response or explanation that is unconvincing or insubstantial

Example: *Her lamely prepared argument failed to sway anyone in the meeting.*

referring to movement or physical actions that are awkward or impaired, like how someone with a limp might move

Example: *He walked lamely after injuring his ankle during the game.*

lamentably /læmˈɛntəbəli/

acting or occurring in a way that is deserving of sorrow or disappointment

Example: *The project was lamentably delayed due to unforeseen issues.*

involving circumstances or outcomes that provoke sadness or regret

Example: *The team's defeat was lamentably disappointing for their fans.*

characterising actions or events that are sadly deficient or problematic

Example: *The report was lamentably filled with errors and inaccuracies.*

lamentingly /læmˈɛntɪŋli/

expressing oneself or acting in a way that conveys sadness or regret

Example: *She spoke lamentingly about the missed opportunities in*
        her life.

performing or communicating something in a way that reflects a
sense of mourning or deep regret

Example: *He sighed lamentingly as he remembered the good times*
        that had passed.

showing or conveying emotions associated with expressing grief or
sorrow, often through tone, language, or behaviour

Example: *She spoke lamentingly about the loss of her beloved pet,*
        her voice filled with sorrow.

landward /ˈlɑndwɝd/
moving or facing in the direction of the land from the sea

Example: *The boat turned landward as it approached the harbour.*

referring to something situated or moving towards the interior of a
landmass rather than towards the coast

Example: *The path led landward, away from the beach and into the*
        forest.

languidly /ˈlɑŋgwɪdli/
performing an action with a sense of fatigue or weakness

Example: *She stretched languidly after a long day at work.*

exhibiting a lack of energy or briskness, often resulting in a slow pace

Example: *He moved languidly through the house, barely able to*
        muster the energy to get up.

acting in a way that conveys a sense of relaxed, dreamy indifference,
often associated with leisure or idleness

Example: *She lounged languidly in the sun, enjoying the lazy*
        afternoon.

languishingly /ˈlɑŋgwɪʃɪŋli/
acting with a noticeable lack of strength or energy

Example: *He languishingly waved goodbye, clearly exhausted from*
        the day's events.

moving or performing tasks with a sense of lethargy or sluggishness

Example: *She worked languishingly through her chores, struggling to find motivation.*

demonstrating signs of weariness, sadness, or a decline in health or vitality

Example: *He looked languishingly out the window, clearly feeling the weight of his illness.*

lankly /ˈlaŋkli/

describing something that appears thin, lean, or lacking in volume

Example: *The lankly tree stood alone in the field, its branches thin and sparse.*

exhibiting a lack of neatness or refinement, often associated with an untidy or dishevelled appearance

Example: *His lankly hair fell over his face, giving him a dishevelled look.*

reflecting a state of being limp or lacking in vitality, as in how something might droop or hang loosely

Example: *The flowers hung lankly from the wilted stems.*

largely /ˈlɑrdʒli/

indicating that something is true or applicable in a significant way

Example: *The event was largely successful, attracting a large crowd and positive feedback.*

referring to the primary or most important aspects of something

Example: *The project's success was largely due to the team's hard work and dedication.*

describing something in a way that reflects its general or overarching nature rather than specific details

Example: *The book is largely about the struggles of overcoming adversity.*

lasciviously /ləsˈɪvɪəsli/
performing actions or making remarks with an overtly sexual or suggestive intent
Example: *He looked at her lasciviously, making her feel uncomfortable.*
exhibiting behaviours or attitudes that are provocative or excessively focused on sexual matters
Example: *He danced lasciviously at the party.*
demonstrating a proclivity for actions or comments that are considered immoral or inappropriate in a sexual context
Example: *His lasciviously suggestive comments were deemed unprofessional by his colleagues.*

last /ˈlɑːs/
referring to something that occurs at the end of a sequence or list
Example: *The last chapter of the book tied up all the loose ends of the story.*
describing something that continues for a significant amount of time
Example: *The meeting lasted three hours and covered many important topics.*
indicating the final stage or last part of something
Example: *She was the last person to leave the party.*

lastingly /ˈlɑːstɪŋli/
indicating that something endures or remains effective for an extended time
Example: *The new policy had a lastingly positive impact on employee morale.*
referring to something that continues or remains on change indefinitely
Example: *The artist's influence on modern design was lastingly significant.*
demonstrating persistence or stability over time

Example: *Her dedication to volunteering has lastingly influenced*
             the community.

lastly /ˈlɑstli/
referring to the last item or point in the series
Example: *Lastly, we discussed the budget for the upcoming project.*
used to introduce the final point or consideration
Example: *Lastly, we need to address the issue of scheduling*
             conflicts.
indicating the final part of a sequence or argument
Example: *Lastly, I want to thank everyone for their hard work on*
             this project.

late /ˈleɪt/
referring to something that occurs or happens after the scheduled or
anticipated time
Example: *He arrived late to the meeting because of traffic.*
describing actions or events that do not occur at the expected time
Example: *The train was late, causing a delay in our plans.*
indicating that something happens or is done later than it ideally
should be
Example: *She submitted the report late, missing the deadline by two*
             days.
referring to something occurring towards the end of the period or
phase
Example: *In the late hours of the evening, the city became quiet and*
             calm.

lately /ˈleɪtli/
referring to events or actions that have taken place not long ago
Example: *I have been feeling more energetic lately.*
indicating that something has been happening or has been the case in
the recent past up to the present

Example: *Lately, she has been spending more time working from home.*

describing something that occurred within a short time frame relative to the present

Example: *Lately, the weather has been unusually warm for this time of year.*

latently /ˈleɪtəntli/

referring to something that exists but is not immediately apparent or observable

Example: *The disease lay latently in his body, showing no symptoms for years.*

describing qualities or conditions that are present but not yet manifested or expressed

Example: *Her talent for music was latently evident even before she started formal lessons.*

indicating that something has the potential to become active or apparent but is not currently so

Example: *The conflict between the two groups was latently simmering beneath the surface.*

later /ˈleɪtɚ/

referring to something happening after a previously mentioned or expected time

Example: *We will discuss the details later in the meeting.*

indicating that an action or event will take place at a point further along in time

Example: *I will call you back later this afternoon.*

used to denote that something happens following a previous event or action

Example: *She completed the report and, later, sent it to her supervisor.*

describing a period towards the end of the time frame

Example: *The project was finished in the later stages of the year.*

laterally /ˈlatɚəˌli/

describing movement or direction that is towards the side or away from the central axis

Example: *The branch grew laterally from the trunk, spreading outwards.*

referring to something that is oriented or happening horizontally rather than vertically

Example: *The machine moved laterally across the floor to reach the other side.*

indicating that something is situated or operates on the side of a structure or within a side

Example: *The control panel was mounted laterally on the wall of the machine.*

latterly /ˈlatəlɪ/

refers to something that has occurred or been the case recently

Example: *Latterly, she has been spending more time at the gym.*

indicates something that happened or was true towards the end of a specific period

Example: *Latterly in his career, he became more focused on mentoring younger colleagues.*

laudably /lˈɔːdəbəli/

when something is done in a manner worthy of commendation or approval

Example: *He laudably volunteered her time to help the community.*

refers to the way an action is performed that merits praise

Example: *He handled the crisis laudably, keeping everyone calm and organized.*

laughably /lˈɑːfəbəli/

describes something so absurd or unreasonable that it causes amusement or derision

Example: The plot of the movie was so implausible that it became laughably ridiculous.

refers to something that is funny or amusing due to its absurdity

Example: The tiny hat on the large dog looked laughably cute.

laughingly /ˈlɑːfɪŋli/

performing an action or making a statement while laughing

Example: He laughingly admitted that he had forgotten his own birthday.

expressing something with a sense of amusement or light-heartedness, often indicating that the speaker finds the situation funny

Example: She laughingly told him that his attempt at cooking was a complete disaster.

lavishly /ˈlavɪʃli/

refers to spending or using resources (such as money, time, or effort) in a way that is abundant or excessive

Example: They decorated the venue lavishly for the wedding.

indicates giving or providing something in large amounts or with great generosity

Example: She was lavishly praised for her outstanding performance.

pertains to something done in a way that reflects luxury or opulence

Example: The mansion was furnished lavishly with golden chandeliers and plush carpets.

lawfully /ˈlɔfəli/

describes actions that are performed in a way that is legal and complies with legal requirements

Example: He acted lawfully by following all the regulations for starting a business.

refers to actions that are permitted or sanctioned by law

Example: She was lawfully allowed to build the new house on her property.

lawlessly /ˈlɔːlɪsli/

refers to actions carried out in ways that are illegal or not in compliance with legal standards

Example: The group was arrested for operating lawlessly without any permits.

indicates behaviour that occurs without regard for legal norms or rules

Example: They acted lawlessly, ignoring all the regulations and guidelines.

laxly /ˈlɑksli/

refers to doing something without sufficient attention to detail or with a lack of thoroughness

Example: He completed the report laxly, missing several important details.

indicates a lack of strictness or rigour, often in the enforcement of rules or standards

Example: The security measures were enforced laxly, leading to frequent breaches.

describes an approach that is not rigorous or systematic

Example: She managed the project laxly, resulting in missed deadlines and errors.

lazily /ˈlɑzəli/

performing an action without urgency or effort

Example: He lazily lounged on the couch all afternoon, watching TV.

doing something with a casual or indifferent attitude

Example: She lazily answered the questions, showing little interest in the exam.

approaching tasks or responsibilities with minimal effort or attention

Example: He lazily completed his chores, barely trying to do them properly.

leadingly /ˈliːdɪŋli/
done in a way that leads or guides someone to a specific conclusion or decision
Example: The lawyer asked leadingly, suggesting the answer he wanted to hear.
implies or hints at something in a manner that directs the listener or reader towards a particular interpretation
Example: Her question was phrased leadingly, hinting at the answer she expected.
presented in a way that seeks to direct or influence someone's thoughts or actions
Example: The advertisement was crafted leadingly to influence customers to buy the product.

leanly /ˈliːnli/
describing something or someone as having a thin or slender form
Example: He trained hard and became leanly muscular, with a toned physique.

leastwise /ˈliːstwaɪz/
used to indicate a minimum or minimal degree
Example: At leastwise, we have made some progress despite the challenges.
used to provide a sense of concession or a degree of acceptance
Example: The project is behind schedule, but leastwise, we are making some headway.

leeringly /lˈiərɪŋli/
refers to looking or acting with a suggestive or furtive expression, often implying dishonesty or deceit
Example: He looked at her leeringly, making her feel uncomfortable with his sly expression.
indicates a manner of looking that is overtly sexual or inappropriate

Example: *The man stared at her leeringly, making her feel uneasy with his inappropriate gaze.*

leeward /ˈliːwəd/
refers to the direction away from the wind
Example: *The boat sailed leeward to avoid the strong winds.*
indicates the side or area that is sheltered from the wind
Example: *We set up our camp on the leeward side of the hill to stay out of the wind.*

left /ˈlɛft/
indicates the direction opposite to the right
Example: *Turn left at the next intersection.*
refers to something that is still available or has not been used up
Example: *There is only one slice of pizza left in the box.*

leftward /ˈlɛftwɚd/
indicates movement or orientation towards the left side
Example: *The path curves leftward as it continues through the forest.*

legalistically /lˌiːgəlˈɪstɪkli/
describes actions are interpretations that strictly follow legal rules or statutes, often to the point of being overly literal or pedantic
Example: *He interpreted the contract legalistically, focusing on every minor detail and clause.*
refers to applying legal principles or regulations in a rigid, formalistic way, possibly ignoring broader context or practical considerations
Example: *She approached the case legalistically, adhering strictly to the letter of the law without considering the broader context.*

legally /ˈligəli/

refers to actions or conditions that conform to legal rules and regulations

Example: *The business operates legally, following all the required permits and regulations.*

indicates that something is achieved or conducted through lawful methods or processes

Example: *She obtained the property legally through a formal purchase agreement.*

legibly /lˈɛdʒəbli/

refers to text or writing that is easy to read due to its clear and distinct appearance

Example: *Please write your name legibly on the form so it can be easily read.*

indicates that something is presented in a way that is easy to understand or interpret

Example: *The instructions were printed legibly, making them easy to follow.*

leisurely /ˈlizɚli/

refers to doing something at a comfortable and unhurried pace, without stress or urgency

Example: *They took a leisurely walk along the beach, enjoying the sunset.*

lengthily /lˈɛŋθili/

refers to something that takes a considerable amount of time

Example: *The meeting was lengthily detailed, lasting over three hours.*

describes actions or discussions that are extended or detailed

Example: *She explained the process lengthily, covering every step in detail.*

lengthwise /ˈlɛŋθwaɪz/

describes something oriented or measured parallel to the length of an object

Example: The board was cut lengthwise to fit the cabinet.

indicates that an action or arrangement is done in the direction of the longest dimension

Example: The fabric was folded lengthwise to make it easier to store.

leniently /ˈlinjəntli/

refers to handling a situation or enforcing rules with a sense of mercy or tolerance, rather than strictness

Example: The teacher graded the assignments leniently, understanding the students' difficult circumstances.

indicates allowing some leeway or being less strict in judgement or enforcement

Example: The judge sentenced him leniently, considering his first offense and good character.

less /ˈlɛs/

indicates a reduction in intensity or extent

Example: She felt less tired after taking a short nap.

refers to a smaller quantity of something

Example: There is less fruit in the basket after you removed some apples.

describes a reduced level or scope of a characteristic or condition

Example: The new software is less complicated than the previous version.

lethally /ˈliːθəlli/

refers to actions or substances that cause death or have fatal consequences

Example: The poison was lethally strong and could kill within minutes.

lethargically /leˈθɑːdʒɪkəlli/
refers to performing actions with a lack of energy or enthusiasm
Example: *He moved lethargically through his chores, barely*
mustering the energy to complete them.
indicates doing something without the usual vigour or alertness
Example: *She answered the questions lethargically, lacking her*
usual enthusiasm.

levelly /ˈlevlli/
refers to doing something in a way that is flat, steady, or consistent
Example: *He spoke levelly, maintaining a calm and steady tone*
throughout the discussion.
indicates handling situations with composure or neutrality, without
emotional fluctuation
Example: *She addressed the complaint levelly, without letting her*
emotions interfere.

lewdly /ˈluːdli/
refers to actions or speech that are offensive due to their crude or
obscene nature
Example: *He made lewdly inappropriate comments that made*
everyone uncomfortable.
indicates behaviour or remarks that have a sexually suggestive or
inappropriate connotation
Example: *He lewdly flirted with his co-worker, crossing the line of*
professional conduct.

lexically /ˈleksɪkəlli/
refers to aspects related to the vocabulary or words of a language
Example: *The dictionary is organized lexically, listing words in*
alphabetical order.
describes how words are employed or defined within a particular
linguistic or semantic framework

Example: *The professor analysed the text lexically, examining how the words were used and defined.*

libellously /lˈaɪbələsli/
refers to making statements that are false and damaging to someone's reputation, usually in writing or other published formats
Example: *The article was criticized for being libellously inaccurate about the politician.*

licentiously /laɪˈsenʃəsli/
refers to actions that are indulgent or disregarding social or moral norms
Example: *He lived licentiously, ignoring the social norms, and indulging in every excess.*
indicates behaviour that is marked by a freedom from conventional moral constraints
Example: *She behaved licentiously, flaunting societal rules and expectations.*

licitly /ˈlɪsɪtli/
refers to doing something in a way that is allowed or authorised by law
Example: *He earned his money licitly through a legitimate business venture.*

light-heartedly /ˈlaɪtˈhɑːtɪdli/
acting or speaking with a cheerful or happy attitude
Example: *She light-heartedly joked about the long meeting, making everyone smile.*
engaging in actions or comments with a playful or fun demeanour
Example: *He light-heartedly teased his friend about their favourite sports team losing.*
approaching something with a relaxed, carefree attitude, without taking it too seriously

Example: *She light-heartedly attempted the puzzle, not worrying about getting it right.*

lightly /ˈlaɪtli/
performing an action with minimal pressure or impact
Example: *He lightly tapped the keys, making barely a sound.*
doing something in a gentle or delicate manner
Example: *She lightly brushed the dust off the old book.*
approaching a subject or situation with a casual or superficial attitude
Example: *He lightly mentioned the issue, not wanting to dwell on it.*
acting in a manner that is easy going or happy
Example: *She laughed lightly, not taking the joke too seriously.*

like /ˈlaɪk/
performing an action in a way that resembles another action
Example: *She danced like a leaf floating in the wind.*
indicating a resemblance or similarity in degree
Example: *The twins look so much alike, it is hard to tell them apart.*
acting in a manner that suggests or implies something
Example: *He spoke like he knew all the answers.*
reflecting the usual characteristics of someone or something
Example: *The old house, with its creaky floors and drafty windows, was just like the one from their childhood.*

likely /ˈlaɪkli/
indicating that something is expected to happen or to be true with a high degree of probability
Example: *It is likely to rain tomorrow based on the weather forecast.*
suggesting that something is reasonable or credible based on available information
Example: *She is likely the best candidate for the job, given her experience and qualifications.*

likewise /ˈlaɪ‚kwaɪz/

used to indicate that something is done in a similar manner or what was previously mentioned

Example: *He enjoyed the movie, and his friend likewise had a great time.*

suggesting that something is like or in agreement with what has been stated before

Example: *She felt nervous about the presentation; likewise, her colleagues were also anxious.*

used to express that. The same applies to another case or situation

Example: *If you need help with the report, she will likewise be available to assist.*

limitedly /ˈlɪmɪtɪdli/

indicating that something is not fully or extensively available, but only within certain limits

Example: *The new software is available only limitedly in select regions.*

performing an action or experiencing something with certain limitations or restrictions

Example: *She could only access the database limitedly due to her user permissions.*

limpidly /ˈlɪmpɪdli/

describing something that is expressed or presented in a clear and easy-to-understand manner

Example: *The professor explained the concept limpidly, making it easy for everyone to grasp.*

used to describe a state of being clear and calm, often in relation to water or other fluids

Example: *The lake was limpidly clear, reflecting the surrounding mountains perfectly.*

limply /ˈlɪmpli/

describing physical movement that is weak, unsteady, or lacking firmness

Example: *She held the book limply, her tired hands barely able to grip it.*

referring to actions or responses that lack strength, enthusiasm, or effectiveness

Example: *His apology was delivered limply, failing to convey genuine regret.*

conveying a sense of being lethargic or lacking in vigour

Example: *He answered the questions limply, showing no interest or energy.*

lineally /ˈlɪnɪəlli/

pertaining to relationships or succession through direct lineage or ancestry

Example: *The estate was passed lineally from father to son for generations.*

involving a straightforward, unbroken line of descent from ancestors

Example: *She could trace her ancestry lineally back to the 18th century.*

linearly /ˈlɪniɚli/

describing movement or arrangement that follows a straight path or direction

Example: *The books were arranged linearly along the shelf.*

referring to a process or progression that follows a logical or sequential order

Example: *The steps in the recipe were explained linearly, from start to finish.*

indicating a direct relationship where one variable changes in a linear proportion to another

Example: *The graph showed that the cost increased linearly with the number of items purchased.*

lingeringly /ˈlɪŋgərɪŋli/

describing an action or state that continues for an extended period, often more than expected or desired

Example: *She stared lingeringly at the old photograph, lost in memories.*

indicating that something is done with continued or reluctant attention, often reflecting a sense of hesitation or deep contemplation

Example: *He spoke lingeringly about his past, as if reluctant to move on.*

lingually /ˈlɪŋgwəlli/

describing something that is done or located with respect to the tongue

Example: *The dentist examined the lingually side of the teeth for any signs of wear.*

referring to aspects related to the language or verbal communication

Example: *The course focused lingually on developing advanced communication skills.*

linguistically /lɪŋgwˈɪstɪkli/

referring to aspects that pertain to language or linguistic features

Example: *The study examined how the new dialect developed linguistically over time.*

describing something with reference to the study of languages, including syntax, semantics, and phonetics

Example: *The professor analysed the sentence structure linguistically to illustrate different grammatical patterns.*

liquidly /ˈlɪkwɪdli/

describing something that flows or moves like a liquid

Example: *The paint spread liquidly across the canvas, creating a smooth, even layer.*

referring to an action or movement that is smooth and continuous, like the flow of a liquid

Example: *Her dance movements were executed liquidly, with a graceful, fluid quality.*

listlessly /ˈlɪstlɪsli/

describing a state of being without enthusiasm, vigour, or motivation

Example: *He watched the movie listlessly, barely reacting to the plot.*

acting or behaving with a lack of concern or emotional involvement

Example: *She answered the questions listlessly, showing no real interest in the discussion.*

literally /ˈlɪtərəlli/

used to indicate that something is true in the most exact sense, without exaggeration or metaphor

Example: *He was so tired that he literally fell asleep on his feet.*

describing something as being true to the actual meaning of the words used, without figurative or symbolic interpretation

Example: *When she said she was "in the middle of nowhere," she literally meant she was far from any town.*

lithely /ˈlaɪðli/

moving in a smooth, agile, and elegant manner

Example: *The dancer moved lithely across the stage, captivating the audience with her grace.*

exhibiting a high degree of physical flexibility and nimbleness

Example: *The gymnast performed lithely, easily executing each difficult manoeuvre.*

little /ˈlɪtl/

used to describe something that occurs or is true to a minimal degree or amount

Example: *She had little time to prepare for the meeting.*

indicating that something is almost not the case or occurs very infrequently

Example: *He knew little about the subject, having only studied it briefly.*

live /ˈlaɪv/

referring to events or broadcasts occurring as they happen, not recorded, or delayed

Example: *The concert was streamed live, so fans could watch it in real time.*

pertaining to experiences or observations that are occurring at the present moment, rather than being discussed or remembered

Example: *She shared her live impressions of the city as she explored it for the first time.*

livelily /lˈaɪvlili/

acting or moving with enthusiasm and vitality

Example: *The children played livelily in the park, their laughter echoing across the field.*

engaging in activities with a high level of excitement or dynamism

Example: *The team celebrated their victory livelily, with cheers and high-fives all around.*

lively /ˈlaɪvli/

acting or moving with enthusiasm and vigour

Example: *The party was lively, with music and dancing that kept everyone energised.*

engaging in an activity with excitement and enthusiasm

Example: *She gave a lively presentation, captivating the audience with her enthusiasm.*

exhibiting characteristics of liveliness, such as being active or full of life

Example: *The garden was lively with colourful flowers and buzzing bees.*

lividly /ˈlɪvɪdli/

describing an action or reaction characterised by extreme anger or rage

Example: *She spoke lividly about the unfair treatment she received.*

livingly /ˈlɪvɪŋli/

describing something done in a way that is full of vitality or vividness, often reflecting a sense of life or energy

Example: *The artist painted the landscape livingly, capturing every vibrant detail of the scene.*

emphasising the aspect of life or liveliness in actions, descriptions, or expressions

Example: *He described his travels livingly, making every experience feel vivid and real.*

loathingly /ˈləʊðɪŋli/

performing an action with a sense of deep repugnance or reluctance

Example: *She accepted the task loathingly, clearly displeased by the assignment.*

doing something in a way that shows clear unwillingness or distaste

Example: *He loathingly agreed to the extra work, knowing it would be tedious.*

locally /ˈloʊkəli/

referring to something that occurs or is relevant with a particular locality or region

Example: *The farm sells produce locally, sourcing ingredients from nearby fields.*

describing something related to or characteristic of a specific geographic area

Example: *The festival features locally made crafts and foods unique to the region.*

referring to activities or issues confined to a specific, often smaller, area rather than a broader or global context

Example: *The community meeting focused on issues locally affecting the neighbourhood*

loftily /l'ɒftɪli/

acting or speaking with an air of superiority or self-importance

Example: *She loftily dismissed their suggestions, believing only her ideas were worth considering.*

describing something done in a way that is metaphorically or literally elevated, or grand

Example: *The speaker loftily described the company's future, envisioning grand successes and achievements.*

performing or expressing something with a sense of high moral or intellectual value

Example: *He loftily spoke about the importance of ethics in business, emphasizing principles over profits.*

logically /'lɑdʒɪkli/

referring to actions or reasoning that is consistent with logic or rational principles

Example: *She logically explained her decision, outlining the clear steps she had taken to reach her conclusion.*

describing something done in a way that follows a logical sequence or structure

Example: *The instructions were arranged logically, making it easy to follow each step.*

acting or thinking in a way that adheres to the rules of logic or sound reasoning

Example: *He approached the problem logically, breaking it down into manageable parts.*

long /ˈlɒŋ/
referring to something lasting or continuing for a considerable amount of time
Example: The movie was so long that it lasted well into the evening.
indicating that something is prolonged in time or distance
Example: The hike took a long time because the trail was much longer than expected.
used to express a strong desire or yearning
Example: She longed to see her family again after many years apart.

longest /ˈlɒŋɡɪst/
describing something that lasts for the most extended period compared to others
Example: The summer vacation was the longest break of the year.
referring to something extending the furthest in terms of physical length or extent
Example: The Nile River is the longest river in the world.

longingly /ˈlɒŋɪŋli/
describing an action or gaze that reflects deep longing or a strong emotional desire for something
Example: She looked longingly at the photo of her old home.
acting in a way that conveys a sense of wistful or nostalgic yearning
Example: He sighed longingly as he watched the sunset over the ocean.

longwise /ˈlɒŋwaɪz/
describing something positioned or oriented along the longer dimension of an object or space
Example: The table was placed longwise along the room to fit more guests.
indicating that something extends or is measured along its longest dimension

Example: *The board was cut longwise to fit the entire length of the shelf.*

loosely /ˈlusli/
describing something that is not tightly fastened or secured
Example: *The lid was placed loosely on the jar, so it fell off easily.*
referring to something done with a lack of exactness or specificity
Example: *The instructions were written loosely, leaving room for interpretation.*
indicating that something is related or organised in a more general or less strict manner
Example: *The meeting was loosely organised, with no set agenda.*
acting or describing something in a way that does not adhere strictly to rules or standards
Example: *The group loosely followed the guidelines but adapted them as needed.*

lopsidedly /ˈlɒpˈsaɪdɪdli/
describing something that is tilted, slanted, or not evenly balanced on one side compared to the other
Example: *The picture hung lopsidedly on the wall, with one side higher than the other.*
referring to a situation or outcome that is on even or disproportionately skewed
Example: *The score was lopsidedly in favour of the home team, with a 7-0 lead.*

lot /lɒt/
indicating a large amount or high degree of something
Example: *She has a lot of books on her shelf.*
describing something that happens regularly or in many instances
Example: *They go to the park a lot on weekends.*

loud /ˈlaʊd/

referring to sounds that are strong, intense, or at a high decibel level

Example: *The music was so loud that it could be heard from across the street.*

describing actions or speech done in a manner that is noticeable or forceful

Example: *He spoke loudly to make sure everyone heard his announcement.*

louder /ˈlaʊdɚ/

referring to a sound that is more intense or has a higher decibel level compared to another sound

Example: *The thunder grew louder as the storm approached.*

describing speech or actions done with greater emphasis or intensity

Example: *She had to speak louder to be heard over the noise of the crowd.*

loudly /ˈlaʊdli/

referring to sounds that are produced at a high intensity or decibel level

Example: *The music played loudly at the party.*

describing actions or speech done in a manner that is forceful, empathic, or noticeable

Example: *He argued loudly to make his point clear.*

indicating that something is expressed or done in a way that is easily noticeable or apparent

Example: *Her laughter rang out loudly in the quiet room.*

lovingly /ˈlʌvɪŋli/

describing actions done with care, warmth, or emotional attachment

Example: *She spoke lovingly to her dog as she patted its head.*

referring to behaviour that demonstrates nurturing or supportive qualities

Example: He hugged his children lovingly before sending them off
to school.

low /ˈloʊ/
describing something that is close to the ground or position at a
minimal height
Example: The cat slept on the low shelf near the floor.
indicating that something is at a small quantity, intensity, or degree
Example: The battery level is low, so you should charge your
phone.
referring to something done with a soft or gentle tone, often in speech
or volume
Example: She spoke in a low voice to avoid waking the baby.
describing actions performed with a sense of humility or lack of
pretension
Example: He took a low-key approach to his promotion, avoiding
any unnecessary attention.

lower /ˈloʊɚ/
referring to something positioned at a decreased height or lower
altitude
Example: The new shelf is set lower than the old one.
indicating a reduction in intensity, amount, or degree
Example: She decided to lower the volume of the music to avoid
disturbing the neighbours.
describing something done with less force, strength, or impact
compared to a higher level
Example: He hit the ball with a lower swing to keep it from going
too high.

lowly /ˈloʊlɪ/
describing actions performed with humility or a lack of pretension
Example: She accepted the award with a lowly demeanour,
showing gratitude without boasting.

referring to someone in a position of low status or rank

Example: *He started his career in a lowly position, but worked his way up through the company.*

indicating something of lesser importance or value

Example: *The task was considered lowly compared to the company's major projects.*

loyally /ˈlɔɪəli/

acting in a manner that shows strong commitment and faithfulness to someone or something

Example: *She loyally supported her friend through every challenge.*

demonstrating dedication and loyalty in one's actions or attitudes

Example: *He loyally attended every team meeting,*

lucidly /ˈluːsɪdli/

referring to communication or explanation that is expressed in a way that is easy to comprehend

Example: *The professor explained the complex theory lucidly, making it easy for everyone to understand.*

describing the presentation of ideas or information in a coherent and transparent way

Example: *She presented her research findings lucidly, ensuring all the key points were clear.*

luckily /ˈlʌkɪli/

describing something that happens because of favourable circumstances or luck

Example: *Luckily, they found a parking spot right in front of the restaurant.*

referring to events or outcomes that are beneficial due to luck

Example: *Luckily, the flight was delayed just long enough for them to catch it.*

ludicrously /ˈludəkrəsli/

describing actions, situations, or ideas that are so unreasonable or
nonsensical that they provoke laughter or disbelief

Example: *The idea of building a roller coaster in the backyard was*
                     ludicrously impractical.

referring to something done in a way that is excessively foolish or
exaggerated

Example: *He dressed ludicrously for the formal event, wearing a*
                     clown costume instead of a suit.

lukewarmly /ˈluːkwɔːmli/

referring to something that is neither hot nor cold, but at a moderate,
tepid temperature

Example: *The coffee was served lukewarmly, lacking the heat*
                     needed to enjoy it fully.

describing an approach or attitude that is lacklustre, showing only
mild enthusiasm or commitment

Example: *She responded lukewarmly to the proposal, showing little*
                     interest or excitement.

lullingly /ˈlʌlɪŋli/

describing something that induces a sense of calm or relaxation, often
making one feel drowsy or at ease

Example: *The gentle rain fell lullingly against the window, making*
                     it easy to drift off to sleep.

referring to an action or condition that creates a temporary sense of
calm or inactivity, potentially leading to a period of quiet or reduced
attention

Example: *The soft music played lullingly in the background,*
                     creating a peaceful atmosphere.

lumberingly /ˈlʌmbərɪŋli/

describing movements or actions that are clumsy, slow, lacking grace,
often characterised by a heavy or burdensome quality

Example: *The bear moved lumberingly through the forest.*
referring to actions performed with a sense of effort or difficulty, typically indicating that they are not done smoothly or efficiently
Example: *He climbed the stairs lumberingly, clearly exhausted from the long day.*

luminously /ˈluːmɪnəsli/
describing something that emits light or appears brightly illuminated
Example: *The moon shone luminously over the quiet lake, casting a soft glow on the water.*
referring to something that is expressed or presented in a clear and vivid manner, often metaphorically implying clarity or brilliance
Example: *Her speech was delivered luminously, capturing everyone's attention with its clarity and insight.*

lusciously /ˈlʌʃəsli/
describing something that is extremely pleasing to the senses, particularly in terms of taste, smell, or appearance
Example: *The fruit salad was lusciously sweet, with a vibrant mix of flavours and colours.*
referring to something that is luxurious or indulgently pleasing
Example: *The hotel room was lusciously decorated with plush fabrics and elegant furnishings.*
describing something that is aesthetically pleasing in a way that is opulent or richly detailed
Example: *The garden was lusciously green, with vibrant flowers and lush foliage everywhere.*

lushly /ˈləʃli/
describing something that is characterised by luxuriant growth or abundance, often related to vegetation or natural beauty
Example: *The hillside was covered lushly with wildflowers and tall, green grasses.*
referring to something that is richly detailed or ornate in appearance

Example: *The ballroom was decorated lushly with intricate*
              patterns and opulent drapes.
indicating a quality of opulence or extravagance
Example: *The novel's descriptions of the palace were lushly*
              detailed.

lustfully /ˈlʌstfʊlli/

describing actions or behaviours driven by strong, often overt, sexual
attraction or passion
Example: *He looked at her lustfully, unable to hide his intense*
              attraction.
referring to an intense, sometimes excessive, yearning for something,
not limited to sexual context
Example: *He gazed lustfully at the rare car, dreaming of owning it*
              one day.

lustily /lˈʌstɪli/

describing actions performed with great energy, enthusiasm, or
strength
Example: *They sang lustily around the campfire.*
referring to actions done with a full and lively spirit, often implying
enjoyment and exuberance
Example: *He ate the feast lustily, savouring every bite.*

luxuriously /lʌgˈzjʊərɪəslɪ/

describing something done with great comfort, indulgence, or
extravagance, often involving high-end or sumptuous quality
Example: *She relaxed luxuriously in the plush spa, enjoying every*
              moment of pampering.
referring to experiences or conditions that are extremely pleasant or
satisfying due to their richness or indulgence
Example: *The hotel room was luxuriously appointed,with a king-*
              sized bed and a marble bathroom.

indicating actions or states that reflect a lifestyle or environment marked by wealth and high comfort

Example: *They dined luxuriously at a five-star restaurant, savouring exquisite dishes and fine wine.*

lyrically /ˈlɪrɪkli/

describing something done in a way that resembles or pertains to the quality of song lyrics, often involving poetic or expressive language

Example: *She spoke lyrically about her travels, painting vivid pictures with her words.*

referring to actions or expressions that are melodious, expressive, or beautifully crafted, like the qualities found in lyrics

Example: *The poet read her verses lyrically, capturing the audience with their melodic flow and beauty.*

describing something done with a sense of emotional depth or aesthetic beauty, akin to the effect of lyrical writing

Example: *The dancer moved lyrically across the stage, conveying deep emotion through her graceful steps.*

Mm

madly /ˈmɑdli/
to an extreme or excessive degree
Example: The dog barked madly at the burglar.

magically /ˈmɑdʒɪkəli/
in a way that seems to use magic
Example: The rabbit magically jumped out of the magician's hat.

magisterially /ˌmɑdʒɪsˈtɪərɪəlli/
in a way that seems to have complete authority
Example: The teacher magisterially walked among the students.

magnanimously /mɑɡˈnɑnɪməsli/
in a way that is generous or forgiving
*Example: After losing the match, Priya magnanimously conversed
            with the winner.*

magnetically /mɑɡˈnɛtɪkəli/
in a way that strongly attracts another person or thing.
Example: The children were magnetically drawn to the games.

magnificently /mɑɡˈnɪfəsəntli/
in a way that is impressive
*Example: The museum is magnificently decorated with intricate
            designs.*

maidenly /ˈmeɪdnlɪ/
in a modest or gentle manner
*Example: She walked through the garden maidenly, admiring the
            flowers with a delicate touch.*

mainly /ˈmeɪnli/
usually or to a large degree
*Example: The bookstore mainly stocks science fiction and fantasy
             novels.*

majestically /məˈdʒɛstɪkəli/
in a beautiful, powerful way, or one that causes great admiration
Example: The Kaieteur waterfall fell majestically down the cliff.

majorly /ˈmeɪdʒəli/
very or to an extreme extent
*Example: She was majorly disappointed when her favourite team
             lost the championship game.*

malevolently /məˈlevələntli/
in a way that causes or wants to cause harm or evil
*Example: He glared at her malevolently, his eyes filled with ill
             intent.*

maliciously /məˈlɪʃɪsli/
in a way that is intended to cause harm, upset or damage
*Example: She spread false rumours about her colleague
             maliciously, intending to ruin his reputation.*

malignantly /məˈlɪgnəntli/
in a way that is related to cancer and is likely to be harmful
*Example: The tumour grew malignantly, spreading its cancerous
             cells throughout the body.*

manfully /ˈmɑnfəli/
with determination and courage, despite great problems
*Example: He faced the difficult challenge manfully, refusing to give
             up despite the overwhelming odds.*

manifestly /ˈmanəfɛstli/

In a way that is clear or obvious to the eye or mind. It indicates that something is apparent or evident.

Example: The truth was manifestly evident, as clear as daylight for everyone to see.

manifoldly /ˈmanɪfəʊldli/

many times, or a great deal

Example: The project improved manifoldly under her leadership.

manly /ˈmanli/

having the qualities that people think a man should have

Example: He displayed a manly courage, stepping forward to protect others without hesitation.

mannerly /ˈmanəlɪ/

following polite ways of treating other people and behaving in public

Example: She always spoke mannerly, using polite language and showing respect to everyone she met.

manually /ˈmanjuəli/

using your hands

Example: He manually assembled the furniture, carefully following the instructions step by step.

not done automatically or using an electronic system

Example: She manually input the data into the spreadsheet, as the system was unable to do it automatically.

marginally /ˈmardʒənəli/

by a very small amount

Example: The price of gas has marginally increased this week.

markedly /ˈmaːktli/

in a way that is easy to notice

Example: *Sam's confidence grew markedly after receiving positive feedback from his supervisor.*

martially /ˈmɑːʃəlli/

in a way that relates to soldiers, war, or life in armed forces

Example: *The commander addressed his troops martially, preparing them for the upcoming battle.*

marvellously /ˈmɑːvələsli/

in a manner that is extraordinarily good or impressive; exceptionally well.

Example: *She performed marvellously in the competition, showcasing her exceptional talent.*

massively /ˈmɑsɪvli/

to a very great degree or extent; extremely.

Example: *The company's new product launch was massively successful.*

masterfully /ˈmɑstɚfəli/

In a very skilful manner or with great expertise.

Example: *He masterfully painted the landscape, capturing every detail with precision and artistry.*

in a way that confidently controls people or situations

Example: *The conductor masterfully led the orchestra through a breath-taking performance.*

masterly /ˈmɑstɚli/

in a way that shows the skill or ability of a master

Example: *The artist's masterly use of colour and light created a breath-taking masterpiece.*

materially /məˈtɪriəli/

in a way that relates to money and possessions

Example: *The company's profits materially increased after they launched their new product line.*

in an important or noticeable manner

Example: *The recent changes to the company's policies materially affected employee morale and productivity.*

maternally /mə'tɜːnlli/

in a way that is like or relates to the characteristics of a mother

Example: *She comforted the child maternally, soothing his fears with a gentle touch and reassuring words.*

in a way that relates to the mother's side of the family

Example: *She inherited her artistic talents maternally from her mother's side of the family.*

mathematically /ˌmɑθɪ'mɑtɪkəlli/

in a way that relates to or involves mathematics

Example: *The teacher solved the problem mathematically, using complex equations to derive the precise solution.*

matrimonially /ˌmɑtrɪ'məʊnjəlli/

in a way that is related to marriage or people who are married

Example: *She approached the legal issue matrimonially, seeking advice on how it would impact her marriage and family life.*

maturely /mə'tjʊəli/

in a grown or responsible manner

Example: *Jane handled the situation maturely, addressing the conflict with calm and understanding*

maximally /m'ɑksɪməli/

to the greatest degree possible

Example: *The athlete trained maximally to prepare for the upcoming championship.*

maybe /ˈmeɪbi/

used to show that something is possible or might be true

Example: *Maybe we can meet for coffee next week if our schedules align.*

used to politely ask for or suggest something

Example: *Maybe we could consider a different approach to the project?*

meagrely /mˈiːɡɐli/

in a way that is very small or not enough in number, amount, or quantity

Example: *The company's profits increased meagrely, falling short of their projected targets.*

meaningfully /ˈminɪŋfəli/

in a way that is intended to express a feeling or thought without saying it directly

Example: *She nodded meaningfully to indicate her agreement with his proposal.*

in a way that has meaning and makes sense

Example: *She spoke meaningfully about her experiences, conveying deep emotions and insights.*

in a useful, serious, or important way

Example: *The new software update meaningfully improved the efficiency of our daily tasks at the office.*

meanly /ˈmiːnlɪ/

in a way that is unkind to others

Example: *He spoke meanly to his younger sibling, mocking them for their mistakes.*

in a way that shows that you are not willing to give or share things, such as money

Example: *He treated his colleagues meanly, refusing to contribute to the office birthday fund.*

meantime /ˈminˌtaɪm/
during the period between two times or events or while something else is happening
Example: *She studied for her exams. In the meantime, her friends went out for a quick lunch.*

meanwhile /ˈminˌwaɪl/
until something expected happens, or while something else is happening
Example: *The builders continued working on the roof; meanwhile, the electricians started wiring the house.*

measly /ˈmizli/
very small and ridiculous in size
Example: *He received a measly amount of pocket money each week.*

mechanically /məˈkɑnɪkli/
using or relating to machines
Example: *He fixed the car mechanically, following the repair manual step by step.*
without thinking about what you are doing, especially because you do something often
Example: *He mechanically answered the phone, his mind occupied with other pressing matters.*

medically /ˈmedɪkəlli/
in a way that is related to people's health or to the treatment of illness and injuries
Example: *The doctor examined the patient medically, conducting tests to diagnose the cause of their symptoms.*

medicinally /meˈdɪsɪnlli/

in a way that relates to medicine, or that is used to cure illnesses

Example: *She brewed the herbal tea medicinally, hoping it would soothe her sore throat.*

meekly /ˈmiːkli/

in a quiet, gentle way and without arguing or expressing your opinions

Example: *Fred accepted the criticism meekly, nodding quietly without offering any defence.*

melancholily /mˈɛlənkˌɒli/

in a depressing manner

Example: *He gazed out of the window melancholily, lost in thoughts of the past.*

mellowly /ˈmeləʊli/

in a way that is pleasant, relaxed and soft

Example: *The jazz musician played the saxophone mellowly, creating a soothing and relaxed atmosphere.*

memorably /ˈmɛmɚəbli/

in a way that is likely to be remembered or worth remembering

Example: *The concert was memorably electrifying, leaving the audience with an unforgettable experience.*

menacingly /ˈmɛnəsɪŋli/

in a way that makes you think that someone is going to do something bad or that something bad is going to happen

Example: *The dark clouds loomed menacingly in the sky, signalling an approaching storm.*

mentally /ˈmɛnəli/
with regard to the mind or its capacity
Example: *John prepared for the exam by mentally reviewing the key concepts and principles*

mercifully /mˈɜːsɪfəli/
in a way that makes you grateful because it stops something that is unpleasant
Example: *The rain mercifully stopped, allowing the outdoor event to continue without interruption.*

mercilessly /ˈmɝsələsli/
in a way that has or shows no mercy
Example: *The villain mercilessly taunted the hero, revelling in his suffering.*

merely /ˈmɪrli/
used to emphasise that you mean exactly what you are saying and nothing more
Example: *His apology was merely a formality, lacking sincerity or remorse.*
used to emphasise that something is not large, important, or effective when compared to something else
Example: *The old smartphone was merely a fraction of the cost of the latest model.*

meridionally /məˈrɪdɪənlli/
regarding the south or the direction of a meridian
Example: *The vines were planted meridionally to maximise sun exposure in the southern hemisphere.*

meritedly /mˈɛrɪtɪdli/
in a way that is deserving or excellent

Example: *She was promoted meritedly due to her outstanding*
performance and dedication to the company.

merrily /ˈmɛrəli/
showing happiness or enjoyment
Example: *They sang merrily as they walked through the park on a*
sunny afternoon.

mesially /ˈmiːzjəlli/
towards the centre of the body or towards the middle of the mouth or
tooth.
Example: *The dentist applied the filling mesially, ensuring it filled*
the cavity towards the centre of the tooth rather than the
sides.

metamerically /ˌmɛtəˈmɪrɪkli/
in a metameric or segmented manner
Example: *The earthworm's body is organised metamerically, with*
distinct segments along its length.

metaphorically /ˌmɛtəˈfɔrɪkli/
relating to or using metaphors
Example: *She described her emotions metaphorically, likening her*
heartbreak to a stormy sea.

metaphysically /ˌmɛtəˈfɪzɪkəlli/
in a way that relates to the part of philosophy that is about
understanding existence and understanding
Example: *She contemplated the nature of reality metaphysically,*
pondering the essence of being and the universe.

methodically /məˈθɑdɪkəli/
In a very ordered and systematic manner, typically involving careful
planning and organization.

Example: She methodically organised her study notes by topic, ensuring each section was neatly labelled.

meticulously /məˈtɪkjələsli/
in a way that shows great care and attention to detail
Example: Jane meticulously arranged the flowers in a perfect bouquet for the event.

metrically /ˈmɛtrɪkəli/
in a way that uses or relates to a system of measurement that uses metres, centimetres, and litres
Example: The length of the field was measured metrically in metres to ensure accuracy for the construction project.
in a way that relates to the metre of a piece of poetry or music
Example: The poem was analysed metrically to understand its rhythmic structure and poetic flow.

microscopically /ˌmaɪkrəˈskɑpɪkli/
in a way that uses or can only be seen with a microscope
Example: The biologist examined the cells microscopically to study their internal structures.

midships /ˈmɪdʃɪps/
in, at or toward the middle of the ship
Example: The cargo was stored midships to maintain balance and stability during the voyage across rough seas.

midst /ˈmɪdst/
in the middle or central part
Example: She stood in the midst of her friends, laughing and chatting.

midway /ˈmɪdˌweɪ/
half the distance between two places

Example: *The hikers stopped for lunch midway between the*
trailhead and the summit.
in the middle of a process or period
Example: *She realised midway through the semester that she*
needed to improve her grade.

midweek /'mɪdˌwik/
in the middle of the week, usually from Tuesday to Thursday
Example: *They planned a midweek dinner gathering to catch up*
with friends who were busy on weekends.

mightily /'maɪtəli/
with great effort
Example: *Pam struggled mightily to lift the heavy box onto the*
shelf.

mighty /'maɪti/
having or showing great strength or power
Example: *The mighty oak tree stood tall and strong, unaffected by*
the storm raging around it.

mildly /'maɪldli/
in a gentle or moderate way
Example: *She spoke mildly, trying not to upset anyone with her*
criticism.

militarily /ˌmɪlə'tɛrəli/
in a way that relates to or involves the armed forces
Example: *The country responded militarily to the threat by*
mobilising its troops and deploying military assets.

milkily /m'ɪlkili/
in a milky manner, as in the appearance and consistency

Example: The tea appeared milky as I poured the cream, creating a smooth and consistent texture.

mimically /'mɪmɪkli/
in an imitative manner
Example: The actor mimically recreated the famous comedian's gestures and expressions.

mincingly /mˈɪnsɪŋli/
using small, delicate steps in a way that does not look natural
Example: She walked mincingly in her new high heels.
in a way that is too delicate or not direct enough
Example: He delivered his critique mincingly, avoiding the harsh truth and softening his words to spare their feelings.

mindlessly /'maɪndləsli/
in a way that does not involve thought or mental effort
Example: She scrolled through social media mindlessly, unaware of the passing time.

minimally /'mɪnəməli/
in a way that is very small in amount
Example: The patient was minimally affected by the surgery, experiencing only mild discomfort.

minionly /'mɪnjənli/
in the manner of a follower or subordinate
Example: She carried out his orders minionly, without question or hesitation.

ministerially /ˌmɪnɪsˈtɪərɪəlli/
in the manner of a minister or clergyman
Example: He spoke ministerially, offering comfort and guidance to the grieving family.

miraculously /mɝˈɑkjələsli/

in a way that is very surprising or difficult to believe

Example: *The patient miraculously recovered overnight, defying all medical expectations.*

miserably /mˈɪzrəbli/)

in a way that is very unpleasant and makes you unhappy

Example: *She failed the exam miserably, feeling dejected and defeated.*

having little value, in a way that is disappointing

Example: *The poorly organised event ended miserably, with attendees leaving early in disappointment.*

mistakenly /mɪstˈeɪkənli/

wrongly or by mistake

Example: *Sally mistakenly took someone else's coat from the restaurant.*

mistily /mˈɪstili/

in a way that is full of mist

Example: *The mountains appeared mistily in the early morning light; their peaks barely visible.*

in a way that is uncertain or mysterious, and often romantic

Example: *She gazed mistily into the distance, lost in a daydream of far-off places and times.*

mistrustingly /mɪstrˈʌstɪŋli/

in a manner that shows distrust or suspicion.

Example: *She looked at him mistrustingly, doubting every word he said.*

mockingly /mˈɒkɪŋli/

in a way that involves laughing at someone unkindly

Example: He raised his eyebrow mockingly as he imitated her
              clumsy attempt at dancing.

modally /ˈməʊdlli/
in a way that pertains to modality or modes, particularly in the
context of music, logic, or philosophy.
Example: The musician explored different keys modally,
              experimenting with various scales and tonalities.

moderately /mˈɒdərətli/
in a way that is neither small nor large, but with reasonable limits in
amount, degree or strength
Example: She exercises moderately to maintain her fitness without
              overexerting herself.

modernly /ˈmɒdənli/
in a way or style that is modern
Example: The building was designed modernly, with sleek lines and
              minimalist aesthetics.

modestly /mˈɒdəstli/
in a way that is not very large in size, amount, or degree, or not
expensive
Example: She lived in a modestly sized apartment that was
              affordable and suited her needs perfectly.

molecularly /məʊˈlekjʊləli/
in a way that relates to molecules
Example: The researchers manipulated the DNA molecularly,
              altering its sequence to study genetic mutations.

momentarily /mˌəʊməntˈɛrəli/
for a very short time or very soon

Example: *He paused momentarily to catch his breath before*
            continuing with his presentation.

monastically /ˌmɑːnəˈstɪkli/

in a way that relates to monks or monasteries, often reflecting the practices, lifestyle, or environment of monastic life.

Example: *The monks lived monastically, dedicating their lives to*
            prayer, meditation, and work within the monastery.

in a simple way, for example with few possessions, no sexual activity, and few people around you

Example: *She chose to live monastically, dedicating herself to*
            solitude, prayer, and a minimalist lifestyle.

monstrously /mˈɒnstrəsli/

in a very cruel way

Example: *The dictator ruled monstrously, with no regard for*
            human life

in an extremely large or abnormal manner.

Example: *The building was monstrously huge, dwarfing everything*
            around it.

morally /mˈɒrəli/

based on principles that you or people in general consider to be right, honest, or acceptable

Example: *Sue made her decision morally, considering the impact*
            on others and sticking to her ethical beliefs.

morbidly /mˈɔːbɪdli/

in a way that shows too much interest in unpleasant subjects, especially death

Example: *She morbidly fascinated her friends with detailed stories*
            of crime scenes and gruesome accidents.

in a way relates to or is caused by disease

Example: He was morbidly obese, facing serious health
complications as a result.

more /mˈɔː/
to a greater or higher degree
Example: She wanted more ice cream after finishing her first bowl.
in addition to what has already been mentioned or done.
Example: He wanted more time to finish his project before the
deadline.

moreover /mɔːrˈəʊvɐ/
used to introduce additional information that supports or enhances a
previous statement.
Example: Jane not only excelled in academics but moreover, she
was also a talented athlete.

mortally /mˈɔːtəli/
severely enough to cause death
Example: The knight was wounded mortally in battle, his injuries
too severe for any hope of recovery.
to an extreme degree
Example: She was mortally afraid of heights, unable to even look
down from the balcony.

most /mˈəʊst/
to the highest of greatest degree
Example: Joe was considered the most talented musician in the
entire orchestra.

mostly /mˈəʊstli/
to a large degree or amount
Example: She mostly enjoys spending her weekends with friends
and family.

musically /mjˈuːzɪkli/

in a way that relates or sounds like music

Example: *He approached the piano musically, coaxing out melodies that filled the room with emotion.*

mutually /mjˈuːtʃuːəli/

felt or done by two or more people or groups in the same way

Example: *They reached a mutually beneficial agreement that satisfied both parties involved.*

mysteriously /mɪstˈɪərɪəsli/

in a way that is strange, not known, or not understood

Example: *She disappeared mysteriously one night, leaving behind only unanswered questions and speculation.*

Nn

naggingly /ˈnɑgɪŋli/
in an unpleasant or annoying way that continues for a long period of time
Example: *She naggingly reminded him to do his chores every day.*

naively /naɪˈiːvli/
in a way that shows you are too willing to believe that someone is telling the truth or that life is pleasant or fair
Example: *Jane naively trusted the stranger with her personal information.*

nakedly /nˈeɪkɪdli/
in a way that is obvious and unpleasant
Example: *The politician's greed was nakedly apparent in his attempts to manipulate the system for personal gain.*

namelessly /ˈneɪmlɪsli/
without a name, or with a name that is not known or shown
Example: *The hero moved through the crowd, helping others namelessly.*

namely /nˈeɪmli/
used to introduce specific details or examples that clarify or elaborate on what has just been mentioned
Example: *Sarah has two favourite hobbies, namely painting and hiking.*

narcotically /nɑːrˈkɑːtɪkli/
in a manner that relates to or involves the use of narcotics, often referring to the effects or administration of drugs.

Example: The patient was sedated narcotically to relieve the pain
after the surgery.

narratively /ˈnɑrətɪvli/
in a way that relates to the act of telling a story or describing a series
of events
Example: The movie unfolds narratively, introducing characters
and building suspense throughout the plot.

narrowingly /nˈɑrəʊɪŋli/
increasing in a narrow way
Example: The candidate narrowly won the election, securing
victory by a margin of only a few votes.

narrowly /nˈɑrəʊli/
by a very small amount or number
Example: She narrowly avoided missing the bus.
carefully or in a way that shows doubt
Example: He watched the stranger narrowly, unsure of his
intentions.

nasally /nˈeɪzəli/
in a way that relates to the nose or is done through the nose
Example: She exhaled nasally, trying to clear her sinuses.

nastily /nˈɑːstɪli/
in a way that is unkind
Example: He nastily criticised her outfit.
in a way that is bad or unpleasant
Example: The milk smelled nastily sour.

nationally /nˈɑʃənəli/
by or to everyone in a nation
Example: The new policy was implemented nationally.

natively /ˈneɪtɪvli/

in a way that relates to one's first or native language

Example: He spoke French natively, having learned it as his first
*   language.*

in a way that relates to plants and animals that are indigenous to a
        particular area.

Example: The redwood trees grow natively along the northern
*   California coast.*

nattily /nˈatɪli/

in a strikingly neat and trim manner

Example: He dressed nattily in a tailored suit and polished shoes.

naturally /nˈatʃərəli/

happening or existing as part of nature and not made or done by
people

Example: The river flowed naturally through the valley, carving its
*   own path over time.*

in a usual or easy way

Example: She naturally excels in mathematics, solving complex
*   problems effortlessly.*

because of an ability or characteristic that you were born with

Example: Susan naturally has a talent for singing, inherited from
*   her mother.*

naturedly /nˈeɪtʃədli/

in a certain way or nature

Example: He naturedly accepted the challenge, showing his
*   competitive spirit.*

naughtily /nˈɔːtɪli/

in a way that shows bad behaviour

Example: The children giggled naughtily as they snuck cookies
*   before dinner.*

in a way that involves or suggests sex
Example: *She winked naughtily, sending his heart racing.*

nauseously /ˈnɔːsjəsli/
in a way that shows that you might vomit, or makes you feel that you might vomit
Example: *The smell of the garbage made her feel nauseously ill.*
in a way that you dislike and disapprove of
Example: *He stared nauseously at the graphic images on the screen, unable to watch any longer.*

nautically /nˈɔːtɪkli/
in a way that relates to ships, sailing or sailors
Example: *The captain navigated nautically, using traditional methods to steer the ship across the ocean.*

navally /ˈneɪvəlli/
with a naval crown
Example: *During the re-enactment, the actor wore his costume navally, proudly displaying the naval crown, a symbol of the Roman military award.*
in a naval manner or from a naval standpoint
Example: *The fleet was strategically deployed navally to ensure maximum protection of the coastline.*

nearly /nˈiəli/
almost, close or not completely
Example: *The project is nearly finished, just needing a few final touches.*

neatly /nˈiːtli/
in a tidy way, with everything in its place
Example: *She arranged the books neatly on the shelf.*
in a clever and simple way

Example: *He solved the puzzle neatly, impressing everyone with his*
quick thinking.

needily /nˈiːdili/
describes a condition of being in need, often related to poverty
Example: *The family lived needily, struggling to afford basic*
necessities.

needly /ˈniːdli/
as an inevitable or natural consequence
Example: *Due to his poor diet, he needly faced health issues.*

negatively /nˈɛɡətˌɪvli/
in a way that expresses "no"
Example: *She responded negatively to the proposal, declining the*
offer.
in a way that is bad or harmful
Example: *The news negatively impacted his mood for the rest of the*
day.
in a way that relates to the type of electrical charge that is carried by electrons
Example: *Electrons are negatively charged particles.*
in a way that shows unhappiness or disapproval
Example: *She spoke negatively about the new policy, expressing*
her disapproval.

neglectfully /nɪˈɡlektfʊlli/
in a way that does not give enough care and attention to someone or something
Example: *He handled the fragile items neglectfully, causing some*
to break during transit.

negligently /nˈɛglɪdʒəntli/

in a way that is not careful enough, or does not give enough attention to people or things that are your responsibility

Example: *James handled the fragile vase negligently, causing it to slip from his hands and break.*

neocortically /ˌniːoʊˈkɔːrtɪkli/

relating to the neocortex, the part of the brain involved in higher-order brain functions

Example: *The information processed neocortically influenced his decision-making in complex ways.*

neolithically /ˌniːəʊˈlɪθɪkli/

in a manner characteristic of the Neolithic era, which is the later part of the Stone Age

Example: *They crafted tools neolithically, using stone and bone for hunting and gathering.*

neonatally /nˈiːəʊnˌeɪtəli/

actions or conditions related to or occurring during the neonatal period

Example: *The paediatrician monitors newborns neonatally to ensure they are healthy and developing well.*

neoterically /ˌniːəʊˈtɛrɪkli/

in a new, recent, or modern manner

Example: *She approached the problem neoterically, using innovative methods that had not been tried before.*

nervously /nˈɜːvəsli/

in a worried or slightly frightened way

Example: *Kim tapped her foot nervously while waiting for the interview to begin.*

netherward /ˈnɛðərwərd/

pertaining to or moving toward the downward or lower part of something.

Example: *The hikers descended netherward into the valley, following a steep trail.*

nettlingly /ˈnɛtɪŋli/

in a way to make someone annoyed or slightly angry

Example: *Her constant interruptions nettlingly disrupted the flow of the meeting.*

neurally /ˈnjʊərəlli/

in a way that involves or relates to a nerve or the system of nerves that includes the brain

Example: *The signal travelled neurally from her fingertip to her brain in milliseconds.*

neurotically /njuːrˈɒtɪkli/

actions or behavior done in a manner that reflects neurosis, which often involves excessive anxiety, worry, or nervousness.

Example: *He cleaned his hands neurotically, as if trying to rid himself of invisible contamination.*

neutrally /njˈuːtrəli/

in a way that does not encourage or support any of the groups involved in something and does not show personal opinion

Example: *The mediator listened neutrally to both sides of the argument without favouring either party.*

using colours such as white, cream, and grey

Example: *The room was painted neutrally with shades of white and beige.*

never /nˈɛvɐ/

something that does not occur at any time or on any occasion

Example: *He never misses his morning jog, regardless of the*
             weather.

newly /njˈuːli/
happening recently or a short time ago
Example: *They moved into their newly renovated house just last*
             month.

nicely /nˈaɪsli/
in a way that is pleasant, polite, or satisfactory
Example: *Susan thanked him nicely for helping her carry the*
             groceries.

niftily /nˈɪftɪli/
in a clever, skillful, or effective manner
Example: *He solved the puzzle niftily, impressing everyone with his*
             quick thinking.

nigglingly /ˈnɪɡlɪŋli/
in a way that worries someone or causes them slight pain, usually for
a long time
Example: *She felt nigglingly anxious about the upcoming exam.*
in a way that criticises someone about small details, or that gives too
much attention to details
Example: *He nigglingly pointed out every minor flaw in her*
             presentation, making her feel overly criticised.

nightly /nˈaɪtli/
something that occurs or is done each night
Example: *Pam took her nightly walk around the neighbourhood*
             before bed.

nightmarishly /ˈnaɪtmeərɪʃli/

in a way that is extremely unpleasant and very upsetting or frightening

Example: *The storm raged nightmarishly, with thunder shaking the windows and lightning flashing across the sky.*

nilpotently /nˈɪlpˈəʊtəntli/

in a manner characteristic of or related to nilpotency

Example: *The equation was solved nilpotently, demonstrating the power of nilpotent matrices in linear algebra.*

nimbly /nˈɪmbli/

in a way that is quick and exact either in movement or thoughts

Example: *The dancer moved nimbly across the stage, executing intricate steps with grace and precision.*

ninthly /ˈnaɪnθlɪ/

in the ninth place

Example: *He finished ninthly in the race, just missing out on a top-eight finish.*

nippingly /ˈnɪpɪŋli/

in a sharp or biting cold manner

Example: *The wind blew nippingly as they walked along the icy path*

nobbily /nˈɒbili/

in a fashionable or stylish manner

Example: *He appeared nobbily dressed in his tailored suit and polished shoes.*

nobly /nˈəʊbli/

in a way that is morally good, brave, honest, or kind

Example: *Sam nobly sacrificed his own comfort to help those in
               need.*

in a way that relates to belonging to a high social rank in a society,
especially by birth

Example: *The princess carried herself nobly, displaying grace and
               elegance at every royal event.*

in a way that causes admiration, especially because of a grand or
impressive appearance

Example: *The statue stood nobly in the centre of the square.*

nocturnally /nɒktˈɜːnəli/

happening at night rather than during the day

Example: *Owls are nocturnally active, hunting for prey under the
               cover of darkness.*

nodally /ˈnəʊdlli/

in a way that is near a node

Example: *The problem was nodally related to the intersection of
               several key factors in the research study.*

nodosely /ˈnəʊdəsli/

in the way of having many protuberances

Example: *The plant grew nodosely, with numerous branches and
               buds forming along its stems.*

noetically /noʊˈɛtɪkli/

in a way relating to the mind or intellect

Example: *Pamela approached the puzzle noetically, considering
               various theories and perspectives.*

nohow /nˈəʊhaʊ/

not in any way

Example: *He could nohow convince her to change her mind about
               the decision.*

noiselessly /ˈnɔɪzlɪsli/
actions done without making noise
Example: *The cat crept noiselessly across the room, stalking its prey.*

noisily /nˈɔɪzɪli/
in a loud or confusing manner, especially containing unwanted sounds
Example: *The children played noisily in the backyard, laughing, and shouting as they ran around.*

noisomely /ˈnɔɪsəmli/
in an offensive or disgusting manner, especially affecting the sense of smell
Example: *The garbage bin smelled noisomely after sitting in the sun for days.*

nominally /nˈɒmɪnəli/
in name or thought but not in fact, or not as things really are
Example: *He was nominally the team captain, but others made all the decisions.*
used when talking about prices or rates that are correct at the present time but do not show the effect of inflation
Example: *The rent was nominally affordable, but with inflation, it became harder to manage.*

nominatively /ˈnɒmɪnətɪvli/
in a manner of a nominative
Example: *Roy spoke nominatively about his achievements during the interview.*

nonchalantly /nˈɒnʃələntli/

in a calm manner, often in a way that suggests you are not interested or do not care

Example: *Sarah shrugged nonchalantly when asked about her upcoming exam.*

non-normally /nˈɒn-nˈɔːməli/

in an irregular way

Example: *The weather behaved non-normally for this time of year, with unexpected cold spells and sudden rain showers.*

non-socially /nˈɒn-sˈəʊʃəlˌi/

in a way that is not concerned with society or social matters

Example: *He preferred to spend his weekends non-socially, focusing on solitary hobbies like reading and hiking.*

non-trivially /nˈɒntrˈɪvɪəli/

in a significant or important manner

Example: *The scientist's research findings have nontrivially contributed to our understanding of climate change.*

nonverbally /nˈɒnvˈɜːbəli/

in a way that does not use words

Example: *She communicated her discomfort nonverbally through gestures and facial expressions.*

normally /nˈɔːməli/

in a way that is natural or expected

Example: *She normally wakes up early in the morning to go jogging.*

normatively /ˈnɔːmətɪvli/

in a way that relates to norms, rules, or standards, especially regarding behaviour

Example: *The teacher spoke normatively to remind the students of the classroom rules.*

north-easterly /nˈɔːθiːstəli/
in a way that relates to the direction to or from the northeast
Example: *The wind blew north-easterly, bringing cold air from the northeast across the region.*

north-eastward /ˈnɔːθiːstwəd/
in the direction of the northeast
Example: *They travelled north-eastward to reach their destination.*

northerly /nˈɔːðəli/
in or towards a northward position or direction
Example: *The birds flew in a northerly direction as they migrated for the winter.*

northward /nˈɔːθwəd/
towards the north
Example: *They embarked on a journey northward, aiming to explore the Arctic Circle.*

north-westward /ˈnɔːθˈwestwəd/
towards the northwest
Example: *They sailed north-westward across the ocean.*

noisily /nˈɔɪzɪli/
in a way that shows too much interest in what other people are doing or a wish to discover more about them than you should
Example: *She noisily peered over her cubicle to see what her colleague was working on.*

notably /nˈəʊtəbli/
to an important degree, or in a way that can or should be noticed

Example: *Paul was notably absent from the meeting, which delayed the decision-making process.*

notarially /nəʊˈteərɪəlli/
in a way of being executed by a notary public
Example: *The document was notarially signed to ensure its legal validity.*

notedly /ˈnəʊtɪdlɪ/
in the way of being well-known by reputation
Example: *She was notedly skilled in solving complex mathematical problems.*

noteworthily /nˈəʊtwɜːðili/
in a way that deserves attention because of being important or interesting
Example: *His research findings were noteworthily ground-breaking in the field of medicine.*

noticeably /nˈəʊtɪsəbli/
in a way that is easy to see or recognize
Example: *Simone had noticeably improved her tennis skills over the summer.*

notionally /nˈəʊʃənəli/
in a way that exists only as an idea, not as something real
Example: *He notionally agreed to the proposal, but actual implementation was uncertain.*

notoriously /nəʊtˈɔːrɪəsli/
in a way that is famous for something bad
Example: *The restaurant was notoriously slow with its service.*

nourishingly /ˈnʌrɪʃɪŋli/
in a way that provides nourishment or food
Example:　*The homemade soup was prepared nourishingly with*
　　　　　fresh vegetables and herbs.

novelly /ˈnɒvəlli/
in a new or original manner
Example:　*The artist approached the project novelly, blending*
　　　　　traditional techniques with modern digital tools.

now /nˈaʊ/
at the present time, not past or future
Example:　*I am currently busy right now.*
used when describing a situation that is the result of what someone
just said or did
Example:　*Ruby realised she needed to leave now that the bus had*
　　　　　arrived.

noxiously /ˈnɒkʃəsli/
in a harmful or unpleasant way
Example:　*The chemical fumes spread noxiously through the*
　　　　　factory.

numberlessly /ˈnʌmbəlɪsli/
in a way that cannot be counted because it is too great
Example:　*The stars filled the sky numberlessly on a clear night in*
　　　　　the countryside.

numerably /ˈnjuːmərəbli/
in a way that can be counted
Example:　*The available seats were numerably listed on the chart*
　　　　　for the event.

numerally /ˈnjuːmərəlli/
in a way that consists of numbers or numerals
Example: *The data was numerally represented in the form of*
             graphs and charts.

numerically /njuːmˈɛrɪkli/
in a way that involves or is expressed in numbers
Example: *She ranked numerically higher than all other participants*
             in the maths competition.

numerously /ˈnjuːmərəslɪ/
in large numbers or many times
Example: *Visitors attended the art exhibition, numerously.*

nutritionally /njuːtrˈɪʃənəli/)
in a way that relates to nutrition
Example: *The cereal was designed to be nutritionally dense,*
             offering a high amount of fibre and protein per serving.

nutritiously /njuːˈtrɪʃəsli/
in a way that relates to food that contains the substances needed for
life and growth
Example: *They prepared a meal that was both delicious and*
             nutritiously balanced.

nutritively /ˈnjuːtrɪtɪvli/
in a way of providing nutriment
Example: *The smoothie was packed nutritively with vitamins and*
             minerals.

oafishly /ˈəʊfɪʃli/
in a stupid, rude, or awkward way
Example:　*He oafishly knocked over the vase as he stumbled
　　　　　　through the room.*

obdurately /ˈɒbdjʊrɪtli/
in a way that shows that someone is extremely determined to act in a
particular way and not to change despite what anyone else says
Example:　*She obdurately refused to apologise, even when she knew
　　　　　　she was wrong.*
in a way that is difficult to deal with or change
Example:　*The old door obdurately resisted all attempts to open it.*

obediently /əʊbˈiːdiəntli/
in a compliant and respectful manner, showing a willingness to
follow rules and authority
Example:　*The dog obediently followed its owner's commands.*

obiter /ˈɒbɪtə/
in an incidental way of passing a remark or opinion
Example:　*She mentioned obiter that she had met the mayor once.*

objectively /ɒbdʒˈɛktɪvli/
in a way that is based on facts and not influenced by personal beliefs
or feelings
Example:　*She evaluated the proposal objectively, considering only
　　　　　　the facts presented.*

obligatorily /əblˈɪɡətərˌili/
in a way that means that something must be done because of a rule or
law

Example: The company obligatorily provides safety training to all
             new employees.
in a way that is expected because it usually happens
Example: Employees must obligatorily wear safety helmets in the
             construction zone to comply with health and safety
             regulations

obligingly /əblˈaɪdʒɪŋli/
in a way that shows that you are willing or eager to help
Example: He obligingly held the door open for the elderly woman
             struggling with her bags.

obliquely /əblˈiːkli/
in a way that is not direct, so that the real meaning is not immediately
clear
Example: She answered obliquely, avoiding the question with a
             subtle change of topic.
in a slanting or sloping manner
Example: The sunlight streamed in obliquely through the window.

obliviously /əˈblɪvɪəsli/
in a way that shows that you are not aware of something, especially
what is happening around you
Example: She walked obliviously through the busy market.

obnoxiously /ɒbnˈɒkʃəsli/
in a very unpleasant or rude way
Example: He spoke obnoxiously, interrupting everyone in the
             meeting.

obscenely /ɒbsˈiːnli/
in a way that is offensive, rude, or shocking, usually because of being
too obviously related to sex or showing sex

Example: *The comedian made an obscenely explicit joke that left*
               the audience uncomfortable.

to a degree that makes you feel dislike or moral disapproval

Example: *The price of the luxury watch was obscenely high.*

obscurely /ɒbskjˈɔːli/

in a way that is not known about by many people

Example: *She lived in an obscurely in a remote location, far from*
               the bustling city life.

in a way that is not clear or is difficult to understand or see

Example: *The message was written obscurely, with vague*
               references that were hard to decipher.

obsequiously /əbˈsiːkwɪəsli/

in a way that is too eager to praise or obey someone

Example: *He behaved obsequiously around his boss.*

observably /ɒbzˈɜːvəbli/

in a way that can be noticed or seen

Example: *The temperature dropped observably as the sun set*
               behind the mountains.

observantly /əbˈzɜːvəntli/

in a way that shows that you are good or quick at noticing things.

Example: *She walked through the museum observantly, taking note*
               of every detail in the artwork.

in a way that obeys religious rules or customs

Example: *He ate observantly during Ramadan, adhering strictly to*
               fasting from dawn until sunset.

observingly /ɒbzˈɜːvɪŋli/

in an attentive or watchful manner

Example: *She looked observingly at the intricate patterns in the*
               fabric.

obsessively /ɒbsˈɛsɪvli/
in a way that involves thinking about something or someone, or doing something, too much or all the time
Example: *He checked his phone obsessively, constantly refreshing his social media feeds.*

obsoletely /ˈɒbsəliːtli/
in a way that tells that it is no longer in use or replaced with something better
Example: *He still uses an obsoletely old computer model.*

obstinately /ˈɒbstɪnˌeɪtli/
in a way that is unreasonably determined, especially by acting in a particular way and not changing at all, despite what anyone else says
Example: *Despite the evidence, he obstinately refused to admit he was wrong.*
in a way that is difficult to deal with, change or solve
Example: *The problem persisted obstinately, despite multiple attempts to resolve it.*

obstreperously /əbˈstrepərəsli/
in a way that is difficult to deal with and noisy
Example: *The children played obstreperously in the yard.*

obtrusively /əbˈtruːsɪvli/
in a way that is too noticeable or prominent, often in an unwelcome manner
Example: *She wore obtrusively bright clothing at the solemn event.*

obtusely /ɒbtjˈuːsli/
in a way that is foolish and slow to understand, or unwilling to try to understand
Example: *He responded obtusely to the professor's question.*

obversely /ˈɒbvɜːsli/

in a manner corresponding to an obverse or opposite side

Example: *Obversely, if one idea holds true, the opposite idea must be false.*

obviously /ˈɒbvɪəsli/

in a way that is easy to understand or see

Example: *He was obviously upset by the news, as tears streamed down his cheeks.*

occasionally /əkˈeɪʒənəli/

in a way that is not often or regular, happens sometimes

Example: *I occasionally go for a run in the park on weekends to relax.*

occultly /ɒˈkʌltli/

in a concealed or hidden manner; relating to supernatural or mystical elements

Example: *The treasure was hidden occultly beneath the old oak tree.*

ocularly /ˈɒkjʊləli/

by means of the eyes or the sight

Example: *She examined the painting ocularly, studying every brushstroke and detail.*

oddly /ˈɒdli/

in a strange or surprising way

Example: *He spoke oddly, using phrases that did not quite fit the conversation.*

odiously /ˈəʊdjəsli/

in an extremely unpleasant way that causes or deserves hate

Example: *The dictator ruled odiously, suppressing dissent, and persecuting those who opposed him.*

offendedly /əfˈɛndɪdli/

in a way that causes or expresses pain or hurt

Example: *She turned away offendedly after hearing his insensitive remark.*

offensively /əfˈɛnsɪvli/

in a way that is likely to upset, annoy, or embarrass someone

Example: *He spoke offensively, making inappropriate jokes that offended several people at the party.*

in a way that relates to attacking someone or something

Example: *The team played offensively, pushing forward aggressively to score goals.*

in a way that relates to getting points in a sport, rather than stopping the other player or team getting points

Example: *The basketball player moved offensively, aiming to score points for his team.*

offhandedly /ˈɒfhandɪdlɪ/

in a way that does not seem to show much interest or careful thought

Example: *She replied offhandedly to the question, not realising its importance.*

officially /əfˈɪʃəlˌi/

in a way agreed to or arranged by people in positions of authority

Example: *The government officially declared the new policy during a press conference.*

as stated, or accepted by people publicly, although it may not be true

Example: *He was officially declared the winner of the race, despite controversy over the timing.*

relating to a position of responsibility

Example: *Officially, the mayor welcomed the new citizens to the city with a speech.*

officiously /əf'ɪʃəsli/
in a way that shows you have too high an opinion of your own importance, and are too eager to tell people what to do
Example: *He officiously directed everyone on how to arrange the meeting room.*

often /'ɒfən/
in a frequent manner
Example: *He often goes jogging in the park in the mornings before work.*

oftentimes /'ɒfɪnt͵aɪmz/
on many occasions
Example: *Oftentimes, they would meet for coffee after work to catch up.*

ofttimes /'ɒfttaɪmz/
many times, at short intervals
Example: *John ofttimes checked his phone for updates throughout the day.*

oilily /'ɔɪlɪli/
in a way that relates to, or consists of oil
Example: *The mechanic's hands were oilily stained after working on the car engine all morning.*

ominously /'ɒmɪnəsli/
in a way that suggests that something unpleasant is likely to happen
Example: *Dark clouds gathered ominously on the horizon, signalling an approaching storm.*

omnipotently /ɒmˈnɪpətəntli/

in a way that involves having unlimited power and being able to do anything

Example: The sorcerer in the story wielded magic omnipotently.

once /wˈɒns/

one time and no more

Example: She visited Paris once, and it was a memorable experience.

onerously /ˈəʊnərəsli/

in a way that needs a large amount of effort, or causes a great deal of difficulty or worry

Example: The new regulations placed onerously high demands on small businesses.

online /ˈɒnlaɪn/

bought, done, or used using the internet

Example: He ordered the book online.

connected to a system

Example: The computer needs to be online to access the latest updates.

only /ˈəʊnli/

to indicate that something is limited to a specific amount or type

Example: She had only one cookie left after the party.

to say that something unpleasant will happen because of an action or a failure to act

Example: He refused to study, only to fail the exam.

to show that you feel sorry about something that cannot happen when explaining why it cannot happen

Example: I can only apologise for the inconvenience caused by the delay in delivery.

onward /ˈɒnwəd/
toward or at a point lying ahead in space or time
Example: *From that day onward, their friendship grew stronger.*

onwards /ˈɒnwədz/
in a way of moving forward or progressing
Example: *They marched onwards through the night.*

opaquely /əʊˈpeɪkli/
in a way that is difficult to understand
Example: *The instructions were written opaquely, leaving the*
students confused about the assignment.

open-handedly /ˈəʊpnˈhandɪdli/
in a generous way and unselfish way.
Example: *He donated open-handedly to the charity.*

openly /ˈəʊpənli/
in a transparent or honest manner
Example: *She admitted her mistake openly during the meeting.*

operosely /ˈɒpəˌroʊsli/
in a laborious or tedious manner
Example: *The students worked operosely through the complex*
maths problems.

opinionatedly /əˈpɪnjəneɪtɪdli/
expressing strong opinions in a forceful and confident manner
Example: *She opinionatedly argued her views on politics.*

opportunely /ˈɒpətjuːnli/
happening at a time that is likely to produce success or that is
convenient

Example: *He arrived opportunely just as the meeting was about to start.*

opportunistically /ˌɒpətjuːnˈɪstɪkli/
in a way that uses a situation to get power or an advantage
Example: *He opportunistically took credit for the project's success.*

opposite /ˈɒpəsˌɪt/
in a position facing someone or something but on the other side
Example: *She sat opposite her friend at the dinner table.*

oppositely /ˈɒpəzɪtli/
on or to an opposing side
Example: *The two teams moved oppositely on the field.*

oppressively /əprˈɛsɪvli/
in a cruel or unfair way that does not allow people the freedom they should have
Example: *The dictator ruled oppressively, denying basic human rights to the citizens.*
in a way that makes people feel worried or uncomfortable
Example: *The heat hung oppressively in the air, making it difficult to breathe comfortably.*

optatively /ˈɒptətɪvli/
in a way to indicate or express a wish, desire, or choice
Example: *She optatively hoped for good weather on her wedding day.*

optically /ˈɒptɪkli/
in a way that relates to light or the ability to see, or to what someone sees
Example: *The artwork was designed optically to create a three-dimensional illusion on a flat surface.*

optimally /ˈɒptɪməli/
in a way that is most likely to bring success or advantage
*Example: To perform optimally in exams, it is important to study
            consistently and manage time effectively.*

optimistically /ˌɒptɪmˈɪstɪkli/
in a way that shows hope or a positive belief about future outcomes.
*Example: She smiled optimistically, confident that things would
            work out despite the challenges.*

optionally /ˈɒpʃənəli/
in a way that shows you chose to do something because you want to
and not because you must
*Example: The dessert could be optionally topped with whipped
            cream.*

opulently /ˈɒpjʊləntli/
in an expensive and luxurious way
*Example: The mansion was decorated opulently with crystal
            chandeliers and velvet drapes.*

oracularly /ɒˈrakjʊləli/
in a manner resembling that of an oracle, providing wise and
prophetic advice
*Example: The old sage spoke oracularly, predicting a prosperous
            future for the kingdom.*

orally /ˈɔːrəli/
expressed in speech, not writing
Example: She presented her findings orally to the class.
entering the body through the mouth
*Example: The medication is available in both pill form and orally
            as a liquid suspension.*

ordinarily /ˌɔːdɪnˈɛrəli/

in a usual or typical manner

Example: *He would ordinarily take the bus to work every morning.*

ordinately /ˈɔːdɪnətli/

in an orderly or regular manner

Example: *The files were stored ordinately in alphabetical order for easy access.*

organizationally /ˌɔːgənəˈzeɪʃənəli/

in a way that relates to the way that the different parts of something are combined or work together

Example: *He focused organizationally on restructuring the company.*

originally /ərˈɪdʒɪnəli/

in the beginning when something first existed

Example: *The company originally started as a small family business in the garage.*

ornamentally /ˌɔːnəmˈɛntəli/

in a manner that is intended to be decorative or for aesthetic purposes rather than functional.

Example: *The garden was planted ornamentally.*

ornately /ɔːnˈeɪtli/

in a manner characterised by elaborate and detailed decoration.

Example: *The cathedral was ornately decorated with intricate carvings and stained-glass windows.*

orthodoxly /ˈɔːθədɒksli/

in a correct, conventional, or proper way

Example: *He strictly adhered to the recipe and cooked the dish orthodoxly.*

ostensibly /ɒstˈɛnsəbli/

in a way that appears or claims to be one thing when it is really something else

Example: The company's decision to downsize was ostensibly due to financial reasons.

ostentatiously /ˌɒstəntˈeɪʃəsli/

in a way that is obvious and is an attempt to make people notice you

Example: The celebrity arrived at the event, ostentatiously displaying their expensive jewellery and designer clothing.

otherwhere /ˈʌðəweə/

in or to another place

Example: She dreamed of travelling otherwhere, imagining distant lands she had never visited.

otherwise /ˈʌðəwaɪz/

differently or in another way and is used to indicate a consequence or alternative

Example: She planned to leave early; otherwise, she would miss the train.

outdoors /aʊtdˈɔːz/

out in the air, not inside a building

Example: They enjoyed having a picnic outdoors on a sunny day.

outerly /ˈaʊtəli/

toward the outside

Example: He carefully applied the sealant outerly.

outlandishly /aʊtlˈændɪʃli/

in a way that is strange and unusual and difficult to accept or like

Example: She dressed outlandishly for the costume party.

outrageously /aʊtrˈeɪdʒəsli/

in a way that is shocking, usually because of being unusual or strange

Example: *The actor's outfit for the awards ceremony was outrageously flamboyant.*

outrightly /ˈaʊtraɪtli/

in a straightforward and direct manner

Example: *She outrightly rejected the proposal without hesitation.*

outside /ˈaʊtˈsaɪd/

not in a room, building or container

Example: *They played soccer outside in the park during the sunny afternoon.*

outspokenly /aʊtspˈəʊkənli/

in a way that expresses strong opinions very directly without worrying if other people are offended

Example: *The activist spoke outspokenly about the need for social change.*

outwardly /ˈaʊtwədli/

in a way that relates to how people, situations, or things seem to be, rather than how they are inside

Example: *Outwardly, he appeared calm and composed, but inside he was nervous about the upcoming presentation.*

outwards /ˈaʊtwədz/

going or pointing away from a particular place or towards the outside

Example: *The branches of the tree spread outwards.*

ovally /ˈəʊvəlli/

in a way that looks like an oval

Example: The mirror was designed ovally, reflecting a distorted image.

over /ˈəʊvɐ/
across a barrier or intervening space
Example: She tossed the ball over the fence to her friend waiting on the other side.

overall /ˈəʊvərɔːl/
in general, on the whole
Example: Overall, the team performed well throughout the season.

overbearingly /ˌəʊvəˈbeərɪŋli/
in the manner of someone who is too confident or too determined to tell other people what to do, especially in a way that is unpleasant
Example: He overbearingly insisted on taking control of the project, disregarding others' suggestions.
in a way that is too strong
Example: Her perfume was overbearingly strong, filling the room with its scent.

overboard /ˌəʊvəbˈɔːd/
over the side of a boat or ship and into the water
Example: He accidentally dropped his hat overboard while leaning too far over the railing.

over-confidently /ˌoʊvɚˈkɑnfɪdəntli/
in a way of having excessive confidence
Example: She spoke over-confidently about her chances of winning the competition, underestimating her opponents' skills.

overhead /ˈəʊvehed/
above your head, usually in the sky

Example: The hot air balloon drifted slowly overhead, offering a
stunning view of the landscape below.

overleaf /ˌəʊvəlˈiːf/
on the other side of a page
Example: The answer to the question can be found overleaf in the
textbook.

overly /ˈəʊvəlˌi/
to an excessive degree
Example: He tends to worry overly about small details.

overmuch /ˌəʊvəmˈʌtʃ/
too much or very much
Example: She worried overmuch about the outcome of the exam.

overseas /ˈəʊvəˈsiːz/
in or to another country or countries, especially across the sea
Example: He travelled overseas to Europe for a business
conference last month.

overtly /əʊvˈɜːtli/
in a way that is done or shown publicly or in an obvious way and not
secret
Example: She overtly expressed her disagreement with the decision
during the meeting.

overwhelmingly /ˌəʊvəwˈɛlmɪŋli/
in an extremely great extent
Example: The team's performance was overwhelmingly positive.

owlishly /ˈaʊlɪʃli/
in a way that seems serious and intelligent, often because someone is
wearing glasses

Example: *She peered owlishly over her glasses as she reviewed the*
                        intricate details of the report.

oxymoronically /ˌɑkˈsiˈmɔrɑnɪkli/
in a way that relates to two words or ideas that are used together, but
have, or seem to have, opposite meanings
Example: *The advertisement's claim of "military intelligence" was*
                        oxymoronically self-contradictory.

Pp

painfully /pˈeɪnfəli/
in a way that causes pain
Example: *The doctor had to provide painfully honest feedback
              about the patient's condition.*
to emphasise a quality, action, or situation that is unpleasant or not
wanted
Example: *The meeting was painfully long and unproductive.*

painlessly /pˈeɪnləsli/
in a way that causes no physical pain
Example: *The dentist removed the tooth painlessly.*
in a way that causes no problems
Example: *The software update installed painlessly.*

palatably /pˈalətəbəli/
in a way that has a pleasant taste
Example: *The chef prepared the dish palatably.*
in a way that is acceptable
Example: *She explained the complex topic palatably, making it easy
              for everyone to understand.*

palely /pˈeɪlli/
in a way that is not bright and strong, especially in colour
Example: *The moon shone palely through the thin clouds.*
in a way that has less colour than usual, especially in the face and
skin
Example: *She smiled palely; her face drained of its usual colour.*

pallidly /ˈpalɪdli/
in a way that looks pale, unhealthy, and not attractive

Example: *He stared pallidly at the mirror, his complexion sickly and* *dull.*

in a way that shows no enthusiasm and excitement

Example: *She greeted us pallidly, lacking her usual enthusiasm.*

palmately /ˈpɑlmɪtli/

in a way the resembles a hand with the fingers spread

Example: *The leaves were arranged palmately, spreading out like fingers from a central point.*

palpably /pˈɑlpəbli/

in a way that is too obvious that it can easily be seen or known

Example: *The disappointment in her voice was palpably clear when she found out the event had been cancelled.*

in a way that feels so strong that it seems as if it can be physically felt

Example: *The excitement in the room was palpably felt as the announcement of the winner was about to begin.*

palterly /ˈpɔːltəli/

in an insincere or deceitful manner

Example: *He answered the questions palterly, avoiding the truth.*

pantingly /pˈɑːntɪŋli/

in a manner that involves rapid breathing or palpitation

Example: *She arrived at the finish line pantingly, gasping for breath.*

papally /ˈpeɪpəlli/

in a way that resembles a pope or that of a pope

Example: *He waved to the crowd papally, exuding a dignified presence.*

paradoxically /ˌpærədˈɒksɪkli/
in a way that seems impossible or difficult to understand because of containing two opposite facts or characteristics
Example: Paradoxically, his fear of failure drove him to take more risks in his career.

parallelly /ˈpærəlelli/
in a parallel direction or manner, such being similar or equal to something else
Example: The two projects were developed parallelly, each following a similar timeline and approach.

pardonably /pˈɑːdəʊnəbəli/
in a way that is possible to forgive
Example: Her mistake was pardonably innocent.

parentally /pəˈrentlli/
relates to actions or responsibilities associated with being a parent
Example: She took on the responsibility parentally, always putting her children first.

parenthetically /ˌpærənˈθetɪkəlli/
in a way that is in addition to the main part of what you are saying or writing
Example: He mentioned, parenthetically, that he had once lived in Paris.

parliamentarily /pˌɑːləmˈentərili/
actions or procedures conducted in a manner consistent with parliamentary practices
Example: The bill was debated parliamentarily before being put to a vote.

parochially /pəˈrəʊkjəlli/
in a way that shows interest only in a narrow range of matters, especially those that directly affect yourself, your town, or your country
Example: *She viewed the issue parochially, focusing only on how it affected her own community.*

partially /pˈɑːʃəlˌi/
to some extent or in some degree, indicating that something is not complete
Example: *The project is partially completed, but there is still work to do.*

particularly /pətˈɪkjʊləli/
to an unusual degree
Example: *She was particularly excited about the upcoming trip.*
in a specific or detailed manner
Example: *He described the event particularly, noting every detail.*

partly /pˈɑːtli/
to some degree, but not completely
Example: *She was partly responsible for the success of the project.*

passably /pˈɑːsəbli/
in a way that is satisfactory but not excellent
Example: *Her performance in the exam was passably good, earning a solid B grade.*

passingly /pˈɑːsɪŋli/
In a manner that is brief or not deeply engaged
Example: *He mentioned her name passingly, not dwelling on the topic for long.*

passionately /pˈaʃənətli/
in a way that shows that you have very strong feelings or emotions
Example: *She spoke passionately about her favourite cause at the rally.*
in a way that shows strong sexual feelings
Example: *He kissed her passionately under the moonlight.*

passively /pˈɑːsɪvli/
in a way that does not act to influence or change a situation
Example: *She watched passively as the decisions were made without her input.*

past /pˈɑːst/
to reach and go beyond a point near at hand
Example: *They walked past the park on their way to the store.*

pastorally /pˈɑːstərəli/
used to refer to the way religious and spiritual leaders do work that involves giving help and advice about religious, emotional, and social matters
Example: *The pastorally minded priest offered comfort and guidance to the grieving family.*
used to refer to the way teachers do work that involves giving help and advice to students about personal matters, not just helping them with schoolwork
Example: *The school counsellor handled the situation pastorally, addressing both academic and personal challenges faced by the students.*

patchily /pˈatʃɪli/
in a way that only exists or happens in some parts or situations
Example: *The rain fell patchily across the city, leaving some areas soaked while others remained dry.*
in a way that is sometimes good and sometimes bad
Example: *Her performance in the play was reviewed patchily.*

patently /pˈeɪtəntli/

in a way that is clear

Example: *His excitement was patently obvious from the huge grin on his face.*

paternally /pəˈtɜːnlli/

 in a manner typical of a father, especially one who is caring and supportive

Example: *He spoke to his son paternally, offering advice and encouragement for the challenges ahead.*

relating to or derived from a father or paternal lineage

Example: *He inherited his strong build and athletic abilities paternally, from his father's side of the family.*

patiently /pˈeɪʃəntli/

in a patient way, with calmness or without complaint or hurry despite delays or difficulties

Example: *She waited patiently for her turn in line at the grocery store, smiling at the cashier.*

patly /ˈpɑtli/

in a pat or appropriate manner

Example: *He responded patly to the interviewer's question, demonstrating his preparedness for the job.*

pausingly /pˈɔːzɪŋli/

with hesitation

Example: *She answered his question pausingly, unsure of how much to reveal.*

peaceably /pˈiːsəbli/

without violence or war, or in a peaceful way

Example: The neighbours resolved their dispute peaceably through calm discussion and compromise.

in a calm way, without arguments or trouble

Example: The children played together peaceably in the park.

peacefully /pˈiːsfəli/

in a way that does not involve violence

Example: The protestors marched peacefully through the streets.

in a quiet or calm way

Example: After a long day of hiking, they rested peacefully by the lake.

peculiarly /pɪkjˈuːliəli/

in a strange, and sometimes unpleasant, way

Example: She behaved peculiarly at the party, talking to herself and avoiding eye contact with others.

in a way that is more than usual

Example: He was peculiarly quiet during the meeting.

peevishly /pˈiːvɪʃli/

in an easily annoyed way

Example: She responded peevishly to the criticism, unable to hide her irritation.

pell-mell /pˈɛlmɛl/

in mingled confusion or disorder

Example: After the announcement, students rushed pell-mell out of the classroom.

in confused haste

Example: The children ran pell-mell through the playground, laughing and shouting.

pellucidly /peˈljuːsɪdli/

in a way that is very clear and easy to understand

Example: *The instructions were written pellucidly, ensuring even beginners could follow them without confusion.*

penally /pˈiːnəli/
in a way that involves punishment given by law
Example: *He was fined penally for violating the traffic laws.*

pendently /ˈpendəntli/
in a pendent manner, as in hanging or suspended
Example: *The chandelier swayed pendently from the ceiling, catching the light beautifully.*

penitently /ˈpenɪtəntli/
in a way that shows that you are sorry for something you have done because you feel it was wrong
Example: *She apologised penitently for her mistake.*

pensively /pˈensɪvli/
in a way that shows that you are thinking in a quiet way, often with a serious expression on your face
Example: *He stared out of the window pensively, contemplating the decision he needed to make.*

perceptibly /pəsˈeptəbəli/
in a way that can be seen, heard, or noticed
Example: *The temperature dropped perceptibly as evening approached.*

perceptively /pəsˈeptɪvli/
in a way that shows the ability to notice and understand things that many people do not notice
Example: *She perceptively identified the underlying issues in the project.*

perfectly /pˈɜːfɛktl̩i/

in a perfect way

Example: *She executed the dance moves perfectly.*

used to emphasise the word that follows

Example: *She was perfectly happy with the way the event turned out.*

to a complete or adequate extent

Example: *The instructions were perfectly clear.*

perhaps /pəhˈɑps/

used to show that something is possible or that you are certain about something

Example: *Perhaps we can meet for lunch tomorrow if you are available.*

used to show that a number or amount is approximate

Example: *There were perhaps twenty people at the meeting, though it is hard to say exactly.*

used when making polite requests or statements of opinion

Example: *Perhaps you could help me with this task if you have a moment.*

perilously /ˈperɪləsli/

in a way that can cause problems

Example: *He balanced perilously on the edge of the cliff, unaware of the danger below.*

periodically /pˌɪərɪˈɒdɪkli/

in a way that is repeated after a particular period

Example: *She checks her email periodically throughout the day to stay updated.*

perkily /pˈɜːkili/

in a happy or energetic way

Example: *She greeted everyone perkily in the morning, brightening up the office atmosphere.*

permanently /pˈɜːmənəntli/
in a permanent manner or in a way that continues without changing or ending
Example: *He decided to move permanently to the countryside.*

permissively /pəˈmɪsɪvli/
in a way that allows behaviour that some people might not allow or might disapprove of
Example: *The teacher managed the classroom permissively, allowing students to choose their own projects.*

perpetually /pəpˈɛtʃuːəli/
in a way that continues forever or for a very long time; constantly
Example: *She was perpetually late for meetings, much to her colleagues' frustration.*

perseveringly /ˌpɜːsɪˈvɪərɪŋli/
in a way that involves continuing to try to do or achieve something, even when this is difficult or takes a long time
Example: *Despite facing numerous setbacks, she perseveringly pursued her dream of becoming a doctor.*

persistently /pəsˈɪstəntli/
continuously or steadily; in a way that does not give up easily
Example: *Even after several rejections, she persistently applied for jobs in her desired field.*
firmly or resolutely; with determination
Example: *Against all odds, she persistently trained for the marathon, determined to finish.*
repeatedly or frequently; in a recurring manner

Example: The alarm clock persistently rang every morning at 6
AM.

personally /pˈɜːsənəli/
used when you give your opinion
Example: Personally, I believe that exercise is essential for
maintaining good health
in a way that is related to one's individual experience or feelings
Example: I took the criticism personally because it attacked my
work directly.
used to refer to an intentionally offensive remark about someone's
character or appearance or which is understood as being critical
Example: She took his comment about her appearance personally,
feeling hurt by his insensitivity.

perspicaciously /ˌpɜːspɪˈkeɪʃəsli/
in a way that shows skill in noticing, understanding, or judging things
accurately
Example: He approached the problem perspicaciously, quickly
identifying the root cause of the issue.

perspicuously /pəˈspɪkjʊəsli/
in a way that is clear and easy to understand
Example: The instructions were written perspicuously, making it
easy for everyone to follow.

persuasively /pəswˈeɪsɪvli/
in a way that makes you want to do or believe something
Example: She argued her case persuasively, convincing the team to
adopt her proposal.

perversely /pəvˈɜːsli/
in a way that is strange and not what most people would expect or
enjoy

Example: *Instead of celebrating their victory, he perversely*
expressed disappointment.

pettily /pˈɛtili/
in a way that gives too much attention to things that are not
important
Example: *She responded pettily to his criticism, focusing on minor*
details instead of the main issue.

pettishly /ˈpetɪʃli/
in an angry, impatient, and rude way, especially about things that are
not important
Example: *She answered pettishly when asked about the missing*
pencil.

petulantly /pˈɛtjʊləntli/
in a way that is petulant, such as being easily annoyed and rude
Example: *He sighed petulantly when asked to clean his room,*
showing his annoyance with a scowl.

phenomenally /fɪnˈɒmɪnəli/
to an exceptional degree or extent, especially in a way that is
surprising
Example: *She performed phenomenally well in her exams.*

philanthropically /fɪlɛnθrˈɒpɪk ˈɔːli/
in a way that helps poor people, especially by giving them money
Example: *He donated philanthropically to various charities.*

philosophically /fˌɪləsˈɒfɪkli/
in a way that calmly accepts a difficult situation
Example: *She took the bad news philosophically, remaining calm*
and composed.

physically /fˈɪzɪkli/

in a way that relates to the body or someone's appearance

Example: *He trains physically every day to maintain his strength and endurance.*

in a way that relates to things you can see or touch or the laws of nature

Example: *The structure was physically impossible to build without advanced technology.*

picturesquely /pˌɪktʃərˈɛskli/

in an attractive way, especially when it is old-fashioned

Example: *The village is picturesquely nestled in the rolling hills.*

piercingly /ˈpɪəsɪŋli/

in a way that makes a high, loud, and unpleasant sound

Example: *The alarm rang piercingly in the middle of the night.*

piously /pˈaɪəsli/

in a way that shows that you have strong religious beliefs

Example: *He piously attended church every Sunday without fail.*

in a way that pretends to be religious or sincere

Example: *She piously spoke about charity, though she rarely gave to any causes.*

piquantly /ˈpiːkəntli/

in an interesting and exciting way

Example: *The movie's plot twist was piquantly surprising and kept everyone on the edge of their seats.*

in a way that is pleasantly sharp or spicy

Example: *The dish was piquantly flavoured with a blend of spices that made it irresistible.*

piteously /pˈɪtiəsli/

in a way that causes you to feel sadness and sympathy

Example: *The abandoned puppy looked up at them piteously,*
                 shivering in the cold.

pithily /pˈɪθɪli/
in a clever way that uses only a few words
Example: *He pithily summarised the book in just one sentence.*

pitiably /pˈɪtɪəbəli/
in a way that makes you feel sympathy
Example: *She pitiably pleaded for help after losing her job.*

pitifully /pˈɪtɪfəli/
in a way that makes people feel sympathy
Example: *The cat looked pitifully at the empty food bowl.*
in a way that is very bad, unsatisfactory, or not enough
Example: *The team performed pitifully in the championship, losing*
                 every game.

pitilessly /pˈɪtɪləsli/
in a cruel way that shows no sympathy for others
Example: *He pitilessly criticised her performance in front of the*
                 entire team.
in a severe or unpleasant manner
Example: *The storm raged pitilessly through the night, causing*
                 widespread damage.

pityingly /ˈpɪtɪɪŋlɪ/
in a way that shows sadness or sympathy for someone else's
unhappiness or difficult situation
Example: *She looked pityingly at the old man struggling with his*
                 groceries.

placidly /plˈɑsɪdli/
in a calm and peaceful way

Example: *He responded placidly to the unexpected news, showing*
             no sign of distress.

plaguily /plˈeɪgli/
in a disagreeable or annoying manner
Example: *The constant noise from the construction site plaguily*
             disrupted their peace.

plainly /plˈeɪnli/
in a clear or obvious way
Example: *She plainly stated her opinion on the matter, leaving no*
             room for doubt.
in a simple way without a lot of decoration
Example: *The room was decorated plainly, with just a few essential*
             pieces of furniture.

plausibly /plˈɔːzəbli/
in a way that is likely to be true, or is possible to believe
Example: *He explained the situation plausibly, making it easy to*
             believe his version of events.

playfully /plˈeɪfəli/
in a way that is funny and not serious
Example: *She playfully teased her friend about the silly mistake*
             they made.

pleadingly /plˈiːdɪŋli/
in an emotional and urgent way that shows that you want something
very much
Example: *She looked pleadingly at her parents, hoping they would*
             let her stay out later.

pleasantly /plˈɛzəntli/
in a way that is enjoyable, attractive, friendly or easy to like

*Example: The weather was pleasantly warm, making the afternoon
picnic enjoyable.*

please /plˈiːz/
in a way that expresses politeness or emphasis in a request
Example: Could you pass the salt, please?
in a way that expresses polite affirmation
Example: Would you like to join us for dinner? Yes, please.
in a way that expresses scornful disagreement, disapproval, or
disbelief
Example: He thinks he can finish the project in one day? Please!

pleasingly /plˈiːzɪŋli/
in a way that gives a sense of enjoyment or satisfaction
*Example: The meal was pleasingly delicious, leaving everyone
satisfied.*

pleasurably /plˈɛʒərəbli/
in an enjoyable way
*Example: She spent the afternoon pleasurably reading her favourite
book by the fireplace.*

ploddingly /ˈplɒdɪŋli/
in a way that is slow, continuous, and not exciting
Example: He worked ploddingly through the tedious paperwork.

pluckily /plˈʌkili/
in a way that shows courage and a strong will to succeed
*Example: She pluckily faced the difficult challenge, determined to
overcome every obstacle.*

plumply /ˈplʌmpli/
in a manner that suggests fullness or roundness.

Example: *The cushions were arranged plumply on the sofa, inviting guests to sit comfortably.*
in a wholehearted manner and without hesitation or circumlocution
Example: *She plumply declared her love for him, leaving no room for doubt.*

plurally /ˈpluərəlli/
in multiple ways
Example: *The artist's work can be interpreted plurally, offering multiple perspectives.*
by more than one person or thing
Example: *The project was completed plurally by the entire team.*
using the form of a word that expresses more than one
Example: *The nouns in the sentence were written plurally to indicate more than one.*

poetically /pəʊˈetɪkli/
in a way that is like or relates to poetry or poets
Example: *She described the sunset poetically, comparing it to a canvas painted by the heavens.*
in a way that is very beautiful or expresses emotion
Example: *He spoke poetically about his love for the old town.*

poignantly /pˈɔɪnjəntli/
in a way that causes or has a very sharp feeling of sadness
Example: *She poignantly recalled her childhood memories, tears welling up in her eyes.*

pointedly /pˈɔɪntɪdli/
in an obvious way, usually to express criticism or disapproval
Example: *He pointedly mentioned her mistake during the meeting.*

politely /pəlˈaɪtli/
in a courteous and respectful manner

Example: *She politely declined the invitation to the party.*

politically /pəlˈɪtɪkli/
in a way that relates to politics
Example: *The senator spoke politically about the new policy*
            changes.

pompously /pˈɒmpəsli/
in a way that is too serious and shows that you think you are very
important
Example: *He spoke pompously about his achievements.*

poorly /pˈɔːli/
in a poor condition or manner, especially in an ill, imperfect, or
inferior way
Example: *The project was executed poorly, leading to numerous*
            errors and delays.

popularly /pˈɒpjʊləli/
in a manner that is widely accepted or favoured by many people
Example: *The new restaurant is popularly known for its delicious*
            pizza.

positively /pˈɒzɪtˌɪvli/
in a good or positive way
Example: *The team responded positively to the new project*
            proposal.

possibly /pˈɒsəbli/
in a possible manner or by any possibility
Example: *The package might possibly arrive by tomorrow if the*
            weather improves.
by merest chance
Example: *He could possibly win the contest if he gets lucky.*

potentially /pət'ɛnʃəlˌi/
in a potential or possible state or condition
Example: *The new technology could potentially revolutionise the*
industry.

potently /p'əʊtəntli/
in a very powerful, forceful or effective way
Example: *The medicine worked potently, relieving her symptoms*
almost immediately.

powerfully /p'aʊəfəli/
in a way that has a very great effect
Example: *The speech was delivered powerfully, leaving the*
audience inspired and moved.
in a way that has a lot of strength or force
Example: *The engine roared powerfully as the car sped down the*
track.

practically /pr'aktɪkli/
in a way that relates to real situations and actions rather than ideas
Example: *The solution is practically effective, addressing the issue*
directly and efficiently.
almost, but not completely or exactly
Example: *The new software is practically identical to the previous*
version.

pragmatically /prɑgm'atɪkli/
in a pragmatic manner, such as approaching situations in a practical
and realistic manner
Example: *She approached the problem pragmatically, focusing on*
workable solutions rather than ideal ones.

prayerfully /ˈpreəfʊlli/
in a way that involves praying or is like praying
Example: *She made her decision prayerfully, seeking guidance and clarity through her faith.*

precisely /prɪsˈaɪsli/
in a way that indicates exactness or accuracy
Example: *The measurements were recorded precisely, ensuring that the results would be reliable.*
in a way that expresses complete agreement with someone or suggest that what they have said is obvious
Example: *He answered, "Precisely, that's exactly what I was thinking."*

predictably /prɪdˈɪktəbli/
in a manner that can be predicted
Example: *The team performed predictably well, maintaining their usual high standards.*
as one could predict or expect
Example: *The weather turned predictably cold as winter approached.*

predominantly /prɪdˈɒmɪnəntli/
to a large extent or mainly
Example: *The population of the city is predominantly young professionals.*

preferably /prˈɛfrəblˌi/
by choice or preference
Example: *I would like to meet in the morning, preferably before noon.*

pregnantly /ˈpregnəntli/
describe something done in a manner related to pregnancy.

Example: *She walked pregnantly across the room, her movements gentle and deliberate.*

prematurely /prɪmətʃˈɔːli/
in a way that happens or is done too soon, especially before the natural or suitable time
Example: *The project was completed prematurely, before all the necessary details were finalised.*

presently /prˈɛzəntlˌi/
at this time
Example: *The manager is presently reviewing the latest sales report.*
not at this time but after a short time in the future
Example: *The results will be available presently, after the analysis is complete.*

pressingly /prˈɛsɪŋli/
in a way that is urgent or needs to be dealt with immediately
Example: *The matter was pressingly important, requiring immediate attention from the team.*

prestigiously /prɛstˈɪdʒəsli/
in a way that is respected and admired very much
Example: *She was prestigiously appointed as the university's new dean.*

presumably /prɪzjˈuːməbli/
by reasonable assumption
Example: *Presumably, he will arrive by noon.*

presumedly /prɪˈzjuːmɪdli/
in a way that is presumed
Example: *She was presumedly the best candidate for the job.*

prettily /prˈɪtili/
In a way that is attractive or pleasing in appearance
*Example: The garden was prettily arranged with colourful flowers
and neatly trimmed hedges.*

pretty /prˈɪti/
to a moderate degree or extent of something
Example: The restaurant is pretty expensive.

prevalently /ˈprevələntli/
in a very common or frequent way
Example: This type of tree grows prevalently in the region.

previously /prˈiːvɪəsli/
before the present time or the time referred to
Example: Marlene had previously visited the museum.

primarily /praɪmˈɛrəli/
for the most part
Example: The store primarily sells electronics.
in the first place
*Example: She went to the conference primarily to network with
other professionals.*

primely /ˈpraɪmlɪ/
in an excellent manner
*Example: The team performed primely during the championship
game.*

primevally /praɪˈmiːvəlli/
in a primaeval manner relating to the earliest ages or the beginning of
time; ancient
Example: The forest looked primevally untouched.

primly /prˈɪmli/
in a very formal or correct way
Example: *Sara addressed the guests primly, ensuring every word and gesture adhered to the highest standards of formality.*

princely /prˈɪnsli/
in a way that relates to a prince
Example: *He lived in a princely estate on the edge of the city.*
in a way that relates to a large or generous amount of money, usually ironic
Example: *The bonus he received was a princely sum.*

principally /prˈɪnsɪpəli/
more than anything else
Example: *The project is principally focused on improving customer satisfaction.*

prissily /prˈɪsili/
in a way that shows too much care about behaving or dressing correctly
Example: *She arranged her desk prissily, making sure everything was perfectly aligned.*

pristinely /prɪstˈiːnli/
in a way that shows that something is new, perfect, or very clean
Example: *The kitchen was pristinely clean after the renovation.*

privately /prˈaɪvətli/
in secret, or with only one or two other people present
Example: *They discussed the plans privately in her office.*
by a person or company and not by the government
Example: *The property is owned privately by a local family.*

not said or done officially or publicly

Example: *She privately expressed her concerns about the project.*

privily /prˈɪvili/

in a way that people do not know or are not told about

Example: *The decision was made privily, without any public announcement.*

proactively /prəʊˈæktɪvli/

in a way that anticipates future problems or needs and takes action to address them before they become issues

Example: *She proactively addressed potential issues before they became problems.*

probably /prˈɒbəbli/

likely to be true or likely to happen

Example: *It will probably rain tomorrow.*

prodigally /ˈprɒdɪɡəlɪ/

in a way that is very generous with money, time, and energy, especially when it is unwise

Example: *He spent his savings prodigally on luxury vacations.*

in a way that is great in amount or degree

Example: *The project required a prodigally large number of resources.*

prodigiously /prədˈɪdʒəsli/

in a way that is extremely great in ability, amount, or strength

Example: *She was prodigiously talented at playing the piano.*

productively /prədˈʌktɪvli/

in a way that produces or results in a large amount of something

Example: *She worked productively throughout the day, completing all her tasks.*

in a way that has good or useful results

Example: *The team brainstormed productively, generating many new ideas.*

in a way that involves active language use (such as speaking or writing), rather than passive understanding

Example: *He focused on productively using the language to enhance his fluency.*

profanely /prəˈfeɪnli/

in a way that shows no respect for a God or a religion, often through using language that is offensive or rude

Example: *He spoke profanely during the heated argument.*

professionally /prəfˈɛʃənəli/

by people with skills or qualifications

Example: *The report was reviewed professionally by the team of experts.*

as a job, not as a hobby

Example: *She plays tennis professionally on the national circuit.*

as a person with a particular job

Example: *He handles client accounts professionally as a financial advisor.*

proficiently /prəfˈɪʃəntli/

in a way that shows skill and experience

Example: *She completed the project proficiently and ahead of schedule.*

profitably /prˈɒfɪtəbli/

making or likely to make a profit

Example: *The company operates profitably, with increasing revenues each year.*

in a way that produces or is likely to produce an advantage

Example: *He invested in the start-up profitably, gaining valuable business insights.*

profoundly /prəfˈaʊndli/
in a way that has a strong effect
Example: *Her speech profoundly impacted the entire audience.*

profusely /prəfjˈuːzli/
with a large amount of something or in large amounts
Example: *He apologised profusely for the mistake.*

progressively /prəgrˈɛsɪvli/
in a gradual or increasing manner
Example: *The pain worsened progressively over the week.*

prolifically /prəlˈɪfɪkli/
in a way that produces a great number or amount of something
Example: *The author wrote prolifically, publishing several books each year.*

prolixly /ˈprəʊlɪksli/
in a prolix manner or at great length
Example: *He explained the process prolixly, going into every detail.*

prominently /prˈɒmɪnəntli/
in a way that can easily be seen or noticed
Example: *The new product was prominently displayed in the store window.*
in a way that sticks out from a surface
Example: *The nameplate was prominently affixed to the door.*
in a way that is important
Example: *The issue was prominently featured in the meeting agenda.*

promisingly /prˈɒmɪsɪŋli/

in a way that shows signs that something is going to be successful or enjoyable

Example: *The new project started promisingly, with early results exceeding expectations.*

promptly /prˈɒmptli/

in a prompt manner, without delay and immediately

Example: *She responded promptly to the email.*

exactly at a particular time or the correct time

Example: *The train arrived promptly at 9:00 AM.*

pronely /ˈprəʊnli/

in a prone manner or position

Example: *He lay pronely on the grass, soaking up the sun.*

properly /prˈɒpəli/

correctly, or in a satisfactory way

Example: *The machine should be set up properly for it to work.*

in a socially and morally acceptable way

Example: *She was dressed properly for the formal event.*

in a way that is right for a particular situation

Example: *It is important to address the audience properly during the presentation.*

prophetically /prɒfˈɛtɪkli/

in a way that correctly tells what will happen in the future

Example: *She spoke prophetically about the coming changes in the industry.*

prosily /prˈəʊzɪli/

in a manner that is dull or monotonous, lacking in imagination or interest.

Example: He described his vacation prosily, focusing on mundane
details and lacking any engaging anecdotes.

prosingly /prˈəʊzɪŋly/
in a manner that is characterised by prose writing or speaking,
especially when it is dull or lacks excitement
Example: She spoke prosingly about her daily routine, presenting it
in a dry and uninspiring way.

prosperously /ˈprɒspərəsli/
in a way that is successful, usually in earning a lot of money
Example: The business expanded prosperously, doubling its profits
in a year.

protectively /prətˈɛktɪvli/
in a way that gives protection or shows that you want to protect
someone from criticism, hurt or danger
Example: He spoke protectively of his younger sister, defending her
from harsh remarks.

proudly /prˈaʊdli/
with feelings of satisfaction and pleasure because of something that
you have achieved, possess, or are a part of
Example: She proudly displayed her award on the mantelpiece.
with respect for yourself, recognizing your own worth
Example: He walked into the room proudly, knowing he had earned
his achievements.

provably /prˈuːvəbli/
in a way that can be proved
Example: The scientist presented data that was provably accurate.

providently /ˈprɒvɪdəntlɪ/

in a way that can provide for future needs, especially by saving money

Example: *She invested providently to ensure a secure retirement.*

provisionally /prəvˈɪʒənəli/

in a way that is true for the present time but could change

Example: *The job offer is provisionally accepted pending background checks.*

proximally /prˈɒksɪməli/

in a way that is nearest to a point of reference in the body

Example: *The injury was located proximally to the shoulder joint.*

prudently /prˈuːdəntli/

in a way that is careful and avoids risks

Example: *She invested her savings prudently, choosing low-risk options.*

prudishly /ˈpruːdɪʃli/

in a way that shows that you are easily shocked by rude things, especially anything relating to sex

Example: *He reacted prudishly to the jokes, clearly uncomfortable with their suggestive content.*

psychically /sˈaɪkɪkli/

in a way that relates to a special mental ability, such as being able to know what will happen in the future or know what people are thinking

Example: *She claimed to have psychically predicted the outcome of the game before it even started.*

in a way that relates to the mind rather than the body

Example: *She felt psychically drained after a long day of intense mental work.*

psychologically /saɪkəlˈɒdʒɪkli/
in a way that relates to the human mind and feelings
Example: *The accident left her psychologically scarred, leading to*
                      anxiety and fear.

publicly /pˈʌblɪkli/
done, owned, or paid for by the government
Example: *The mayor publicly announced the new city initiative*
                      during the press conference.
so that anyone can see and hear
Example: *The singer publicly performed her latest song in the*
                      crowded park for everyone to see and hear.

puckishly /ˈpʌkɪʃli/
in a playful or mischievous manner
Example: *She winked puckishly at her friend, indicating her playful*
                      mood.

puerilely /ˈpjʊəraɪlli/
in a puerile or childish manner
Example: *The comedian puerilely made faces at the audience,*
                      hoping to elicit laughter.

puffingly /pˈʌfɪŋli/
with puffing
Example: *He ran puffingly to catch the bus.*

punctually /pˈʌŋktʃuːəli/
at the expected or correct time and not late
Example: *He always arrives punctually for his appointments.*

pungently /pˈʌndʒəntli/
in a way that smells or tastes very strong, sometimes unpleasantly

Example: The onions were chopped pungently, making everyone's eyes water.

in a way that has a strong effect

Example: The cheese was pungently strong, filling the room with its odour.

punily /pjˈuːnili/

in a puny or weak manner

Example: The plant grew punily in the shadow of the large trees.

punishingly /pˈʌnɪʃɪŋli/

in a way that is very difficult to do or cope with, or makes you feel very tired

Example: The workout was punishingly intense, leaving everyone exhausted.

punitively /pjˈuːnɪtˌɪvli/

in a way that is intended as a punishment

Example: The company fined him punitively for the violation of the policy.

in a way that is difficult to pay

Example: The fines were set punitively high, making them hard to afford.

purely /pjˈɔːli/

to a full extent

Example: The decision was purely based on the available evidence.

without a mixture of anything injurious or foreign

Example: The product is made from purely natural ingredients.

in a chaste or innocent manner

Example: She approached the task purely, focusing only on its true purpose.

for only one reason or purpose

Example: He attended the seminar purely to gain new skills.

purposefully /pˈɜːpəsfəli/

in a way that shows that you know what you want to do

Example: *He walked purposefully towards the podium to give his speech.*

purposely /pˈɜːpəsli/

with a specific intent

Example: *She purposely left the door open to let in fresh air.*

puzzlingly /ˈpʌzlɪŋli/

in a way that is difficult to explain or understand

Example: *The sudden change in his behaviour was puzzlingly unexplained.*

Qq

quadrennially /kwɒˈdrenɪəlli/
occurring every four years
Example: *The Olympics are held quadrennially, attracting athletes from around the world.*

quadruply /kwɑˈdrupəli/
in a way that is four times as big, many or often
Example: *The investment's value increased quadruply over the past decade.*

quaintly /kwˈeɪntli/
in a way that is attractive because of being unusual and often old fashioned
Example: *The village was quaintly charming, with its narrow streets and historical buildings.*

qualifiedly /ˈkwɒlɪfaɪdli/
in a manner that is conditional, limited, or restricted
Example: *He accepted the offer qualifiedly, noting that it depended on further negotiations.*

qualitatively /kwˈɒlɪtˌeɪtɪvli/
in a way that relates to how good or bad something is
Example: *The new product was qualitatively superior to the previous version.*
in a way that relates to what something or someone is like
Example: *The two artworks were qualitatively different, each showcasing a unique style and technique.*

quantifiably /kwˈɒntɪfˌaɪəbəli/
in a way that can be measured

Example: The project's success was quantifiably assessed through detailed performance metrics.

quantitatively /kwˈɒntɪtˌeɪtɪvli/
in a way that relates to numbers or amounts
Example: The team evaluated the results quantitatively, focusing on the precise measurements and figures.

quarterly /kwˈɔːtəli/
in heraldic quarters or quarterings
Example: The family crest was divided quarterly, each section displaying a different emblem.
at three-month intervals
Example: The company sends out financial reports quarterly.

quaveringly /kwˈeɪvərɪŋli/
with a voice that is shaking because of strong emotion
Example: She spoke quaveringly, her voice trembling with emotion as she delivered the heartfelt speech.

queasily /ˈkwiːzɪlɪ/
in a way that makes you feel likely to vomit
Example: The sight of the rotting food made her feel queasily.
in a way that makes you feel worried, unhappy, or uncertain
Example: He looked queasily at the unfamiliar paperwork.

queenly /kwˈiːnli/
in a manner befitting a queen
Example: She accepted the award with a queenly grace.

queerly /ˈkwɪəli/
in a way that is strange, unusual, or not expected
Example: The old house was decorated queerly.

queryingly /kwˈiərɪŋli/
in a manner that involves asking questions or seeking information
*Example: He looked at the instructions queryingly, unsure if he had
             understood them correctly.*

questionably /kwˈɛstʃənəbli/
in a way that seems uncertain, or wrong in some way
*Example: The decision was questionably made, raising doubts
             about its fairness and accuracy.*

questioningly /kwˈɛstʃənɪŋli/
in a way that expresses doubt about the value or truth of something,
or that shows you want an answer from someone
*Example: She looked at him questioningly, waiting for an
             explanation.*

questward /kwˈɛstwˈɔːd/
in the direction of or toward a quest or pursuit
*Example: They journeyed questward, eager to uncover the secrets
             of the ancient ruins.*

quickly /kwˈɪkli/
in a speedy manner
Example: She finished her homework quickly and went out to play.

quietly /kwˈaɪətli/
without making much noise
Example: She closed the door quietly to avoid waking the baby.
in a way that is not obvious to other people because you do not say
much
Example: He quietly supported his friend through the difficult time.

quintuply /kwɪnˈtʌpli/
in a manner that involves a fivefold increase or quantity

Example: The company's revenue increased quintuply over the five-year period, showing remarkable growth.

quizzically /kwˈɪzɪkli/
in a way that seems to ask a question
Example: He glanced at the strange instructions quizzically, unsure of what they meant.

quotationally /kwəʊtˈeɪʃən/ˈɔːli/
pertains to quotation or by use of quotations
Example: The essay was quotationally rich, incorporating several famous lines to support its arguments.

Rr

racially /rˈeɪʃəlˌi/

in a way that is based on someone's perceived race, especially when this is unfair or harmful

Example: The hiring decision was criticized for being racially biased.

in a way that relates to race or people of different races

Example: The conference addressed issues racially, focusing on how different racial groups experience inequality.

racily /rˈeɪsɪli/

in an exciting and slightly shocking way, especially because of relating to or suggesting sex

Example: The novel was written racily, with provocative themes and scenes that captured the readers' attention.

radially /rˈeɪdɪəli/

in a way that spreads out from a central point

Example: The flowers were arranged radially around the centrepiece.

radiantly /rˈeɪdɪəntli/

in a way that is obviously very happy, very beautiful or very attractive

Example: She smiled radiantly, her joy lighting up the entire room.

radically /rˈɑdɪkli/

in a radical or extreme manner

Example: The company's approach to innovation changed radically.

in a way that removes all diseased tissue

Example: The surgeon removed the tumour radically, ensuring all
             diseased tissue was excised.
in a way that supports or relates to the belief that there should be
great or extreme social or political change
Example: The activist advocated radically for social reform.

radioactively /ˈreɪdɪəʊˈæktɪvli/
in a way that involves powerful and dangerous energy that comes
from the breaking up of atoms
Example: The waste was handled radioactively, requiring special
             precautions due to its hazardous nature.
in a way that is very dangerous or harmful
Example: The area was deemed unsafe because it was
             contaminated radioactively.

raggedly /ˈragɪdli/
wearing clothes that are torn and not in good condition
Example: The homeless man wandered raggedly through the
             streets.
with an edge that is not smooth
Example: The paper was torn raggedly, leaving uneven edges and a
             frayed appearance.
in a way that is not regular or controlled
Example: His breathing was raggedly uneven after the intense run.
in a way that is not very good, because of not being organized
Example: The meeting ended raggedly, with disorganized notes and
             unfinished discussions.

rakishly /ˈreɪkɪʃli/
in a confidently careless and informal way
Example: He wore his hat rakishly tilted to one side.
in an immoral way, used especially in relation to a man who has sex
with a lot of women

Example: His rakishly behaviour was often the talk of the town, known for his numerous romantic entanglements.

rampantly /rˈampəntli/
in a way that is uncontrolled and increasing quickly, especially in a negative way
Example: The disease spread rampantly through the town, affecting more people each day.

rancidly /ˈransɪdli/
in a manner that is unpleasantly stale or spoiled
Example: The butter had gone rancidly sour.

randomly /rˈandəmli/
in a way that is unexpected or does not seem to have any reason or cause
Example: The names were drawn randomly from a hat.

rankly /ˈraŋkli/
in a way that smells or tastes very unpleasant
Example: The garbage was left out too long and smelled rankly, making the entire room unbearable.
in a complete or extreme manner, especially of something bad
Example: The policy was rankly unfair, disadvantaging the most vulnerable members of the community.

rantingly /rˈɑːntɪŋli/
with ranting; speaking loudly and angrily
Example: He spoke rantingly about the new regulations, his voice rising with frustration and anger.

rapaciously /rəpˈeɪʃəsli/

in a way that has or shows a strong wish to take things for yourself, usually using unfair methods or force

Example: *The corporation acquired resources rapaciously, using aggressive tactics to outmanoeuvre its competitors.*

rapidly /rˈapɪdli/

at a fast pace or speed

Example: *The car accelerated rapidly, quickly reaching its top speed on the highway.*

rapturously /rˈaptʃəɹəsli/

in a way that shows extreme pleasure and happiness or excitement

Example: *The audience cheered rapturously at the final performance.*

rarely /rˈeəli/

not often

Example: *She rarely eats out, preferring to cook at home instead.*

with rare skill

Example: *Her ability to play the violin so beautifully was rarely achieved.*

in an extreme or exceptional manner

Example: *Her performance was rarely matched, showcasing an extraordinary level of talent.*

rashly /rˈaʃli/

in a careless or unwise way, without thought for what might happen or result

Example: *He rashly invested all his savings in the volatile stock market, without proper research or consideration.*

raspingly /ˈrɑːspɪŋli/
in a voice that sounds unpleasantly rough
Example: *She spoke raspingly, her voice rough and grating from the cold.*

rationally /rˈaʃənəli/
in a way that is based on reason and clear thought, rather than emotions
Example: *She approached the problem rationally, carefully weighing all the evidence before deciding.*

raucously /rˈɔːkəsli/
in a loud and energetic way
Example: *The crowd cheered raucously at the concert, their excitement filling the entire stadium.*

ravenously /rˈavənəsli/
in an extremely hungry way
Example: *After the long hike, they ate ravenously, devouring every bit of food they had.*
in a way that shows that you want something very much or want a lot of something
Example: *She ravenously pursued every opportunity to advance her career, never missing a chance to improve her skills.*

ravishingly /rˈavɪʃɪŋli/
in a way that is very beautiful
Example: *She looked ravishingly beautiful in her elegant evening gown.*

rawly /ˈrɔːli/
in a way that is natural, not controlled, and often full of emotion
Example: *He expressed his feelings rawly, sharing his pain and frustration without any filter.*

in a way that does not try to hide anything about a subject

Example: *The documentary presented the issues rawly, showing the unfiltered realities of life in the war zone.*

readably /rˈiːdəbəli/

in a way that makes something easy and enjoyable to read

Example: *The book was written readably, with clear language and engaging stories that captivated the reader.*

readily /rˈɛdɪli/

in a ready manner without hesitating or without much difficulty

Example: *She agreed to help with the project readily, eager to contribute.*

realistically /riəlˈɪstɪkli/

in a manner that is according to the facts and what is possible

Example: *The budget was set realistically, reflecting the actual costs and financial constraints of the project.*

in a way that seems as if it exists

Example: *The special effects in the film were designed realistically.*

really /rˈiəli/

in reality or to emphasize an assertion

Example: *She was not really upset; it was just a misunderstanding.*

in a way to emphasize an assertion

Example: *The view from the mountaintop was really breath-taking.*

rearward /rˈiəwəd/

in a direction toward or at the rear

Example: *The pilot adjusted the aircraft's controls to move the plane rearward for a better approach to the runway.*

rearwards /ˈrɪəwədz/

towards or in the rear

Example: The seats in the theatre were arranged rearwards,
allowing everyone to have a clear view of the stage.

reasonably /rˈiːzənəbli/
in a way that shows good judgement
Example: She made a reasonably decision, weighing all the options
before choosing the best one.
in a satisfactory way
Example: The project was completed reasonably on time, meeting
all the necessary deadlines.
at a price that is not too expensive
Example: The restaurant offered a variety of dishes reasonably
priced for a quality meal.

reassuringly /rˌiːəʃjˈɔːrɪŋli/
in a way that makes someone feel less worried
Example: She spoke reassuringly, calming him down with her
confident and soothing words.

rebelliously /rɪˈbeljəsli/
in a way that shows someone does not want to be controlled or to
behave as other people expect
Example: He acted rebelliously, choosing to wear mismatched
clothes despite the dress code.
in a way that opposes the ideas of people in authority and plans to
change the system
Example: The students protested rebelliously, challenging the
administration's new policies, and calling for reform.

rebukingly /rɪbjˈuːkɪŋli/
in a manner that expresses sharp disapproval or criticism
Example: She spoke rebukingly, clearly upset by his careless
mistake and scolding him for it.

recently /rˈiːsəntli/
at a time that started not too long ago
Example: She has recently moved to a new city.

receptively /rɪˈsptɪvli/
in a way that shows that you are willing to listen to and accept new
ideas and suggestions
*Example: He responded receptively to the feedback, open to new
                ideas and eager to improve.*
in a way that relates to the ability to understand language, rather than
produce it
*Example: She listened receptively during the language class,
                focusing on understanding the new vocabulary.*

reciprocally /rɪˈsɪprəkəlli/
in a way that involves two people, or groups of people, who behave in
the same way towards each other or agree to help each other
*Example: The two teams worked reciprocally to achieve their
                common goal.*

recklessly /rˈɛkləsli/
in a way that is dangerous and shows that you are not thinking about
the risks and possible results of your behaviour
Example: He drove recklessly through the crowded streets.

recognizably /rˈɛkəgnˌaɪzəbəli/
in a way that is easy to recognize
*Example: The building was recognizably different after the
                renovation.*

recurrently /rɪkˈʌɹəntli/
in a way that happens again many times
Example: She recurrently checked her email throughout the day.

redly /rˈɛdli/
in a red manner or with a red colour
Example:　*The sun set redly over the horizon.*

reflectively /rɪflˈɛktɪvli/
in a way that shows that you are thinking carefully and quietly
Example:　*He stared reflectively out the window, lost in thought.*

reflexively /rɪflˈɛksɪvli/
in a way that is caused by an uncontrolled physical reaction
Example:　*She blinked reflexively when the light suddenly flashed.*

reflexly /ˈriːfleksli/
in a reflex manner or by means of reflexes
Example:　*He withdrew his hand reflexly from the hot surface.*

refreshingly /rɪfrˈɛʃɪŋli/
in a way that is pleasantly different and interesting
Example:　*The new restaurant's menu was refreshingly unique.*
in a way that makes you feel less hot or tired
Example:　*The cool breeze was refreshingly soothing on the hot
　　　　　　summer day.*

regally /rˈiːɡəli/
in a way that is very special and suitable for a king or queen
Example:　*She walked regally into the grand hall, wearing a
　　　　　　stunning crown.*

regardless /rɪɡˈɑːdləs/
despite what has been said or done
Example:　*She decided to go for a walk regardless of the rain.*

regimentally /ˌrɛdʒɪˈmentlli/
in a regimental way or by regiment

Example: *The soldiers lined up regimentally for inspection.*

regionally /rˈiːdʒənəli/
in a way that relates to a particular part of a country
Example: *The festival featured regionally inspired foods and crafts.*

regretfully /rɪgrˈɛtfəli/
in a way that shows that you feel sorry about something
Example: *He regretfully apologized for missing the meeting.*

regrettably /rɪgrˈɛtəbli/
in a way that makes you feel sad and sorry about something
Example: *Regrettably, we had to cancel the event due to the weather.*

regularly /rˈɛgjuːləli/
occurring at fixed intervals or following a pattern
Example: *She exercises regularly every morning at 7 a.m.*

relatively /rˈɛlətˌɪvli/
to a certain degree or extent, especially in comparison with something else
Example: *The test was relatively easy compared to the previous one.*

relentlessly /rɪlˈɛntləsli/
in an extreme way that continues without stopping
Example: *The storm raged relentlessly through the night.*

relevantly /rˈɛlɪvəntli/
in a way that relates to what is happening or being discussed
Example: *She spoke relevantly about the topic, providing valuable insights for the meeting.*

reliably /rɪlˈaɪəbli/
in a way that can be trusted or believed
Example: The train arrived reliably on time every morning.

religiously /rɪlˈɪdʒəsli/
in ways or subjects relating to religion
Example: She attended church services religiously every Sunday.
in a very careful or regular manner
*Example: He followed his workout routine religiously, never
                missing a session.*

reluctantly /rɪlˈʌktəntli/
in a way that shows that you are not willing to do something and are
therefore slow to do it
*Example: She reluctantly agreed to help with the project after much
                persuasion.*

remarkably /rɪmˈɑːkəbli/
in a manner that is extraordinary or worthy of notice
Example: The athlete performed remarkably well, setting a record.

reminiscently /ˌremɪˈnɪsntli/
recalls or evokes memories of the past
*Example: She spoke reminiscently about her childhood summers
                spent at the lake.*

remorsefully /rɪˈmɔːsfʊlli/
in a way that shows that you feel sad and guilty
Example: He apologized remorsefully for forgetting her birthday.

remorselessly /rɪmˈɔːsləsli/
in a way that shows no sadness or guilt about doing something
wrong

Example: He remorselessly took credit for the project, even though it was a team effort.

in a way that never stops or is impossible to stop

Example: The storm raged remorselessly, battering the coast for hours.

remotely /rɪmˈəʊtli/

in a remote place

Example: The cabin was located remotely in the mountains, far from any nearby towns.

from a distance

Example: She controlled the drone remotely from her tablet.

in a remote or very slightly way

Example: The new policy is only remotely related to the original proposal.

renownedly /rɪˈnaʊndli/

with renown

Example: The chef was renownedly celebrated for his innovative dishes.

reparably /rɪˈpɛrəbli/

in a way is capable of being repaired

Example: The chair was reparably damaged, so they decided to have it fixed.

repeatedly /rɪpˈiːtɪdli/

at frequent intervals

Example: She asked the question repeatedly until she got an answer.

repellently /rɪˈpeləntli/

in a way that makes you feel strong disapproval or that makes you not want to be involved with someone or something

Example: The mouldy smell in the old house repellently
discouraged potential buyers.

repellingly /rəˈpɛlɪŋli/
in a way that repels or causes aversion
Example: The dirty, overcrowded room was repellingly
uncomfortable to stay in.

repetitively /rɪpˈɛtɪtɪvli/
in a way that involves doing or saying the same thing several times,
especially in a way that is boring
Example: She tapped her pencil repetitively on the desk while
waiting for the teacher.

reportedly /rɪpˈɔːtɪdli/
according to what many people might say about something
Example: The new restaurant is reportedly the best in town,
according to local reviews.

reprehensibly /rɪprɪhˈɛnsəbəli/
in an extremely bad or unacceptable way
Example: His behaviour was reprehensibly rude, causing
discomfort among his colleagues.

reproachfully /rɪˈprəʊʧfʊlɪ/
in a way that expresses criticism
Example: She looked at him reproachfully after he forgot their
anniversary.

reprovingly /rɪprˈuːvɪŋli/
in a way that shows that you disapprove of someone's bad or silly
behaviour

434

Example: *He spoke reprovingly after she broke the vase, reminding*
              her to be more careful.

repulsively /rɪˈpʌlsɪvli/
in an extremely unpleasant or unacceptable way
Example: *The old, decaying food smelled repulsively, driving*
              everyone out of the room.

reputably /rɪpjˈuːtəbli/
according to what is said about someone or something
Example: *The hotel is reputably known for its excellent service and*
              luxurious amenities.
in a way that has a good reputation and can be trusted
Example: *She works for a reputably honest company, known for its*
              integrity and fairness.

reputedly /rɪpjˈuːtɪdli/
in a way that is said to be true, although it is not known to be certain
Example: *The mansion is reputedly haunted, though no one has*
              confirmed the stories.

resentfully /rɪsˈɛntfəli/
in a way that shows that you feel angry because you have been forced
to accept something that you do not like
Example: *He resentfully agreed to the new rules, feeling they were*
              unfairly imposed.

reservedly /rɪˈzɜːvɪdlɪ/
in a reserved manner; without openness or frankness
Example: *She smiled reservedly, not revealing her true feelings*
              about the news.

residentially /ˌrezɪˈdenʃəlli/
in a way that relates to where people live

Example: *The area was zoned residentially, with only houses and*
             no commercial buildings.

resignedly /rɪˈzaɪndli/
in a way that shows that you accept something will happen although
you do not like it
Example: *She nodded resignedly, knowing there was no changing*
             the decision.

resiliently /rɪsˈɪliəntli/
in a way that allows you to be happy or successful again after
something difficult or bad has happened
Example: *He bounced back resiliently from the setback, quickly*
             finding new opportunities.
in a way that allows something to quickly return to its usual shape
after being bent, stretched, or pressed
Example: *The rubber band stretched but resiliently returned to its*
             original shape.

resolutely /rˈɛzəlˌuːtli/
in a determined and unwavering manner, showing firm determination
or purpose
Example: *She resolutely continued her workout despite the*
             challenging weather.

resonantly /rˈɛzənəntli/
produces a deep, clear, and continuing sound, or in a way that evokes
or suggests strong emotions or ideas.
Example: *The bell rang resonantly through the quiet hall.*

resoundingly /rɪzˈaʊndɪŋli/
in a complete or a very definite way with a loud, clear, or emphatic
effect

Example: The team won the match resoundingly, with a score of 5-0.

resourcefully /rɪzˈɔːsfəli/
in a way that shows that you are skilled at solving problems and making decisions on your own
Example: She resourcefully fixed the broken machine using only a few household tools.

respectably /rɪspˈɛktəbli/
in a respectable way
Example: He dressed respectably for the important meeting.
in a way that achieves a reasonable result
Example: The team performed respectably, finishing third in the competition.

respectfully /rɪspˈɛktfəli/
in a way that shows that you want to be polite or honour someone
Example: She spoke respectfully to her elders, always mindful of their wisdom.
in a way that shows that you admire someone or something
Example: He listened respectfully to the accomplished musician's advice.

respectively /rɪspˈɛktɪvli/
in a way that relates or belongs to each of the separate people or things you have mentioned
Example: Alice and Bob won first and second place, respectively.

resplendently /rɪsˈplendəntli/
in a way that has a very bright or beautiful appearance
Example: The bride walked down the aisle resplendently in her sparkling gown.

responsibly /rɪspˈɒnsəbli/

in a way that shows that you have good judgement and the ability to act correctly and make decisions on your own

Example: *He managed his finances responsibly, saving a portion of his income each month.*

responsively /rɪsˈpɒnsɪvli/

as a positive or quick reaction to something or someone else

Example: *The customer service representative responded responsively to each inquiry.*

restfully /ˈrestfʊlli/

in a way that produces a feeling of being calm and relaxed

Example: *She slept restfully after a long day at the spa.*

restively /ˈrestɪvli/

in a way that is unwilling to be controlled or be patient

Example: *The crowd grew restively as they waited for the concert to start.*

restlessly /ˈrestlɪsli/

in a way that is unwilling or unable to stay still or to be quiet and calm, because you are worried or bored

Example: *He paced restlessly around the room while waiting for the test results.*

restoratively /rɪsˈtɒrətɪvli/

in a manner that helps to restore health, strength, or well-being

Example: *The yoga session was conducted restoratively, helping everyone feel refreshed and rejuvenated.*

restrictively /rɪsˈtrɪktɪvli/

in a way that imposes limitations or restrictions, thereby limiting freedom or the degree of something

Example: *The new policy was applied restrictively, limiting employees' access to certain resources.*

retroactively /rˌɛtrəʊˈæktɪvli/
in a way that has effect from a date before it was approved
Example: *The new law was applied retroactively, affecting transactions made six months prior.*

retrospectively /rˌɛtrəʊspˈɛktɪvli/
in a way that relates to or involves thinking about something that happened in the past
Example: *Retrospectively, she realized that the early signs were there all along.*
with effect from a date in the past before a law or decision was approved
Example: *The tax changes were applied retrospectively, affecting returns filed from the beginning of the year.*

revengefully /rɪˈvendʒfʊlli/
 shows a desire for revenge or vindictiveness
Example: *He acted revengefully after discovering the betrayal.*

reverentially /ˌrevəˈrenʃəlli/
in a way that shows a lot of respect and admiration
Example: *The students spoke reverentially about their inspiring teacher.*

reverently /rˈɛvrəntli/
in a way that shows great respect and admiration
Example: *They stood reverently as the national anthem played.*

reversedly /rɪvˈɜːsdli/
in a manner that is reversed or contrary to a previous state or direction.

reversibly /rɪvˈɜːsəbli/

in a way that can be undone or changed back to what it was before

Example: The changes to the document were made reversibly,
allowing easy restoration to the original version.

revoltingly /rɪvˈəʊltɪŋli/

in an extremely unpleasant way

Example: The garbage was left outside in a revoltingly foul state.

rewardingly /rɪˈwɔːdɪŋli/

in a way that makes you feel satisfied that you have done something
important or useful, or that something has been done well

Example: The community service project was completed
rewardingly, leaving everyone with a sense of
accomplishment.

rhapsodically /rɑpˈsɒdɪkəlli/

in a way that expresses great enthusiasm about something

Example: She spoke rhapsodically about the new art exhibit,
praising every detail with excitement.

in a way that relates to a rhapsody

Example: The composer crafted the piece rhapsodically, capturing
the emotional highs and lows of the story.

rhetorically /rɛtˈɒrɪkli/

in a way that makes a statement that does not expect an answer

Example: He asked rhetorically, "Who doesn't want to be
successful?"

in a way that relates to using language effectively

Example: The speaker spoke rhetorically, carefully choosing words
to persuade the audience.

rhythmically /rˈɪðmɪkli/

in a way that has a regular, repeated movement or beat

Example: *The drummer tapped rhythmically, setting the beat for the entire band.*

richly /rˈɪtʃli/

in a very special or valuable way, or in a way that is greater than usual

Example: *The room was richly decorated with ornate furniture and fine art.*

to a great degree

Example: *The novel is richly detailed, providing a vivid portrayal of the era.*

ridiculously /rəˈdɪkjələsli/

in a way that is stupid or unreasonable and deserves to be laughed at

Example: *The costume was ridiculously oversized.*

right /ˈraɪt/

according to right

Example: *She made the right decision, considering all the facts and ethical implications.*

in the exact location, position, or moment

Example: *He stood right next to the entrance, waiting for the others to arrive.*

in a suitable, proper, or desired manner

Example: *She handled the situation right, ensuring everyone was heard and respected.*

in a direct line, course, or manner

Example: *The path went right through the centre of the park.*

according to fact or truth

Example: *Her answer was right, confirming the accuracy of her calculations.*

all the way or in a complete manner

Example: He ate the sandwich right down to the last crumb.

without delay

Example: She responded right away to the urgent email.

to a great degree

Example: The view from the mountaintop was right breath-taking.

on or to the right

*Example: The coffee shop is right across the street from the
            bookstore.*

righteously /ˈraɪtʃəsli/

in a way that is morally correct

*Example: She righteously defended her friend, standing up for what
            was right.*

in a way that shows you believe that you are morally correct

*Example: He righteously argued his point, convinced that he was
            on the side of justice.*

rightfully /ˈraɪtfəli/

in a morally or legally correct way

*Example: She was rightfully awarded the prize for her outstanding
            achievements.*

rightly /ˈraɪtli/

in a way that is morally good or acceptable or fair

*Example: He was rightly praised for his honest and fair approach
            to the problem.*

in a correct or exact way

*Example: She rightly answered the question, providing the exact
            information needed.*

with good judgement

*Example: He rightly chose to invest in the company, based on
            thorough research and analysis.*

with freedom from doubt

Example: *She could rightly assume that the meeting was scheduled*
              for 3 PM, as it was confirmed in the email.

rightward /ˈraɪtwɚd/
at, toward or to the right
Example: *The path turned rightward, leading us to the garden*
              entrance.

rigidly /ˈrɪdʒɪdli/
in a stiff or fixed way, without bending or moving
Example: *The statue stood rigidly on its pedestal, unmoving despite*
              the wind.
not willing or able to change according to circumstances
Example: *He rigidly adhered to the old procedures, refusing to*
              adapt to the new system.
in a way that does not permit change
Example: *The rules were applied rigidly, leaving no room for*
              exceptions or adjustments.

rigorously /ˈrɪgɚəsli/
in a careful way so that every part of something is looked at or
considered to make certain that it is correct or safe
Example: *The researchers tested the new drug rigorously to ensure*
              its safety and effectiveness.
in a way that controls behaviour severely
Example: *The school enforced the dress code rigorously, with strict*
              penalties for any violations.

ringingly /ˈrɪŋɪŋli/
in a very clear and powerful way
Example: *The victory was announced ringingly, with cheers*
              echoing through the stadium.

riotously /ˈraɪətəsli/
in a very loud and uncontrolled way that is full of energy
Example: The crowd cheered riotously at the concert.

ripely /ˈraɪpli/
in a rich and colourful way
Example: The autumn leaves ripely adorned the landscape.

riskily /rˈɪskili/
in a way that involves the possibility of something bad happening
Example: He invested riskily in the volatile stock market, hoping
             for a big return despite the dangers.
in a risky way
Example: She drove riskily through the storm, pushing the limits of
             her car's performance.

ritually /ˈrɪtʃʊəlli/
in a way that is done as part of a ritual
Example: The family ritually gathered around the table every
             Sunday for their traditional meal.
in a way that is done because it is a normal thing to do
Example: He ritually checks his email first thing every morning
             before starting his workday.

roaringly /ˈrɔːrɪŋli/
in an extreme manner or to a great degree
Example: The crowd cheered roaringly as the winning goal was
             scored in the final seconds.

robustly /rəʊˈbʌstli/
in a strong or determined way
Example: She robustly defended her ideas during the meeting.

roguishly /ˈrəʊgɪʃli/
in a way that suggests that someone is doing something that is
slightly wrong or bad, but it is not too serious
*Example: He smiled roguishly as he playfully teased his friend
            about the surprise party.*

romantically /roʊˈmæntɪkəli/
in a way that relates to love or a close loving relationship
Example: They strolled romantically along the beach.
in an exciting and mysterious way that has a strong effect on your
emotions
Example: The old castle was romantically lit by moonlight.
in a way that is not practical and involves ideas that are not related to
real life
*Example: She viewed their long-distance relationship romantically,
            imagining a perfect reunion despite the challenges.*

Rome-ward /ˈroʊmwərd/
toward Rome or Roman Catholicism
*Example: The pilgrimage led the travellers Rome-ward, guiding
            them toward the sacred sites of Rome.*

rompingly /rˈɒmpɪŋli/
in a playful manner that is rough, exciting, and noisy
Example: The kids played rompingly in the backyard.

roomily /rˈuːmili/
with ample or spacious room
*Example: The new apartment was roomily designed, offering plenty
            of space for all their belongings.*

ropily /rˈəʊpɪli/
in a manner that is below par

Example: The old bridge swayed ropily under the weight of the passing vehicles.

rosily /rˈəʊzili/
in an optimistic manner
Example: She spoke rosily about the future, believing that everything would work out perfectly.
with a colour or tinge between pink and red
Example: The sunset painted the sky rosily, casting a warm pink glow over the horizon.

rottenly /ˈrɒtnli/
in a very bad or terrible manner
Example: The food smelled rottenly, making everyone hesitant to taste it.

rotundly /rəʊˈtʌndli/
in a way that is round or rounded in shape, especially of a person
Example: He smiled rotundly, his round face glowing with cheerfulness.

roughly /ˈrʌflɪ/
in a harsh or violent manner
Example: The workers handled the materials roughly, causing some items to get damaged.
in crude fashion
Example: The table was built roughly, with uneven edges and splintered wood.
without completeness or exactness
Example: The estimate was roughly calculated, lacking precise details.

roundly /ˈraʊndlɪ/
in a complete or thorough manner

Example: The book was roundly praised by critics for its depth and
insight.

by nearly everyone

Example: The proposal was roundly accepted by all members of the
committee.

in a plainspoken manner

Example: She roundly criticized the plan, expressing her concerns
clearly and directly.

with vigour or asperity

Example: The coach roundly condemned the team's poor
performance, addressing them with stern words.

rousingly /ˈraʊzɪŋli/
in a way that makes people feel excited and proud or ready to take
action

Example: The speaker rousingly rallied the crowd, inspiring them
with a powerful and motivational speech.

routinely /ruːtˈiːnli/
as a matter of regular occurrence

Example: She routinely checks her email every morning before
starting her workday.

rovingly /ˈroʊvɪŋli/
in a wandering or roaming manner

Example: He wandered rovingly through the city, exploring new
neighbourhoods without a set destination.

rowdily /rˈaʊdili/
in a way that is noisy and disorderly

Example: The fans celebrated rowdily after the big game.

royally /rˈɔɪəli/
by persons of a royal rank or lineage

Example: The event was royally attended, with members of the royal family gracing the occasion.

to a standard befitting royalty

Example: The wedding was celebrated royally, with elaborate decorations and a grand feast.

to a high degree

Example: She was royally impressed by the stunning performance of the orchestra.

ruddily /rˈʌdili/

in a way that is red in colour

Example: The sunset painted the sky ruddily, casting a warm red hue over the horizon.

rudely /rˈuːdli/

in a way that is not polite

Example: He spoke rudely to the server, showing no regard for their feelings.

in a way that relates to sex or going to the toilet

Example: The joke was rudely explicit, making everyone uncomfortable with its inappropriate content.

in a way that is sudden and unpleasant

Example: The meeting ended rudely when the power outage abruptly cut off the discussion.

in a very simple and rough way

Example: The instructions were written rudely on a scrap of paper, lacking any detail or clarity.

ruefully /rˈuːfəli/

in a way that shows that you are feeling sorry and wishing that something had not happened

Example: She smiled ruefully as she looked at the broken vase, wishing she had been more careful.

ruggedly /rˈʌgɪdli/

in a wild and uneven way that is difficult to travel over

Example: *The hikers trekked ruggedly across the rocky terrain,*
navigating the challenging path with effort.

in a way that is strong, simple, and not delicate

Example: *He built the cabin ruggedly, using sturdy materials that*
would withstand harsh weather.

in a way that is attractive and strong

Example: *He was ruggedly handsome, with a strong jawline and a*
weathered look that many found appealing.

ruinously /rˈuːɪnəsli/

in a way that causes great harm

Example: *The company's poor financial decisions were ruinously*
costly, leading to its eventual collapse.

rumblingly /rˈʌmblɪŋli/

in a way that involves a deep resonant sound

Example: *The engine roared rumblingly as the old truck struggled*
up the steep hill.

ruminantly /ˈruːmɪnəntli/

in a slow quiet way that may involve meditation or contemplation

Example: *The cow chewed ruminantly in the field, slowly*
processing its food.

runningly /ˈrʌnɪŋli/

in a rapid or flowing manner

Example: *The river flowed runningly over the rocks, creating a*
steady and soothing current.

rurally /rˈɔːrəli/

in the countryside, or in a way that relates to the countryside or
farming

Example: *They decided to live rurally, enjoying the peace and quiet of the countryside.*

rustily /ˈrʌstɪkli/

in a way that is covered in rust or old and lost its strength

Example: *The old gate creaked rustily as it swung open.*

in a way that shows that something or someone needs more practice

Example: *His performance on the piano sounded rustily, revealing that he had not played in a while.*

ruthlessly /rˈuːθləsli/

in a way that shows no thought or worry about pain caused to others when deciding what you need to do

Example: *The manager acted ruthlessly, cutting jobs without regard for the employees' well-being.*

rustically /ˈrʌstɪkli/

in a way that is simple and often rough in appearance, or typical of the countryside

Example: *The cabin was decorated rustically, with handmade furniture and rough wooden beams.*

Ss

sacrilegiously /ˌsækrɪˈlɪdʒəsli/
in a way that treats something holy or important without respect
Example: *He spoke sacrilegiously about the sacred traditions of the church.*

sadly /sˈɑdli/
in a way that shows unhappiness
Example: *She looked sadly out the window as the rain began to fall.*
in a way that is very bad or unsatisfactory
Example: *The project was sadly lacking in organization and effort.*

safely /sˈeɪfli/
in a way that does not involve experiencing or causing danger or harm
Example: *She drove safely through the storm.*

sagely /sˈeɪdʒli/
in a wise way, especially as a result of great experience
Example: *He nodded sagely, offering his wisdom to the discussion.*

same /sˈeɪm/
in a manner that is identical
Example: *They responded to the question in the same way.*

sanctimoniously /ˌsæŋktɪˈməʊnjəsli/
in a way that suggests that you are morally better than others
Example: *He spoke sanctimoniously about the importance of charity.*

sanely /sˈeɪnli/

in a way that shows that someone has a healthy mind and is not mentally ill

Example: She addressed the issue sanely, offering practical solutions without getting emotional.

in a way that shows good judgement and understanding

Example: He evaluated the situation sanely and made a well-informed decision.

sappily /sˈɑpili/

in an emotional or sweet manner

Example: The movie ended sappily with a predictable and overly sentimental scene.

sardonically /sɑːdˈɒnɪkli/

humorously, but in an unkind way that shows that you do not respect someone or something

Example: He commented sardonically on her new project.

sartorially /sɑːtˈɔːrɪəli/

in a way that relates to someone's way of dressing

Example: He was always sartorially impeccable, wearing tailored suits to every event.

satirically /sɐtˈɪrɪkli/

in a way that criticizes people or ideas in a humorous way, especially to make a political point

Example: The comedian spoke satirically about the new policy, using humour to expose its flaws.

savagely /sˈavɪdʒli/

in a violent, cruel, or very severe way

Example: The tiger attacked savagely, showing no mercy to its prey.

scalably /skˈeɪləbəli/
in a way that allows adjustments to meet different demands or levels of activity
Example: *The new software was designed scalably, allowing it to handle increased user demand smoothly.*

scantily/skˈɑːntɪli/
in a manner that is barely enough or lacks fullness
Example: *The report was scantily detailed, missing many important facts and figures.*

scarcely /skˈeəsli/
by a narrow margin or hardly at all
Example: *She scarcely finished the race before the timer ran out.*
in a way that suggests that something is unlikely
Example: *He could scarcely believe the news when he heard it.*

scarifyingly /skˈɑrɪfˌaɪŋli/
in a way that is frightening
Example: *The movie's scarifyingly realistic scenes left the audience trembling.*
in a way that shows strong disapproval of something or someone, and is usually cruel or unkind
Example: *Her scarifyingly harsh critique of his work made him feel demoralized.*

schemingly /skˈiːmɪŋli/
in a manner that is devious or cunning
Example: *He looked at her schemingly, planning his next move.*

school-ward /skˈuːlwˈɔːd/
toward school

Example: *The children walked school-ward, chatting excitedly*
            about the day's lessons.

scintillatingly /sˈɪntɪlˌeɪtɪŋli/
in a very lively and interesting way
Example: *She spoke scintillatingly about her adventures.*

scoffingly /skˈɒfɪŋli/
in a manner that shows a lack of respect
Example: *He replied scoffingly, dismissing the idea as ridiculous.*

scornfully /skˈɔːnfəli/
in a way that shows that you have no respect for someone or
something and think they are stupid
Example: *She looked at him scornfully, clearly unimpressed by his*
            excuse.

scraggily /skrˈɑgili/
in a scrawny or unkempt manner
Example: *The stray dog wandered scraggily down the alley.*

scripturally /ˈskrɪptʃərəlli/
in a way that relates to the holy writings of a religion
Example: *He explained the tradition scripturally, citing verses from*
            the sacred texts.

scrumptiously /skrˈʌmpʃəsli/
in a way that tastes extremely good
Example: *The pie was scrumptiously sweet, leaving everyone*
            wanting more.

sculpturally /ˈskʌlptʃərəlli/
in a way that relates to making something by shaping a material such
as wood, clay, metal, or stone

*Example: The building was designed sculpturally, with elegant
lines and curves.*

seamlessly /sˈiːmləsli/
without any sudden changes, interruptions, or problems
*Example: The new software integrates seamlessly with the existing
system.*

searchingly /sˈɜːtʃɪŋli/
in a way that is intended to find out the truth about something
*Example: She looked at him searchingly, trying to gauge whether
he was telling the truth.*

seasonably /sˈiːzənəbli/
in a way that is expected at or suitable for a particular time of the
year
Example: The holiday decorations were seasonably festive.

seawards /sˈiːwədz/
toward the sea
Example: The boat sailed seawards, leaving the shore behind.

secondly /sˈɛkəndli/
in the second place
*Example: Firstly, we need to gather information; secondly, we
should analyse the data.*

secretly /sˈiːkrətli/
in a way that people do not know or are not told about
Example: She secretly planned a surprise party for his birthday.

secularly /ˈsekjʊləli/
in a way that does not have any connection with religion
Example: The school curriculum was secularly designed.

securely /sɪkjˈɔːli/

in a way that avoids someone, or something being harmed by any risk, danger, or threat

Example: *The data was securely encrypted to protect it from unauthorized access.*

positioned or fastened firmly and correctly and therefore not likely to move, fall, or break

Example: *The shelf was securely mounted on the wall.*

seedily /sˈiːdili/

in a way that looks dirty or in bad condition and likely to be involved in dishonest or illegal activities

Example: *The alley was seedily lit, with trash strewn about and signs of neglect.*

seemingly /sˈiːmɪŋli/

appearing to be something, especially when this is not true

Example: *The plan was seemingly perfect, but it had several hidden flaws.*

according to the facts that you know

Example: *Seemingly, the project was on track, based on the latest progress reports.*

seldom /ˈseldəm/

in few instances

Example: *She seldom visits the museum, only going once a year.*

self-consciously /ˈselfˈkɒnʃəsli/

in a nervous or uncomfortable way because you are worried about what other people think about you or your actions

Example: *She smiled self-consciously, unsure of how her joke was received.*

in a way that is intentional, especially to impress people

Example: *He adjusted his tie self-consciously, hoping to make a good impression at the meeting.*

selfishly /sˈɛlfɪʃli/
in a manner that is solely concerned with one's own interest often at the expense of others
Example: *He acted selfishly, taking all the credit for the team's success.*

selflessly /sˈɛlfləsli/
in a manner that involves caring about other people more than themselves
Example: *She volunteered selflessly, dedicating her time to help those in need.*

semi-annually /ˈsɛmɪˈɑnjʊəlli/
every six months or twice a year
Example: *The company holds semi-annually meetings to review its progress and set new goals.*

sensationally /sɛnsˈeɪʃənəli/
in an extreme manner that emphasizes positive adjectives or adverbs
Example: *The concert was sensationally amazing, leaving the audience in awe.*
in an extremely interesting or exciting way
Example: *The movie was sensationally captivating, keeping everyone on the edge of their seats.*

sensitively /sˈɛnsɪˌɪvli/
in a careful way to avoid upsetting people
Example: *She spoke sensitively about the sensitive topic, making sure not to offend anyone.*
in a way that shows you understand a character in a play, story, or the feelings in a piece of music

Example: *The actor portrayed the character sensitively, capturing*
             every nuance of their emotions.

in a way that reacts quickly to small changes or easily records small
changes

Example: *The touch screen was designed to work sensitively,*
             registering even the lightest tap.

in a way that involves becoming upset or angry easily

Example: *He reacted sensitively to criticism, quickly becoming*
             upset over the smallest remarks.

sensorily /sˈɛnsərˌili/

in a way that relates to the physical senses of touch, smell, taste,
hearing, and sight

Example: *The artist designed the exhibit sensorily, engaging sight,*
             sound, and touch to create a fully immersive experience.

sensuously /ˈsensjʊəsli/

in a way that affects or relates to the physical senses, rather than
pleasing the mind or the intelligence

Example: *The perfume was sensuously rich, with a fragrance that*
             delighted the senses.

in a way that expresses or suggests physical, especially sexual,
pleasure or satisfaction

Example: *The dance was performed sensuously, with movements*
             that conveyed deep physical allure.

sentimentally /sˌɛntɪmˈɛntəli/

in a way that is influenced by or relates to emotional feelings,
especially about the past

Example: *She looked at the old photos sentimentally, reminiscing*
             about her childhood.

in a way that gives too much importance to emotions, especially love
and sadness

Example: He spoke sentimentally about their past relationship.

separately /sˈɛprətli/
in a way that involves keeping actions or items distinct from one another
Example: The documents were filed separately, each in its own folder.

septentrionally /sepˈtentrɪənəlli/
in the direction of the north
Example: The path led septentrionally, guiding travellers toward the northern mountains.

sequentially /siːkwˈɛnʃəlˌi/
in a way that follows a particular or fixed order
Example: The steps were completed sequentially, each one building on the previous task.

serenely /sərˈiːnli/
in a peaceful and calm way
Example: She smiled serenely, enjoying the calm morning breeze.

seriocomically /sˈiərɪəkˈɒmɪkɔli/
in a way that is both serious and funny
Example: The play was performed seriocomically, blending moments of deep emotion with witty humour.

seriously /sˈiərɪəsli/
in a sincere manner
Example: He spoke seriously about the importance of the project, emphasizing its impact.
to a severe or extreme extent
Example: The company took the issue seriously, addressing it with immediate and thorough action.

serologically /sˌɛrəlˈɒdʒɪkəli/
as pertains to or with respect to serology
Example: *The researchers tested the samples serologically to detect*
the presence of antibodies.

seventhly /ˈsevnθli/
in the seventh place
Example: *Seventhly, the report covered the environmental impact*
of the new project.

severely /sɪvˈiəli/
in a very bad or serious way
Example: *The storm severely damaged the coastal buildings,*
leaving them in ruins.
in a way that is not kind or does not show sympathy
Example: *He criticized her performance severely, offering no*
words *of encouragement.*
very plainly
Example: *The room was decorated severely, with only the essential*
furniture and no embellishments.

sexlessly /ˈsekslɪsli/
in a way that does not involve sex
Example: *They maintained their relationship sexlessly, focusing*
solely on emotional support and friendship.
in a way that is not sexually attractive
Example: *The office space was arranged sexlessly, with plain decor*
and utilitarian furniture.

sexually /sˈɛkʃuːəli/
in a way that has to do with sexual activity
Example: *The workshop addressed sexually transmitted diseases*
and safe practices.

in a way that has to do with male or female
Example: *The study explored sexually dimorphic traits, examining*
              differences between male and female animals.

shadily /ʃˈeɪdɪli/
in a way that is dishonest or illegal
Example: *He conducted his business shadily, avoiding clear*
              records and transparent practices.
in a way that is sheltered from direct light from the sun
Example: *The picnic table was placed shadily under the large oak*
              tree.

shakily /ʃˈeɪkɪli/
in a way that involves someone trembling because of being weak, ill,
or not very confident
Example: *He held the cup shakily, his nerves getting the best of him*
              during the speech.
in a way that involves small movements from side to side
Example: *The ladder stood shakily against the wall, swaying*
slightly   *with every breeze.*
in a way that seems likely to be unsuccessful
Example: *The plan was shakily outlined, with many unresolved*
              issues and uncertainties.

shallowly /ʃˈaləʊli/
in a way that measures only a short distance from the top to the
bottom, or from where something is to the ground or surface
Example: *The pond was shallowly filled with water, barely*
              covering the stones at the bottom.
in a way that is not completely certain or convincing
Example: *The argument was shallowly presented, lacking depth*
              and solid evidence.
in a way that involves taking in only a small amount of air with each
breath

Example: ` She breathed shallowly, struggling to get enough air after running up the stairs.*

in a way that does not show serious or careful thought

Example: *He addressed the issue shallowly, without considering its deeper implications.*

shamefacedly /ʃˈeɪmfeɪsˌɪdli/

in a way that is awkward and embarrassed, or ashamed

Example: *She shamefacedly admitted she had forgotten their anniversary.*

sharply /ʃˈɑːpli/

in a sudden and immediately noticeable way

Example: *The temperature dropped sharply as the sun set.*

in a way that will cut or make a hole

Example: *The glass shattered sharply when it hit the floor.*

in a strong way that is intended to be painful

Example: *She spoke sharply, making it clear she was displeased.*

in a way that is easy to see or understand

Example: *The contrast between the two colours was sharply defined.*

in a fashionable or groomed manner

Example: *He dressed sharply for the important meeting.*

in a way that is strongly felt or that has a strong effect

Example: *The movie's ending sharply affected everyone in the theatre.*

sheepishly /ʃˈiːpɪʃli/

in a way that is embarrassed because you have done something wrong or silly

Example: *He smiled sheepishly after realizing he had forgotten his lines.*

shiftily /ʃˈɪftili/
in a way that looks or seems dishonest
Example: *He glanced shiftily around the room, avoiding eye*
contact.

shimmeringly /ʃˈɪmərɪŋli/
in a manner that shines with a faint, unsteady light or has an unclear,
unsteady appearance
Example: *The lake surface glistened shimmeringly in the*
moonlight.

shoddily /ʃˈɒdɪli/
in a way that is careless, of poor quality, and that uses low quality
materials
Example: *The furniture was built shoddily, with uneven legs and*
rough edges.
in a way that involves treating someone without respect, thought, or
care
Example: *He spoke shoddily to his colleagues, dismissing their*
ideas without consideration.

shortly /ʃˈɔːtli/
in a few words
Example: *She explained the plan shortly, getting straight to the*
point.
in an abrupt manner
Example: *He answered the question shortly, without elaborating.*
in a short time
Example: *The train will arrive shortly at the next station.*
at a short interval
Example: *She checks her email shortly throughout the day.*

short-sightedly /ˈʃɔːtˈsaɪtɪdli/

in a way that does not think enough about how an action will affect the future

Example: *He short-sightedly invested all his savings in a risky venture.*

in a way that shows that a person can only clearly see objects that are close to them

Example: *She viewed the small print short-sightedly, struggling to read without her glasses.*

showily /ˈʃəʊili/

in a way that is intended to be noticed or to attract attention

Example: *He dressed showily for the party, wearing a bright, sequined suit.*

shriekingly /ʃrˈiːkɪŋli/

in a manner that involves or resembles a loud, high-pitched or piercing sound

Example: *She shriekingly called for help when she saw the spider.*

shrilly /ʃrˈɪlli/

in a way that is loud, high, and unpleasant or painful to listen to

Example: *The teacher spoke shrilly, her voice echoing through the hallway.*

in a way that is too forceful in its arguments or criticisms

Example: *He criticized the proposal shrilly, ignoring any counter arguments.*

shudderingly /ʃˈʌdərɪŋli/

in a manner that involves or is accompanied by a sudden, involuntary movement typically caused by fear, cold or strong emotion

Example: *She recalled the horror movie shudderingly, her skin crawling with the memory.*

shyly /ˈʃaɪli/
in a manner that shows timidity or reserve
Example: *She smiled shyly when introduced to the new classmates.*

sibilantly /ˈsɪbɪləntli/
in a way that makes a "*s*" or "*sh*" sound
Example: *The snake hissed sibilantly as it slithered through the*
               grass.

significantly /sɪgnˈɪfɪkəntli/
in a way that is easy to see or by a large amount
Example: *The company's profits increased significantly after the*
               new marketing campaign.
in a way that that suggests a special meaning
Example: *She looked at him significantly, hinting that she knew*
               more than she was saying.

silently /sˈaɪləntli/
without talking or making any noise
Example: *She listened silently, absorbing every word of the lecture.*
in an unnoticeable manner
Example: *He moved silently through the house, careful not to wake*
               anyone.

silkenly /ˈsɪlkənli/
in a manner that is smooth, soft, or delicate
Example: *The cat's fur felt silkenly smooth under her fingers.*

similarly /sˈɪmɪləli/
in a way that indicates that two or more things are alike
Example: *She decorated her room similarly to how she did her*
               living room.

simply /sˈɪmpli/

in a way that is easy to understand or do

Example: He explained the instructions simply so everyone could follow them easily.

in a way that provides emphasis

Example: The solution is simply brilliant.

in a direct way, without using a lot of words

Example: She answered the question simply, with just a yes or no.

in a plain way, without unnecessary things or decorations

Example: The room was decorated simply, with only a few essential pieces of furniture.

just; only

Example: She was simply too tired to continue working.

simultaneously /sˌɪməltˈeɪniəsli/

in a way that actions or events are happening at the same moment

Example: The dancers moved simultaneously, creating a perfectly synchronized performance.

sincerely /sɪnsˈiəli/

in a way that you really mean or feeling something, instead of pretending

Example: She apologized sincerely for her mistake.

in a way that is used as a complimentary close with or without "Yours"

Example: He signed the letter with "Sincerely," followed by his name.

sinfully /sˈɪnfəli/

in a way that is against the rules of a religion or morally wrong

Example: The decadent chocolate cake was sinfully rich and indulgent.

in a way that is bad for you, but enjoyable

Example: *She ate the ice cream sinfully, savouring every bite*
              despite knowing it was unhealthy.

singularly /sˈɪŋɡjʊləli/
to a way that is very great or remarkable
Example: *The book was singularly captivating, holding her*
              attention from start to finish.

sinusoidally /ˌsaɪnʊˈsɔɪdəli/
in a manner that relates to a sine curve
Example: *The signal fluctuated sinusoidally, creating smooth,*
              wave-like patterns on the graph.

sixthly /ˈsɪksθlɪ/
in the sixth position
Example: *Sixthly, he addressed the issue of team communication in*
              his presentation.

sizably /sˈaɪzəbli/
in a quite large way
Example: *The company's profits increased sizably after the new*
              product launch.

sizzlingly /ˈsɪzlɪŋli/
in a manner that is very hot or makes a sound similar to the sound of
cooking on a hot surface
Example: *The bacon was frying sizzlingly in the pan.*

skilfully /skˈɪlfəli/
in a way that shows that someone can do something well
Example: *She skilfully played the piano, impressing everyone with*
              her performance.

skulkingly /skˈʌlkɪŋli/
in a manner that is stealthy, often to avoid notice
*Example: He moved skulkingly through the shadows, trying not to
be seen.*

slackly /slˈɑkli/
in a loose or not tight manner
Example: The rope hung slackly from the tree branch.
in a manner that is careless or with less effort than usual
*Example: He worked slackly on the project, putting in minimal
effort.*

slantingly /slˈɑːntɪŋli/
in a way that slopes in one direction
*Example: The roof was designed slantingly to allow for better rain
runoff.*

slashingly /ˈslaʃɪŋli/
with a violent motion
Example: He cut through the air slashingly with his sword.

slaughterously /ˈslɔːtərəsli/
in a manner that involves extreme violence or killing
*Example: The scene was described slaughterously, depicting the
brutal and excessive violence of the battle.*

sleepily /slˈiːpɪli/
in a way that shows you are tired and want to sleep
Example: She yawned sleepily as she made her way to bed.

sleeplessly /ˈsliːplɪsli/
in a manner that involves a lack of sleep
Example: He tossed and turned sleeplessly throughout the night.

slickly /slˈɪkli/

in a way that operates or happens skilfully and effectively, without problems and without seeming to need effort

Example: *The presenter delivered the speech slickly, handling every question with ease.*

in a way that is skilful and effective but not sincere or honest

Example: *He handled the negotiations slickly, but his smooth talk concealed his true intentions.*

in a way that is smooth, and moves easily

Example: *The car glided slickly over the wet pavement.*

in a way that is very clever or attractive, but lacks real meaning or importance

Example: *The advertisement was slickly designed, but it did not offer any substantial information.*

slidingly /slˈaɪdɪŋli/

in a manner that involves moving smoothly and continuously along a surface

Example: *The ball moved slidingly across the smooth surface of the table.*

slightly /slˈaɪtli/

in a small amount or degree

Example: *The temperature dropped slightly as the sun began to set.*

slipperily /slˈɪpərili/

in a manner that is smooth

Example: *The snake moved slipperily through the grass.*

sloppily /slˈɒpɪli/

in an untidy way, in clothes that are too large and loose

Example: *He dressed sloppily in oversized clothes that hung loosely on him.*

in a messy or careless way

Example: *She wrote the notes sloppily, with smudged ink and crooked lines.*

in a way that has a lot of liquid, often unpleasantly so

Example: *The soup was served sloppily, with broth spilling over the sides of the bowl.*

slothfully /ˈsləʊθfʊlli/

in a way that is lazy and unable to make an effort to work

Example: *He spent the entire afternoon slothfully lounging on the couch.*

slowly /slˈəʊli/

in a manner that is without much speed

Example: *The tortoise moved slowly across the field.*

slumberously /ˈslʌmbərəsli/

in a way that induces sleep or drowsiness

Example: *The gentle, slumberously swaying hammock lulled him into a deep sleep.*

slily /slˈaɪli/

in a way that suggests that you know secrets

Example: *She smiled slily, hinting that she had a surprise planned.*

in a clever way, especially when it deceives people to get what you want

Example: *He slily maneuverer the conversation to his advantage.*

smokelessly /ˈsməʊklɪsli/

in a manner that does not involve smoke

Example: *The new fireplace burned smokelessly, leaving the air clean and clear.*

smoothly /smˈuːðli/

in an easy way and without interruption or difficulty

Example: *The car glided smoothly down the freshly paved road.*
in a manner that is without any sudden movements or changes
Example: *The dancer moved smoothly across the stage.*

socially /sˈəʊʃəlˌi/
in a way that relates to society or the way that society is organized
Example: *He interacted socially with his co-workers at the office party.*
at activities in which people spend time together to enjoy themselves
Example: *They gathered socially every weekend to play board games.*

softly /sˈɒftli/
in a manner that is very gentle and has no force or harshness
Example: *She spoke softly, so as not to wake the baby.*

solely /sˈəʊlli/
in a manner that is to the exclusion of all else
Example: *He is solely responsible for the project's success.*
in a manner that is without another
Example: *She travelled solely, enjoying the solitude of her journey.*

solemnly /sˈɒləmli/
in a manner that is very serious and sincere
Example: *He solemnly swore to tell the truth in court.*

someday /sˈʌmdeɪ/
in a manner that involves some time in the future that is not yet known or not stated
Example: *Someday, I hope to visit all the countries on my list.*

sometimes /sˈʌmtaɪmz/
in a manner that involves some occasions but not always or often
Example: *Sometimes, she prefers to work from home rather than the office.*

soon /sˈuːn/
in a manner that involves in or within a short time; quickly
Example: *The rain will stop soon, and we can go for a walk.*

specially /spˈɛʃəlˌi/
in a particular way or for a particular purpose
Example: *The cake was decorated specially for the anniversary party.*

specifically /spəsˈɪfɪkli/
in a way that is definite or exact
Example: *He asked for the report specifically by noon.*
in a manner that is for a particular reason or purpose
Example: *She bought the dress specifically for the upcoming wedding.*

speedily /spˈiːdɪli/
in a way that is very quick
Example: *The team completed the project speedily to meet the deadline.*

spiritually /spˈɪrɪtʃˌuːəli/
in a way that relates to deep feelings and beliefs, especially religious beliefs
Example: *She practices meditation spiritually to find inner peace.*

spitefully /spˈaɪtfəli/
in a way that shows that you want to annoy, upset, or hurt another person, because you feel anger towards them
Example: *He spitefully refused to help her after their argument.*

steadily /stˈɛdɪli/
in a way that is calm and controlled

Example: *She spoke steadily, maintaining her composure during the interview.*

in a way that is gradual and regular over a period

Example: *The garden has been growing steadily since the start of spring.*

stealthily /stˈɛlθɪli/

in a manner that is quiet and careful in order not to be seen or heard

Example: *He stealthily entered the room to avoid waking anyone.*

in a secretive manner, so that people do not realise what is happening

Example: *She stealthily slipped the note into his pocket without him noticing.*

sternly /stˈɜːnli/

in a way that shows disapproval

Example: *The teacher spoke sternly to the students about their behaviour.*

still /stˈɪl/

in a manner that does not involve motion

Example: *The lake was perfectly still, reflecting the trees like a mirror.*

in a manner that is progressive

Example: *She still works on improving her skills every day.*

in spite of that

Example: *He was tired, but he still finished the project on time.*

to an even greater degree or in an even greater amount

Example: *The movie was entertaining, but the sequel was still more exciting.*

stilly /ˈstɪlɪ/

in a manner that is quiet or calm

Example: *She smiled stilly, enjoying the peaceful morning.*

strategically /strəˈtiːdʒɪkli/

in a way that helps to achieve a plan, such as in business or politics

Example: *They positioned the advertising strategically to reach their target audience.*

in a way that provides military forces with an advantage

Example: *The army placed their defences strategically to block the enemy's advance.*

strictly /stˈɪktli/

in a way that would bring severe punishment if not obeyed

Example: *The rules were enforced strictly to ensure everyone's safety.*

in a way that is very limited or limiting

Example: *The diet was followed strictly to achieve the best results.*

in way that is exact or correct

Example: *The recipe must be followed strictly to get the best flavour.*

strongly /strˈɒŋli/

very much or in a very serious way

Example: *She strongly believes in the importance of education.*

in a way or form that is difficult to break

Example: *The bridge was built strongly to withstand heavy traffic.*

in a persuasive or determined way

Example: *He argued strongly for the need to protect the environment.*

in a way that shows that something is performing well or improving a lot

Example: *The company's sales have grown strongly over the past year.*

stubbornly /stˈʌbənli/

in a way that shows you are determined to do what you want and refuse to do anything else

Example: *She stubbornly refused to change her mind, despite the new evidence.*

in a way that is difficult to move, change, or deal with

Example: *The old machinery stubbornly resisted any attempts to repair it.*

stupidly /stjˈuːpɪdli/

in a way that is silly or unwise, or shows little intelligence

Example: *He stupidly forgot to bring his umbrella on a rainy day.*

subsequently /sˈʌbsɪkwəntli/

in a way that indicates that one action or event follows another in time

Example: *She graduated from college and subsequently started her first job.*

substantially /səbstˈɑnʃəlˌi/

in a way that relates to a large degree

Example: *The new policy substantially improved employee satisfaction.*

successfully /səksˈɛsfəli/

in a way that achieves the results wanted or hoped for

Example: *She successfully completed the marathon in under four hours.*

suddenly /sˈʌdənli/

in a manner that is very quick or unexpected

Example: *The lights suddenly went out, plunging the room into darkness.*

sufficiently /səfˈɪʃəntli/

in a manner that meets the required needs or standards

Example: *The report was sufficiently detailed to answer all the questions.*

summarily /sʌmˈɛrəli/
in a sudden manner, without discussion or a legal process
Example: *He was summarily dismissed from his job for misconduct.*

superficially /sˈuːpəfˈɪʃəlˌi/
in a way that seems to be real or important when this is not true or correct
Example: *The problem was superficially resolved, but deeper issues remained.*
in a way that is not complete and involves only the most obvious things
Example: *She examined the report superficially and missed several key details.*
in a way that only affects the surface of something
Example: *The scratch was only superficially damaging, not affecting the car's structure.*

supposedly /sʌpˈəʊzɪdli/
according to what someone told you, or according to what is believed by many people to be true
Example: *The restaurant is supposedly the best in town, according to the reviews.*

surely /ʃˈɔːli/
certainly; without any doubt
Example: *She will surely arrive on time for the meeting.*
in a way that expresses surprise that something has happened or is going to happen
Example: *Surely, you did not expect to win the contest with just one try!*

surprisingly /səpˈraɪzɪŋli/

in a way that is unexpected or unusual

Example: *Surprisingly, the quiet student gave the most impressive presentation.*

suspiciously /səspˈɪʃəsli/

in a way that makes you think that something is wrong

Example: *She glanced suspiciously at the unfamiliar package left on her doorstep.*

in a way that makes you think that someone is guilty of something wrong or illegal

Example: *The man was behaving suspiciously, avoiding eye contact and fidgeting.*

in a way that makes you think something may be true

Example: *She smiled suspiciously when asked about her surprise party plans.*

sweetly /swˈiːtli/

in a manner that is pleasant, kind or gentle

Example: *She spoke sweetly to the children, making them feel comfortable.*

swiftly /swˈɪftli/

in a way that is very quick or without delay

Example: *The cheetah moved swiftly across the savannah in pursuit of its prey.*

sympathetically /sˌɪmpəθˈɛtɪkli/

in a way that shows you understand and care about someone else's suffering

Example: *She listened sympathetically as her friend described her troubles.*

in a way that shows you agree with or support someone or something

Example: He nodded *sympathetically to show he supported her decision.*

in a style that is suitable, goes well with other things that are in the same place, and considers the feelings and needs of people who use that place

Example: *The interior was designed sympathetically to match the historical architecture of the building.*

Tt

tacitly /tˈasɪtli/

in a manner that is understood or implied without expressing directly

Example: *She tacitly agreed to the plan by nodding, without saying a word.*

taciturnly /ˈtasɪtɜːnli/

in a manner that is reserved, silent, or uncommunicative

Example: *He responded taciturnly, giving short, clipped answers to the questions.*

tactfully /tˈaktfəli/

in a way that avoids saying or doing anything that could upset someone

Example: *She tactfully suggested a different approach to avoid offending her colleague.*

tactically /tˈaktɪkli/

in a way that relates to a planned method of achieving something

Example: *He placed the pieces tactically on the board to ensure a strategic advantage.*

in a way that relates to the organization and use of soldiers and equipment in war

Example: *The general moved the troops tactically to gain the upper hand in the battle.*

tactilely /ˈtaktaɪlli/

in a way that relates to the sense of touch, to the action of touching people or things, or to how things feel when you touch them

Example: *The fabric felt soft and smooth tactilely, making it pleasant to touch.*

in a way that makes something seem real, as if it can be touched or physically felt

Example: *The artist's detailed brushwork made the painting tactilely vivid, almost as if you could feel the texture.*

tactlessly /ˈtɑktlɪsli/

in a way that shows you are not being careful to avoid upsetting someone

Example: *He tactlessly commented on her appearance, causing her to feel hurt.*

tactually /ˈtɑktjʊəlli/

in a way that relates to the tactile sense or the organs of touch

Example: *The blind man read the book tactually, feeling the raised dots on the pages.*

talkatively /ˈtɔːkətɪvli/

in a manner that involves talking a great deal

Example: *He spoke talkatively about his weekend plans.*

tamely /tˈeɪmli/

in a way that does not involve an animal being wild, dangerous, or frightened of humans

Example: *The lion sat tamely in the enclosure, completely at ease with the visitors.*

in a way that is not interesting or exciting

Example: *The movie ended tamely, without any surprising twists or excitement.*

in a way that suggests a lack of power or effort

Example: *The protest was held tamely, with only a few participants and minimal noise.*

tandem /tˈɑndəm/

one after or behind another

tangentially /tandʒˈɛnʃəlˌi/
in a way that is different from or not directly connected with
something that you were talking about or doing before
Example: *His comment was tangentially related to the main topic.*
in a way that is along a tangent
Example: *The road ran tangentially to the main highway, offering a
scenic alternative route.*

tangibly /tˈandʒəbli/
in a real way that you can touch, feel, see, or experience
Example: *The improvements in the office were tangibly noticeable.*

tanglingly /tˈaŋgəlɪŋli/
in a manner involves becoming twisted or knotted
Example: *The vines grew tanglingly around the old fence.*

tantalizingly /tˈɑːntəlˌaɪzɪŋli/
in a way that makes you feel excited and hope that you might get or
do something, especially when this does not in fact happen
Example: *The scent of fresh cookies tantalizingly wafted through
the house, making everyone eager for a taste.*

tantivy /tanˈtɪvɪ/
at a gallop or at full speed
Example: *The horse charged tantivy across the field.*

tardily /tˈɑːdili/
in a manner that is slow, delayed or late
Example: *He arrived tardily to the meeting, missing the first few
important updates.*

tartly /tˈɑːtli/

in a way that is quick or sharp, and slightly unkind

Example: *She responded tartly to his comment, clearly annoyed by his question.*

tastefully /tˈeɪstfəli/

in a way that shows style and quality and is not likely to offend anyone

Example: *The room was tastefully decorated with elegant furniture and neutral colours.*

tastelessly /tˈeɪstləsli/

in a way that is likely to upset or offend someone

Example: *His joke about the accident was tastelessly made, causing discomfort among the guests.*

in a way that is not stylish

Example: *The room was decorated tastelessly, with clashing colours and mismatched furniture.*

tastily /tˈeɪstɪli/

in a way that has a pleasant flavour

Example: *The chef seasoned the dish tastily, making every bite delightful.*

in a way that is funny or enjoyable

Example: *The comedian performed tastily, leaving the audience laughing throughout the show.*

tattily /tˈatili/

in a manner that is worn out or unkempt

Example: *Her old sweater looked tattily worn, with frayed edges and faded colours.*

tauntingly /tˈɔːntɪŋli/
in a way that is intending to annoy or upset someone else by making unkind remarks or laughing unkindly at them
Example: She smiled tauntingly as she pointed out his error.

tautly /tˈɔːtli/
in a way that is tightly or completely stretched
Example: The rope was pulled tautly across the field.
in an excited or nervous way
Example: He waited tautly for the results, his nerves on edge with anticipation.
in a way that is controlled, clear or short
Example: She delivered her presentation tautly, making every point clearly and concisely.

tawdrily /tˈɔːdrili/
in a way that is of low quality
Example: The decorations were hung tawdrily, with cheap materials and clashing colours.
in a way that shows or has low moral standards
Example: The movie depicted tawdrily scenes, focusing on sensationalism rather than substance.

tearfully /tˈɪəfəli/
done while crying or likely to cry
Example: She spoke tearfully about her departure, unable to hold back her emotions.

tearily /tˈɪərily/
with tears or weeping
Example: He apologized tearily, his eyes brimming with tears.

teasingly /tˈiːzɪŋli/

in a way that shows that you are laughing at someone or saying unkind things about them, either because you are joking or because you want to upset that person

Example: He winked teasingly at her after making a playful
*   comment about her cooking.*

in a way that causes interest or excitement, especially sexual excitement

Example: Her dress was cut teasingly low, adding an element of
*   allure to her appearance.*

technically /tˈɛknɪkli/

with regard or in accordance with a strict or literal interpretation of something

Example: Technically, the project was completed on time.

with regard to technology

Example: Technically, the new software update improves
*   performance and adds several advanced features.*

with regard to technique, as in a performance or technique

Example: Technically, her performance was flawless, with every
*   movement executed with precision.*

tediously /tˈiːdɪəsli/

in a boring way that continues for a long time

Example: He worked tediously on the report, spending hours on
*   each detail without much variety.*

teetotally /tiːˈtəʊtlli/

in a manner that involves abstaining from alcoholic drink

Example: He avoided the party's bar teetotally, sticking to his
*   commitment of not drinking alcohol.*

tellingly /tˈɛlɪŋli/
in a way that shows the truth about a situation, or what someone really thinks
Example: *She glanced at him tellingly, revealing her disappointment without saying a word.*

temerariously /ˌtɛməˈreərɪəsli/
in an audacious manner
Example: *He acted temerariously, diving into the risky venture without a second thought.*

temperamentally /tˌɛmprəmˈɛntəli/
in a way that relates to someone's character and feelings
Example: *Temperamentally, she was suited for the role.*
in a way that shows someone's mood often changes suddenly
Example: *Temperamentally, he was unpredictable, switching from cheerful to irritable without warning.*
in a way that involves something working well sometimes and not working at other times
Example: *Temperamentally, the old machine was unreliable.*

temperately /ˈtɛmpərɪtli/
in a calm and controlled manner
Example: *He responded temperately to the criticism.*

tempestuously /temˈpestjʊəsli/
in a way that is full of strong emotions
Example: *She argued tempestuously, her voice rising with frustration and passion.*

temporally /tˈɛmpərəli/
in a way that relates to time
Example: *The events were arranged temporally, with each one occurring in the correct sequence over the years.*

temporarily /tˌempərˈerəli/

in a way that does not last for long or forever

Example: *He moved to the city temporarily for the summer internship.*

temptingly /tˈemptɪŋli/

in a way that makes you want to do or have something

Example: *The bakery displayed its pastries temptingly, making it hard to resist buying one.*

tenaciously /tɛnˈeɪʃəsli/

in a very determined way and do not give up easily

Example: *She pursued her goals tenaciously, never giving up despite the obstacles.*

in a way that continues to have an influence for a long time

Example: *The old traditions were tenaciously upheld by the community.*

tenderly /tˈendəli/

in a gentle, loving, or kind way

Example: *He held the baby tenderly, whispering soothing words to calm her.*

tensely /tˈensli/

in a worried or nervous way

Example: *He waited tensely for the test results; his hands clenched in anxiety.*

with the muscles in your body or part of your body stretched tight and stiff

Example: *He sat tensely in the chair, his shoulders hunched and his muscles stiff.*

tentatively /tˈɛntətˌɪvli/
in a way that shows you are not certain or confident
Example: *He tentatively suggested a new plan, unsure if it would be accepted.*
in a way that may be changed later
Example: *The meeting was tentatively scheduled for next Tuesday, subject to confirmation,*

tenthly /ˈtenθli/
in the tenth position
Example: *She finished the race in tenthly place.*

tenuously /tˈɛnjuːəsli/
connected in a way that is not strong or certain
Example: *The two theories were tenuously linked, with only a few vague similarities between them.*
in a way that is weak, and easily broken
Example: *The old bridge was held together tenuously, with its beams barely supporting the weight.*

tepidly /ˈtepɪdli/
in a way that is not enthusiastic
Example: *He responded tepidly to the new proposal, showing little interest or excitement.*

terminally /tˈɜːmɪnəli/
very seriously; in a way that will lead to death
Example: *She was diagnosed terminally ill, with the doctors giving her only a few months to live.*

terribly /tˈɛrəbli/
to an extreme degree
Example: *The weather was terribly hot, making it unbearable to be outside for long.*

in a way that is very bad, poor, or unpleasant
Example: *The meal was terribly cooked, with under-seasoned meat and overcooked vegetables.*

very much
Example: *I missed you terribly while you were away.*

terrifically /tər'ɪfɪkli/
in an extremely good way
Example: *The concert was terrifically enjoyable, with a performance that thrilled the entire audience.*

terrifyingly /t'ɛrɪf͵aɪŋli/
in a way that makes you feel very frightened
Example: *The movie's suspenseful scenes were terrifyingly intense, leaving everyone on edge.*

territorially /t͵ɛrɪt'ɔːrɪəli/)
in a way that relates to an area that an animal or person tries to control or thinks belongs to them
Example: *The dogs barked territorially at any stranger who approached their yard.*

in a way that relates to an area of land, or sometimes sea, that is considered as belonging to, or connected with a particular country, group, or person
Example: *The countries negotiated territorially over the disputed border, each claiming rights to the land.*

tersely /'tɜːsli/
using few words, sometimes in a way that seems rude or unfriendly
Example: *He responded tersely to the question, offering no more than a brief, curt answer.*

testily /t'ɛstɪli/
in a way that shows you are easily annoyed and not patient

Example: She answered the repeated questions testily, clearly
frustrated by the lack of understanding.

tetchily /tˈɛtʃɪli/
in a way that shows you get angry or annoyed easily
Example: He responded tetchily to the minor criticism, his patience
wearing thin.

textually /tˈɛkstʃuːəli/
in a way that relates to written or printed material
Example: The editor reviewed the manuscript textually, focusing on
grammar and consistency.
relating to the way in which something has been written
Example: The professor analysed the novel textually, examining the
author's choice of language and style.

thankfully /θˈaŋkfəli/
used, usually at the beginning of a sentence, to show you are happy or
grateful about something
Example: Thankfully, the storm passed quickly, and we were able to
continue our plan.

thanklessly /ˈθaŋklɪsli/
without being thanked for something, especially for doing something
difficult or unpleasant
Example: He worked thanklessly on the project, putting in long
hours without any acknowledgment from the team.
without thanking someone or being grateful for what they have done
Example: She completed the tasks thanklessly, with no one
expressing any gratitude for her efforts.

theatrically /θiːˈatrɪkli/
in a way that belongs or relates to the theatre, or to the performance
or writing of plays, opera or films

Example: *He gestured theatrically, adding dramatic flair to his*
                         storytelling.

in cinemas

Example: *The film was released theatrically, premiering in theatres*
                         across the country.

in a way that is very extreme and not sincere, and is intended to attract attention

Example: *She reacted theatrically to the news, making a dramatic*
                         scene to draw everyone's attention.

then /ð'ɛn/

next or after that

Example: *We had dinner, and then we watched a movie.*

in addition

Example: *She can play the piano, and then she can also sing.*

as a result; in that case; also used as a way of joining a statement to an earlier piece of conversation

Example: *If you finish your homework, then you can go outside to*
                         play.

theoretically /θiər'ɛtɪkli/

in a way that obeys some rules but is not likely

Example: *The new system should, theoretically, improve efficiency,*
                         though its success in practice is uncertain.

used to say what is possible, although it may not actually happen

Example: *The new policy could, theoretically, reduce costs, but its*
                         actual impact remains to be seen.

in a way that relates to ideas and theories rather than practical actions

Example: *The class discussed the issue theoretically, focusing on*
                         abstract concepts rather than practical solutions.

therapeutically /θˌɛrəpjˈuːtɪkli/

in a way that relates to the curing of a disease or medical condition

Example: *The new medication was administered therapeutically,*
               aimed at alleviating the patient's symptoms.

there /ð'eə/
in or at that place
Example: *The book you are looking for is over there on the shelf.*
to or into that place
Example: *She went there to visit her friend over the weekend.*
at that point or stage
Example: *At that point, there was no turning back.*
in that matter, respect or relation
Example: *His expertise is impressive, and there lies the key to his*
               success.
used interjectionally to express satisfaction, approval, encouragement
or sympathy, or defiance
Example: *There you go! You did a great job," he said, giving her a*
               thumbs-up.
used to introduce the subject of a sentence, especially before the
verbs *be*, *seem*, and *appear*
Example: *There is a new restaurant opening downtown next week.*
used to begin some children's stories written in a traditional style
Example: *There was once a little girl who lived in a small cottage*
               in the woods.

thereby /ðeəb'aɪ/
by that: by that means
Example: *He signed the contract, thereby agreeing to all the terms*
               and conditions.
connected with or with reference to that
Example: *She completed the project on time, thereby ensuring the*
               team met its deadline.

thermally /θ'ɜːməli/
in a way that is connected to heat

Example: The building is designed thermally to maintain a comfortable temperature throughout the year.

thickly /θ'ɪkli/

in a way that makes a wide piece of something

Example: The painter applied the colour thickly, creating a rich, textured effect on the canvas.

in a way that covers or fills something with a deep layer of something

Example: The snow fell thickly, blanketing the entire town in a deep layer of white.

in a way that involves many people or things that are very close together

Example: The crowd gathered thickly around the stage, eager to get a glimpse of the performer.

in a way that shows clearly which country or part of a country someone comes from

Example: He spoke thickly with a regional accent, revealing his origins from the southern part of the country.

in a way that is not clear because someone is tired, ill or upset

Example: He spoke thickly, his words slurring due to his high fever.

made or done so that something has a large distance between two opposite sides

Example: The book was bound thickly, with a spine that stood out prominently on the shelf.

thievishly /'θiːvɪʃlɪ/

in the manner of someone who steals or is dishonest

Example: She glanced around thievishly before slipping the small item into her pocket.

thinly /θ'ɪnli/

made or done so that something is not thick

Example: She sliced the cucumber thinly for the salad.

with only a small number of people or things, or without the people or things being close to each other

Example: Guests were seated thinly across the large dining hall.

in a way that is not difficult to see through or to recognize

Example: The fog was thinly covering the landscape, barely obscuring the view.

with few people buying or selling shares

Example: The stock was traded thinly, with only a few buyers and sellers active in the market.

without enough money, people or supplies to operate, do a job, or provide what is needed

Example: The small charity was thinly staffed and struggled to meet all its commitments.

thirdly /θˈɜːdli/

used to introduce the third thing in a list

Example: Firstly, we need to finalize the budget; secondly, we should plan the event details; and thirdly, we must coordinate with the vendors.

thirstily /θˈɜːstli/

in a way that shows that you need to drink

Example: He drank the water thirstily after his long run.

thornily /θˈɔːnili/

in a way that is bearing or covered in sharp points

Example: The rose bushes grew thornily along the garden path.

thoroughly /θˈʌrəli/

in a very careful or detailed way so that nothing is forgotten

Example: She cleaned the kitchen thoroughly, leaving no spot untouched.

to emphasize the great degree or extent of something

Example: He was thoroughly convinced that the plan would work.

though /ðˈəʊ/

used to indicate that the information in a clause contrast with or modifies information given in a previous sentence or sentences

Example: *I wanted to go to the beach; though, it started raining, so we stayed indoors instead.*

thoughtfully /θˈɔːtfəli/

in a way that shows that you are thinking a lot about something

Example: *She stared thoughtfully out the window, lost in her own world.*

in a way that is kind and shows you are thinking about other people's needs

Example: *He thoughtfully brought her a cup of tea when she was feeling unwell.*

in a way that has been planned well and thought about carefully

Example: *The gift was thoughtfully chosen to match her interests*

thoughtlessly /θˈɔːtləsli/

in a way that does not consider how your actions or words may upset someone

Example: *He spoke thoughtlessly, hurting her feelings without realizing it.*

threateningly /θrˈɛtənɪŋli/

in a way that expresses a threat of something unpleasant or violent

Example: *He pointed the stick threateningly at the stray dog.*

thriftily /θrˈɪftɪli/

in a way that shows careful use of money or resources

Example: *She shopped thriftily, always looking for the best deals.*

thrillingly /θrˈɪlɪŋli/

in an extremely exciting and enjoyable way

494

Example: *The roller coaster raced thrillingly down the steep track.*

thrivingly /θrˈaɪvɪŋli/
in a way that involves growing strongly and vigorously
Example: *The garden grew thrivingly under her care.*

throatily /θrˈəʊtili/
in a way that low and rough
Example: *He laughed throatily at the joke.*

throbbingly /θrˈɒbɪŋli/
in a manner that is pulsating or beating repeatedly, especially with increased force
Example: *She held her throbbingly painful ankle after the fall.*

through /θrˈuː/
from one end or side to the other
Example: *The tunnel goes through the mountain.*
from beginning to the end
Example: *She read the book through in one sitting.*
to the core
Example: *The storm was through and through devastating, affecting every part of the town.*
into the open
Example: *The deer emerged through the trees into the open field.*

thumpingly /ˈθʌmpɪŋli/
in an extreme or resounding manner
Example: *The bass in the music pulsed thumpingly through the speakers.*

thunderingly /ˈθʌndərɪŋli/
with great noise or fury

Example: The crowd cheered thunderingly as the team scored the winning goal

thunderously /ˈθʌndərəsli/
in a manner that involves noise resembling thunder
Example: The audience applauded thunderously at the end of the performance.

ticklishly /ˈtɪklɪʃli/
in a way that touches your skin lightly and makes you feel uncomfortable
Example: He was ticklishly unsettled by the light touch of the feather on his arm.
in a way that makes your laugh
Example: The kitten tickled her feet ticklishly, making her laugh uncontrollably.
in a way that forces you to act very carefully
Example: The situation was ticklishly delicate, requiring careful handling to avoid any missteps.

tidily /tˈaɪdili/
in an ordered way, with everything arranged in the right place
Example: She arranged the books tidily on the shelf.

tightly /tˈaɪtli/
in a strongly controlled way
Example: He held the reins tightly to guide the horse.
in a sound manner
Example: The lid was screwed on tightly to keep the jar sealed.
in a firm or close manner
Example: They hugged each other tightly before saying goodbye.

timelessly /tˈaɪmləsli/

in a way that does not change as the years go past, or as fashion changes

Example: Her classic style is timelessly elegant, never going out of fashion.

timeously /ˈtaɪmiəsli/

in good time; sufficiently early

Example: She submitted the report timeously to meet the deadline.

timidly /tˈɪmɪdli/

in way that shows shyness or nervousness

Example: He raised his hand timidly to ask a question.

timorously /ˈtɪmərəsli/

in a way that is nervous and without confidence

Example: She spoke timorously during her first presentation, unsure of herself.

tinglingly /tˈɪŋgəlɪŋli/

in a way that causes a feeling as if a lot of sharp points are being put quickly and lightly into your body

Example: The cold air made her fingers tingle tinglingly.

in a way that involves strong emotions, such as excitement or fear

Example: The thrilling news made her feel tinglingly excited.

tinklingly /tˈɪŋklɪŋli/

in a manner that involves a series of short high ringing or clinking sounds

Example: "The wind chimes rang tinklingly in the breeze.

tipsily /tˈɪpsili/

in a manner that is slightly drunk

Example: *He danced tipsily at the party, laughing and swaying with each step.*

tiredly /ˈtaɪədli/
in a way that shows a need to rest or sleep
Example: *She sighed tiredly after a long day at work and sank into the couch.*

tirelessly /tˈaɪələsli/
in an energetic and continuous way
Example: *He worked tirelessly to complete the project before the deadline.*

tiresomely /ˈtaɪəsəmli/
in a way that is annoying and makes you lose patience
Example: *The endless meetings dragged on tiresomely, testing everyone's patience.*

tiringly /ˈtaɪərɪŋli/
in a way that causes weariness or lack of strength or energy
Example: *The long hike up the mountain was tiringly exhausting.*

titularly /ˈtɪtjʊləli/
in a way that exists in name only
Example: *He was titularly the head of the department, but someone else handled the day-to-day operations.*

today /tədˈeɪ/
on or for this day
Example: *We have a meeting scheduled for today at noon.*
at the present time
Example: *Technology plays a crucial role in our lives today.*

together /təɡˈɛðɐ/
in or into one place, mass, collection, or group
Example: *The team gathered together to discuss their strategy.*
in or into contact, connection, collision, or union
Example: *The puzzle pieces fit together perfectly.*
at one time
Example: *We all arrived together at the party.*
by combined action
Example: *They solved the problem together by pooling their ideas.*
with each other
Example: *They enjoyed spending time together at the park.*

tolerably /tˈɒlərəbli/
to a limited degree or quite
Example: *The weather was tolerably warm for a winter day.*

tolerantly /ˈtɒlərəntli/
in a way that involves the willingness to accept the behaviours or
beliefs that are different from your own
Example: *She listened tolerantly to their differing opinions.*

tomorrow /təmˈɒrəʊ/
on or for the day after today
Example: *We have a meeting scheduled for tomorrow morning.*

tonelessly /ˈtəʊnlɪsli/
in a way that does not express any emotion
Example: *He spoke tonelessly, revealing no hint of his true feelings.*

tonight /tənˈaɪt/
on this present night or the night following this present day
Example: *We are going out for dinner tonight to celebrate.*

too /tˈuː/
more than is needed or wanted
Example: *The soup is too hot to eat right now.*
in addition
Example: *I will have a coffee, and I'll take a piece of cake too.*
used to show surprise
Example: *She won the contest? I did not expect that at all—me too!*

toothily /tˈuːθili/
in a manner that shows numerous, large or projects teeth
Example: *He grinned toothily at the compliment.*

topically /tˈɒpɪkli/
in a way that is of interest at the present time, or that relates to things
that are happening at present
Example: *The news article discussed the issue topically, focusing
on the latest developments.*
in a way that relates to a particular subject
Example: *The lecture was delivered topically, addressing the key
points of the subject.*
used on the outside of the body
Example: *The doctor recommended applying the cream topically to
the affected area.*

tormentedly /tɔːmˈɛntɪdli/
in a manner that is strained and with great pain
Example: *He spoke tormentedly about the challenges he faced
during the project.*

tormentingly /tɔːmˈɛntɪŋli/
in a straining or trying manner
Example: *The long wait for the results was tormentingly stressful.*

torpidly /ˈtɔːpɪdli/
in a manner that involves being unable to move or feel
Example: *He moved torpidly after the long flight, exhausted and*
            slow to react.

torridly /ˈtɒrɪdli/
in a way that involves strong emotions, especially those of sexual
love
Example: *They exchanged torridly passionate letters throughout*
            their long-distance relationship.
with great heat
Example: *The desert sun beat down torridly, making it difficult to*
            stay outside for long.

tortiously /tˈɔːʃəsli/
in a way that involves a tort
Example: *The lawyer argued tortiously, citing various cases of*
            negligence to support the claim.

tortuously /tˈɔːtʃuːəsli/
with many turns and changes of direction
Example: *The path wound tortuously through the dense forest,*
            making it hard to find the way.
in a way that is not direct or simple
Example: *He explained the process tortuously, making it difficult to*
            follow his instructions.

torturously /tˈɔːtʃərəsli/
in a way that involves a lot of suffering or difficulty
Example: *The long wait for the test results was torturously*
            stressful.

tossily /tˈɒsɪli/
in an impudent or scornful manner

Example: *She waved her hand tossily, dismissing his concerns*
           without a second thought.

totally /t'əʊtəli/
to a complete degree
Example: *The project was totally completed by the end of the day.*

touchily /t'ʌtʃili/
in a way that shows that someone is easily offended or upset
Example: *He responded touchily to the criticism, clearly upset by*
           the feedback.

touchingly /t'ʌtʃɪŋli/
in a way that makes you feel emotion, especially sadness or
sympathy
Example: *The movie ended touchingly, leaving the audience with a*
           sense of warmth and reflection.

toughly /t'ʌfli/
in a way that is not easily broken or made weaker
Example: *The backpack was toughly constructed to withstand*
           rough conditions.
in a forceful and determined way
Example: *He argued toughly for his position, not backing down*
           despite the opposition.
in a way that is difficult to deal with or do
Example: *The negotiation process was toughly demanding,*
           requiring careful consideration of every detail.

toweringly /'taʊərɪŋli/
in a way that is very tall, often making people feel respect
Example: *The skyscraper rose toweringly above the city,*
           impressing everyone who saw it.
extremely

Example: *The film was toweringly successful, breaking box office records worldwide.*

toxically /tˈɒksɪkli/
in a manner that is harmful or damaging
Example: *The chemicals were handled toxically, posing a serious health risk.*

traditionally /trædˈɪʃənəli/
in a manner that involves past practices or established conventions
Example: *The festival is traditionally celebrated with music and dancing*

tragically /trˈɑdʒɪkli/
in a way that is very sad, and often involving death and suffering
Example: *He tragically lost his life in the accident.*
in a way that relates to tragedy
Example: *Her story ended tragically, echoing the themes of the novel.*

traitorously /ˈtreɪtərəsli/
in a way that is not loyal to your own country, social group, or beliefs
Example: *He acted traitorously by secretly sharing sensitive information with the rival group.*

tranquilly /ˈtraŋkwɪlli/
in a calm manner, without noise, violence, or worry
Example: *The lake lay tranquilly under the moonlight, undisturbed by any sound.*

transcendentally /ˌtrɑnsenˈdentlli/
in a way that is extremely special and unusual and cannot be understood in ordinary ways

Example: *"The experience was transcendentally beautiful, leaving everyone in awe.*

translucently /trænz'luːsntli/
in a way that allows light to pass through in an attractive way
Example: *The curtains hung translucently, casting a soft glow across the room.*

transparently /trænsp'ærəntli/
in a way that is clear and easy to understand or recognize
Example: *The instructions were written transparently, making them easy to follow.*
in a way that is open and honest
Example: *She spoke transparently about the project's challenges and progress.*

trashily /tr'æʃili/
in a way that involves things of low quality or little value
Example: *The decorations were arranged trashily, making the room look cluttered and cheap.*

traumatically /trɔːm'ætɪkli/
in a way that causes severe and lasting emotional shock and pain
Example: *The accident affected her traumatically, leaving her with lasting emotional scars.*
in a way that upsets or worries someone
Example: *The unexpected news was traumatically upsetting for her.*
in a way that causes or relates to physical injury by violence or an accident
Example: *The car crash caused traumatically severe injuries to several passengers.*

treacherously /trˈɛtʃərəsli/

in a way that is extremely dangerous, especially because of bad weather conditions

Example: The mountain trail was treacherously icy, making the hike extremely dangerous.

in a way that involves deceiving or behaving badly to someone who trusts you

Example: He acted treacherously by betraying his friend's trust for personal gain.

treasonably /trˈiːzənəbəli/

in a way that harms, or is considered to harm, your country or government, especially by helping its enemies

Example: His actions were deemed treasonably, as he secretly provided information to the enemy.

trebly /tˈɛbli/

to three times the extent or degree

Example: The price was trebly high during the peak season.

tremblingly /trˈɛmbəlɪŋli/

in a manner that involves shaking involuntarily, as with cold or fear

Example: She spoke tremblingly, her voice shaking with fear.

tremendously /trəmˈɛndəsli/

to a very great amount or level, or extremely well

Example: The team performed tremendously well, exceeding all expectations.

tremulously /ˈtremjʊləsli/

in an unsteady manner, often because you are nervous or frightened

Example: He spoke tremulously, his voice shaking with anxiety.

trenchantly /trˈɛntʃəntli/
in a way that expresses criticism or opinions forcefully and clearly
Example: *She spoke trenchantly about the need for reform, leaving no room for misinterpretation.*

triangularly /traɪˈaŋgjʊləli/
in a way that is shaped like a triangle
Example: *The table was arranged triangularly, with each seat positioned at one corner*

trickily /trˈɪkili/
in a way that is difficult to deal with and needs careful attention or skill
Example: *The puzzle was trickily designed, requiring careful attention to solve.*
in a way that is likely to deceive people
Example: *The salesman trickily presented the deal, making it seem more advantageous than it was.*

trimly /trˈɪmli/
in a manner that is neat, tidy and attractive
Example: *She dressed trimly in a well-fitted suit for the important meeting.*

trippingly /ˈtrɪpɪŋlɪ/
in a nimble or lively manner
Example: *She danced trippingly across the stage, moving with graceful ease.*

tristfully /ˈtrɪstfʊlli/
in a sad or melancholy manner
Example: *He spoke tristfully about the end of their friendship, reflecting on the lost memories.*

tritely /ˈtraɪtli/
in a way that has been said or expressed too often to be interesting
Example: *His apology sounded tritely rehearsed, lacking any*
genuine emotion.

triumphantly /traɪˈʌmfəntli/
in a way that suggests that you have achieved a victory or feel happy
because of achieving a victory
Example: *She raised her trophy triumphantly, celebrating her*
victory in the competition.

trivially /trɪˈvɪəli/
in a way that presents no important or serious issues to consider
Example: *The problem was solved trivially with a quick fix.*

tropically /trɒˈɒpɪkli/
in a manner that relates to characteristics of the tropics
Example: *The garden was designed tropically, with vibrant flowers*
and lush greenery.

troubledly /ˈtrʌbldli/
in a manner that exhibits worries or concern
Example: *She spoke troubledly about the recent changes at work.*

truculently /ˈtrʌkjʊləntli/
in a manner that is aggressively self-assertive
Example: *He responded truculently, challenging everyone who*
disagreed with him.

truly /trˈuːli/
in all sincerity
Example: *I am truly grateful for your help.*
in agreement with fact
Example: *She is truly the best candidate for the job.*

without feigning, falsity, or inaccuracy in truth or fact

Example: *He truly believed in the importance of honesty.*

with exactness or construction or operation

Example: *The machine operates truly, with no errors in measurement.*

in a proper or suitable manner

Example: *She dressed truly for the formal occasion.*

trustfully /ˈtrʌstfʊlli/

in a manner that is characterized by a tendency or readiness to trust others

Example: *He spoke trustfully, believing in their promises.*

trustily /trˈʌstili/

in a manner that is reliable or faithful

Example: *She completed her tasks trustily, always meeting deadlines.*

trustingly /trˈʌstɪŋli/

in a way that shows that you believe that other people are good or honest

Example: *He looked trustingly at his friends, confident they would support him.*

trustworthily /trˈʌstwɜːðili/

in a manner that is honest, reliable or dependable

Example: *He handled the sensitive information trustworthily, keeping it confidential.*

truthfully /trˈuːθfəli/

in a way that is honest and does not contain or tell any lies

Example: *She answered all the questions truthfully during the interview.*

tuggingly /tˈʌgɪŋli/
with laborious pulling
*Example: He pulled the heavy rope tuggingly, struggling to move
the load.*

tumidly /ˈtjuːmɪdli/
in a manner that is pompous or fulsome
Example: His tumidly exaggerated claims were hard to believe.

tumultuously /tjuːˈmʌltjʊəsli/
in a way that is loud, excited and emotional
Example: The crowd cheered tumultuously after the team's victory

tunefully /ˈtjuːnfʊlli/
in a way that involves a series of musical notes that is pleasant
*Example: She sang tunefully, captivating everyone with her
melodious voice.*

tunelessly /ˈtjuːnlɪsli/
in a way that has no tune and does not sound pleasant
*Example: He sang tunelessly, making it hard for anyone to enjoy
the performance.*

turbidly /ˈtɜːbɪdli/
in a muddy, thick or cloudy manner
Example: The river flowed turbidly after the heavy rains.

turbulently /tˈɜːbjʊləntli/
in a stormy or violent manner
Example: The plane shook turbulently during the storm.

turgidly /ˈtɜːdʒɪdli/
in a way that is boring and difficult to understand

Example: *The professor spoke turgidly, making the lecture hard to*
follow and less engaging.

twice /twˈaɪs/
on two occasions
Example: *I have visited that museum twice this year.*
two times: in doubled quantity or degree
Example: *She ate twice as much as usual at the feast.*

typically /tˈɪpɪkli/
in a manner that something usually happens in the way that you are
describing
Example: *She typically enjoys a quiet evening at home after work.*
in a manner to indicate that someone has behaved in a way that they
usually do
Example: *She typically dresses in bright colours for casual outings.*

Uu

ulteriorly /ʌlˈtɪərɪəli/
in a manner that goes beyond what is openly said or done
Example: *He ulteriorly agreed to the plan, hiding his true*
intentions.

ultimately /ˈʌltɪmətli/
finally, used after a series of things have happened
Example: *Ultimately, they decided to move to a new city.*
used to emphasize the most important fact in a situation
Example: *Ultimately, it is your health that matters most.*

unabashedly /ˌʌnæbˈæʃɪdli/
in a way that shows that someone is not ashamed or shy
Example: *She unabashedly expressed her opinion in the meeting.*

unaccountably /ˌʌnækˈaʊntəbli/
in a way that cannot be explained or understood
Example: *He unaccountably missed the important deadline.*

unaffectedly /ˌʌnəfˈɛktɪdli/
in a way that is natural and sincere
Example: *She smiled unaffectedly at the compliment.*

unanimously /juːnˈanɪməsli/
in a way that is agreed or supported by everyone in a group
Example: *The committee unanimously approved the proposal.*

unarguably /ʌnˈɑːgjuːəbli/
in a way that is obviously true and that nobody can disagree with
Example: *She is unarguably the best player on the team.*

unashamedly /ʌnɐʃˈeɪmɪdli/
in a way that shows someone is not embarrassed
Example: He unashamedly admitted his mistake.

unassumingly /ʌnɐsˈuːmɪŋli/
in a manner that is modest or unpretentious
Example: She unassumingly joined the conversation and shared her ideas.

unattractively /ˌʌnəˈtraktɪvli/
in a way that is unpleasant to look at
Example: The room was unattractively cluttered with old furniture.
in a way that lacks good or positive features that make someone want to do something
Example: The job offer was unattractively low-paying and lacked benefits.

unavoidably /ʌnɐvˈɔɪdəbli/
in a way that is impossible to avoid or prevent
Example: The meeting was unavoidably delayed due to technical issues.

unbearably /ʌnbˈeərəbli/
in a way that is too painful or unpleasant for you to continue to experience
Example: The heat was unbearably intense during the hike.

unbecomingly /ˈʌnbɪˈkʌmɪŋli/
in an unbecoming manner
Example: He behaved unbecomingly during the formal event.

unbelievably /ʌnbɪlˈiːvəbli/
in a way that is very surprising or difficult to believe
Example: The news was unbelievably good.

unbelievingly /ʌnbɪlˈiːvɪŋli/
in a manner that is hard to believe or astonishing
Example: *She looked at the results unbelievingly.*

unbiasedly /ˈʌnˈbaɪəstli/
in a manner that is fair and not likely to support one particular person
or group involved in something
Example: *The judge reviewed the evidence unbiasedly.*

unblinkingly /ʌnblˈɪŋkɪŋli/
in a way that involves looking directly and continuously at a person
or thing
Example: *He stared unblinkingly at the screen, focused on the
             details.*
in a way that is completely clear, or shows no doubt or fear
Example: *She spoke unblinkingly about her plans for the future.*

unblushingly /ʌnˈblʌʃɪŋli/
in a manner that is shameless and immodest
Example: *He unblushingly admitted to taking the credit for the
             project.*

uncannily /ʌnkˈɑnɪli/
in a way that is strange and difficult to explain
Example: *The twins looked uncannily alike.*

uncertainly /ʌnsˈɜːtənli/
in a way that shows that you do not know what to do or believe, or
are not able to decide about something
Example: *She spoke uncertainly about her plans for the weekend.*

unchangingly /ʌntʃˈeɪndʒɪŋli/
in a manner that always stays the same and not becoming different

Example: *The weather remained unchangingly warm throughout the week.*

uncharitably /ʌntʃˈarɪtəbli/
in a way that is unkind or ungenerous
Example: *He uncharitably criticized his colleague's work.*

unchastely /ʌntʃˈeɪstli/
in a manner that is impure or indecent
Example: *She behaved unchastely at the party.*

uncheerfully /ʌntʃˈiəfəli/
in a manner that is gloomy or miserable
Example: *He uncheerfully accepted the news of the delay.*

unchivalrously /ʌnʃˈɪvəlrəsli/
in a manner that is not gallant or courteous
Example: *He unchivalrously ignored her request for assistance.*

uncivilly /ˈʌnˈsɪvlli/
in a way that lacks good manners or is not polite
Example: *He spoke uncivilly to his co-workers during the meeting.*

unclearly /ʌnklˈiəli/
in a way that is not obvious or easy to see, understand, or know
Example: *The instructions were unclearly written, causing confusion.*

uncomfortably /ʌnkˈʌmftəbli/
in a way that does not feel comfortable and pleasant
Example: *The chair was uncomfortably hard and made sitting difficult.*
in a way that makes you feel slightly embarrassed, or that shows that you feel slightly embarrassed

Example: She smiled uncomfortably after tripping in front of
everyone.

uncommonly /ʌnkˈɒmənli/
to an unusual degree or in a manner that is rare
Example: The weather was uncommonly warm for this time of year.

unconcernedly /ˈʌnkənˈsɜːndli/
in a way that shows someone is not worried or interested
Example: He unconcernedly brushed off the minor error in the
report.

unconsciously /ʌnkˈɒnʃəsli/
without being aware of what you are doing
Example: He unconsciously tapped his fingers on the table while
thinking.

uncontrollably /ʌnkəntrˈəʊləbli/
in a way that is too strong or violent to be controlled
Example: She laughed uncontrollably at the joke.

unconvincingly /ʌnkənvˈɪnsɪŋli/
in a way that does not seem true or real
Example: He explained the situation unconvincingly, leaving
everyone doubtful.

uncouthly /ʌnˈkuːθli/
in a manner that lacks good manners, refinement or grace
Example: He behaved uncouthly at the formal dinner, speaking
loudly, and making inappropriate jokes.

uncritically /ˈʌnˈkrɪtɪkəlli/
in a manner that is not severely judgemental

Example: *She accepted the information uncritically, without*
             questioning its accuracy.

unctuously /ˈʌŋktjʊəsli/
in a way that is friendly or that gives praise which is not sincere and
is therefore unpleasant
Example: *He complimented her unctuously, making her feel*
             uncomfortable.

undauntedly /ʌnˈdɔːntɪdli/
in a manner that shows that you are not afraid or worried about
dealing with something
Example: *She undauntedly faced the challenging project despite the*
             difficulties.

undecidedly /ˈʌndɪˈsaɪdɪdli/
in a manner that involves not having made up one's mind
Example: *He spoke undecidedly about his plans for the weekend.*

undeniably /ˌʌndɪnˈaɪəbli/
in a way that is certainly true
Example: *The results are undeniably impressive.*

understandingly /ˌʌndəˈstandɪŋli/
in a way that shows sympathy for other people's problems and the
ability to forgive them when they do something wrong
Example: *She smiled understandingly, acknowledging his difficult*
             situation.

understatedly /ˌʌndəstˈeɪtɪdli/
in a manner that avoids obvious emphasis or embellishment
Example: *He understatedly mentioned his achievements,*
             downplaying his success.

undeservingly /ˈʌndɪˈzɜːvɪŋli/
in a way that is not right or that someone does not deserve
Example: *She felt that she was undeservingly praised for the team's work.*

undividedly /ˈʌndɪˈvaɪdɪdli/
in an manner that is complete or total
Example: *He listened undividedly to her concerns, giving her his full attention.*

undoubtedly /ʌndˈaʊtɪdli/
used to emphasize that something is true
Example: *She is undoubtedly the best candidate for the job.*

unduly /ˈʌnˈdjuːlɪ/
more than is necessary, acceptable, or reasonable
Example: *The project was delayed unduly due to unforeseen complications.*

uneasily /ʌnˈiːzɪli/
in a way that shows you are slightly worried or uncomfortable about a particular situation
Example: *She glanced uneasily at the darkening sky.*
in a way that does not fit well or seems awkward or unlikely
Example: *The solution seemed uneasily fitting for the complex problem.*

unemotionally /ʌnɪmˈəʊʃənəli/
without the expression of strong feeling
Example: *He explained the situation unemotionally, keeping his feelings in check.*

unendingly /ʌnˈendɪŋli/
in a way that does not stop, or seems to have no end

Example: The meeting seemed to drag on unendingly.

unenviously /ʌnˈɛnvɪəsli/
in a manner that is marked by an absence of envy
Example: She accepted the award unenviously, genuinely happy for her colleague.

unequally /ʌnˈiːkwəli/
unfairly and not in the same way
Example: The resources were distributed unequally among the team members.
not in equal amounts
Example: The funds were divided unequally between the two projects.

unequivocally /ʌnɪkwˈɪvəkəli/
in a way that is total, or expressed very clearly with no doubt
Example: She unequivocally stated her position on the matter.

unerringly /ʌnˈɜːrɪŋli/
in a way that hits a target without failing
Example: He unerringly made every shot during the competition.
in a way that is always accurate or good, never failing or making a mistake
Example: She unerringly followed the recipe, ensuring a perfect dish every time.

unethically /ʌnˈɛθɪkli/
in a manner that is not morally acceptable
Example: He unethically used insider information to gain an advantage.

unevenly /ʌnˈiːvənli/
in a way that is not level, equal, flat, or continuous

518

Example: *The tiles were laid unevenly across the floor.*
in a way that is not always of a good quality
Example: *The team's performance varied unevenly throughout the season.*

unexpectedly /ˌʌnɛkspˈɛktɪdli/
in a manner that surprises you because you did not think that it was likely to happen
Example: *The rain arrived unexpectedly, catching everyone off guard.*

unfailingly /ʌnfˈeɪlɪŋli/
in a way that always shows itself
Example: *She unfailingly arrives at work early every day.*

unfairly /ʌnfˈeəli/
in a way that is not right or does not involve equal treatment
Example: *The decision was made unfairly, favouring one side over the other.*

unfaithfully /ˈʌnˈfeɪθfʊlli/
in a manner that does not adhere to vows, allegiance or duty
Example: *He acted unfaithfully by breaking his promises.*

unfalteringly /ʌnˈfɔːltərɪŋli/
in a constant manner
Example: *She worked unfalteringly until the project was complete.*

unfamiliarly /ˈʌnfəˈmɪljəli/
in a manner that is not known or experienced
Example: *He spoke unfamiliarly, using words he rarely used.*

unfashionably /ʌnfˈaʃənəbli/
in a way that is not popular or fashionable at a particular time

Example: *She dressed unfashionably, wearing clothes from last*
                  season.

unfavourably /ʌnˈeɪvərəbli/
in a way that does not give you an advantage or a good chance of success
Example: *The new policy was viewed unfavourably by the*
                  employees.
in a negative way that shows that you do not like something
Example: *She spoke unfavourably about the changes to the plan.*

unfeelingly /ʌnˈfiːlɪŋli/
in a manner without sympathy
Example: *He responded unfeelingly, showing no concern for her*
                  emotions.

unflaggingly /ʌnˈflɑɡɪŋli/
in a consistently strong or tireless manner
Example: *She worked unflaggingly to complete the project on time.*

unflappably /ʌnˈflɑpəbli/
in a manner that is composed or hard to upset
Example: *He handled the crisis unflappably, remaining calm and*
                  composed throughout.

unflinchingly /ʌnflˈɪntʃɪŋli/
in a way that shows someone is not frightened or is not trying to avoid something
Example: *She faced the tough questions unflinchingly during the*
                  interview.

unfortunately /ʌnfˈɔːtʃənətli/
used to say that something is sad, disappointing, or has a bad effect

Example: *Unfortunately, the meeting was cancelled due to a*
             scheduling conflict.
in a regrettable, unlucky, or unsuitable manner
Example: *Unfortunately, the weather was too stormy for our picnic.*
`

ungallantly /ʌnˈɡaləntli/
in a way that is not marked by courtesy or valour
Example: *He acted ungallantly by interrupting her speech without*
             any apology.

ungenerously /ʌndʒˈɛnərəsli/
in a way that shows unwillingness to give money or help
Example: *He answered the request for a donation ungenerously,*
             offering only a small amount.
in a way that is unkind or unfair, because someone deserves better
Example: *She responded ungenerously to his heartfelt apology,*
             refusing to forgive him.

ungenially /ʌndʒˈiːnɪəli/
in a manner that is not pleasant or cheerful
Example: *He greeted the guests ungenially, barely acknowledging*
             their presence.

ungraciously /ˈʌnˈɡreɪʃəsli/
in a way that is not polite or friendly, especially towards somebody
who is being kind to you
Example: *She accepted the compliment ungraciously, barely*
             thanking him.

ungratefully /ʌnˈɡreɪtfʊlli/
in a way that does not show or express thanks for something that
somebody has done for you or given to you opposite gratefully
Example: *He reacted ungratefully to the generous gift, complaining*
             about its size.

ungrudgingly /ˈʌnˈɡrʌdʒɪŋli/

in a manner without envy or reluctance

Example: *She accepted the help ungrudgingly, appreciating the support.*

unguardedly /ˈʌnˈɡɑːdɪdli/

in a manner that is open or frank

Example: *He spoke unguardedly about his personal life during the interview.*

unhappily /ʌnhˈapɪli/

in a way that shows or involves sadness

Example: *He answered the question unhappily, his disappointment clear.*

unhealthily /ʌnhˈɛlθɪli/

in a way that is not good for your health

Example: *She ate unhealthily, consuming too much junk food and sugary drinks.*

in a way that is not good for someone or not acceptable because it does not seem normal

Example: *His behaviour changed unhealthily, becoming increasingly erratic and unpredictable.*

unheedingly /ˈʌnˈhiːdɪŋli/

in a manner that shows no awareness or gives no attention

Example: *She walked unheedingly past the warning signs, unaware of the danger.*

unhelpfully /ʌnhˈɛlpfəli/

in a way that does not offer assistance

Example: *He responded unhelpfully to her questions, giving vague and confusing answers.*

unhesitatingly /ʌnhˈɛsɪtˌeɪtɪŋli/
in an immediate or confident manner, without any doubt or anxiety
Example: *He unhesitatingly agreed to help with the project.*

unhurriedly /ˈʌnˈhʌrɪdli/
in a relaxed and calm way; not too quickly
Example: *She walked unhurriedly through the park, enjoying the peaceful surroundings.*

uniformly /jˈuːnɪfˌɔːmli/
in a way that is the same everywhere or for everyone
Example: *The paint was applied uniformly across the entire wall.*

unilaterally /jˌuːnɪlˈatərəli/
in a way that involves doing or deciding something without first asking or agreeing with another person, group or country
Example: *He made the decision unilaterally, without consulting the rest of the team.*

unimpeachably /ˌʌnɪmpˈiːtʃəbli/
in a manner that unquestionable as to honesty
Example: *Her conduct was unimpeachably ethical throughout the investigation.*

unimpressively /ʌnɪmprˈɛsɪvli/
in a manner that is not attracting or deserving particular attention, admiration or attention
Example: *The performance ended unimpressively, leaving the audience underwhelmed.*

uninhibitedly /ˈʌnɪnˈhɪbɪtɪdli/
in a manner that is free from inhibition

Example: She danced uninhibitedly, letting the music guide her every move.

unintelligently /ˈʌnɪnˈtelɪdʒəntli/
in a way that shows a lack of intelligence
Example: He answered the questions unintelligently, clearly not understanding the topic.

unintelligibly /ˌʌnɪntˈɛlɪdʒəbəli/
in a way that is impossible to understand
Example: She spoke unintelligibly, her words slurring together and making no sense.

uninterestedly /ˈʌnˈɪntrɪstɪdli/
in a manner that does not have the mind or feelings engaged
Example: He listened uninterestedly to the presentation, clearly bored by the topic.

uninvitingly /ˈʌnɪnˈvaɪtɪŋli/
in a manner that is not appealing or attractive
Example: The dark, cluttered room looked uninvitingly cold and unwelcoming.

uniquely /juːnˈiːkli/
in a way that is unusual or special in some way
Example: Her artwork was uniquely vibrant, setting it apart from the others.

unitedly /ˈjʊˈnaɪtɪdli/
in a manner that is harmonious or that involves being in agreement
Example: The team worked unitedly to achieve their common goal.

universally /jˌuːnɪvˈɜːsəli/
in a way that exists everywhere, or involves everyone

Example: *The need for clean water is universally acknowledged as a basic human right.*

univocally /jˈuːnivˈəʊkəli/
in a manner that has one meaning only
Example: *The instructions were given univocally, leaving no room for misunderstanding.*

unjustly /ʌndʒˈʌstli/
in a way that is not in accordance with accepted standards of fairness or justice
Example: *He was punished unjustly, as he had not committed the offense.*

unkindly /ʌnkˈaɪndli/
in a way that does not treat someone very well, or does not consider someone's feelings
Example: *She spoke unkindly, ignoring how her words would hurt his feelings.*

unknowingly /ʌnnˈəʊɪŋli/
in a way that is not conscious of a particular situation or problem
Example: *He unknowingly entered the restricted area, unaware of the security rules.*

unlawfully /ʌnlˈɔːfəli/
in a way that is not allowed by law
Example: *He was charged with operating the business unlawfully, without the necessary permits.*

unluckily /ʌnlˈʌkili/
used in a way to comment on something bad or unpleasant that happens to someone
Example: *Unluckily, the car broke down in the middle of the trip.*

unmelodiously /ʌnmɛlˈəʊdɪəsli/

in a manner that is not sweet or agreeable in sound

Example: *The music played unmelodiously, producing discordant and jarring sounds.*

unmercifully /ʌnmˈɜːsɪfəli/

in a manner that is done a lot, showing no pity

Example: *The critic reviewed the play unmercifully, highlighting every flaw without compassion.*

unmindfully /ʌnˈmaɪndfʊlli/

in a careless or forgetful fashion

Example: *She spoke unmindfully, not realizing her words would offend him.*

unmusically /ˈʌnˈmjuːzɪkəlli/

in a manner that is not harmonious

Example: *The piano was played so unmusically that it hurt my ears.*

unnaturally /ʌnnˈatʃəɹəli/

in a way that is not in accordance with nature

Example: *The flowers bloomed unnaturally in the middle of winter.*

unnecessarily /ʌnnˌɛsɪsˈɛɹəli/

in a way that is not needed or wanted, or more than is needed or wanted

Example: *He unnecessarily added extra salt to the soup.*

unnervingly /ʌnnˈɜːvɪŋli/

in a way that makes you feel less confident and slightly frightened

Example: *The dark hallway was unnervingly silent.*

unobtrusively /ʌnɒbtrˈuːsɪvli/
in a way that is not easily noticed
Example: He unobtrusively left the meeting early.

unofficially /ʌnəfˈɪʃəlˌi/
in a way that is not official, or not from a person in authority or the government
Example: She unofficially announced her candidacy to her friends.

unorthodoxly /ʌnˈɔːθədˌɒksli/
in a manner that is not conventional in belief, behaviour or custom
Example: He unorthodoxly solved the puzzle by thinking outside the box.

unpleasantly /ʌnplˈɛzəntli/
in a way that is not enjoyable or gives you bad feelings
Example: The food tasted unpleasantly bitter.

unprecedentedly /ʌnprɪsˈɛdəntˌɪdli/
in a way that has not happened or existed before
Example: The company achieved unprecedentedly high sales this quarter.

unpredictably /ʌnprɪdˈɪktəbli/
in a way that is likely to change suddenly and without reason
Example: The weather changed unpredictably from sunny to stormy.

unpreparedly /ˈʌnprɪˈpeədli/
in a manner that have made inadequate preparations
Example: She unpreparedly walked into the meeting without any notes.

unproductively /ˈʌnprəˈdʌktɪvli/
in a manner that does not yield any good results
Example: *She worked unproductively for hours, unable to focus.*

unpropitiously /ʌnprəpˈɪʃəsli/
in a manner that is not favourable or advantageous
Example: *The project began unpropitiously with several unexpected setbacks.*

unquestionably /ʌnkwˈɛstʃənəbli/
in a way that is obvious and impossible to doubt
Example: *The team's victory was unquestionably the highlight of the season.*

unquestioningly /ʌnkwˈɛstʃənɪŋli/
in a manner that accepts something without expressing doubt or uncertainty
Example: *She followed the instructions unquestioningly, trusting the guide completely.*

unquietly /ˈʌnˈkwaɪətli/
in a manner that characterized by disorder, unrest, or tumult
Example: *The room was unquietly filled with whispers and restless movements.*

unreadably /ʌnrˈiːdəbli/
in a manner that is difficult or tedious to read
Example: *The handwriting was so messy that it was unreadably scrawled on the page.*

unrealistically /ʌnriəlˈɪstɪkli/
in a way that is not based on facts or not likely to be successful
Example: *Her expectations were unrealistically high for the project's completion.*

unreally /ˈʌnˈrɪəlli/

in a manner that is imaginary or fanciful or seemingly so

Example: *The movie's special effects were unreally flashy and over-the-top.*

unreasonably /ʌnrˈiːzənəbli/

in a way that is not fair or acceptable

Example: *The store's prices were unreasonably high for such basic items.*

unrelentingly /ˌʌnrɪlˈɛntɪŋli/

in a way that never becomes less or better

Example: *She worked unrelentingly to finish the project on time.*

unreliably /ʌnrɪlˈaɪəbli/

in a manner that is not fit or suitable to be dependent on

Example: *The old car started unreliably, often leaving him stranded.*

unrepentantly /ˈʌnrɪˈpentəntli/

in a manner that does not feel or exhibit shame or remorse

Example: *She unrepentantly continued her behaviour despite the consequences.*

unreservedly /ˌʌnrɪsˈɜːvɪdli/

completely, without doubts or feeling of being uncertain

Example: *She unreservedly supported his decision, trusting it completely.*

unresponsively /ˈʌnrɪsˈpɒnsɪvli/

in a way that shows no reaction to something

Example: *He stared unresponsively at the screen, not reacting to the news.*

unrestrainedly /ˈʌnrɪsˈtreɪndli/

in a way that is not limited or controlled

Example: *She laughed unrestrainedly at the joke, not caring who heard.*

unromantically /ʌnrəʊmˈantɪkli/

in a way that is not typical of romantic love

Example: *He unromantically handed her a list of household chores instead of a heartfelt gift.*

in a way that is not exciting, mysterious, or special, but instead in a way that is practical or ordinary

Example: *They unromantically discussed their weekend plans over coffee*

unscrupulously /ʌnskrˈuːpjʊləsli/

in a way that is dishonest or unfair, to get what you want

Example: *She unscrupulously took credit for her colleague's work to advance her career.*

unseasonably /ʌnsˈiːzənəbli/

in a way that is not usual or expected for the time of the year

Example: *The weather was unseasonably warm for a December day.*

unselfishly /ʌnsˈɛlfɪʃli/

in a way that shows you are thinking about what is good for other people rather than yourself

Example: *She unselfishly donated her time to help the community centre.*

unsettlingly /ʌnsˈɛtəlɪŋli/

in a way that causes someone to feel worried or uncomfortable

Example: *The silence in the abandoned house was unsettlingly eerie.*

unshakeably /ʌnʃˈeɪkəbli/
in a way that shows a firm belief that cannot be made weaker or destroyed
Example: *She remained unshakeably confident in her decision despite the criticism.*

unskilfully /ʌnskˈɪlfəli/
in a way that lacks proficiency or dexterity
Example: *He unskilfully attempted to fix the leaky sink, making the problem worse.*

unsociably /ʌnsˈəʊʃiəbli/
in a way that shows someone does not like to meet people or spend time with them
Example: *He unsociably stayed in his room during the party.*
happening at unusual times
Example: *The meeting was scheduled unsociably early, making it difficult for everyone to attend.*

unsparingly /ʌnspˈeərɪŋli/
in a way that shows no kindness or no wish to hide unpleasant truths
Example: *She criticized the report unsparingly, pointing out every flaw and error.*
in a way that is extremely generous with money, time or help
Example: *He donated unsparingly to the charity.*

unspeakably /ʌnspˈiːkəbli/
in a way that cannot be expressed in words, usually because it is too bad or shocking
Example: *The tragedy left them feeling unspeakably devastated and heartbroken.*

unsteadily /ʌnstˈɛdɪli/

in a way that involves moving slightly from side to side, as if you might fall

Example: *He walked unsteadily after standing up too quickly, trying to regain his balance.*

in a way that is not smooth or regular

Example: *The car drove unsteadily over the rough, uneven road.*

in a way that often changes or is likely to change

Example: *Her mood shifted unsteadily throughout the day, making it hard to predict her reactions.*

unstintingly /ʌnstˈɪntɪŋli/

in a way that is extremely generous with time, money, praise or help

Example: *She volunteered unstintingly, always offering her time and support to those in need.*

unstoppably /ʌnstˈɒpəbli/

in a way that incapable of being stopped or prevented from developing

Example: *The wildfire spread unstoppably across the forest, despite all efforts to contain it.*

unsubtly /ʌnsˈʌtəlˌi/

in a way that is noticeable, obvious, or direct

Example: *She unsubtly hinted that she wanted a promotion by mentioning her extra hours at work.*

unsuccessfully /ʌnsəksˈɛsfəli/

in a way that does not succeed or achieve the hoped-for result

Example: *He tried unsuccessfully to fix the broken faucet.*

unsuitably /ʌnsˈuːtəbli/

in a way that is not acceptable or right for something or someone

Example: *She was dressed unsuitably for the formal event.*

unsurprisingly /ʌnsəprˈaɪzɪŋli/
in a way that is not unexpected
Example: *Unsurprisingly, the test was difficult for everyone who had not studied.*

unsuspectingly /ʌnsəspˈɛktɪŋli/
in a manner that is unaware of any danger or threat
Example: *He unsuspectingly walked into the surprise party.*

unswervingly /ʌnswˈɜːvɪŋli/
in a manner that is constant, without turning aside
Example: *She pursued her goals unswervingly, no matter the obstacles in her path.*

unthinkingly /ʌnθˈɪŋkɪŋli/
without someone seriously thinking about or intending something
Example: *She unthinkingly gave away her friend's secret.*

untidily /ʌntˈaɪdili/
in a way that is not neat or well arranged
Example: *She left her room untidily, with clothes scattered everywhere.*

untruly /ˈʌnˈtruːli/
in a manner that is not according with the facts
Example: *He untruly claimed that he had finished the project.*

untruthfully /ʌntrˈuːθfəli/
in a way that involves telling lies, or not telling the complete truth
Example: *He answered the question untruthfully to avoid getting in trouble.*

unusually /ʌnjˈuːʒuːəli/

more than is usual or expected, or in a way that is not usual

Example: The weather was unusually warm for early spring.

unwarily /ʌnwˈeərili/

in a way that shows someone is not careful about possible risks and dangers

Example: He unwarily walked into the dark alley without checking for safety.

unwaveringly /ʌnˈweɪvərɪŋli/

without changing or becoming weaker

Example: She supported her friend unwaveringly through all the challenges.

without moving or looking away

Example: He stared unwaveringly at the distant horizon.

unwillingly /ʌnwˈɪlɪŋli/

in a way that involves someone doing something they do not want to do

Example: She unwillingly agreed to work on the weekend.

unwisely /ʌnwˈaɪzli/

in a way that shows a lack of good judgement

Example: He unwisely spent all his savings on a risky investment.

unwittingly /ʌnwˈɪtɪŋli/

in a way that is done without knowing or planning

Example: She unwittingly revealed the surprise party details.

unwontedly /ʌnˈwəʊntɪdli/

in a manner that is rare or out of the ordinary

Example: He spoke unwontedly about his personal life at the meeting.

unworthily /ʌnwˈɜːðɪli/
in a way that deserves no respect, admiration, or support
Example: *He was unworthily praised for his lack of effort.*

unyieldingly /ʌnˈjiːldɪŋli/
in a way that shows someone is completely unwilling to change a decision, opinion, or demand
Example: *She unyieldingly refused to compromise on her principles.*

upright /ˈʌpraɪt/
in a vertically upward position
Example: *She stood upright to get a better view of the parade.*

uprightly /ˈʌpˌraɪtlɪ/
in an honest, responsible, and moral way
Example: *He acted uprightly in every business transaction, earning everyone's trust.*

uproariously /ʌprˈɔːrɪəsli/
in an extremely noisy and confused way
Example: *The crowd laughed uproariously at the comedian's jokes.*
in an extremely funny way
Example: *The movie was uproariously funny, making everyone laugh out loud.*

upsettingly /ʌpsˈɛtɪŋli/
in a manner that is mentally or emotionally troubling or disturbing
Example: *The news was upsettingly distressing to everyone who heard it.*

upward /ˈʌpwəd/
in a direction from lower to higher

Example: *The balloon floated upward into the sky.*

towards a higher or better condition or level

Example: *Her career has been moving upward since she earned her promotion.*

to an indefinitely greater amount, figure, or rank

Example: *The company's profits have been trending upward for the past year.*

toward or into later years

Example: *As he grew older, his interests shifted upward to more mature topics.*

upwardly /ˈʌpwədli/

towards or situated in a higher place or level

Example: *The bird flew upwardly into the clouds.*

urbanely /ɜːˈbeɪnli/

in a manner that is notably polite or polished

Example: *He urbanely navigated the social event with grace and charm.*

urgently /ˈɜːdʒəntli/

in a way that needs attention very soon, especially before anything else, because of being very important

Example: *She called the doctor urgently after feeling severe pain.*

in a determined way that shows you want something very much or think it is very important

Example: *He urged the committee urgently to address the pressing issue.*

usefully /jˈuːzfəli/

in an effective or helpful way

Example: *She used the tool usefully to complete the repair quickly.*

uselessly /juːsləsli/

in a way that is of no use, or that is not working or achieving what is needed

Example: *The broken machine ran uselessly, producing no results.*

usually /juːʒuːəli/

in the way most often happens

Example: *She usually drinks coffee every morning.*

utterly /ˈʌtəli/

to an absolute or extreme degree

Example: *The movie was utterly captivating from start to finish.*

uxoriously /ʌkˈsɔːrɪəsli/

in a way that shows too much love or need for your wife

Example: *He uxoriously followed her every command, eager to please.*

Vv

vacantly /vˈeɪkəntli/
in a manner that shows no interest or mental activity
Example: *She stared vacantly out the window, lost in thought.*

vacuously /ˈvɑkjʊəsli/
in a way that shows no intelligent thought
Example: *She smiled vacuously as if she had not understood a word.*

vagally /vˈɑgəli/
in a way that relates to or passes through the vagus nerve
Example: *The doctor explained that the symptoms could be vagally related to the nerve's influence.*

vagariously /vəˈgeərɪəsli/
in a manner that is characterized or caused by vagaries; irregular or erratic
Example: *His behaviour was vagariously unpredictable.*

vaginally /vˈɑdʒɪnəli/
through or in the vagina
Example: *The medication was administered vaginally for better absorption.*

vagrantly /ˈveɪgrəntli/
in a manner that involves wandering from place to place usually with no means of support
Example: *He wandered vagrantly from place to place.*

vaguely /vˈeɪgli/
in a way that is not clearly expressed, known, described, or decided

Example: *She vaguely remembered meeting him at the party last year.*

without giving many details or facts, especially because you do not want to tell someone everything that you know

Example: *He vaguely mentioned the meeting without revealing any specific details.*

to some degree or to a slight degree

Example: *The weather was vaguely warm, hinting at the approaching spring.*

vainly /vˈeɪnli/

in a manner that involves having or showing undue or excessive pride in one's appearance or achievements

Example: *She vainly checked her appearance in the mirror for the umpteenth time.*

valiantly /vˈalɪəntli/

in a way that is brave or determined when a situation is very difficult

Example: *The soldiers fought valiantly to defend their homeland.*

validly /vˈalɪdli/

in a way that is based on truth or reason, or that can be accepted

Example: *Her argument was validly supported by solid evidence.*

in a way that has legal force, or that is legally acceptable

Example: *The contract was validly signed by both parties, making it legally binding.*

valorously /ˈvalərəsli/

in a way that shows great courage

Example: *He acted valorously during the emergency, saving several lives.*

vanishingly /vˈanɪʃɪŋli/

to be almost non-existent or invisible

Example: The distant ship became vanishingly small on the
horizon.

vapidly /ˈvɑpɪdli/
in a way that shows no intelligence or imagination
Example: The lecture was delivered vapidly, with no interesting
insights or engagement.

vaporously /ˈveɪpərəsli/
in a manner that contains or is obscured by vapors
Example: The mist rolled in vaporously, obscuring the view of the
valley.

variably /vˈeərɪəbəli/
in a way that changes often and not in a regular way
Example: The weather in the region varies variably from day to
day.

variedly /ˈveərɪdli/
in a manner that is displaying or characterized by variety; diverse
Example: The students answered the questions variedly,
showcasing their different perspectives.

variously /vˈeərɪəsli/
in several different ways, at several different times, or by several
different people
Example: The proposal was variously criticized by experts and
stakeholders.

varyingly /vˈeərɪŋli/
in a way that changes or is different in amount or level, especially
among similar things
Example: The students' performances were varyingly impressive
throughout the semester.

vascularly /ˈvɑskjʊləli/
in a manner that relates to or having vessels that conduct or circulate liquids
Example: *The medication is administered vascularly to ensure rapid absorption.*

vastly /vˈɑːstli/
to a very great or vast degree or extent
Example: *The new technology vastly improved the efficiency of the process.*

vauntingly /vˈɔːntɪŋli/
in a way that shows great pride and confidence, especially in a way that is more than is acceptable or reasonable
Example: *He spoke vauntingly about his achievements.*

veeringly /vˈiərɪŋli/
in a manner that involves directing to a different course
Example: *The car swerved veeringly to avoid the obstacle.*

vegetatively /vˈɛdʒɪtˌeɪtɪvli/
in a manner that involves growing or having the power of growing
Example: *The seeds spread vegetatively through the garden soil.*

vehemently /vˈiəməntli/
in a manner that involves having very strong feelings and opinions and expressing them forcefully
Example: *She protested vehemently against the proposed changes.*

venally /ˈviːnlli/
in a way that is easily bribed or corrupted
Example: *The official acted venally, accepting bribes in exchange for favours.*

venerably /vˈɛnərəbəli/

in a way that shows someone, or something is very old and deserves care and respect

Example: *The old professor, venerably dressed in his traditional academic robes, delivered his lecture with the wisdom of decades of experience.*

venereally /vɪˈnɪərɪəlli/

in a manner that relates to or involves the genitals

Example: *The doctor discussed the symptoms venereally during the consultation.*

vengefully /ˈvɛndʒfʊlli/

in a way that expresses a strong wish to punish someone who has harmed you

Example: *She vengefully plotted her revenge against those who had wronged her.*

venially /ˈviːnjəlli/

in a manner that is not serious and therefore easy to forgive

Example: *He committed the error venially, knowing it was a minor mistake.*

venomously /ˈvɛnəməsli/

in a way that is full of anger or hate

Example: *She spoke venomously about her rival during the heated debate.*

venously /ˈviːnəsli/

in terms of, or by means of, the vein

Example: *The medication was administered venously through an intravenous drip.*

ventrally /vˈɛntrəli/

in a position or direction towards the front of the human body or the underside of an animal

Example: *The surgeon made the incision ventrally to access the internal organs.*

veraciously /vəˈreɪʃəsli/

in a manner that is marked by truth

Example: *She spoke veraciously, providing accurate and truthful information.*

verbally /vˈɜːbəli/

in a way that is spoken rather than written

Example: *He explained the instructions verbally during the meeting.*

in a way that relates to words

Example: *The coach provided feedback both verbally and in writing.*

verbosely /vɜːˈbəʊsli/

in a way that uses too many words

Example: *He explained the process verbosely, making it difficult to follow.*

verdantly /ˈvɜːdəntli/

in a manner that is covered with green vegetation

Example: *The garden flourished verdantly with lush green plants and trees.*

verifiably /vˈɛrɪfˌaɪəbli/

in a way that can be checked, proved to be true or correct

Example: *The data was verifiably accurate, with all sources clearly documented.*

verily /vˈɛrɪli/

in a completely honest way

Example: *He spoke verily about his feelings, sharing his true thoughts.*

verisimilarly /ˌverɪˈsɪmɪləli/

in a way that suggests truthfulness

Example: *The actor portrayed the character verisimilarly, capturing the essence of the real person.*

veritably /ˈvɛrɪtəbli/

in actual fact

Example: *The project was veritably successful, exceeding all expectations.*

vernacularly /vəˈnɑkjʊləli/

in a way that involves using a language or dialect native to a region or country

Example: *He spoke vernacularly, using the local dialect that everyone understood.*

vernally /ˈvɜːnlli/

in a manner that is fresh and new like the spring

Example: *The garden was renewed vernally with vibrant flowers and fresh greenery.*

versatilely /ˈvɜːsətaɪlli/

in a manner that involves being capable of or adapted for many different uses or skills

Example: *She handled the various tasks versatilely, adapting to each challenge with ease.*

vertically /vˈɜːtɪkli/

straight up or at an angle of 90 degrees to a horizontal surface or line

Example: *The flagpole stood vertically, reaching high into the sky.*

vertiginously /vɜːˈtɪdʒɪnəsli/
in a manner that is causing or tending to cause dizziness
Example: *The view from the cliff was vertiginously thrilling,*
making her feel dizzy.

very /vˈɛri/
to a high degree
Example: *The cake was very delicious, much better than I expected.*
in actual fact
Example: *The book was very interesting, exactly as the reviews*
described.

vestigially /vesˈtɪdʒɪəlli/
in a way that has almost disappeared, or that is a small remaining part
of something
Example: *The building's original architecture was vestigially*
preserved in the modern renovation.

vexatiously /vɛksˈeɪʃəsli/
in a way that has little chance of succeeding in law, but is intended to
annoy or cause problems for someone
Example: *The lawsuit was filed vexatiously, meant more to harass*
than to achieve any real legal outcome.
in a way that is annoying or difficult to deal with
Example: *he repeated phone calls were vexatiously disruptive,*
making it hard to focus on work.

viably /vˈaɪəbli/
in a way that is able to succeed or to work as intended
Example: *The new business plan was viably structured to ensure*
long-term success.

in a way that is able to continue to exist or develop into a living being

Example: *The seeds were planted in conditions that would viably support their growth.*

vibrantly /vˈaɪbrəntli/
in a way that is energetic, exciting, and full of enthusiasm

Example: *The festival was vibrantly alive with colourful decorations and lively music.*

in a way that is bright and strong

Example: *The flowers bloomed vibrantly, with bright colours that caught everyone's eye.*

vicariously /vɪkˈeərɪəsli/
in a manner that involves being experienced through the activities of other people, rather than by doing something by yourself

Example: *She lived vicariously through her friend's exciting travel stories.*

viceregally /ˈvaɪsˈriːgəlli/
in a manner that relates to a viceroy or viceroyalty

Example: *The governor addressed the assembly viceregally, reflecting his high status and authority.*

viciously /vˈɪʃəsli/
in a way that is cruel and shows an intention to hurt or upset someone

Example: *He attacked his opponent viciously, with harsh words and bitter accusations.*

in a violent way that causes great pain

Example: *The dog bit the intruder viciously, causing severe injuries.*

victoriously /vɪktˈɔːrɪəsli/
in a way that involves defeating an adversary
Example: *The team celebrated victoriously after winning the*
championship game.

vigilantly /vˈɪdʒɪləntli/
in a way that is always careful to notice things
Example: *She monitored the security cameras vigilantly, watching*
for any signs of suspicious activity.

vigorously /vˈɪgərəsli/
in a way that is very forceful or energetic
Example: *He exercised vigorously every morning to stay in shape.*
in a way that is healthy and strong
Example: *The plants grew vigorously in the rich, well-nourished*
soil.

vilely /vˈaɪlli/
in a way that is very unpleasant and usually immoral and
unacceptable
Example: *The dictator ruled vilely, oppressing his people with*
harsh and unjust policies.

villainously /ˈvɪlənəsli/
in a way that involves evil behaviour, or that involves being a bad or
harmful person or character
Example: *She plotted villainously against her rivals.*

vindictively /vɪndˈɪktɪvli/
in a way that shows a wish to harm someone because you think they
have harmed you
Example: *He acted vindictively after losing the game.*

vinously /ˈvaɪnəsli/
in a manner that shows the effects of the use of wine
Example: He spoke vinously, as if he had had a few glasses of wine.

violently /vˈaɪələntli/
in a forceful way that causes people to be hurt
Example: The storm hit violently, causing widespread damage.
in a strong or extreme way
Example: He reacted violently to the unexpected news.

viperously /ˈvaɪpərəsli/
in a manner that involves having the qualities attributed to a viper
Example: He glared at them viperously, full of hostility.

virally /vˈaɪərəli/
in a way that is caused by a virus
Example: She developed a rash virally after catching the flu.
used to describe how something quickly becomes very popular or well known by being published on the internet or sent from person to person by email or phone
Example: The video spread virally across social media within hours.

virginally /ˈvɜːdʒɪnlli/
in a way that relates to being a virgin
Example: She wore a virginally white dress for her wedding day.
in a way that seems very new, pure, or clean, rather than old, used, or spoiled
Example: The old house looked virginally fresh after its renovation.

virtually /vˈɜːtʃuːəli/
almost entirely
Example: The project is virtually complete, with just a few minor details left.

by means of a computer or computer network: in a virtual location

Example: *They attended the conference virtually from their home offices.*

virtuosically /ˌvɜːrtʃuˈɑːsɪkli/
in the matter of one who excels in the technique of an art

Example: *She played the piano virtuosically, impressing everyone with her skill.*

virtuously /vˈɜːtʃuːəsli/
in a way that shows good moral qualities and behaviour

Example: *He lived virtuously, always helping those in need.*

in a way that shows too much satisfaction, because you think you have done the right thing

Example: *She smiled virtuously after pointing out her colleague's mistake.*

virulently /vˈɪrələntli/
in a manner that is extremely bitter or hostile

Example: *He spoke virulently against the new policy, expressing strong opposition.*

viscerally /vˈɪsərəli/
in a way that is based on deep feeling and emotional reactions rather than on reason or thought

Example: *She reacted viscerally to the news, feeling a deep, immediate sadness.*

viscidly /ˈvɪsɪdli/
in a manner that cohesive an

Example: *The syrup flowed viscidly, sticking to everything it touched.*

viscously /'vɪskəsli/
in a way that is thick and sticky, or that has viscosity
Example: *The paint was applied viscously, covering the wall with a thick layer.*

visibly /v'ɪzəbli/
in a way that can be noticed; obviously
Example: *She was visibly excited about the upcoming vacation.*

visigothically /ˌvɪzɪ'gɒθɪkli/
in a manner that involves or is concerned with Visigoths
Example: *The architecture of the old cathedral was decorated visigothically.*

visually /v'ɪʒuːəli/
in a matter that relates to seeing or appearance
Example: *The room was visually stunning, with its vibrant colours and elegant decor.*

vitally /v'aɪtəli/
in a way that is extremely important, or necessary for the success or continued existence of something
Example: *Good communication is vitally important for a successful team.*
energetically, or in a way that is full of life
Example: *She danced vitally, full of energy and enthusiasm.*

vituperatively /vɪ'tjuːpərətɪvli/
in a way that involves criticizing and attacking someone or something angrily in speech or writing
Example: *She addressed the issue vituperatively, unleashing a barrage of harsh criticisms.*

vivaciously /vɪˈveɪʃəsli/
in a way that is attractively energetic and enthusiastic
Example: *She spoke vivaciously, her energy lighting up the room.*

vividly /vˈɪvɪdli/
in a way that is very clear, powerful, and detailed in your mind
Example: *She described the sunset so vividly that I could almost see the colours in my mind.*
in a way that is very brightly coloured
Example: *The artist painted the room vividly, with bright colours that made it come alive.*

vocalically /voʊˈkɑlɪkli/
in terms of, or by means of, a vowel
Example: *The linguist analysed the words vocalically to understand their pronunciation better.*

vocally /vˈəʊkəli/
in a way that relates to or is produced by the voice, either in singing or speaking
Example: *She expressed her concerns vocally during the meeting.*
by expressing opinions and complaints often
Example: *He vocally criticized the new policy at every opportunity.*

vocationally /vəʊkˈeɪʃənəli/
in a way that provides skills that prepare you for a job, or that relates to a particular type of work
Example: *She attended a vocationally focused training program to become a skilled technician.*

vociferously /vəʊsˈɪfərəsli/
in a loud and repeated manner
Example: *The crowd vociferously cheered for their team throughout the game.*

voicelessly /ˈvɔɪslɪsli/

in a mute manner

Example: She communicated her disapproval voicelessly with a
disappointed look.

volcanically /vɒlkˈɑnɪkli/

in a manner of, relating to or produced by a volcano

Example: The eruption occurred volcanically, sending lava and ash
high into the sky.

volitionally /vəʊˈlɪʃnəlli/

in a manner that involves making a choice or decision

Example: She volunteered for the project volitionally, eager to
contribute her skills.

volubly /vˈɒlʌbli/

in a way that involves a lot of words, spoken confidently and
forcefully

Example: She spoke volubly about her ideas, confidently and
persuasively sharing her views.

volumetrically /ˌvɑːljuˈmɛtrɪkli/

in a manner pertaining to the measurement or analysis of volume

Example: The researcher measured the liquid volumetrically to
ensure accurate results."

voluminously /vəˈljuːmɪnəsli/

in a way that involves writing or speaking a lot, often in detail

Example: The author wrote voluminously about the history of the
region, covering every detail.

in a way that involves producing or using a great amount of
something

Example: *The factory produced voluminously, churning out*
thousands of items each day.

used for saying that a piece of clothing is large and consists of a lot of
cloth

Example: *She wore a voluminously flowing gown that swirled*
around her as she danced.

voluntarily /vˌplənt'ɛrəli/

in a manner that involves proceeding from the will or from one's own
choice or consent

Example: *He joined the community service project voluntarily,*
eager to help.

voluptuously /vəˈlʌptjʊəsli/

in a way that is soft, curved, and sexually attractive

Example: *The dress hugged her figure voluptuously, accentuating*
her curves.

in a way that gives you a lot of pleasure because it feels extremely
soft and comfortable, or sounds and looks extremely beautiful

Example: *She sank into the voluptuously soft cushions of the*
armchair, enjoying their luxurious comfort.

voraciously /vɔːrˈeɪʃəsli/

in a way that is very eager to have a lot of something

Example: *He devoured the book voraciously, unable to put it down.*

vortically /ˈvɔːtɪkəlli/

in a manner related to or resembling a vortex, characterised by
swirling or rotational motion

Example: *The water spun vortically down the drain.*

votively /ˈvəʊtɪvli/

in a manner related to or done as a vow or offering, often for religious
or devotional purposes

Example: *She lit the candles votively in hopes of bringing good*
            fortune.

voyeuristically /ˌvɔɪəˈrɪstɪkli/
in a way that involves getting pleasure from watching other people, or
from knowing about their life, especially when watching sad
situations without helping
Example: *The crowd gathered voyeuristically, taking interest in the*
            personal struggles of the celebrities.
in a way that involves getting sexual pleasure from secretly watching
other people in sexual situations
Example: *He watched voyeuristically through the keyhole, gaining*
            a forbidden thrill from the private moments.

vulgarly /vˈʌlgəli/
in a way that is not suitable, simple, or beautiful, or not in the style
preferred by rich or well-educated people
Example: *She spoke vulgarly, using crude language that offended*
            her refined friends.
in a way that is rude and likely to upset or anger people, especially by
referring to sex or the body
Example: *He made vulgarly inappropriate jokes that made*
            everyone uncomfortable.

vulnerably /vˈʌlnərəbli/
in a way that makes it easy for someone to be physically or mentally
hurt, influenced, or attacked, or that makes them look as if this could
happen
Example: *She spoke vulnerably about her fears, exposing her*
            deepest insecurities to the group.

Ww

wackily /wˈɑkili/
in a pleasing and exciting or silly and unusual way
Example: She dressed wackily for the party.

waddlingly /wˈɒdlɪŋli/
in a manner of walking with short steps and a swaying motion, like a duck
Example: The duck moved waddlingly across the pond.

waggishly /ˈwɑgɪʃli/
in a way that is funny and usually very clever
Example: She waggishly suggested that the meeting's only purpose was to consume endless coffee.

wailingly /wˈeɪlɪŋli/
to make a prolonged, high-pitched cry or sound, typically expressing grief or pain
Example: The baby cried wailingly throughout the night, unable to be soothed.

wakefully /ˈweɪkfʊlli/
in the manner of someone who is not sleeping or not able to sleep
Example: He stared at the ceiling wakefully, unable to shake off his insomnia.

wanderingly /ˈwɒndərɪŋli/
in a manner that describes moving aimlessly or without a fixed course
Example: His gaze drifted wanderingly across the room, lost in thought.

wantonly /ˈwɒntənli/

in a way that is intentional or shows no care about bad things that might result

Example: *He spent money wantonly, ignoring the consequences of his reckless spending.*

in a way that is, or appears to be, very sexual

Example: *She danced wantonly at the party, drawing everyone's attention with her provocative moves.*

warily /ˈweərɪli/

in a way that is cautious or vigilant

Example: *She approached the unfamiliar dog warily, unsure of its temperament.*

warmly /wˈɔːmli/

in a way that makes or keeps you warm

Example: *She wrapped the blanket warmly around herself on the chilly evening.*

in a very friendly or approving way

Example: *He was warmly welcomed by his old friends at the reunion.*

warningly /ˈwɔːnɪŋli/

in a way that serves as an alarm, signal, summons, or admonition

Example: *She glanced warningly at him, hoping he would understand the danger of his actions.*

waspishly /ˈwɒspɪʃli/

in a way that is angry or unpleasant, often using sharp, slightly cruel remarks

Example: *She responded waspishly to his criticism; her words laced with irritation.*

wastefully /wˈeɪstfəli/

in a way that uses more of something than is necessary

Example: *He used the paint wastefully, covering the entire wall with several unnecessary coats.*

watchfully /ˈwɒtʃfʊlli/

being alert and attentive to potential dangers or changes

Example: *She kept her eyes watchfully on the kids as they played near the street.*

waveringly /ˈweɪvərɪŋli/

in a way that changes in strength, determination, or purpose

Example: *He spoke waveringly, his confidence faltering as he presented his argument.*

in a way that suggests you are unable to decide which possibility to choose

Example: *She answered waveringly, unsure whether to accept the job offer or not.*

waywardly /ˈweɪwədli/

in a manner that describes someone or something that is unpredictable, difficult to control, or inclined to go off course

Example: *He behaved waywardly, frequently changing his plans without any clear direction.*

weakly /wˈiːkli/

in a way that is not physically strong

Example: *She lifted the box weakly, struggling with its weight.*

in a way that is not strong in character, so that you are not able to make decisions or to persuade or lead other people

Example: *He argued weakly, failing to convince anyone of his point.*

in a way that is not likely to be accepted or believed

Example: *Her excuse was weakly defended and easily dismissed.*

wealthily /wˈɛlθɪli/
in the manner of someone who has a lot of money
Example: They lived wealthily in a grand mansion with luxury cars.

wearily /wˈiəɹɪli/
in a way that shows that you are very tired
Example: She wearily trudged home after a long day at work.
in a way that is boring, or that shows that you are bored with
something because you have experienced too much of it
Example: He wearily listened to the same old stories repeatedly.

wearisomely /ˈwɪərɪsəmli/
in a way that causes a person to be tired or bored
*Example: The lecture went on wearisomely, leaving everyone
            exhausted and bored.*

weekly /wˈiːkli/
every week: once a week: by the week
Example: She goes to the gym weekly to stay fit.

weepily /ˈwiːpɪli/
in a manner that describes something characterised by or causing
tears or sadness
Example: She spoke weepily about her lost pet.

weepingly /ˈwiːpɪŋli/
to cry or shed tears
*Example: He told the story weepingly, his voice breaking with
            emotion.*

weightily /ˈweɪtɪli/
in a way that feels very heavy

Example: *The book was weightily placed on the shelf, its presence*
undeniable.

in a way that is very serious or important

Example: *The CEO spoke weightily about the company's future*
direction.

weirdly /wˈiədli/

in a way that is strange and unusual

Example: *He acted weirdly, talking to himself in the middle of the*
street.

well /wˈɛl/

in a good or proper manner

Example: *She sings well, impressing everyone with her talent.*

in a kindly or friendly manner

Example: *He greeted us well, with a warm smile and a firm*
handshake.

with skill or aptitude

Example: *She performed the task well, finishing ahead of schedule.*

with careful or close attention

Example: *He examined the report well before making any*
decisions.

to a high degree

Example: *The movie was well received by critics and audiences*
alike.

in a way appropriate to the facts or circumstances

Example: *Her response was well suited to the situation.*

in accordance with the occasion or circumstances

Example: *The dress she wore was well chosen for the formal event.*

as one could wish

Example: *He did the project well, meeting all his goals and*
expectations.

in all likelihood

Example: *She will well attend the meeting tomorrow.*

in a prosperous or affluent manner

*Example: They live well in a beautiful home with all the comforts
            they could wish for.*

to an extent approaching completeness

*Example: The plan is well developed, covering all necessary
            details.*

without doubt or question

Example: She is well the best candidate for the job.

in a familiar manner

Example: He greeted her well, like an old friend.

to a large extent or degree

*Example: The new software is well received by users for its ease of
            use.*

westward /wˈɛstwəd/

towards the west

Example: The travellers headed westward across the desert.

westwardly /ˈwestwədli/

in a direction that is towards the west

Example: The boat sailed westward to reach the distant island.

wetly /wˈɛtli/

in a way that involves water or another liquid

*Example: The rain fell wetly on the pavement, creating puddles
            everywhere.*

in a weak way, without any confidence

Example: He spoke wetly, unsure of his own argument.

whatever /wɒtˈɛvɐ/

in any case: whatever the case may be

Example: We'll support the decision, whatever the outcome may be.

whatsoever /wɒtsˌəʊˈɛvɐ/
used after a negative phrase to add emphasis to the idea that is being expressed
Example: *She had no interest in the topic whatsoever.*

wheedlingly /ˈwiːdlɪŋli/
in a manner that uses flattery or persuasion to achieve a desired outcome
Example: *He asked wheedlingly for an extension on his deadline.*

wheezily /wˈiːzili/
in a way that involves or sounds like a husky, rasping, or whistling sound or breathing
Example: *He spoke wheezily, struggling to catch his breath.*

wheezingly /wˈiːzɪŋli/
with a whistling or rattling sound, typically due to a respiratory issue
Example: *She laughed wheezingly after running up the stairs.*

when /wˈɛn/
at what time
Example: *When does the meeting start?*
at or during which time
Example: *She was nervous when the exam began.*
at a former and usually less prosperous time
Example: *When I was younger, we lived in a much smaller house.*

whenever /wɛnˈɛvɐ/
at whatever time
Example: *You can call me whenever you need help.*

where /wˈeə/
at, in or to what place
Example: *Where did you leave your keys?*

in what situation

Example:　*Where do we stand on the project deadline?*

used when referring to a particular stage in a process or activity

Example:　*We're at a point where we need to finalize the design before moving on.*

whereby /wˈeəbaɪ/

by what means

Example:　*She explained the procedure, whereby each step must be completed before the next can begin.*

wherever /weərˈɛvɐ/

where in the world

Example:　*Wherever you go, remember to stay safe and have fun.*

anywhere at all

Example:　*You can find the best coffee, wherever you choose to look.*

whiggishly /ˈwɪɡɪʃli/

something done in a manner characteristic of Whig principles, often implying a progressive or reformist attitude

Example:　*The historian wrote whiggishly, presenting historical events as a steady progress toward modernity.*

whimperingly /wˈɪmpərɪŋli/

to make low, feeble, or plaintive sounds, often in response to pain or distress

Example:　*The puppy looked up at her whimperingly, wanting to be let inside.*

whimsically /ˈwɪmzɪkəlli/

describes something that is playfully quaint or fanciful, often in an unpredictable or capricious manner

Example: She decorated the room whimsically, with bright colours
            and playful patterns.

whiningly /wˈaɪnɪŋli/
in an annoying way that shows that you are disappointed or unhappy
Example: She spoke whiningly about the changes to her favourite
            show, clearly disappointed with the new direction.

whisperingly /ˈwɪspərɪŋli/
with a low sound like a sibilant
Example: The leaves rustled whisperingly in the quiet forest.
in a quiet or secret way that suggests something that may or may not
be true
Example: The group spoke whisperingly about the surprise party

wholeheartedly /hˈəʊlhɑːtˌɪdli/
in a way that is completely enthusiastic and without any doubt
Example: She supported the project wholeheartedly, believing in its
            potential to make a difference.

wholesomely /ˈhəʊlsəmli/
in a way that shows that someone is morally good and physically
healthy
Example: He lived wholesomely, focusing on a balanced diet and
            positive relationships.
in a way that produces good physical or mental health
Example: She enjoyed the fresh air and exercise wholesomely,
            benefiting both her body and mind.

wholly /hˈəʊli/
to the full or entire extent
Example: She was wholly committed to completing the project on
            time.
to the exclusion of other things

Example: He was wholly focused on his studies, ignoring all other distractions.

wickedly /wˈɪkɪdli/
in a way that is morally bad or evil
Example: The villain laughed wickedly.
in a way that is slightly morally bad or bad for you, but attractive
Example: She enjoyed the wickedly rich chocolate cake, despite knowing it was not the healthiest choice.
in an extreme manner
Example: The car sped wickedly down the highway.

widely /wˈaɪdli/
including a lot of different places, people, or subjects
Example: The new book was widely acclaimed, reaching readers across many countries and cultures.

wildly /wˈaɪldli/
in an uncontrolled or extreme way
Example: The crowd cheered wildly as the team scored the winning goal.

wilfully /wˈɪlfəli/
in a way that is describes actions or attitudes that are done or expressed deliberately, especially with the intention of causing someone harm
Example: He wilfully ignored the instructions, choosing to do things his own way.

willingly /wˈɪlɪŋli/
in a way that shows that you are happy to do something if it is needed
Example: She willingly stayed late at the office to help her colleague finish the project.

windily /ˈwɪndili/

in a way that is confident and continues for a long time, but does not say anything useful or interesting

Example: The politician spoke windily for hours, filling time without offering any concrete solutions.

windingly /ˈwɪndɪŋli/

with a curving or sinuous motion or pattern

Example: The road wound windingly through the mountains, curving around each bend.

winkingly /ˈwɪŋkɪŋli/

in a manner that involves shutting one eye briefly as a signal or in teasing

Example: He winkingly acknowledged the inside joke, letting his friend know he understood.

winningly /wˈɪnɪŋli/

in a way that is friendly and pleasant and makes people like you

Example: She smiled winningly at everyone she met, quickly making friends wherever she went.

in a way that people like

Example: His charming speech was delivered winningly, earning applause from the audience.

winsomely /ˈwɪnsəmli/

in a way that is attractive and pleasing, with simple qualities

Example: She spoke winsomely, her genuine kindness and sincerity winning everyone over.

wintrily /ˈwɪntrɪli/

in a way that describes something characteristic of winter, such as cold, bleak, or frosty conditions

Example: *The landscape looked wintrily beautiful, with snow*
                covering the ground and frost on the trees.

wisely /wˈaɪzli/
in a way that shows good judgement
Example: *She wisely saved a portion of her pay-check each month*
                for future emergencies.

wishfully /ˈwɪʃfʊlli/
in a way that imagines or discusses what you wish or hope for,
especially when this is very unlikely to happen
Example: *She looked wishfully at the luxury car, dreaming of one*
                day owning it.

wispily /wˈɪspili/
in a way that is thin and delicate, like a small, thin line of cloud,
smoke, or steam
Example: *The fog rose wispily from the lake, creating a delicate,*
                ethereal mist.
thin and not growing thickly
Example: *The hair fell wispily around her face, light and airy*
                without any volume.
in a way that is not loud or strong
Example: *The music played wispily in the background, barely*
                audible over the conversation.

wistfully /wˈɪstfəli/
in a way that is sad and shows someone is thinking about something
that is impossible or in the past
Example: *She gazed wistfully at the old photographs, reminiscing*
                about days long gone.

wistly /ˈwɪstli/
in an intent or observing manner

Example: *He stared wistly at the horizon, focused on the distant goals he aimed to achieve.*

witheringly /wˈɪðərɪŋli/
in a way that criticizes someone severely, or that is intended to make someone feel ashamed
Example: *She looked at him witheringly, clearly disapproving of his careless mistake.*

witlessly /ˈwɪtlɪsli/
in a way that is foolish, or that shows no intelligence
Example: *He spoke witlessly about the complex issue, revealing a lack of understanding.*

wittily /ˈwɪtɪlɪ/
in a way that uses words in a clever and funny way
Example: *She wittily defused the awkward situation with a clever joke that had everyone laughing.*

wittingly /ˈwɪtɪŋlɪ/
in a way that involves knowing or planning what you are doing
Example: *He wittingly chose his words to avoid any misunderstandings during the sensitive discussion.*

woefully /wˈəʊfəli/
used to emphasize how bad a situation is
Example: *The project's progress was woefully behind schedule, causing concern among the team.*

wolfishly /ˈwʊlfɪʃli/
in a way that looks as though you want to trick or harm someone
Example: *He smiled wolfishly as he plotted his next move, his intentions clear in his cunning gaze.*

wonderfully /wˈʌndəfəli/

in a way or to an extent that excites wonder, astonishment, or amazement

Example: *The sunrise painted the sky wonderfully, casting vibrant hues across the horizon.*

in a way or to an extent that is extremely or unusually good or pleasing

Example: *The meal turned out wonderfully, exceeding all our expectations with its delicious flavours.*

wonderingly /wˈʌndərɪŋli/

in a way that feels curiosity or doubt

Example: *He asked the question wonderingly, curious about the mysterious answer.*

wondrously /ˈwʌndrəsli/

in a manner that describes something as strange and beautiful or impressive

Example: *The performance was wondrously captivating, leaving the audience spellbound.*

wontedly /ˈwəʊntɪdli/

in a manner that is usual or ordinary especially by reason of established habit

Example: *She wontedly started her day with a cup of coffee and a newspaper.*

woodenly /ˈwʊdnli/

in an awkward way or showing no expression

Example: *He replied woodenly, his face betraying no emotion despite the surprising news.*

wooingly /wˈuːɪŋli/

in an attractive or alluring manner

Example: He spoke wooingly, trying to win her favour with
charming compliments and kind words.

woozily /wˈuːzili/
in a way that shows you feel weak or ill and unable to think clearly
Example: She spoke woozily after the long flight, struggling to stay
awake and focused.

wordily /wˈɜːdili/
in a way that contains a lot of words, or too many words
Example: His explanation was wordily detailed, making it hard to
follow his main point.

wordlessly /wˈɜːdləsli/
in a way that is not expressed in or accompanied by words
Example: They exchanged a glance wordlessly, understanding each
other's feelings without saying a word.

worriedly /wˈʌrɪdli/
in an unhappy way because you are thinking about problems or
unpleasant things that might happen
Example: She looked worriedly at the weather forecast, concerned
about the upcoming storm.

worrisomely /ˈwʌrɪsəmli/
in a way that is vexing or causes distress
Example: The weather forecast worrisomely predicted severe
storms for the weekend.

worryingly /wˈʌrɪɪŋli/
in a way that is troubling or creates reason to worry
Example: She spoke worryingly about the upcoming changes at
work.

worshipfully /ˈwɜːʃɪpfʊlli/
in a way that shows great respect or admiration for someone or something
Example: *He looked worshipfully at the famous artist's painting.*

worthily /wˈɜːðɪli/
in a way that deserves respect, admiration, or support
Example: *She was honoured for her worthily contributions to the community.*
in a way that is not very interesting but should be admired for its good and useful qualities
Example: *The book is worthily written, offering practical advice even if it is not very exciting.*

worthlessly /ˈwɜːθlɪsli/
in a way that has no worth or value in money
Example: *The old coins were worthlessly tossed aside after the appraisal.*
in a way that is not important or useful
Example: *The lengthy report was worthlessly detailed, adding no new insights.*

wrathfully /ˈrɒθfʊlli/
in a raging or furious manner
Example: *She shouted wrathfully at the delay in the project.*

wrathily /rˈɑθɪli/
in an extremely angry manner
Example: *He responded wrathily to the unfair criticism.*

wrenchingly /rˈɛntʃɪŋli/
in a way that makes you feel emotional pain
Example: *The movie ended wrenchingly, leaving everyone in tears.*

wretchedly /rˈɛtʃɪdli/
extremely, when referring to something unpleasant or of low quality
Example: *The old house was wretchedly in disrepair, with broken windows and rotting wood.*

wrong /ɹˈɒŋ/
without accuracy
Example: *The directions he gave were wrong, leading us far off course.*
without regard of what is proper or just
Example: *It was wrong of him to take credit for someone else's work.*
in a wrong direction
Example: *We went in the wrong direction and ended up lost in the woods.*
in an unsuccessful or unfortunate way
Example: *The project went wrong, resulting in missed deadlines and wasted resources.*
in a false light
Example: *The article portrayed the situation wrong, leading to public misunderstanding.*

wrongfully /rˈɒŋfəli/
in a way that is unfair or illegal
Example: *She was wrongfully accused of the crime and lost her job.*

wrongly /rˈɒŋli/
in a way that is incorrect and not in accordance with the facts
Example: *He answered the question wrongly on the test, losing points.*

wryly /rˈaɪli/
in a way that shows you find a bad or difficult situation slightly funny
Example: *She wryly noted the irony of getting stuck in traffic on her day off.*

Xx

xenophobically /zˌɛnəfˈəʊbɪkɔ:li/

in a way that shows or expresses an extreme dislike or fear of people from foreign countries

Example: *His comments were xenophobically charged, reflecting a strong distrust of people from other cultures.*

xerically /ˈzɪərɪkli/

in a manner that relates to growing in dry conditions

Example: *The desert plant thrived xerically, efficiently conserving water in the arid environment.*

xerographically /ˌzɛtəˈɡrɑfɪkli/

in a way that involves copying graphic matter by the action of light on an electrically charged photoconductive insulating surface in which the latent image is developed with a resinous powder, such as toner

Example: *The document was reproduced xerographically, using a dry copying process to make the copies.*

Yy

yappingly /jˈɑpɪŋli/
in a way that involves quick sharp barking
Example: *The small dog barked yappingly at every passerby,*
creating a constant noise.

yawningly /jˈɔːnɪŋli/
in a way that shows fatigue or boredom by yawns
Example: *The lengthy and repetitive speech was yawningly dull,*
making everyone in the audience sleepy.
in a way that is very large, wide, or empty
Example: *The yawningly vast desert stretched out as far as the eye*
could see, with no signs of life.

yearly /jˈiəli/
each or every year
Example: *They take a vacation yearly to explore a new country*
together.

yearningly /ˈjɜːnɪŋli/
in a way that expresses a strong feeling of wishing for something,
especially something that you cannot have or get easily
Example: *He gazed yearningly at the distant mountains, wishing he*
could explore their peaks.

yeastily /jˈiːstili/
in a manner that is fermenting or causes fermentation
Example: *The dough rose yeastily, filling the kitchen with its warm,*
bread-like aroma.

yeomanly /ˈjəʊmənli/
in a manner befitting a yeoman

Example: She performed her duties yeomanly, showing dedication
and skill in every task.

yesterday /jˈɛstədˌeɪ/
on the day before today
Example: We went to the park yesterday and had a great time
playing soccer.
at a time not long past
Example: The technology in that old phone feels outdated, as if it
were from yesterday.

yester-even /jˈɛstɐˈiːvən/
on the evening of yesterday
Example: We had a lovely dinner yester-even at the new restaurant
downtown.

yester-night /ˈjestəˈnaɪt/
on the night last past
Example: The storm that hit yester-night caused significant damage
to the neighbourhood.

yieldingly /ˈjiːldɪŋli/
in a manner that is compliant, submissive or flexible
Example: She spoke yieldingly, accommodating their concerns and
agreeing to their suggestions.

youthfully /jˈuːθfəli/
in a way that is like, typical of, or relates to young people
Example: He danced youthfully, with energy and enthusiasm that
belied his age.

Zz

zanily /zˈeɪnɪli/
in a way that is humorously strange, surprising, or uncontrolled
Example: *The comedian acted zanily on stage, making the audience burst into laughter.*

zealously /ˈzeləsli/
in a very enthusiastic and eager way
Example: *She zealously pursued her goals, never letting obstacles stand in her way.*

zestfully /ˈzɛstfəlli/
in a way that is invigorating and involves keen enjoyment
Example: *She tackled the new project zestfully, bringing fresh energy and excitement to the team.*

zestily /zˈɛstili/
in a way that shows a lot of energy and enthusiasm
Example: *He danced zestily at the party, filling the room with his infectious enthusiasm.*
with a lot of flavour
Example: *The chef seasoned the dish zestily, adding a burst of vibrant flavour to every bite.*

zigzaggedly /zˈɪgzɑgdli/
in a manner that involves having short sharp turns or angles
Example: *The path zigzaggedly wound through the forest.*

zionward /ˈzaɪənˈwɔrd/
toward Zion or heavenward
Example: *The pilgrims journeyed zionward, drawn by their faith and hope for a future in the promised land.*

zonally /ˈzəʊnlli/

involving or relating or having the form of an area that has particular features or characteristics

Example: *The climate was zonally categorized, with different regions experiencing distinct weather patterns.*

zoologically /zˌuːəlˈɒdʒɪkli/

in a matter relating to the classification and the properties and vital phenomena of animals

Example: *The exhibit was designed zoologically, showcasing detailed information about animal behaviour and habitats.*